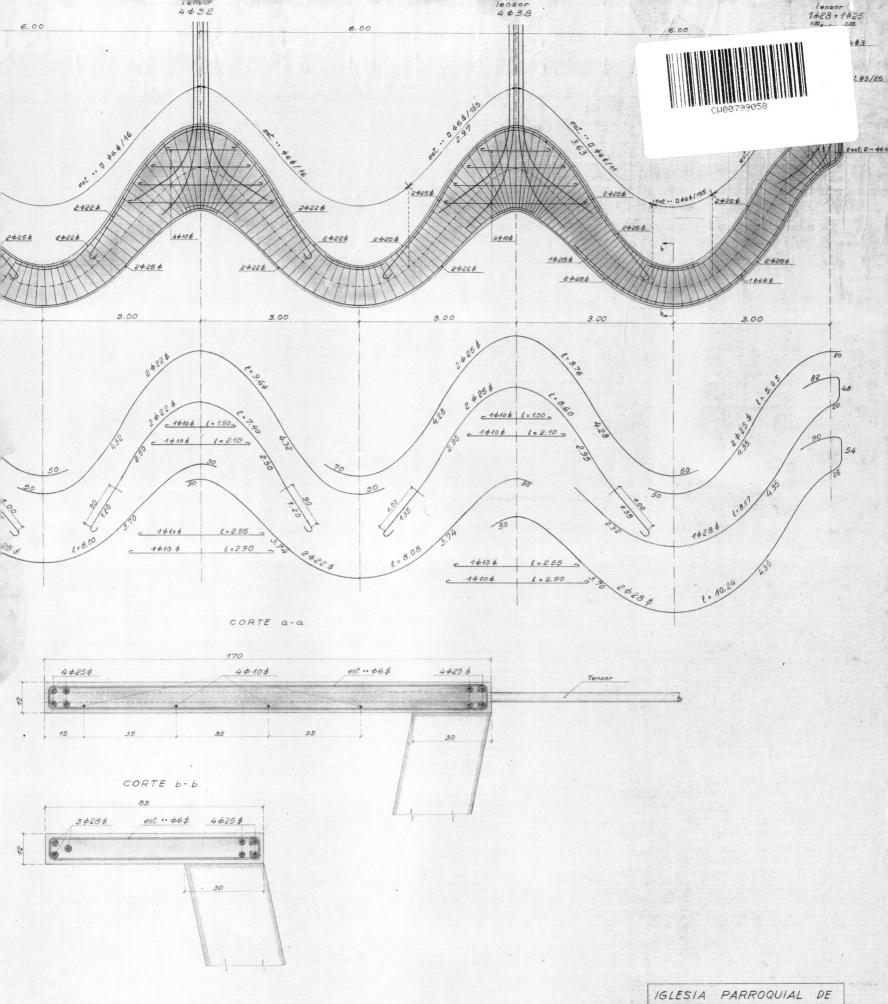

CORTE a-a

CORTE b-b

IGLESIA PARROQUIAL DE
A T L A N T I D A
V I G A   P R I N C I P A L
Escalas   1/25

2.

3.

4.

Latin America in Construction: Architecture 1955–1980

Barry Bergdoll
Carlos Eduardo Comas
Jorge Francisco Liernur
Patricio del Real

The Museum of Modern Art, New York

5.

6.

7.

8.

9.

Contents

10.

Foreword

It is now sixty years ago that The Museum of Modern Art staged *Latin American Architecture since 1945*, an influential showcase of then-contemporary architecture of the vast and complex region between Tierra del Fuego and the Rio Grande. That show, along with *Brazil Builds* of 1943, marked a moment of the Museum's intense involvement with Latin America, as well as continuing the ethos, predominant since the Department of Architecture's founding in 1932, of creating exhibitions from newly commissioned photographs.

It has been a much more challenging undertaking, for *Latin America in Construction*, to evaluate retrospectively the quarter of a century between 1955 and 1980 by assembling the materials of architectural production and dissemination: design and construction drawings, models, and period photographs and films. In contrast to earlier exhibitions, this show proposes an intellectual laboratory for exploring a vibrant architectural culture marked by great growth but often shadowed by dictatorship and brutal military rule. Our South American guest curators, Carlos Eduardo Comas and Jorge Francisco Liernur, have worked with Barry Bergdoll and Patricio del Real, of the Department of Architecture & Design, to open new lines of inquiry. Their travels have taken them to archives, libraries, museums, government agencies, foundations, and the offices and homes of architects and their families to collect a rich and unprecedented array of original materials.

The title *Latin America in Construction* has a meaning in addition to the obvious architectural and political ones, signaling an exhibition and publication that function as an ongoing laboratory for constructing new histories. This catalogue is conceived as an opening for new research; we have placed its bibliography on-line, so that it may continue to grow. We are immensely grateful to the scholars from the region who have contributed precious advice to the curators and texts to the catalogue. We are equally indebted to the teams that have realized new materials for the exhibition: handsome didactic models produced under the direction of Jeannette Plaut and Marcelo Sarovic at the Pontificia Universidad Católica de Chile in Santiago, and under Jean-François Lejeune at the University of Miami; engaging anthologies of films researched and edited by Joey Forsyte; and the stunning new photography of Leonardo Finotti.

We greatly appreciate the scores of lenders on three continents who have made the show possible. My thanks go to the curators for their unflagging determination in assembling these materials and for their creative interpretation in laying them out, in an exhibition that will stimulate debate and new studies and in a book intended as a point of reference. I would like to thank the members of the Museum's Acquisition Committee on Architecture & Design, who have supported a robust program of enhancing the permanent collection, including the specific gifts of Patricia Phelps de Cisneros, Elise Jaffe + Jeffrey Brown, André Aranha Corrêa do Lago, and Alice Tisch, the committee's chair. Additional help has come from the Embassies of Argentina and Chile in the United States.

The Museum is enormously grateful for a major contribution made by Emilio Ambasz. Major support is also provided by The International Council of The Museum of Modern Art. Additional funding came from The Reed Foundation, the Mexican Agency for International Development Cooperation (AMEXCID) with the Mexican Cultural Institute of New York, the Government of Chile, the Consulate General of Brazil in New York, and the Consulate General of the Argentine Republic in New York.

Glenn D. Lowry
Director, The Museum of Modern Art, New York

Peruvian president Fernando Belaunde Terry at the construction site of
the San Felipe housing complex, Lima. 1968. From *El comercio* magazine

Learning from Latin America:
Public Space, Housing, and Landscape

Barry Bergdoll

The spectacular urbanization of Latin America after 1945 transformed architectural culture in the vast region and became the catalyst for some of the most heated and productive debates of the mid-twentieth century. For the first time, architecture and urban planning in Latin America—in particular in Mexico, Brazil, and Venezuela—seemed not the belated reflection of examples set in Europe or in the Americas north of the Rio Grande but previsions of a modernization to come: lessons from the "underdeveloped" world (as the region was classified after 1945 in the debates over models of development) useful even for the "developed" world to contemplate in the 1950s and '60s.

Although Buenos Aires attracted worldwide attention in the opening decades of the twentieth century—particularly around 1900, when Argentina's soaring gross domestic product evinced the fastest growth of any country in the world to date—the shape of the city's boulevards and monuments, captured in newsreels and magazine reports, was still entirely in line with the late-nineteenth-century transformation and growth of Paris and Madrid, as well as with the City Beautiful ideology in the United States. During World War II, by contrast, when architectural production in Europe and the United States had all but halted, Rio de Janeiro, São Paulo, Havana, Bogotá, Caracas, and Mexico City seemed to offer avant-garde visions of future cities and of possibilities for Europe, rebuilding after the war, and the United States, gearing up for urban renewal. In the 1940s the lead in architectural experimentation was first taken by Mexico and then, and especially, by Brazil, which would be celebrated as a veritable crucible of new inventions in the forms of modern architecture and in new approaches to public housing, in projects such as Affonso Eduardo Reidy's Pedregulho complex, in Rio de Janeiro (1946–58). Brazil had made headlines as early as 1939, at the New York World's Fair, when critics had considered the Brazil Pavilion (along with Alvar Aalto's Finland Pavilion) to be evidence of a wholly new experimental modernism, from countries that had rarely garnered attention in previous decades (fig. 1). Brazil's pavilion, along with Venezuela's, in Flushing Meadows was radically different from the streamlined late–Art Deco imagery that dominated the fair, or the traditional, largely neocolonial imagery in sectors such as the housing display *The Town of Tomorrow*. Venezuela had turned to Skidmore, Owings & Merrill, an all-but-untried American firm, thus announcing the alignment of the fastest-growing petroleum-producing country in the world with the United States. But Brazil offered an inventive modernist vision unlike anything seen before in the United States, one even quite distinct from the European version that had been celebrated in 1932 in *Modern Architecture: International Exhibition*, at The Museum of Modern Art, the

1. Brazil Pavilion, New York World's Fair. 1939.
Oscar Niemeyer (Brazilian, 1907–2012), Lucio Costa
(Brazilian, born France. 1902–1998). Exterior view.
Architecture & Design Study Center, The Museum
of Modern Art, New York

event that had coined the term "International Style"—paradoxically enough, since whole continents, including South America, were not mentioned, let alone illustrated, in its publications. Lucio Costa and Oscar Niemeyer's pavilion announced a fresh idiom that integrated nature, site, a play of indoor and outdoor spaces, ramps and light-and-shade-monitoring brise-soleils. The painter Cândido Portinari, a collaborator on the esteemed Ministério da Educação e Saúde in Rio (1936–45), was featured in the Hall of the Good Neighbor. In 1943 a model of the (already demolished) pavilion was featured in MoMA's *Brazil Builds*, which was widely covered in the press, with headlines that linked Brazil's new ideas about architecture to its role on the world stage: "Brazil Builds for the Future," "Brazil Blazes Modern Trail in Architecture," "Brazil Has Much to Offer US," "Brazil Leads US in Modern Architecture," "Brazil Builds for Peace" (fig. 2).[1] This status was reasserted in 1949—as the United Nations Headquarters was under construction, following a design drawn up by an international committee headed by Wallace K. Harrison and including Le Corbusier, the Brazilian Niemeyer, the Uruguayan Julio Vilamajó, and others (fig. 3; see also page 262, fig. 1)—in MoMA's exhibition *From Le Corbusier to Niemeyer, 1929–1949*.

MoMA had helped to launch a trend, one that both reinforced Brazil's self-perception through modern architecture and showed an image of a progressive country to the rest of the world. Brazil, initially hesitant to join the Allies in World War II, was enlisted by the Museum in an ongoing aesthetic battle: "The Brazilian Government leads all other national governments in the Western Hemisphere in its discriminating and active encouragement of modern architecture," began the press release for *Brazil Builds*, which continued,

Other capital cities of the world lag far behind Rio de Janeiro in architectural design. While Federal classic in Washington, Royal Academy archaeology in London, Nazi classic in Munich, and neoimperial in Moscow are still triumphant, Brazil has had the courage to break away from safe and easy

2. Installation view of *Brazil Builds*, The Museum of Modern Art, New York, January 13–February 28, 1943. Photograph by Soichi Sunami. The Museum of Modern Art Archives, New York

*conservatism. Its fearless departure from the slavery of traditionalism has put a depth charge under the
antiquated routine of governmental thought and has set free the spirit of creative design. The capitals
of the world that will need rebuilding after the war can look to no finer models than the modern buildings
of … Brazil.*[2]

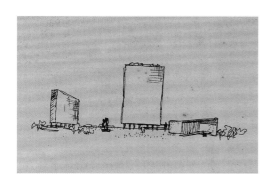

3. **United Nations Headquarters, New York.
1947–49.** Oscar Niemeyer (Brazilian, 1907–2012).
Proposal, perspective sketch (detail). c. 1947. Ink
on paper. Fundação Oscar Niemeyer

The Mexican architect Carlos Obregón Santacilia solicited *Brazil Builds* for Mexico City,
where it was shown in the summer of 1943 at the Palacio de Bellas Artes (one can hardly imagine a
greater contrast with the building, one of the great Beaux Arts monuments of Latin America). MoMA
had discussed a possible *Uruguay Builds*, and Santacilia hoped for a *Mexico Builds*, although neither
came to pass.

As the war came to an end and transatlantic travel again became possible, European
architectural journals devoted special issues to Brazil, including the British *Architectural Review* in
March 1944, the French *Architecture d'aujourd'hui* in September 1947, and the Italian *Domus* and the
German *Werk* in January 1948. Newspaper and magazine coverage soon spread beyond Brazil, with
reports on such works as Horacio Acevedo's small housing projects for workers in Chile and Mario
Pani's Centro Urbano Presidente Alemán in Mexico City.[3] By 1955 most of Latin America was involved
in modernist architectural explorations, as Arthur Drexler wrote in his preface to Henry-Russell
Hitchcock's *Latin American Architecture since 1945*: "The quality of current Latin American building
exceeds our own, the appearances there of predominantly 'modern' cities gives us the opportunity to
observe effects, which we ourselves still only anticipate."[4]

Buenos Aires was no longer the only city experiencing daunting change and rapid population
growth: between 1950 and 1955 Mexico City, Rio de Janeiro, and São Paulo each added nearly a million
citizens, with over a million more to come by 1960. São Paulo in these decades was growing faster than
any city in the world, closely followed by Caracas. Hitchcock was astonished, noting in 1955 that

*from Mexico City in North America, whose size has tripled in fifteen years, to Caracas, which positively
seems to expand under the visitor's eye, the tremendous rate of population growth (3% a year—double
the rate in the rest of the world) and the increasing vitality of the local economy, have induced a rate
of building production unequalled in the Western World. Today, Mexico City and Rio de Janeiro are
both much larger than Rome; and of the six largest cities in the Western Hemisphere, four are in Latin
America.*[5]

That Latin America's future was urban, and that the future of the urban was best observed
in Latin America, emerged as a dominant theme both of production within the region and observation
from outside, at every level—from architectural discourse to the politics of development and foreign
aid. In the quarter century from 1955 to 1980, Lima went from a city with a population hovering around
1 million to a sprawling, formless city of 4 million people, spreading unplanned far over the arid plateau
of the central Peruvian coast. Santiago de Chile grew from 1.6 to 3.7 million. By 1980 the doctrines of
developmentalism that had been both engines of and solutions to urban growth were being called into
question by rising neoliberal economics. By then, as well, Latin America was home to megacities with
the kinds of problems that are characteristic of our current global situation. In the decades since then,
Latin American cities have become emblems of extreme urban malaise—lack of security, intense and
entrenched-seeming poverty, rampant ad hoc housing and squatter settlements, poor infrastructure,
an ever-widening gap between rich and poor—and it is often forgotten that in the 1950s this same
region was heralded as offering promising signs of better urban futures. At that point the informal

nature of much of the great expansion had been seen as a temporary byproduct of growth rather than a formidable challenge to the underlying assumptions of planning and development ideology.

Latin America in Construction: Architecture, 1955–1980 opens in the mid-1950s, a period of challenges to the traditional practice and imagery of architecture in Latin America, when the first results of modernism were being debated and the unchecked euphoria of the 1940s had been shaken by reappraisals from critics both at home and abroad, including Max Bill's notorious critique of Brazilian modernist architecture in 1953. In 1955 Hitchcock was careful to ignore, for the most part, the storm clouds gathering over the achievements of Latin American architects, in Brazil in particular. But we take this moment of conflict as our starting point, in order to reopen for consideration a complex body of innovative designs that grappled with the role of architecture in a rapidly urbanizing culture at every level, from the relationship of the building with its immediate public setting to the struggle to respond to the swelling populations—much of it due to internal immigration from South America's rural areas—and the growing need to control the vast territory of the interior even as those rural areas became, as a result, less populated.

Hitchcock ended his catalogue by compiling fictive streetscapes (fig. 4), using buildings taken from various burgeoning Latin American cities to compose an ideal urban fabric. Our curatorial team, rather than searching for an essential Latin American architecture or positing a unified view of a style, is instead eager to reveal different urban cultures of architecture in all their specificity, a plurality of positions, all of which were formed in a climate increasingly dominated by the practices and philosophy of development and even of its transformation into an –ism: *desarrollismo*, or developmentalism. As Jorge Francisco Liernur argues so persuasively in his essay in this volume, development theory—the notion that it was the role of the state to promote modernization and to attend to the urban challenges it brought—was a challenge reflected across the entire political spectrum, in the countries ruled by leaders who grasped power (Fidel Castro in Cuba, Marcos Pérez Jiménez in Venezuela) and those governed by leaders democratically elected, even if for brief intervals (Fernando Belaunde Terry in Peru, Salvador Allende in Chile).

4. Henry-Russell Hitchcock, *Latin American Architecture since 1945* (New York: The Museum of Modern Art, 1955)

Storm Clouds: Responses to a Critique

It wasn't only exhibitions that promoted modernism and modernization: publications, newsreels, and films brought images of cities in transformation to movie houses and television screens throughout the developed world.[6] Many of them directly equated architecture with progress and development, thus echoing the very message intended by state investment in much of the most visible architecture of the period. But in the mid-1950s such messages began to find themselves in competition with doubting voices. The opening salvo came from the British journal *Architectural Review*, in a series of reports aimed at demystifying the extent and quality of modern architecture in Brazil. "What gives the architectural scene in Brazil its special character," the *Review* asserted, "is the fact that the very wealthy and (to some extent) the government have constituted themselves the patrons of modern architecture; the result has been that most of the best modern buildings belong to luxury types; there are very few developments in working-class housing, and town planning is still regarded as the province of the traffic engineer."[7]

Bill, the Swiss artist, designer, and architect who had taken the top prize at the first Bienal de São Paulo, in 1951, took the opportunity, on a return visit in 1953, of lecturing the Brazilians on the ideological and formal flaws—sins, even, in his eyes—of their architecture. This, for him, was an urgent task: students flocking to Brazil's architectural schools would "fashion the look of the cities of tomorrow," he held, and Brazilian influence was on the rise from the United States to Europe and even to Australia.[8] In particular Bill attacked the rise of the organic form, in what he saw as an overall casualness in Brazilian modernism, a capricious individualism, a quality made all the more dangerous by Brazil's status as "the boom-province of the Modern Movement":

I saw some shocking things, modern architecture sunk to the depths, a riot of anti-social waste, lacking any sense of responsibility towards either the business occupant or his customers.... Here is utter anarchy in building, jungle growth in the worst sense.... One is baffled to account for such barbarism as this exemplifies being able to break out in a country where there is a CIAM group, a country in which international congresses on modern architecture are held, where a journal like Habitat *is published and where there is a biennial exhibition of architecture. For such works are born of a spirit devoid of all decency.*[9]

The Brazilians might have detected here a strong sense of Swiss puritanism, and no doubt Bill was using them to some degree as proxies for the growing fascination with organic form that was increasingly challenging the geometric rigor cultivated at the Ulm Hochschule für Gestaltung, his home base.

In 1953 critics also turned to Mexico and its much-publicized new campus for the Universidad Nacional Autónoma. Sibyl Moholy-Nagy, who, like Bill, was involved with the creation of a "new Bauhaus," this one in Chicago, set the tone, criticizing the "restless scale" of the new campus, which, to her mind, amounted to a wasteful use of materials and forms.[10] In the "monumental quiet and unity" of the site she found an "essay contest in concrete, determining what 'Mexican architecture' means to a dozen different men."

For US and European critics, Latin American architecture was haunted by the specter of individualism, which challenged the ideal of modernism as a universal and communal project. Nikolaus Pevsner declared as much in the revised edition of *Pioneers of Modern Design* (first published as *Pioneers of the Modern Movement* in 1936). A new edition appeared in 1960, just as Brasília was being inaugurated. Pevsner extended the warnings of what he had called, in the first edition, the "short interlude" of German Expressionism after World War I in order to counter what he now saw as a post–World War II reprise: "The structural acrobatics of the Brazilians and all of those who imitate them are attempts to satisfy the craving of architects for individual expression, the craving of the public for the surprising and the fantastic, and for an escape out of reality into a fairy world."[11]

Eero Saarinen, in his Dulles airport (1969), seemed to confirm Pevsner's worst fears. Although the 1969 books *Arquitectura latinoamericana, 1930–1970*, and *New Directions in Latin American Architecture*, by the Argentine architect and critic Francisco Bullrich, provided a counter-argument in the form of a survey of vibrant innovation in building across the region, Pevsner's view would continue to surface in influential histories.[12] As late as 1976, in *Architettura contemporanea*, Manfredo Tafuri and Francesco Dal Co noted that "Oscar Niemeyer . . . attempted to mold his architectural objects as unexpected events, spectacles of the absurd, euphoric fragments of nature crystallized. . . . Niemeyer had already shown the limits of his approach in the new capital of Brazil. This approach was used in Brazil ad nauseum."[13] Like a number of other historians, Tafuri and Dal Co made an exception for Reidy's Pedregulho housing (fig. 5), in which they felt that social purpose and landscape and urban approach were consonant with a love of curved forms and facades rendered as permeable screens—in this case of terracotta blocks—not only as formal gestures but as elements of a more appropriate communion with nature and climate.

In Latin America, where Bill's attack circulated in journals such as *Arquitectura México*, *Nuestra arquitectura*, and *El arquitecto peruano*, the response was swift.[14] Critics countered Bill's insinuation that Niemeyer's architecture lacked the gravitas and ideological conviction of European modernism of the interwar years (an odd claim given Niemeyer's avowed commitment to Brazilian communism), insisting that Brasília remained one of the most concrete embodiments of the central role architecture would play in different projects of national construction.

But the most influential and daring Latin American designs of the postwar years had resonance across the region and beyond: if they were not examples of the canonical International Style, they were certainly of international significance. It is our hypothesis that the period after 1955 was characterized by position taking, and by Latin America's new role a catalyst for regional and national debates, in such gatherings as the foundation of the Federación Panamericana de Asociaciones de Arquitectos in Montevideo, in 1950 (following the foundation there, thirty years earlier, of the Congreso Panamericano de Arquitectos), or the seminal seventh meeting of the International Union of Architects in Havana, in 1963, devoted to "La arquitectura en los países en vías de desarrollo" (Architecture of developing countries), where different visions of what development might mean were vigorously debated. We close our study around 1980, since by the mid-1980s many Latin American countries were falling in line with the neoliberal vision emanating from the administrations of Ronald Reagan and Margaret Thatcher, of a limited role for the state in matters of development and infrastructure and a greater advancement of market principles.

By the 1950s Latin America had become the source not only of new forms but also of new attitudes, of experiments—some spectacularly successful, others ultimately failures—by individuals and by nation-states in building both architecture and citizenry. Critical positions and new ideas came from architects who questioned the dominant ideology of development theory, or in some cases subtly resisted the demands of a dictatorship, to their own peril, in particular in the school that formed around João Batista Vilanova Artigas and Paulo Mendes da Rocha in São Paulo; or those who found a modernism that could marry handwork with new technologies, even in traditional materials, such as in the brick architecture of Eladio Dieste in Uruguay; or in the engagement of Lina Bo Bardi in the native and Afro-Brazilian cultures of Salvador de Bahia; as well as in the more obvious countermodels such as the Ciudad Abierta (Open city) of the Escuela de Arquitectura in Valparaíso, and in

5. **Pedregulho complex, Rio de Janeiro. 1947–52.** Affonso Eduardo Reidy (Brazilian, born France. 1909–1964). View of the school, with housing in the background. 1972. Photograph by Paolo Gasparini

the official utopian architecture for Castro's radical new Cuba in its earliest phase. Far from an essential Latin America, of the sort that Hitchcock was seeking in 1955, these and other engaged stances defined a vast panorama of positions in the next quarter century, from alternative practices to those that aligned with and promoted the mainstream developmentalist agenda of the state. It is the heightened sense of experimentation, of projecting a future and not simply building a present, that is the common thread in this array of attitudes, forms, and convictions.

Campuses as Fragments of a Future City: The Stage of Civil Society

For nearly two centuries, beginning with Thomas Jefferson's University of Virginia (1819), college campuses in the United States have functioned as architectural laboratories, as spatialized visions of community, even of the polis. At the dawn of the twentieth century, under the ideology of the City Beautiful movement, the urban campuses of Columbia University, New York University (in the Bronx), and the University of California, Berkeley, advanced the hypothesis of the campus as a fragment of an ideal city, a harmonic mediator between landscape and urban form, private use and civic expression, education as refuge and as engagement. The City Beautiful campus was characterized by highly formal axial plans and Beaux Arts–style architecture, focusing on a great symbolic building usually approached by a monumental stair—a plan deliberately reminiscent of the ancient Roman fora. The influence of these new urban campuses was considerable in Latin America, for example in the planning of the new campus of the Universidad de la Habana in the Vedado neighborhood from 1905 into the 1930s, and in Fritz Karsen and Leopold Rother's master plan for the Universidad Nacional de Colombia in Bogotá in 1937–45 (page 174, fig. 1). If US influence can still be seen, even in the hybrid forms of Henry Klumb's extension to the Río Pedras campus of the Universidad de Puerto Rico (fig. 6), in the 1950s Latin American campuses developed increasingly in terms both local and axiomatic for postwar modernism.

Design work had already begun in the late 1940s on two projects, both charged with representing the identity of aspiring nation-states. Both were unprecedented architectural experiments: the Universidad Nacional Autónoma de México (UNAM), for which Pani and Enrique del Moral first made sketches in 1947 (inspired by the preliminary parti of the young student architect Teodoro González de León), and the Universidad Central de Venezuela (UCV) in Caracas, where Carlos Raúl Villanueva began his decades-long involvement in 1945. Both were national and public, but they were protected by bureaucratic structures meant to render them autonomous and free from political influence, even though the projects were deeply engaged with national politics of development. Both were built in record time, providing training grounds for younger architects during design and construction. Both employed large, on-site architects' offices and included purpose-built edifices for their architecture schools, which symbolized the project as a whole and were granted prominent locations at the core of their respective master plans. Both became at once symbols and motors of the modernizing nation-state, boosting the building industry and new technologies and establishing exemplars of urban solutions for architects and planners throughout the region. Each campus was set at the edge of a burgeoning city, offering new forms of public space and interaction and becoming a pole of attraction for orderly urban expansion in a period when migration from rural areas was increasingly creating informal settlements that escaped the control of planners both economic and physical. UNAM was at the then-southern edge of Mexico City, adjacent to El Pedregal, Luis Barragán's great architectural, landscape, and real estate experiment developed in the same years. In Caracas the plan for UCV transformed the leafy grounds of a former hacienda into a landscaped city quarter. Both campuses established new forms of collaboration among architects, engineers, and artists, as well as new landscape approaches to architecture that pushed the technologies of the moment to their edge.

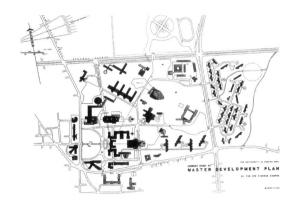

6. **Río Piedras campus, Universidad de Puerto Rico, San Juan. 1946–66.** Henry Klumb (US, born Germany. 1905–1984). Master plan. Pencil on vellum, 28 ½ x 40 in. (72.4 x 101.6 cm). Archivo de Arquitectura y Construcción, Universidad de Puerto Rico, San Juan

7. **Universidad Nacional Autónoma de México (UNAM), Mexico City. 1947–54.** Mario Pani (Mexican, 1911–1993), Enrique del Moral (Mexican, 1905–1987), and others. Aerial view of the campus. 1951. Photograph by Compañía Mexicana Aerofoto. Fundación Ingenieros Civiles Asociados (FICA), México

8. **Estadio Olímpico Universitario, UNAM, Mexico City. 1950–52.** Augusto Perez Palacios (Mexican, 1909–2002), Raúl Salinas Moro (Mexican, born 1920), Jorge Bravo Jiménez (Mexican, born 1922). Aerial view of stadium. 1954. Photograph by Compañía Mexicana Aerofoto. Fundación Ingenieros Civiles Asociados (FICA), México

9. **Central library, UNAM, Mexico City. 1950.** Juan O'Gorman (Mexican, 1905–1982), Gustavo M. Saavedra (Mexican, born 1905), Juan Martínez Velasco (Mexican, born 1924). View of the southern facade. 1951–53. Photograph by Rollie McKenna. Architecture & Design Study Center, The Museum of Modern Art, New York

On the lava fields south of the city, in a wild, primordial landscape set before active volcanoes, UNAM's campus is laid out both in and on the land (fig. 7). Historians have celebrated the coordinated contributions of more than seventy architects, but it was the overall intertwining of urban and landscape approaches that makes the campus exemplary. Complex overlapping axes order the buildings, and the composition shifts from a pedestrian's perspective—slower and more attentive to detail and texture, on paths that crisscross the campus without ever meeting a street—to that of a passing motorist—at a larger scale and higher velocity, on the carefully orchestrated ring road around the campus that predates Mexico City's peripheral highway. The campus's plazas become increasingly contained from west to east, from the great open spaces around the stadium, itself a crater in dialogue with the landscape (fig. 8), to the interior courtyards of the classrooms and the more intimate spaces of the planned (but never completed) residential quarter, which would have been set at a diagonal to the more formal academic campus.

Almost overnight the campus attracted attention from the press, in everything from daily newspapers to in-flight magazines. Many of the articles featured the campus's individual buildings (which continue to appear in architectural surveys to this day), perhaps most frequently the emblematic Biblioteca Central by Juan O'Gorman, Gustavo M. Saavedra, and Juan Martínez Velasco, with its blank box of library stacks adorned with a monumental pictogram rendered in mosaic (fig. 9)—an ancient work in a new polychromatic medium, perfect for photographic spreads in color. Such *integración plástica* (integration of the arts), born of a distinctly Mexican concern with harnessing the fine arts toward civic ends (and echoed in debates at the time in the United States), became one of the ideals of Mexican public architecture and had in fact been so since the didactic muralist program launched in the 1920s during the Mexican Revolution by the education minister José Vasconcelos. David Alfaro Siqueiros's *El pueblo a la universidad, la universidad al pueblo* on the side of the rectorate, the main administration building, is an experiment in merging perspectives from different vantage points viewed at various velocities in a single work, much as the architects and planners did in the detailing of their buildings in both the quick silhouettes glimpsed by motorists and the finer texture of pedestrian encounters in the lower ranges (an effect nowhere more clearly achieved than in the rectorate tower, originally opened to pedestrians at the ground floor).

The campus's greatest achievement is a masterful synthesis of the analytical functionalist recommendations emerging from the Congrès Internationaux d'Architecture Moderne (CIAM), with references to the monumental sculptural effects and spatial enclosure of the great pre-Columbian compositions of Monte Albán, in Oaxaca, and Teotihuacan, along with an approach to landscape that responds to the nature of the site itself. The site plan is a powerful revision of CIAM's functionalist planning—of the separation of work, study, residence, and traffic—with terracing that allows movement through spaces, as well as provides communal places of gathering and repose. Attention has been paid to the emotive and visual relationships between buildings, particularly the great horizontal sweep of the classroom buildings, with their narrow plan of classrooms with ample daylight set above open walkways behind *pilotis* creating a distinct recollection of colonial arcaded streets. The sublime scale of this horizontal skyscraper—combining three buildings by three architectural teams—holds its own against views of the distant volcanoes on the high Mexican plateau.[15]

UNAM and the neighboring residential community of El Pedregal present an impressive array of modern Mexican architectural solutions practiced simultaneously in the 1950s. El Pedregal is primarily known for Barragán's innovative houses of colorful stucco walls, such as Casa Prieto (1947–51), which the architect and his followers would proclaim to be the path to a Mexican modernism, at one with colonial and vernacular tradition, thus existing in a transcendent time frame set apart from the forward march of progress. But it also contained glazed modernist structures that could hold their own with Miesian developments in Chicago and the new case study houses in Los Angeles, most notably in houses that integrated interior and gardens, designed by José Antonio Attolini Lack, Augusto H. Álvarez, and Francisco Artigas. All of the El Pedregal houses are set behind high stone walls, so that the lava landscape is largely privatized, except for several small, brilliant parks that are masterly orchestrations of geology and botany.[16] At UNAM, by contrast, gardens, patios, buildings, and landscape are woven together to create the most powerful public space since Mexico City's grand Zócalo plaza, where the university had been located for centuries before its move.

At UNAM, in nuce, was a series of projects that would define Mexican architectural creation for the next two decades: the thin shell vaults of Félix Candela in the diminutive but monumentally scaled Pabellón de Rayos Cósmicos (Cosmic-ray pavilion) (fig. 10); the curtain walls between the exposed concrete slabs of the long humanities building by a team that included Vladimir Kaspé, Enrique de la Mora, and Federico Mariscal, among others; the vigorous collages of different materials in which abstract building planes play against highly figurative art work, as in Pani, del Moral, and Salvador Ortega's rectorate. By far the most original declaration of a new typology is the stadium by Augusto Pérez Palacios, Raúl Salinas Moro, and Jorge Bravo Jiménez, in which all the lessons of the pre-Columbian ruins—ramped planes, land berms, and monumental rubble construction—are orchestrated to create a gathering place for the university community. Here Diego Rivera's three-dimensional murals merge perfectly with the rubble wall, emerging naturally and forcefully from the stadium's svelte, lava-stone forms. It seems poetically to create an artificial volcano to communicate with the real ones still visible from Mexico City, not yet choked by automobile exhaust.[17]

UNAM developed as a national collaborative architectural work; Villanueva's work in Caracas, by contrast, was a single-author project, albeit one with rich contributions of international visual artists. Villanueva's approach evolved rapidly and dramatically, as the design shifted away from a formal Beaux Arts campus plan indebted to the Universidad Nacional de Colombia, which Villanueva had visited, to a modernist experiment. The great oval perimeter road of Bogotá is echoed in the first Caracas plan of 1944, and in both plans the shape resonates within an overall symmetry; by 1949, however, Villanueva's plans show the morphology of the buildings beginning slowly to transform,

10. **Pabellón de Rayos Cósmicos, UNAM, Mexico City. 1951.** Félix Candela (Mexican, born Spain. 1910–1997), Jorge González Reyna (Mexican, 1920–1969). Exterior view. 2013. Photograph by Leonardo Finotti

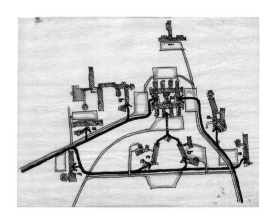

11. Ciudad Universitaria, Caracas. 1945–70.
Carlos Raúl Villanueva (Venezuelan, born England. 1900–1975). Plan of the medical center. c. 1952. Ink on tracing paper, 16 9/16 x 11 11/16 in. (42 x 29.7 cm). Fundación Villanueva

with the campus anchored in the west by a heroic cantilevered concrete stadium (finished in 1951), similar in position to its Mexican contemporary although ultimately altogether different in form (fig. 11). The earliest buildings he designed for the campus, such as the medical center in the early 1950s, clearly betray his Beaux Arts training, but in a revised master plan from 1955 the central auditorium has been transformed from a fan shape—lifted directly from the history of the amphitheater—into a looser form, seemingly amorphous, embedded in surrounding plazas that obscure any reading of it as a whole. The auditorium emerges as the central nodal point of the campus, with paths circulating around it and forms within it empirically developed for movement, expressive of structural experimentation, and clearly influenced by Villanueva's friendships with artists of biomorphic abstraction.

Villanueva developed an architecture of experience, one that links circulation with stasis and places for public assembly with settings for integrated abstract artworks, in a plan that unfolds haptically rather than axially, seeming to follow the rhythms of the body and of the sun. The most famous integration of art and architecture resulted from his collaboration with the American sculptor Alexander Calder in the Aula Magna, where Calder's colorful "clouds"—acoustic devices developed with the American engineers Bolt, Beranek & Newman—create an interior landscape for the campus's central gathering place (page 279, fig. 4). Outside the buildings a rich, sensorial architecture of light and shadow, created by arcades, broad ramps, and perforated masonry screens in various forms, both echoes the rapidly changing skies over the high valley and gives protection from them. In these same years Tomás José Sanabria, Villanueva's former student and close friend, began a daily meteorological record of the effects of the encounter between the moist air of the Caribbean and the great landmass of Cerro El Ávila, the mountain that dominates Caracas, atop which he built his Hotel Humboldt, in 1956 (page 280) to serve as a beacon for the city. In many respects the preoccupation of Alexander von Humboldt (the nineteenth-century German natural scientist and explorer for whom the hotel is named) with the specific relationship of geography to culture resonates still in Sanabria's and Villanueva's architecture.

The acclaim in the international architectural press for both campuses was immediate and widespread. The British *Builder* picked out UCV for special praise amid the "surfeit of brilliant modern architecture" in booming Venezuela, saying that "it could be said it contains the germ of a Venezuelan style of architecture."[18] If it did contain such a germ, it was not a question of the brise-soleils that had, when exhibited at MoMA, caused so much controversy over the death of composition; it was not a kit of parts, a Latin American set of elements, but rather the creation of a modern agora connected by cantilevered pathways that exploited the most advanced engineering to conduct students and visitors through the spaces of the campus. Covered paths cutting great diagonal connections had been employed earlier on a modest scale in Frank Lloyd Wright's Florida Southern College (first designed in 1938), but Villanueva created a whole network of differentiated vaulted spaces that extend outward almost like tentacles from the mollusk- or crab-shaped central acropolis, or Plaza Cubierta (Covered plaza), through the lush plantings of the tropical campus. Villanueva's growing affinity with developments in Brazil, in particular with the astounding freeform public plaza that connects Niemeyer's contemporary buildings in Parque Ibirapuera in São Paulo (inaugurated in 1954) or later with the early urban plans for Brasília (beginning in 1957), was reflected in his own teaching at UCV's architecture school, housed in one of his most accomplished buildings on the campus, where he lectured to the students on a wide range of contemporary architecture (fig. 12).

The optimism of Villanueva's vision of the modern university campus as an ideal city was not without its immediate paradoxes, for although the site was purchased in the early 1940s under the

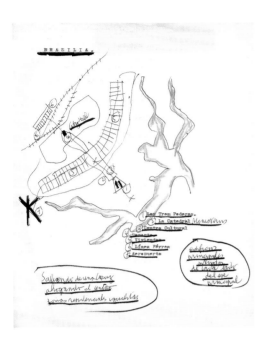

12. Notes for a classroom lecture on Brasília. c. 1965. Carlos Raúl Villanueva (Venezuelan, born England. 1900–1975). Ink on paper, 11 x 8 ½ in. (27.9 x 21.6 cm). Fundación Villanueva

13. Plan for Brasília. 1957. Rino Levi (Brazilian, 1901–1965). Competition entry, model. Acervo Digital Rino Levi, Pontifícia Universidade Católica de Campinas

democratically elected Isaías Medina Angarita, the campus plan evolved into its final form a decade later, under the progressive dictatorship of Pérez Jiménez, a regime that in a few short years would sponsor Caracas's radical transformation into a city organized around a major highway connecting it to the sea. Venezuelan urbanism not only took on the power of the territory—it began to transform it.

New Cities: The Ordering of the Territory

Architectural modernism has almost always allied itself with the larger forces of modernization, in particular the rationalization of infrastructure and, thus, control over entire territories; this notion was established in the engineering tradition of France during the Enlightenment and was dramatically visible in the efforts to bring the vast interiors of South America under control. No project is more emblematic than the new Brazilian capital, treated at greater length by Carlos Eduardo Comas in this volume. There, in a period of only three years, an entire city, zoned for administration, residence, commerce, and transportation, was laid out deep in the interior, in a location reachable primarily by airplane (air travel in these decades was increasingly rewriting the maps of many countries and of regional relationships).[19] Brasília was inaugurated on April 21, 1960, after which it was visited by heads of state, including Queen Elizabeth II and Josep Broz Tito, and captured media attention in the architectural and daily presses, television, and even feature films, such as the construction-site chase scenes in Philippe de Broca's highly popular *L'Homme de Rio* (*That Man from Rio*) (1964).

Costa's winning entry in the competition for the city's plan—selected from among schemes showing more of a European influence, by Rino Levi (fig. 13), Artigas, and others—both conquered and established the territory. It was the first urban layout to feature a transportation center as the veritable navel of a growing city, an ideal first imagined in 1914 by the Italian Futurist Antonio Sant'Elia, and by Tony Garnier in his Cité Industrielle in 1917, and partly implemented in the Centro Bolívar in Caracas in the 1950s.[20] The Brazilian president Juscelino Kubitschek and Niemeyer represented a formidable artistic-political alliance, with a vision of a modern nation comparable to that of the Sun King and Louis Le Vau in the planning of Versailles. Niemeyer defined the prime geometries of the congress, with its twin towers and monumental, abstracted domes, one inverted, flanked on either side by the colonnaded ministries of foreign affairs and justice. The central green lawn esplanade was clearly reminiscent of the mall in Washington, D.C., but it was Costa's subtle planning of the residential and shopping quarters that made Brasília more than an exercise in the new monumentality so hotly debated by CIAM after World War II.

Brasília's design was rapidly criticized as an apotheosis of the errors of international modernist planning. But the criticism, which reached an apex in Bruno Zevi's and Moholy Nagy's condemnations—the latter entitled "Brasília: Majestic Concept or Autocratic Monument?"—overlooked the new city's subtle change in scale from representational to residential quarters and, above all, its innovative model for integrating recreation, shopping, housing, and the automobile in Costa's *superquadras*, or superblocks.[21] Rather than employing the rationalized slab-housing constructions associated with modernism—in everything from Ludwig Hilberseimer's vision for Berlin (1927) to Villanueva's 23 de Enero housing project in Caracas (1955–57, page 290), one of the largest in South America at the time—Costa brilliantly merged architecture, landscape planning, and planting, and he demonstrated mastery of circulation and parking. In the *superquadras* (which refer to the neighborhood units, rather than the individual buildings) parking is recessed below the datum of dwelling, so that clear sightlines through the glazed lobbies of slabs raised on *pilotis* afford uninterrupted vistas from landscape court to landscape court, defining a flowing public ground plane in a dense housing quarter replete with well-defined exterior spaces for leisure. Photographs of Ludwig Mies van der Rohe and Costa viewing

14. Lucio Costa (center), and Ludwig Mies van der Rohe (right) examining a model of *superquadras*. c. 1957. Photograph by Mario Fontenelle. Archivo Público do Distrito Federal, Brasília

models of this housing together in 1959 point to the parallel nature of their discoveries rather than a flow of influence between Brazilian design and the contemporary work by Mies, Hilbersheimer, and landscape designer Alfred Caldwell for the Lafayette Park neighborhood in Detroit, also built in 1958–60 (fig. 14).

Brasília established the modernity of Brazil and the maturity of its urbanism on a world stage, creating a public image to replace those of the land of underdevelopment and tropical paradise. For a time this achievement crowded out discussion of the mushrooming informal settlements or favelas, not only on the hills of Rio de Janeiro and surrounding São Paulo but even in the unplanned satellite suburbs of Brasília, where many of the temporary workers lived.[22]

The creation of infrastructure and monumental representation of the state in the South American interior were dominant themes in the 1950s and '60s. Argentina integrated the distant inland pampas through projects such as the Centro Cívico of the new provincial capital of Santa Rosa de La Pampa (1955–63, page 100), Clorindo Testa's first great success. Meanwhile, in Chile, the architects of the Escuela de Arquitectura were developing a poetic approach to the territory through an alternative architectural pedagogy: an open-ended search for the autochthonous and unknown that would resist the certainties of the modernist conquest of space and land. In 1952, with the joint appointment of the architect Alberto Cruz and the poet Godofredo Iommi, the architecture school in Valparaíso underwent a fundamental transformation of curriculum and outlook, a radical rethinking of the very notion of architecture that would mark the school as one of the most experimental architectural programs on the continent. The school recast all of South America as a mythical landscape, Amereida—combining America with *Eneida*, Spanish for *Aeneid*—and developed a metaphoric and performative relationship to both land and territory, ignoring national borders as teachers and students made pilgrimage journeys, or *travesías*, starting in 1965, in search of a primordial American essence. In addition to pilgrimage, the *travesías* involved the creation of temporary dwellings from transportable and found materials spontaneously adapted to chance and terrain, to let the travelers lightly occupy the land.[23] With the founding in 1970 of the Ciudad Abierta at Ritoque, on the coast north of Valparaíso, the group adopted a landscape of sand dunes and ravines in which to craft their living spaces, as well as a cemetery designed with Juan Ignacio Baixas, a teacher. The city was built by hand, by students and teachers in a process of discovery of both materials—in particular of the capacities of brick—and landscape. The school was also able to establish a dialogue with existing cities, in such projects as the competition entry for the naval academy at Valparaíso (1956–57, page 157). One notable and innovative (although unexecuted) project wove Valparaíso and its coastline into a more meaningful relationship with the city and the territory, in a proposed restructuring of Avenida del Mar (page 168) along the seafront. This project thus put forward an approach to territorial planning that would work in consonance with the found landscape, in contrast to the state-sponsored attempts to conquer new and distant territories for resource extraction or to open up the coastline for the development of tourist infrastructure, as did the Mexican government in the Yucatán and along the Pacific Coast, or President Belaunde with his project for an Andean highway in Peru.

Outside of Brazil, the growth of architecture linked to large-scale infrastructure was nowhere more impressive and fast paced than in Venezuela, where ambitious engineering projects transformed Caracas in the 1950s. New highways organized the city around the twin towers of the Centro Simón Bolívar and connected it to the coast and the airport. Sanabria's Hotel Humboldt, atop Cerro El Ávila, was linked by cable cars on both sides of the mountain it crowned, one linking it to the city in the high valley, the other to the port. The landscape scale of these projects reached an unprecedented size in 1961, with the construction of El Helicoide de la Roca Tarpeya (page 282), a privately funded mixed-use commercial megastructure that attracted a great deal of international attention. Construction began in 1958 under the Jiménez regime, but the center was inaugurated with the return of democratic rule in the second administration of President Rómulo Betancourt, who in the same year announced plans for a new city for 2.5 million, to be called Ciudad Guayana, in the sparsely populated southeast.

El Helicoide was nothing less than the transformation of a lower peak in the Cordillera de la Costa mountain chain, which forms Caracas's dramatic, omnipresent backdrop, by large-scale terracing—an ancient Andean tradition. The building is formed of a continual coil of intertwined road and structures, thus creating a man-made mountain cap, a meeting of pre-Columbian earthwork with shopping center, albeit one more advanced than the US models that were cropping up everywhere in the Venezuelan capital. Designed by the team of Pedro Neuberger, Dirk Bornhorst, and Jorge Romero Gutiérrez, El Helicoide was also a perfect intersection of northern and southern influences: at once apotheosis of Wright's "automobile objective"—his park for the automotive age—and landscape translation of the megascale Latin American mixed-use project, a type launched in 1956 with David Libeskind's Conjunto Nacional, a residential and commercial center on Avenida Paulista in São Paulo. In the Conjunto Nacional internal circulation takes place via a ramp similar to the one then under construction in Wright's Guggenheim Museum, in New York, but here linking underground parking with ground-level arcades connecting the adjacent streets to multiple floors of shops around an open atrium (fig. 15). A *Delirious São Paulo* or *Delirious Caracas*—with apologies to Rem Koolhaas's influential 1978 book, which posits New York as a capital of modernist hybridity—might well have celebrated these Brazilian and Venezuelan disavowals of monofunctional planning in favor of intensified metropolitan energy and public interaction.

In 1961, the same year that MoMA celebrated El Helicoide in the exhibition *Roads* (fig. 16), the Betancourt administration launched Ciudad Guayana, which was located at the conjuncture of the Orinoco and Caroní rivers, two key South American transportation axes.[24] The Caroní is a major link between the Atlantic Ocean and inland Venezuela and Colombia; Humboldt had identified this location as a major geographic and economic feature of northern South America as far back as 1800. In much the same way that the area around Lake Maracaibo, in the west of the country, was being developed to take advantage of a limitless-seeming supply of petroleum, Ciudad Guayana, in the east, would bring rationalized city planning to a territory rich in iron ore and bauxite, along with waterfalls for the

15. **Conjunto Nacional, São Paulo. 1952–56.** David Libeskind (Brazilian, 1928–2014). View of the ground floor and ramp leading from subterranean parking to the roof terrace. 2012. Photograph by Leonardo Finotti

16. Installation view of *Roads*, with photographs of El Helicoide de la Roca Tarpeya, Caracas, at The Museum of Modern Art, New York, August 14– September 17, 1961. Photograph by George Barrows. The Museum of Modern Art Archives, New York

generation of electricity. Thus the raw materials of modern architecture were intimately linked to the materials of the national resource export economy. Planning was initially done in collaboration with the Joint Center for Urban Studies at MIT and Harvard, which provided technical assistance in the first five years of development, but the key architectural components of the city center were designed by Venezuelan architects.

Jesús Tenreiro-Degwitz's headquarters for the Corporación Venezolana de Guayana (CVG) (page 288 and portfolio 1), which at the time offered a new model for office space, is no doubt the masterwork of the new city: an open steel-frame structure that creates a flow from interior to exterior, with rows of screens framing views of the landscape and creating tranquil exterior zones within the building's protective footprint. In a rather pointed irony Tenreiro's building—a symbol of steel as an engine of development and the first large-scale steel-frame structure in Venezuela since the construction of the Centro Bolívar had begun the transformation of Caracas into a city of skyscrapers—ultimately required steel imported from the United States. The CVG headquarters was one of a group of buildings intended to encourage South American steel industries, including two experimental high-rises: Mario Roberto Álvarez's SOMISA building in Buenos Aires (1971–78, page 119)—the headquarters for the Sociedad Mixta Siderúrgica Argentina, founded in 1947 to promote national steel production—and Ricardo Legorreta's headquarters in Mexico City for the Celanese chemical firm (1968, page 239), in which a lightweight steel frame is held in tension, hung from a single mastlike elevator core. Each of these buildings represents the linking of industry with economic development and, through experiments in the capacities of steel and glass, proposes new relationships between the realms of work and civic life, in plazas and interpenetrating corporate and civic spaces, and between workers and the surrounding urban fabric.

In an interview Tenreiro described his ambition to create both a monument and a porous, hybrid structure poised between building and civic realm, and his subsequent disappointment: "The building stood lonely for many years. However, the archetypal image was strong enough to overcome the shameful city that eventually grew up around it."[25] No less disillusioned by the city's development was the American anthropologist Lisa Redfield Peattie, one of the original consultants, whose experiences during the city's formative years catalyzed her advocacy of participatory design in place of technocratic approach. In *The View from the Barrio*, from 1968, she offered a searing critique of top-down planning in the vein of Jane Jacobs's *The Death and Life of Great American Cities* (1961).

Memories of Underdevelopment, Dreams of Development

The debate over the means and prospects of development can be read in many different contrasting examples from the 1960s and early 1970s. Here it is useful to juxtapose three contemporaneous projects, each the result of a major policy decision or political event with international resonance: the decision to make Santiago the headquarters for the United Nations Comisión Económica para América Latina (CEPAL), which was founded in 1947; the decision, in 1959, by the Banco de Londres y América del Sur to build its new headquarters in Buenos Aires (with branch banks in then-less-stable locations around South and Central America); and the success of Castro and his rebel army, in 1959, in finally sending the corrupt Fulgencio Batista into exile and instituting a revolutionary, and highly experimental, government in Cuba. Although the Argentine bank building was the most visible symbol of capitalist approaches to development, it would be CEPAL that would prove the more sustained advocate of the dependency theory of development. This was especially true from 1950 to 1963, under the leadership of Raúl Prebisch, the Argentine economist and author of the influential

Economic Development of Latin America and Its Principle Problems (1950), which advocated compensation to developing countries for the unequal global distribution of the gains of productivity.[26] Castro, in Cuba—one of the most outspoken among the countries of the Non-Aligned Movement—would spend the 1960s seeking a countermodel for development and progress, not only domestically but also as an export model for the third world. Cuba, indeed, was watched by many intellectuals and politicians throughout Latin America.

The headquarters of the Banco de Londres in Buenos Aires's financial district, designed by the SEPRA studio with Clorindo Testa, is one of the architectural masterpieces of the period, and it can be as profitably studied architecturally, for its radical revision of the physical relationship of a bank to the civic realm, as for its innovations in prefabrication and its new conception of a working environment (page 102). Like the Manufacturers Trust Company branch on Fifth Avenue and Forty-Third Street in New York, built five years earlier, in which a glazed curtain wall created a modernized and urbane space for retail banking, the Banco de Londres was one of a series of Argentine buildings, along with the branches designed for the Banco de la Ciudad (page 106) by the firm of Manteola, Petchersky, Sánchez Gómez, Santos, Solsona, Viñoly, that proposed new exemplars of the bank as a transparent, interactive civic monument. Occupying its site as a provocative counterargument to the neo-Baroque bank buildings on the other three chamfered corners of the intersection, the bank's concrete frame elements billow out, creating room beneath them for the sidewalk, all the while allowing the bank to occupy the maximum volume on its site. The corner itself is dramatically opened, almost like the parting of a theater curtain's wings—an effect made clear in lively sketches Testa made after the fact—to offer dramatic views from the interior to the street and from the street into the inner workings of the bank. The interior is organized in trays of office space set around a great atrium. In short, the building is conceived as a dramatic platform for public interaction, rather than a sanctuary set behind solid, vaultlike doors, and as a breaking down of the barrier between facade and interior; it is also a precursor of the rethinking of an urban museum a decade later in the Centre Georges Pompidou in Paris (1971–77).

The Santiago CEPAL headquarters (page 162) was the result of a competition held in 1960 for a new building for the UN and its agencies, which was won by the Chilean architect Emilio Duhart.[27] It may be the most coherent and unified of the forays into modern architecture made by the United Nations, which began with its New York headquarters (1947–49), in which Niemeyer played a key role, and continued with the competition for the UNESCO headquarters in Paris (1958). Duhart's design places a more overt emphasis on monumental and symbolic form, including a powerful integration of the building both within its immediate surroundings and in its dramatic setting against the chain of the Andes—and by implication, with the entire continent. The extensive grounds, designed by Burle Marx but much altered in execution, would form a new link in a system of green parks along the Mapocho River laid out a half century earlier, the first of which was Jorge Dubois's Parque Forestal. The UN rhetoric about fostering a world architecture gave way to discourses on regionalism, like those emerging from the debates taking place in many Latin American countries at the time, as in the brief noting that the site was "a suitable setting for exhibiting the types of wood, stone, and marble to be found in the American continent."[28] The design reflects both the UN's ideal of a "Workshop for the New Latin America" and the increased interest, starting in the 1950s, in having a rugged naturalism of exposed concrete enrich the vocabulary of modern architecture.

One of the most pressing issues for Duhart was how to control the intense Chilean sunlight in and around his building in both summer and winter. He was fresh from the atelier of Le Corbusier, where he had worked on buildings for the new Punjab capital in Chandigarh, and he had absorbed the lessons of that project's experiments with the brise-soleil as both sun-control mechanism and powerful plastic feature with a symbolic duty. But in integrating the spaces of daily work and occasional assembly into a more flowing and interconnected whole, Duhart made clear that he had also learned from the problems of the work environments in the previous UN buildings, both of them campuses of connected elements in asymmetrical groupings with offices organized vertically in slabs. Duhart's parti offered a departure, with the offices on a single raised floor surrounding two exceptional structures for large meetings, ceremonies, and events—one shaped as cone and the other (built many years later) as a diamond. These were set within the ample perimeter of offices raised on powerful piers and protected under a great overhanging soffit, all enjoying panoramic views; the landscape also entered the ground level courtyard through the continuous covered passages formed by the piers, blurring, in the days of less-heightened security concerns, the institutional and civic realms. Duhart's solution was a complex composition held tightly in architectonic form, the symbolism of its forms so sculptural that they were later reworked by Uruguayan sculptor Gonzalo Fonseca in his *Torre de los vientos* (Tower of the winds) created for the Ruta de la Amistad (Route of friendship), one of a series of sculptures erected in Mexico City for the 1968 Olympics (fig. 17).

By describing the building's relation to the "cosmic complexity of the Andes" and its duality, constituting "at once a house and a monument"—recalling Le Corbusier's *Une Maison—un palais*, written in 1928 in defense of his rejected League of Nations design of that year—Duhart situated the building between the national and the global, between the depth of historical learning and the search for contemporary expression.[29] He explained that his design invoked Spanish colonial town planning and traditional Chilean house types, with the offices set above a *zócalo*. A second courtyard beyond the first was intended to be more private, and Duhart here made reference to Chilean haciendas. The great cone of the assembly hall, with its ramp ascending to a *mirador*, or observatory, is at once reminiscent of pre-Columbian monuments and of the latest Corbusian expression in Chandigarh. It is literally given a stamp of the Americas in various pictograms worked into the concrete, to be discovered like fossils while ascending to the view of the distant snow-capped mountains (fig. 18).

These two masterpieces, in Buenos Aires and in Santiago, are now part of architectural history, but an alternative history might trace their influence beyond their brilliant architectural expression: here are two of the main agencies whose control of the flow of money is inscribed in the architectural projects of the period in ways not yet elucidated. Such a history would include not only national—and nationalist—projects but also the agendas that were shaping the region's cities and territories, including those of the World Bank, the United States–based Alliance for Progress, launched by the US president John F. Kennedy in 1961, and the UN, as well as bilateral arrangements such as the transfer of technology between the Soviet Union and Cuba and, later, Chile, especially in the field of prefabricated construction. An accounting of the financial and ideological chains of connection—perhaps along the itinerary suggested by this exhibition and publication—might well offer new insight into the period.

The history of postrevolutionary Cuban architecture clearly lays out the debate between issues of architectural form and technique and issues of development and international politics, via the country's dramatic economic shift from being symbiotically linked to the United States in the 1950s to courting both the Soviet Union and autonomy after 1959. Cuba had attracted considerable attention in the international architectural press for the high quality and innovation of its architecture in the 1950s, largely in the design of houses, well-appointed apartment buildings such as the Evangelina Aristigueta de Vidaña apartment building, by Mario Romañach (1956, page 199), and tourist hotels and nightclubs. The first decade of Castro's leadership did nothing to detract from this achievement, even

17. *La torre de los vientos*, Ruta de la Amistad, Mexico City. 1968. Gonzalo Fonseca (Uruguayan, 1922–1997)

18. **Comisión Económica para América Latina (CEPAL), Santiago. 1960–66.** Emilio Duhart (Chilean, 1917–2006). View of a courtyard and assembly hall with pictographs. 1972. Photograph by Paolo Gasparini

if the whole ideology of architecture radically changed. Although many Cuban architects went into exile, mostly to the United States and, later, like Ricardo Porro, to Europe, architects from abroad were attracted to the new regime's countrywide experiment in spatial and social forms. The early 1960s was a particularly fluid time, as both the revolution and its building projects searched for ideal forms of expression; the Cuban construction industry was hard hit by the material restrictions brought about by the US embargo, so that technical experimentation was at once a necessity and a creative release. The Escuelas Nacionales de Arte were the result of a decision made in 1961 by Castro and his close advisor Che Guevara to turn a Cubanacán country club into an egalitarian center of Cuban cultural expression (pages 206–10). The Cuban Porro was joined by the Italian émigrés Roberto Gottardi and Vittorio Garatti in designing experimental brick structures with details that would evoke Cuba's African (rather than Spanish) origins. Each of the five schools was designed by a single architect, although all of them conformed to a material and technical palette of brick and Catalan vaults—materials thought to express self-reliance, material modesty, and craft, and to facilitate an organic handling of space and form and an autochthonous authenticity. But the schools were an exception to the growing culture. Left unfinished by Castro after a few years, they were soon overshadowed by the very different project of furthering a more industrial Cuba through standardized prefabrication.

The largest project of the period, Unidad no. 1 of the Habana del Este housing project (page 201), was begun under Batista but was pushed forward by the revolution to advance the new regime's promise to provide housing for everyone. In February 1959 Castro convened a team of young architects at the Colegio de Arquitectos to form the Instituto Nacional de Ahorro y Vivienda (National institute of savings and housing). These architects, with Mario González and Hugo D'Acosta, designed a new neighborhood of low-, medium-, and high-rise houses, for 80 acres east of Havana, expropriated from a former Batista loyalist, with the intent of encouraging eastward growth of the capital. As in the *superquadras* of Brasília—although with little of the landscaping finesse—internal vehicular circulation was subordinated to pedestrian movement, creating a zone with a day care center, social club, green lawns calculated at 215 square feet (20 square meters) per resident, sports facilities, shopping, and parking. Construction was completed very quickly, with fifty-eight buildings containing 1,306 apartments completed in 677 working days, largely through the orchestration of hand labor, since the means for large-scale prefabrication were not yet available.[30]

Prefabrication had been studied by Cuban architects in the 1950s, but it became an official priority in 1963, in the wake of both Hurricane Flora, which left some 1,200 Cubans homeless, and the ideological standoff that came to a head in the Cuban Missile Crisis. Not long afterward, the Soviet Union donated the components of its I-646 factory system for producing concrete panels for prefabricated housing, which was transforming Moscow, Leningrad, and cities throughout the Eastern Bloc. In Cuba, after 1965, it was put into production for housing, first in Santiago de Cuba and later in other cities. D'Acosta, who was among the most inventive of those who adapted the Soviet system to Cuban needs and capacities, carved and perforated the panels to lighten them and make them both resilient to high winds and conducive to cross-ventilation in a tropical climate. In the 1970s the Soviet sphere of influence was extended even further, when Leonid Brezhnev donated the same system and equipment to Allende's short-lived left-wing government in Chile.[31]

In Cuba the panels were not deployed exclusively in regimented rows for mass-housing estates. One of the most unpretentious—albeit inventive —uses was not in an urban situation at all but a rural one, as part of the attempt to disseminate the benefits of the revolution, in particular literacy and better living conditions, in order to stem the tide of rural exodus and maintain an agricultural labor force. In the westernmost province of Pinar del Río, the new settlement of Las Terrazas was laid out with housing units of different dimensions, as well as a school and community center, each made up of a simple number of parts—a half-size panel, a bathroom/kitchen unit, and tile roofs (page 204). The smaller panel dimensions allowed for a hybrid of machine production and assembly by hand, as well as for buildings that could be more readily adapted to the terrain and to community needs, in a hilly landscape that would soon become the object of agricultural reform and reforestation as Cuba's first biosphere reserve.

Learning from Latin America

So dominant has the narrative been of Latin America as a testing site for the architectural and urban-planning ideas of Mies van der Rohe, José Luis Sert, and Le Corbusier (helped along by the Uruguayan, Colombian, Mexican, and Argentine architects who trained in the latter's atelier) that the originality of many key Latin American projects is often obscured from historical view. Equally overlooked is the extent to which Latin American architects worked abroad, thus exporting New World ideas not only to other Latin American countries but to Europe, the United States, and Canada, and even to other third world countries in Asia and Africa—such as Niemeyer's apartment building in Hansaviertel (1957), Berlin's model housing estate, or his Communist Party headquarters in Paris (1967–81); Candela's church of Nuestra Señora de Guadalupe in Madrid (1962–63); and the Los Angeles houses of Niemeyer (Strick House, 1963) and Legorreta (Montalbán House, 1985)—not to mention Costa's planning for Nigeria (fig. 19) and the schools designed by the Mexican architect Pedro Ramírez Vázquez (1958, page 234) for worldwide export.

Much of the architecture of the period emphasized technical mastery, lyrical expression, and unprecedented form—often with heroic overtones of the capacity of architecture and infrastructure to accelerate modernization, economic and social development, and the integration of resource-rich economies into the global economy. Architecture marched hand in hand with intense political and economic debates on modernization. Octavio Paz said as much of Mexico when he wrote, "Modernity, for the last one hundred years, has been our style. It is the universal style. Wanting to be modern seems like madness, we are condemned to be modern."[32] Yet despite anxieties about uncritical modernization, the architectural record of the period is also filled with remarkable achievements, buildings that created novel types of social spaces and interaction and projects both tectonic and programmatic whose potential has not yet been exhausted. What, for example, of the work of Dieste? The Uruguayan engineer united complex structural calculations with handwork, and he used this alliance of the everyday with the sophisticated to produce some of the most moving and beloved buildings of the period, in parish churches in rural Uruguay beginning in 1958 with the church of Cristo Obrero (Christ the worker) (page 266) in Atlántida and culminating in what is perhaps his masterpiece, the parish church of San Pedro in Durazno, in 1967 (page 267 and portfolio 2).

Or what of the Brazilian practice of the Italian émigré Bo Bardi? She adapted a glass, steel, and concrete idiom in such heroic and canonical works as the Museu de Arte de São Paulo (MASP) (page 144), but she also explored buildings of simple and nativist means during her years in Salvador. For MASP, according to a legend propagated by Pietro Maria Bardi, the engineer Joaquim Eugênio de Lima had made a gift of his land on the rapidly densifying Avenida Paulista, but he stipulated that once cleared of the Belvedere Trianon, a popular social space consisting of a single-story pavilion set in a small park, the public views of the city must be preserved.[33] Bo Bardi, having already skillfully juxtaposed different structural and typological solutions in her own Casa do Vidro in São Paulo (1951–52)—a glazed box raised on *pilotis* set before a traditionally constructed earthbound courtyard—worked with the engineer José Carlos de Figueiredo Ferraz to collage together two vastly different structures and graft them into the hillside, in a disjunctive composition that can hardly

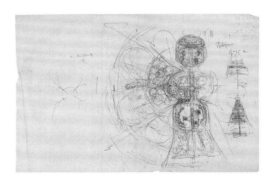

19. **Plan for a new capital of Nigeria. 1970–79.** Lucio Costa (Brazilian, born France. 1902–1998). **Sketch.** Ink on paper, 8 9/16 x 12 7/8 in. (21.9 x 32.7 cm). Casa de Lucio Costa

ever be perceived as whole. A large, two-story, fully glazed gallery space appears to be suspended 26 feet (8 meters) above the site, hanging from two powerful transverse beams and thus becoming an urban frame between powerful concrete pylons that were originally unpainted. Within the upper volume, which has become an urban landmark, Bo Bardi refused to allow paintings to be hung conventionally on walls and instead created an interior vista as impressive as the one framed below, with works placed on upright glass panels in a single large, open space, like so many totems on transparent easels, at once ready for close-up inspection and forming a panorama of display. The building's exterior spaces unfold from sidewalk to great urban plaza for enjoying the view and other activities, passing between the pylons, which are set in basins of water. The plaza is in fact the roof of the museum's second component—a large mixed-used building set into the site's slope atop a highway tunnel—and is home to the events Bo Bardi imagined taking place there, which included a popular circus. MASP was inaugurated in 1968, the same year of Mies van der Rohe's Neue Nationalgalerie in Berlin, a building of similarly complex section, at once a glazed pavilion and a plaza atop the roof of a museum below it. Unlike Mies, Bo Bardi set out to join civic solemnity and popular culture on the same urban stage.

Bo Bardi's vision combined innovative display techniques with the notion of the museum's potential for creating social activity across classes and horizons, ideas she had developed between 1959 and 1964 when she designed and then became the director of the Museu de Arte Moderna da Bahia, in Salvador, in Brazil's northeast. There she became fascinated by the rich mixture of active and unhomogenized cultures, of the encounters between native peoples, Afro-Brazilians, and the Portuguese settlers who had arrived in the sixteenth century. That experience, and the creativity it unleashed, remained with Bo Bardi as she reconceptualized the role of architecture and the architect in the mushrooming metropolis of São Paulo. In her architecture Bo Bardi claimed to promote the "pursuit of freedom" and declared, "I never look for beauty, only purity."[34]

The culmination of Bo Bardi's socially engaged architecture was her masterpiece of adaptive reuse, the cultural and sports center Serviço Social do Comércio (SESC) Pompeia, which opened in a disused steel-drum factory in 1982. Bo Bardi designed spaces for multiple uses, different age groups, and various tempos, with zones of use and of quiet established by furniture, of her own design, that could be reconfigured for various uses. Like MASP, the SESC building imports the energy of the neighborhood and reframes existing structures to create new relationships, all the while offering an urban oasis. It was a pioneering vision of the postindustrial metropolis in a country perceived by the rest of the world to be an underdeveloped nation.

Colombia in the 1950s and '60s was a country of entrenched and endemic violence, including a bloody standoff between the government and the guerrilla armies of the Fuerzas Armadas Revolucionarias de Colombia; nevertheless it is in Bogotá that we find the Torres del Parque apartment complex (1964–70, page 184), one of the most accomplished examples of architecture synthesizing private and public space, indeed one of the only projects in which this was achieved anywhere in the world in this period. The complex was funded by El Banco Central Hipotecario, as part of a program begun in the 1930s to encourage housing production and, by extension, to keep the middle class from deserting the city center for the city's northern reaches in a pattern of class polarization taking place throughout the Americas in the 1960s. Land for the project was available on the lower slopes of the Cerro de Monserrate range, which dominates the capital, adjacent to the Parque de la Independencia, laid out in 1910 and one of the city's oldest parks, and to the Plaza de Toros, the main bullfighting ring, a circular neo-Romanesque stadium that opened in 1931.

The complex was designed by Rogelio Salmona, who in the late 1950s had worked in Le Corbusier's office in Paris. On his return he launched himself immediately into innovative housing-design projects, starting with El Polo in Bogotá (1960–63, page 186), designed with Guillermo Bermúdez. His initial design for the Torres del Parque aligned slab apartment buildings in a neat row at the uppermost part of the site, adjacent to the major north-south thoroughfare of Carrera 7a. But as the design evolved, Salmona curved the slabs, as if to embrace the bullring and to echo the serrated landscape of the mountain range behind the project, thus visually connecting the city with its towering landscape. Torres del Parque's curves became more pronounced in each new iteration, so that the buildings seem to torque with the elegance of bullfighter, as well as to respond to one another, aided by specially shaped bricks. The narrow, curved buildings yield apartment layouts of enormous variety, many with views in multiple directions, as well as generous balconies splayed and cascading down the sides of the buildings, further echoing the landscape, and planted with verdant gardens. The design enhanced the public sphere in a manner unusual for a middle-class urban apartment complex, with the buildings set in a picturesque network of paths, plazas, and gardens that merges seamlessly with the adjacent park and seems to shape the buildings as much as the buildings shape it. Paths and spaces open to the public are not set off by fences but by simple bronze plaques that denote the legal limit between public and private, a limit rarely perceptible in the project's weaving of the two into the fabric of Bogotá, a rapidly densifying downtown otherwise given over to commercial use, offices, and hotels.

Salmona's complex acts as a complement to the nearby multilevel urban-redevelopment scheme used in the Centro Internacional Tequendama (1952–82), a prototypical urban renewal-project with raised pedestrian plazas, underground parking, and bridge connections, of the type that came to characterize urban centers throughout Europe and the United States, in which the open space often seems left over, rather than deliberately designed. At Torres del Parque a different approach to urban fabric is essayed, and nearly seventy-five percent of the site, which holds 294 apartments, is given over to space shared among residents and other citizens of Bogotá. For Salmona—who, like other Colombian architects such as Fernando Martínez Sanabria, worked in a formal language that increasingly recalled the organic planning of Aalto more than any allegiance to Le Corbusier—the aim was to "create the building through open space, as a generator of covered space."[35]

The 1950s, '60s, and '70s were a particularly experimental era in Latin American housing, from the integration of site planning and elevated open-air walkways in the Portales development in Santiago (1955–68, page 164), by the firm of Bresciani Valdés Castillo Huidobro, to the remarkable integration of private and public spaces in the Bulevar Artigas housing complex in Montevideo (1971–74; page 272 and portfolio 11), by Héctor Vigliecca, Ramiro Bascáns, Thomas Sprechmann, and Arturo Villaamil.[36] Perhaps no project is riper for renewed evaluation than the Proyecto Experimental de Vivienda (PREVI) in Lima (pages 256–59), one of the most ambitious and complex housing and development experiments of the period, and one that is currently being rediscovered by architects and urban theorists.[37] PREVI was sponsored by the UN and conceived under the administration of President Belaunde, himself an architect, in conjunction with Luis Ortiz de Zevallos, also an architect and, at the time, the director of Banco de la Vivienda del Perú, the national housing bank; its design and implementation were entrusted to the British architect and planner Peter Land. The development was intended to produce urban and rural housing—which were desperately needed in Peru and nowhere more so than in Lima, where a vast rural exodus was creating rapidly growing squatter settlements at the city's edges—as pilot experiments that the United Nations Development Program could bring to other developing countries. The most famous of the four proposals was for an entire neighborhood in Lima. Land, like many architects, was inspired by the ideas of John Turner, a British architect who made extensive stays in Peru in the 1960s and who argued that self-built projects were more propitious for social development than top-down state construction. Land proposed an international competition for low-rise, high-density housing schemes, in particular in Lima, although rural models were also sought. He invited a who's who of international architects—Georges Candilis, Alexis Josic, and Shadrach Woods, from France; Christopher Alexander, from the United States; Atelier 5, from Switzerland; Aldo van Eyck, from the Netherlands; Oskar Hansen, from Poland; Fumihiko Maki and Kiyonori Kikutake, from Japan; James Stirling, from the United Kingdom; Charles Correa, from India; and Germán Samper, from Colombia, among others, to work alongside an equal number of Peruvian teams, including Frederick Cooper Llosa, Miguel Alvariño, and Manuel Llanos Jhon. In October 1968 Belaunde was overthrown by a leftist military junta that turned its focus to rural development. Nevertheless, since the UN funding was already in place, the new regime decided that work on PREVI would continue in Lima.

The competition entries were so compelling that Land jettisoned the quest for a single master plan in favor of a patchwork of different approaches to create both urban variety and a potent set of laboratory results for future action. A team in the Peruvian ministry of housing would design the open spaces between projects while the invited architects focused on the relationship between units, which could be expanded and upgraded by their owners, and the neighborhood, which would retain its character even as the houses changed. Thus the teams designed not only themes and variations on a model dwelling but also scenarios for possible growth. The target population was lower middle class, and it was hoped that the housing would empower its residents, who would own rather than renting their units, and in this respect PREVI was as experimental in its financial model as in its architectural one.

Many of the architects—notably Stirling—imagined the base units as entirely prefabricated structures, which would require uniformity and large-scale production, both qualities at odds with the small scale and intended growth of the project. Questions were left unanswered: Would the residents have to order new factory-produced parts only for the specific system of their neighborhood, or could they work in an ad hoc manner? How would ongoing architectural and building advice be provided? It turned out, too, that the needs and desires of the units' owners were at odds with the ideals of design. Van Eyck, having made the trenchant observation that household life in Lima's *barriadas* revolved around the kitchen, emulated this feature in his units, which he designed on a grid of diamond sites with triangular outdoor areas. The orientation of the sites created a brilliantly integrated system of cross-ventilation that risked being compromised if the owners were given full freedom to expand as they wished. Indeed Van Eyck hoped to direct future growth away from that inevitable tendency, but for the most part the ingenuity of the owners exceeded his design's incentives and disincentives. In many cases the openness and permeability he sought to design into the system was lost.

Although few of these projects have found their rightful place in modern architectural history, they have, in recent years, found advocates among architects who believe that architecture need not entirely surrender to market forces. The growing interest on the part of architects in incremental solutions, such as those highlighted in *Small Scale, Big Change: New Architectures of Social Engagement* at MoMA in 2010, might at first suggest that the large-scale ambitions of the developmentalist projects of the 1960s and '70s have little to offer us in the present day. But the attention paid to public space in buildings as diverse as Bo Bardi's museum and Salmona's middle-class housing continue to speak to an ethos of the power of individual projects to craft spaces of meaningful public interaction. At the same time the increased interest in alliances between infrastructural and architectural projects, between merging the landscape and engineering concerns of the very networks of our cities, allows us to look with fresh eyes at MASP and CEPAL, where transportation, public parks and promenades, and public facilities are all interwoven in complex ways. The integration of public land-scape into private or restricted-access building is a lesson of Salmona's Torres del Parque and the work of González de León in his Colegio de México in 1974–76 (page 244). PREVI, a supposedly failed housing project, has become a valuable lesson in providing houses that can be expanded according to the changing needs of their inhabitants, as much attention has been turned to the successes of Chilean architect Alejandro Aravena's experiments with similar incremental housing (minus prefabrication) in recent projects in Chile and Mexico.

The economic and social conditions of the twenty-first century seem quite remote from the period of state developmentalism featured in this book; even the role of municipal government has emerged in new ways, with the work of architect-mayor Jaime Lerner in Curitiba, Brazil, in the early 1990s, and more recently with the commissioning, by Sergio Fajardo, the mayor of Medellín, of libraries connected to the city's transit system by cable cars, a feature also seen in the work of Jorge Mario Jáuregui in the favelas of Rio and of Urban Think Tank in Caracas. Many architecture and urbanism critics have joined the growing praise of recent efforts to extend the acupunctural urbanism of the 1990s to the underprivileged barrios and favelas of Latin American cities; a very few, notably Justin McGuirk, have understood the roots of these ideas in an earlier period.[38] But complex historical under-standing is a vital prerequisite for responding to the challenges facing globalizing cities today, in a period in which market approaches have largely replaced any notion of developmentalism.

Visiting PREVI today, it is hard to discern at first glance the characteristics of the individual buildings that are so readily apparent on the presentation drawings. Nor, on arrival, is it readily apparent where PREVI ends and adjacent neighborhoods begin. But the quality of the exterior spaces is so successful, and has been so successfully maintained, that the lessons of the project are immediately perceptible. It is the aim of *Latin America in Construction*—a historical laboratory animated by many such projects—to provide the materials for a historical and contemporary reevaluation of the architectural legacy of one of the most complex periods in Latin American history.

1   The best analysis of the press is Zilah Quezado Deckker, *Brazil Built: The Architecture of the Modern Movement in Brazil* (London: Spon Press, 2001), p. 151. For MoMA history see also Barry Bergdoll, "Good Neighbors: The Museum of Modern Art and Latin America; A Journey through the MoMA Archives," in Louise Noelle and Iván San Martín, eds., *Modernidad Urbana/Urban Modernity* (Mexico City: Mexico Docomomo, 2012), pp. 41–75; and Bergdoll, "Good Neighbors: MoMA and Latin America, 1933–1955," in Thordis Arrhenius, Mari Lending, et al., eds., *Place and Displacement: Exhibition Architecture* (Zurich: Lars Müller, 2014), pp. 113–28.

2   Philip L. Goodwin, "Museum Notes," *The Bulletin of the Museum of Modern Art* 10, no. 3 (1943): 23.

3   "Laborers' House Development in Chile," *Arts & Architecture*, April 1949.

4   Henry-Russell Hitchcock, *Latin American Architecture since 1945* (New York: The Museum of Modern Art, 1955), p. 9.

5   Ibid., p. 11.

6   For example, a show on Brazilian architecture was presented at the Building Centre in London in July 1953, under the auspices of the Anglo-Brazilian Society. See *Concrete Quarterly* 18 (April–June 1953).

7   Alf Byden, "Report on Brazil," *Architectural Review* 108, no. 464 (October 1950): 221–22.

8   The Vienna-born architect Harry Seidler worked for Oscar Niemeyer for three months in 1948 before emigrating to Australia. See Helen O'Neill, *A Singular Vision: Harry Seidler* (Sydney: Harper Collins Australia, 2013), pp. 111–13.

9   Max Bill, "Report on Brazil," *Architectural Review* 116 (October 1954): 238–39.

10 Sibyl Moholy-Nagy, "Mexican Critique," *Progressive Architecture* 34 (November 1953): 109, 70, 72, 75–76.

11 Nikolaus Pevsner, *Pioneers of Modern Design: From William Morris to Walter Gropius*, rev. ed. (1936; London: Penguin, 1960), p. 217. It was published in Spanish in 1958 as *Pioneros del diseño moderno* (Buenos Aires: Infinito, 1958).

12 Francisco Bullrich, *New Directions in Latin American Architecture* (New York: Braziller, 1969). Published in Spanish as *Nuevos caminos de la arquitectura latinoamericana* (Barcelona: Blume, 1969).

13 Manfredo Tafuri and Francesco Dal Co, *Modern Architecture* (New York: Harry N. Abrams, 1979), pp. 378–79.

14 See, for example, Bill, "Declaraciones de Max Bill," *Nuestra arquitectura*, no. 294 (1954): 6–7.

15 The humanities and philosophy school was designed by Enrique de la Mora, Manuel de la Colina, and Enrique Landa; the law school by Alonso Mariscal and Ernesto Gómez Gallardo; and the economics school by Vladimir Kaspé and José Hanhausen.

16 Alfonso Pérez-Méndez and Alejandro Aptilon, *Las casas del Pedregal, 1947–1968* (Barcelona: Editorial Gustavo Gili, 2007).

17 This transformed landscape figures prominently in Luis Buñuel's 1955 film *El río y la muerte*, which is not surprising.

18 Derek Matthews, "Caracas, City of Uninhibited Modern Architecture," *Builder* 197 (October 1959): 472.

19 See Hugo Mondragón López, "Aviation, Electrification, and the Nation: Visions from Colombia and Chile," in Patricio del Real and Helen Gyger, eds., *Latin American Modern Architectures: Ambiguous Territories* (London: Routledge, 2013), pp. 235–50.

20 See Carlos Brillembourg, "Caracas: Towards a New City, 1938–1955," *Archivos de arquitectura antillana* 34 (September 2009): 100–13.

21 Bruno Zevi, "Inchiesta su Brasilia: Sei? Sulla nuova capitale sudamericana," *L'architettura: Cronache e storia*, no. 51 (January 1960): 608–19; and Moholy-Nagy, "Brasilia: Majestic Concept or Autocratic Monument?," *Progressive Architecture* 40, no. 10 (October 1959): 88–89. These, it must be said, were later appreciated by more balanced scholarly treatment, notably in Norma Evenson's *Two Brazilian Capitals* (New Haven: Yale University Press, 1973), but this did not appear until 1973, by which time the tone of the argument had been set.

22 See Joaquim Pedro de Andrade's moving film *Brasília: Contradições de uma cidade* (1968).

23 See, most recently, *Drifts and Derivations: Experiences, Journeys and Morphologies* (Madrid: Museo Nacional Centro de Arte Reina Sofia, 2010).

24 El Helicoide was celebrated in Bernard Rudofsky's exhibition *Roads* at MoMA in 1961, but by the middle of the decade the project had run into trouble; it was largely abandoned by 1970, only to be—ironically enough—taken over by the state for administrative uses, including the Dirección de los Servicios de Inteligencia y Prevención.

25 Jesús Tenreiro-Degwitz, interview with Brillembourg, *Bomb*, no. 86 (December 2003): 46.

26 Albert O. Hirschman, "Ideologies of Economic Development in Latin America," in Hirschman, ed., *Latin American Issues: Essays and Comments* (New York: The 20th Century Fund, 1961), pp. 3–42.

27 My remarks about CEPAL are derived from my longer essay in Jeanette Plaut and Marcelo Sarovic, eds., *CEPAL 1962–1966, United Nations Building, Emilio Duhart Arquitecto* (Santiago de Chile: Constructo, 2012).

28 CEPAL Documento EGLA/30-50-9.

29 Le Corbusier, *Une maison—un palais* (Paris: Éditions Crès, 1928).

30 Mario González Sedeño, "About Habana del Este and the INAV," in Lisa Schmidt-Colinet et al., *Pabellón Cuba 4D–4Dimensions 4Decades* (Berlin: b-books, 2008), p. 81.

31 Pedro Ignacio Alonso and Hugo Palmarola Sagredo, "A Panel's Tale: The Soviet I-646 System and the Politics of Assemblage," in del Real and Gyger, eds., *Latin American Modern Architectures*, pp. 153–69. Their research was further developed in the Chile Pavilion at the Venice Biennial in 2014.

32 Octavio Paz, *Poesía en movimiento: México, 1915–1966*. This quote served as the overall theme for the Mexico Pavilion at the Venice Architecture Biennial in 2014.

33 Pietro Maria Bardi, *História do MASP* (São Paulo: Instituto Quadrante/Empresa das Artes, 1992), p.31. See also Maria Cristina Machado Freire, *Além dos mapas: Monumentos no imaginário urbano contemporâneo* (São Paulo: Ed. Annablume, 1997), p. 267.

34 Lina Bo Bardi, "An Architectural Lesson," 1990, and the afterword by Marcelo Ferraz, in Bo Bardi, *Stones against Diamonds* (London: AA Publications, 2012), pp. 112, 129.

35 Le Corbusier had offered his own master plan for Bogotá in 1947. See María Cecilia O'Byrne Orozco, ed., *Le Corbusier en Bogotá, 1947–1951* (Bogotá: Universidad de los Andes, Facultad de Arquitectura y Diseño, 2010). Agustín Infante K., "Torres del Parque—Rogelio Salmona," *Plataforma arquitectura* website, September 17, 2009, www.plataformaarquitectura.cl/cl/02-27395/torres-del-parque-rogelio-salmona.

36 Umberto Bonomo Tria, "The Portales Neighborhood Unit: Change and Continuity of a Housing Project in Santiago de Chile," in D. van den Heuvel, M. Mesman, and W. Quist, eds., *The Challenge of Change: Dealing with the Legacy of the Modern Movement* (Rotterdam: Docomomo, 2008), pp. 429–31.

37 The best firsthand account is Peter Land, "El Proyecto Experimental de Vivienda (PREVI) de Lima: Antecedents e ideas/The Experimental Housing Project (PREVI), Lima: Antecedents and Ideas," in Fernando García-Huidobro, Diego Torres Torriti, and Nicólas Tugas, *¡El tiempo construye!/Time Builds* (Barcelona: Editorial Gustavo Gili, 2008), pp. 10–25. See also "Experimental Nature: Interview with Peter Land," *Digital Architecture Papers* 9 (2012), www.architectural-papers.ch/index.php?ID=89. The best recent treatment is Sharif S. Kahatt, *PREVI-Lima: Architettura come opera aperta collettiva; Idee di housing sociale nell'architettura moderna peruviana* (Rome: Fondazione Bruno Zevi, n.d). See also Anahi Ballent, "*Learning from Lima,*" *Block* 6 (Buenos Aires), March 2004, pp. 86–95.

38 Justin McGuirk points very much in the right direction, although his argument is hampered by a number of historical misunderstandings of the earlier projects, notably PREVI, which are evoked, in both their architectural and political contexts. McGuirk, *Radical Cities: Across Latin America in Search of a New Architecture* (London: Verso Books, 2014).

Edifício COPAN, São Paulo. 1952–66. Oscar Niemeyer (Brazilian, 1907–2012).
Exterior view. c. 1960. Photograph by Marcel André Félix Gautherot. Instituto
Moreira Salles Collection

The Poetics of Development:
Notes on Two Brazilian Schools

Carlos Eduardo Comas

Brazilian modern architecture was supported by the country's increasing industrialization, from the revolutionary and then authoritarian presidency of Getúlio Vargas, from 1930 to 1945, to the economic boom of 1968–73 that took place during the military dictatorship of 1964–85. In the 1990s European and American historians and practitioners started to reconsider that architecture. Long demonized, Brasília became an object of some curiosity, along with its devalued antecedent, the work of the Carioca (Rio de Janeiro–based) school led by Lucio Costa, Jorge Moreira, Oscar Niemeyer, Affonso Eduardo Reidy, and the Roberto brothers, all born in the first decade of the twentieth century. The historians and practitioners then discovered the Paulista (São Paulo–based) school—flourishing during the design, construction, and consolidation of Brasília—of João Batista Vilanova Artigas and Lina Bo Bardi, born in the 1910s, and Carlos Millan, Paulo Mendes da Rocha, Fábio Penteado, and Joaquim Guedes, among others, all born in the 1920s and '30s. The plan for Brasília and Niemeyer's later work remained controversial, but Bo Bardi's and Mendes da Rocha's ongoing efforts were winning acclaim. And two facts seemed obvious. Brasília extended Rio and was even a jumping-off point for Rio-trained contemporaries of Mendes da Rocha, such as João "Lelé" Filgueiras Lima. And São Paulo reacted against Rio.

A close reading of Carioca and Paulista designs, buildings, and texts suggests a more complex situation: that the two schools' divergence from each other did not preclude continuity between them.[1] In different ways, both schools conceived modern architecture to be an inclusive and diverse system based on structure, a view delineated by Costa in two seminal texts.[2] Moreover, Costa presented modern architecture not only as the child of the machine but also as the heir to the academic tradition. A former student of the Escola Nacional de Belas Artes, in Rio, Costa served as its dean in 1930–31, soon after converting to modern architecture. For him, shunning historicism did not exclude the equation of good architecture with correct composition endowed with proper character, the legitimate source of architectural diversity for the late-nineteenth-century French theorist Julien Guadet.[3] Using similar strategies, both schools demonstrated the fecundity of Costa's reliance on academic thought, which was supposedly incompatible with modern architecture. As Costa knew, whatever factors may affect the creation of architectural form, already existing form is one of them—and form follows form by deliberate dissent as well as agreement.[4] Industrialization alone did not determine the physique and morale of Brazilian modern architecture, even as architects experimented with the prefabrication of building components.

Foundation

According to Costa, the independent skeleton was the characteristic feature of building in an industrial society, but modern architecture's normal structure consisted of parallel flat floor slabs cantilevered from a regular grid of supports—the specific independent skeleton rhetorically promoted by Le Corbusier in five points (1927) and four compositions (1929) after his Dom-ino scheme (1915).[5] Costa recognized that modern architecture was indebted iconographically to avant-garde art as well as to vehicle shapes, engineering feats, and utilitarian or vernacular buildings, but it was founded on building and distinguished from it: "Architecture is construction with plastic intention."[6]

That normal structure was later aptly described as "pancakes on pins" by the British critic Colin Rowe, and it admitted multiple compositional possibilities; "normal" meant preferable, not imperative.[7] The flat floor slabs assured maximum freedom of plan, and the cantilevers assured maximum freedom of facade. Horizontality, repetition, and orthogonality were the structure's prime attributes, qualified by the necessity of vertical circulation. The slabs could be punched or cut out to introduce vertical accents, the grids could follow complex rhythms, the cantilevers could vary in length on different sides of floor slabs, rectilinear geometries could counterpoint curvilinear ones. Exposed beams and designs without cantilevers were borderline cases. The term *pilotis* was used for a display of columns on the ground floor, which nevertheless could range from totally open to totally enclosed. Inclined and vaulted roofs were as acceptable as roof terraces. The columns could be freestanding or coplanar with walls. Although they were ideally realized in reinforced concrete, "pancakes on pins" could also be made in steel or wood. The structure suited both a picturesque, additive play of volumes and a compact or hollowed-out box, with walls going from minimally holed to maximally glazed. Design could flower from within to without, or crystallize from without to within.

Auditoriums, theaters, churches, terminals, warehouses, and industrial plants might require special structures. An example was the Aula Magna in Costa's plan for the Universidade do Brasil (fig. 1): the same squat, smaller version of the Palace of the Soviets proposed by Le Corbusier in his rejected master plan, from earlier the same year, for the same campus.[8] With its parabolic arch and suspended frames as legible as flying buttresses, it would oppose the tall rectorate building, designed by Costa, a pure prism with a normal structure for the university's administration. Low-rise projects might justify load-bearing masonry walls in columnless or hybrid structures, after the example of many single-family houses of the 1920s, such as those in São Paulo by Gregori Warchavchik, a pioneer of modern architecture in Brazil.

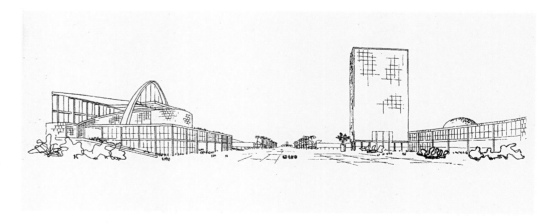

1. **Project for the Universidade do Brasil, Rio de Janeiro. 1936.** Lucio Costa (Brazilian, born France. 1902–1998). Perspective of entrance plaza. Ink on paper, 13 x 8 9⁄16 in. (33 x 21.8 cm). Casa de Lucio Costa

Thus modern architecture was a formal system articulated in three levels, a typology of structures connected with a typology of programs that recognized both a normal situation and two kinds of special occasions. Still, deeming columnless structures a borderline case, Costa mixed types of structure with intimations of lineage and emotional mood, defining modern architecture as an inclusive proposition in which two hitherto opposed architectural conceptions met and complemented each other: Gothic-Oriental drama and Greek-Roman serenity.[9]

Costa was not considering a synthetic fusion of those two conceptions. He was just affirming that modern buildings with classical overtones, such as the rectorate building, could stand next to modern buildings with Gothic overtones, such as the Aula Magna; and parts of modern buildings with classical overtones could join parts of modern buildings with Gothic overtones. He was also hinting at two basic strategies of characterization in academic practice: the reference to relevant precedents and the creation of suitable ambiences to provoke thought and induce sensation. The lack of ornament in modern architecture did not preclude recalling architectural forms from the past, whether erudite or vernacular and utilitarian, whether abstract types and styles or real buildings and part of buildings. "Pancakes on pins" and special structures generated different atmospheres.

Costa recognized the existence of pressures leading both to the diversification and the standardization of architectural forms, and he stressed the importance of "[giving] to each building the character that suits its purposes without losing the family traits that identify a true style."[10] Situation, he felt, modified both program and style, as Guadet had suggested in an analysis of programmatically and stylistically similar Italian buildings in Rome and Italian-derived buildings in Paris.[11] Inflected internationalism was perfectly compatible with the expression of genius loci and affirmation of national identity. Echoing the words of the late-eighteenth-century theorist Antoine Chrysôthome Quatremère de Quincy, Costa argued that modern architecture was international, since technology knew no frontiers, but it could acquire a local character with representative plans, materials, facings, finishes, and vegetation. [12]

Costa would later minimize the importance of the white boxes he designed with Warchavchik during 1931–33.[13] Even before them, his solo designs featured wooden louvered shutters that recall those in Eileen Gray's Villa E-1027 (1929) and rustic stone walls that recall the semicircular shape of Ludwig Mies van der Rohe's dining room screen at the Villa Tugendhat in Brno (1928–30). He mixed vernacular and erudite references, transposing or transforming them. Ground-floor *pilotis* are treated as verandahs rather than garages, contradicting the urban precepts of Le Corbusier. Costa's competition entry for the Monlevade workers' village (fig. 2) includes a take on Auguste Perret's

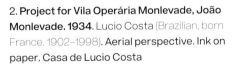

2. **Project for Vila Operária Monlevade, João Monlevade. 1934.** Lucio Costa (Brazilian, born France. 1902–1998). **Aerial perspective. Ink on paper.** Casa de Lucio Costa

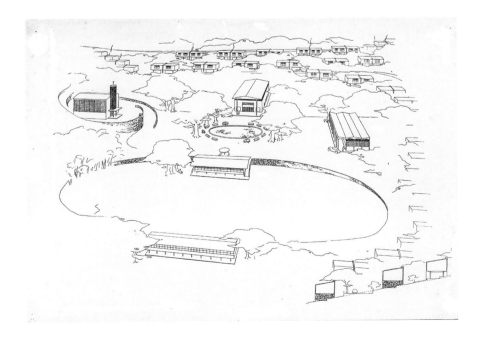

seminal church at Le Raincy (1922–23) and two peristyled public buildings for monumental effect, a movie theater and a general store; the semidetached houses he envisioned were wattle-and-daub boxes with asbestos-cement roofs over a concrete tray of cantilevered slabs and tapering beams on stilts, recalling Le Corbusier's Maisons Loucheur (1929) and Swiss Pavilion (1931–33) while perfecting an old technique used in most Brazilian housing at the time.

Costa lost the Monlevade competition. His Universidade do Brasil project was rejected, too. Yet from 1936 to 1945 Brazil offered more opportunities for modern architects than any other country, thanks to the support of a few influential segments of the Vargas administration. The commissions that launched the Carioca school were mostly state sponsored, on downtown open spaces created by razed hills and landfill or subdivisions of big estates, including leisure and transportation facilities as well as workplaces and dwellings in elevator buildings and walk-ups. The landscape architect Roberto Burle Marx was a key collaborator in such projects, as were structural engineers such as Emílio Baumgart and Joaquim Cardozo, who devised ways to make the taller buildings resist the lateral forces denied by the formal system and calculated thin concrete shells as skillfully as the Swiss engineer Robert Maillart.

The Carioca architects fully explored the visual autonomy that "pancakes on pins" afforded to walls, columns, and slabs. Structure was independent of enclosure, but both had the same rank. As in earlier modern practice, the absence of *poché*, or volumes of concealed space, created conceptual transparency. The generic scheme is tripartite: slab buildings with blank end walls (for bracing) and glazed long sides (for light and lightness) that stand on differentiated bases and are crowned by attics or partially built-up terraces. The bases and crowns contain special program elements, and the body of the building holds repeating ones; the formal distinction of key program elements serves both operational and expressive needs, as in the late Beaux Arts tradition.[14] Sunscreens or sunbreakers, laid over glass panes, are discrete shading devices that add texture, reinforcing the contrast between the facades and the virtual decomposition of the built volume into its constituent planes. Inner and outer service cores also provide bracing.

Bases stand over ground treated as a garden or a platform or both: the definition of a man-made topography is a design's primary, conquering architectural act. Bases often present volumes both contained within the limits of the ground-floor *pilotis* and expanding under or beyond the cantilevered body of the building. Recurrently porous, with intermediate voids serving as open public passages, bases promote elaborate *promenades architecturales*. The colossal column is a favorite motif, either freestanding or requiring a cantileverless intermediary floor slab, first prefigured in the nave and choir of Perret's church at Le Raincy. Colonnades are sometimes combined with the immodest exposition of building entrails, first prefigured in the open corner of Mies's Barcelona Pavilion (1929). Crowns add to the formal diversity, appearing as additive compositions, stepped volumes, walled gardens, penthouses with cantilevered pergolas, or monopitch tiled roofs.

The contrast between smooth and textured, layered surfaces on the opposite sides of a building is often reinforced by a contrast between volumetric containment and sprawl, stratification and verticality, tautness and hollowing out. The Cariocas, like Alvar Aalto, prized curves as much as straight lines, at times using them exclusively, unlike Mies (who very rarely used them) or Le Corbusier (who tended to treat them as episodes). Costa remarked that curves imparted Ionian grace and elegance with a baroque twist to the Brazil Pavilion at the New York's World Fair of 1939, designed by him and Niemeyer, in contrast to the Doric severity of the Ministério da Educação e Saúde in Rio (1936–45), by Costa, Niemeyer, Moreira, Reidy, Carlos Leão, and Ernani Vasconcelos: the former is a bent slab building enlivened by the occasional straight line; the latter, a straight slab

3. **Pampulha complex, Belo Horizonte. 1940–45.**
Oscar Niemeyer (Brazilian, 1907–2012). Perspective
sketch of the casino. Ink on vellum. Fundação
Oscar Niemeyer

building enlivened by the curves of the auditorium and water tanks.[15] Columns add to the distinction
between the two, in granite-clad concrete with a circular section for the ministry, and steel profiles
clad in metal sheet with a volute-shaped section for the pavilion. Niemeyer's Pampulha complex
(fig. 3) proposes a wholly curvilinear dance hall, a mainly straight yacht club, and a casino that mixes
the two. Characterization of program and situation observed the tension between their generic
and particular features. All available strategies were used.

Colossal columns at the base of office buildings lend dignity without grandiloquence. The
ABI building in Rio (1936–39), designed by the Roberto brothers, is an L-shaped slab integrated into
the built perimeter of its block like a travertine-clad *palazzetto* on a corner lot. Here, shops flank an
open vestibule, which expands the sidewalk and communicates with the block's central courtyard.
Sunbreakers create striated facades, and the blank and translucent surfaces above them externally
register the gallery and the auditorium. The Ministério da Educação is a taller *palazzo*, a straight slab
across a whole block, a T-shaped composition with gallery and auditorium wings at the base. The
centrally open *pilotis* is a hypostyle hall, a portico linking two public forecourts. Painted azulejo panels
update a Luso-Brazilian tradition. The rooftop, fashioned after a ship's superstructure, is a clear
case of stylized figuration. A grid holding mobile sunbreakers protects the glazed north facade like a
giant *mashrabiya*. Nearby, the Robertos' Santos Dumont airport (1938–46; page 127, fig.4) extends
between public gardens and the landing strip, the whole treated like a stoa, with marble-clad double-
and quadruple-height colonnades.

Single-height ground-floor columns suit apartment buildings, such as those that Costa
designed for the upscale Parque Guinle (1943–53). Each block-length slab building has a staircase
protruding from the back and is topped by a penthouse. One building completes a corridor street.
The others define a curved one-sided street, and together they half-enclose the park's sloping
grounds while keeping the economic advantages of repetition. Level differences, paving, and vegetation assure privacy at each building's base, whether it is open and serving as a porte cochère or
closed and containing shops.

The Brazil Pavilion was a theatrical, distorted, waving miniature version of the ministry, recalling the Roman house and its offspring, the French *hôtel particulier* and the Brazilian sugar-plantation house. In Ouro Preto, a preserved eighteenth-century city, Niemeyer's Grande Hotel (1940–44) achieved dramatic spatial effects with brown-painted square pillars of Tuscan plainness. In Nova Friburgo, a mountain resort, Costa built the small Park Hotel (1945) with rustic poles and a free plan. Modern architecture was about a new spatiality rather than new materials. Rusticity and urbanity could be two sides of the same coin, the one associated with subjective coziness and the other with impersonal objectivity.[16]

Niemeyer's design for Pampulha updates the picturesque park scheme to anchor an upscale garden suburb. A dammed river becomes a liquid plaza, and follies stand along it as in mid-eighteenth-century Stourhead in England, or late-nineteenth-century Quinta da Boa Vista in Rio. A one-story dance hall on a small island is all matronly grace, at once a round, primitive hut, an Amazonian *maloca*, and a docked barge. The narrow, virile yacht club is built on land but resembles an angular caricature of a houseboat slipping into water, a stratified pyramidal composition mixing Le Corbusier's Citrohan and Errazuris houses (1922, 1930). A big casino sits atop a promontory: a two-story box for gambling and a drum for dancing define a square facing the water; a T-shaped entrance marquee and service wing extend the composition. Colossal columns at the entrance convey grandeur; clad in stainless steel inside, they flirt with Corinthian splendor. A *casino* was first a recreation cottage and then a suburban villa, and Niemeyer, exploiting the site's beauty, presents his as a villa belvedere, akin to Andrea Palladio's Villa Rotonda (1566) and Le Corbusier's Villa Savoye (1928–31). The drum-and-box theme is more extreme in the bigger structure of the hotel. The box becomes a linear block of apartments, bent like a crescent with a slanted facade. The drum turns into a grounded volume with scalloped glass walls bounding lounges and dining rooms.

These designs use "pancakes on pins" to re-create the formal diversity of picturesque park follies without stylistic eclecticism. Niemeyer resorted to a special structure to characterize the São Francisco de Assis chapel. Its nave has a parabolic section, trapezoidal projection, and truncated conic volume, rising with a neo-Gothic, Gaudi-esque, or Expressionist flavor while recalling Maillart's Zementhalle (Cement hall) (1939) in Zurich; it fits into the altar shell between service rooms under lower shells, below which a lustrous panel of painted azulejos seems weightless. Squat, with a single belfry and narthex, the chapel miniaturizes characteristic traits of the Franciscan order's grand churches in Brazil. Nevertheless, the entrance facade appears as an ideogram of spiritual elevation that mixes vernacular and industrial notes. Metallic fins shield a transparent upper panel, evoking both the wooden rods in the entrance of sixteenth-century Brazilian plantation chapels and the pipes of an organ. Columnless plastered buildings provide the final touch: the house for then-mayor and patron Juscelino Kubitschek, with its butterfly roof, and the golf club, with a shallow vault between inclined slabs.

Niemeyer's choice of structure for the chapel was not determined by the requirements of a clear-span roof, which would not have ruled out a normal structure. Yet a "pancake on pins" would not be as immediately representative of the program and its relative singularity; it would not advance as fully the view of modern architecture as an inclusive and diverse proposition. As in earlier modern Brazilian work, there are multiple references, some of them easily understood, some only by cognoscenti. This is double coding, and in the hands of Niemeyer, an avowed communist, it suggests an alternative to Socialist Realism, a way of communicating with both the people and the intelligentsia without resorting to pastiche.[17]

Niemeyer's chapel can be compared to the SOTREq headquarters (1944–46) in Rio, a Caterpillar dealership designed by the Roberto brothers. Segmental arched wooden trusses,

140 feet (43 meters) in span, rise from the ground to shelter the showroom, allowing for maximum freedom in the display of tractors and providing a striking logo for the firm, while evoking utilitarian but grand nineteenth-century sheds such as railroad terminals, or even barns such as Hugo Häring's Gut Garkau (1923–26), near Lübeck, Germany. The particularities of the geometry and materiality of SOTREq point to productivity rather than piety. And unlike Niemeyer's chapel, defined inside and out by continuous curved surfaces that could be described as bent slabs, the interior volume of the showroom is defined by the parallel exposed trusses. By contrast, Niemeyer's Teatro das Artes, the state theater in Belo Horizonte (1943), is a trapezoidal volume held by an exoskeleton of trapezoidal frames with exposed columns that taper toward the base, a more straightforward solution for a smaller theater than that of the Palace of the Soviets. Much like "pancakes on pins," special structures could be manipulated to generate formal diversity within recognizable families, and those families could be mixed. Niemeyer and Baumgart designed the Estádio Nacional (1941) for one hundred thousand people with a symmetrical entrance plaza and an asymmetrical plan, evoking the Centre National de Réjouissances Populaires project (1936) by Le Corbusier and Pierre Jeanneret. Part of the roof slab rests on half-trapezoidal frames, and part of it is suspended from steel cables tied to a parabolic arch after that of the Palace of the Soviets; both arches are at once landmarks and tools.

Rule

Costa and his fellow Carioca architects were a minority in their profession during the Vargas presidency. Their prestige did not diminish with the deposition of Vargas and the beginning of the democratic interlude of 1946–64. Praise from abroad had solidified their position, and after World War II modern architecture triumphed in Brazil, as elsewhere. Commissions grew out of accelerated industrialization and urbanization in southern and southeastern Brazil. Apartment buildings replaced older residences in prestigious neighborhoods. Office buildings, hotels, and mixed-use projects transformed city centers. Government-sponsored projects included university campuses and housing. Designs built on the achievements of the 1930s and early 1940s.

Costa and his fellow Carioca architects knew that Mies had been pursuing a classic distinctive character for his work since the start of the war, while Le Corbusier was in the search of the archaic. They were aware of these new directions but saw no reason to substantially change their views and ways in the first decade after the war. Architects all over Brazil followed their lead, including Rino Levi, another pioneer of modern architecture, in São Paulo, and Artigas, who had started as a follower of Frank Lloyd Wright. They accepted, as Costa proposed, that grace was the essential character of the native genius manifest in Niemeyer's architecture.[18]

Among the outstanding examples of Niemeyer's abundant and inventive work are three mixed-use projects for private developers that recall North American grand hotels in their functional complexity and public role, all the while meeting the standards of public social housing. All three projects leave the *pilotis* on view atop an expanded base. For the Mauá mountain resort (1950), he designed a vertical leisure city that enormously enlarges the scheme of his Pampulha hotel, introducing skip-stop circulation and duplex units that challenge the layout of Le Corbusier's Unité d'Habitation (1946–52), then under construction in Marseille. An urban counterpart is the Juscelino Kubitschek complex (1951–70) in Belo Horizonte, which fills two adjacent blocks with slab buildings placed at right angles to each other, on stepped bases containing shops, banks, services, a hotel, a museum, and state agencies. Only partially built, the complex embodies a metropolitan culture of congestion, as does the sinuous, awe-inspiring COPAN building (page 40) in São Paulo. This city-within-a-city housing two thousand people makes the most of its irregular lot, defining an equally

4. **Palácio da Agricultura, Parque Ibirapuera, São Paulo. 1951–54.** Oscar Niemeyer (Brazilian, 1907–2012). View of columns during construction. c. 1954. Fundação Oscar Niemeyer

sinuous inner street and the corner where it meets a major avenue. The inclined floor of the shopping gallery is an extension of the sloping sidewalk—an amplified version of the ABI building's open vestibule—and the rounded corners of the shop clusters facilitate fluid pedestrian movement. The same extension of sidewalk happens at the smaller, straight but triple-folded Eiffel building (1953–56) nearby, which fits into a trapezoidal corner lot with three frontages.

COPAN is also remarkable for its accordionlike facade; sunlight control is achieved, in part, with the structure itself, or, more exactly, with the cantilevers of the floor slabs. Two horizontal fins over continuous glazed panes divide each floor, on the outside replicating the cantilevers and appearing inside as surprisingly wide slits that frame expansive views. The idea reappears on lots with a rounded corner. At the residential Montreal building (1951–54), in São Paulo, and offices for Banco Mineiro da Produção (1953–55), in Belo Horizonte, the fins stop at midcorner and create a striking pattern, at once superimposed on and juxtaposed with a glazed facade. The enclosed base on the ground floor is shaped by economics, with exposed columns in front of cool glass-brick walls and glass panes and curving ramps that lead to both basement and mezzanine, leaving most of the ground floor available for commercial use.

By contrast, Niemeyer's upscale curvilinear apartment building (1954–60, portfolio 8) in Belo Horizonte, named for the architect, rises from a triangular block on irregularly disposed piers, creating a totally open ground floor. The floor slabs resemble trilobed leaves stuck to the stem of a thin cylindrical staircase. Here, between the fins of the undulating facade, are panels covered with azulejo tiles in a pattern suggesting stones embedded in whitewashed masonry, a recurrent motif in local middle-class bungalows of the 1940s. Dealing with social housing proper in a German park setting, in Berlin's Hansaviertel, Niemeyer radically minimized the use of elevators, which were expensive at the time. In his first proposal, three stops serve three piles of three-storied walk-ups forming a slab apartment building with an open ground-floor *pilotis* (1956).

In Niemeyer's Parque Ibirapuera complex (fig. 4) in São Paulo, mixed structures accompany mixed geometries: an extensive amoeboid marquee over the sloping ground creates a covered plaza connecting a pair of opaque facilities, the domed Palácio das Artes and an unbuilt theater, to three elongated, boxy, transparent pavilions. Here topographical stylization is associated with architectural memories: the marquee's outline resembles that of the artificial lake gracing the picturesque garden in Rio's Quinta da Boa Vista, and the vast dome evokes both hill and cave. Such mixed structures and geometries remained internal in the Museo de Arte Moderno project in Caracas (1954), a bold inverted pyramid mirroring the peak on which it would stand.

Fully externalized frames appeared in different guises in different programs—spidery in the proposal for the Ministério da Educação auditorium (1948), double arcuated in the Duchen plant in São Paulo (1950), and zoomorphic in both cases. In the two-story Hotel Tijuco (1951) in Diamantina—a bold proposal to be located in a preserved eighteenth-century town—bifurcated inclined supports of unequal height support the roof slab and the upper floor like branches of a tree. The Tijuco example is one among many of a treelike column, which enlarged the distance between columns and minimized spatial obstruction at the ground floor, turning metaphorical the real tree trunks that Costa used at the Park Hotel. It became a motif, re-creating the ancient connection of architecture with nature, reinforcing the figurative connotations of the tripartite scheme and combining the classical with the archaic. Niemeyer's inventions included colossal columns tapering toward the base and receiving the load from two vertical lines of supports at each shoulder; on the same load-bearing principle, equally colossal V-, W-, and Y-shaped columns that transpose an idea of Eugène Viollet-le-Duc; post-and-bracket set-ups; and the lone tree-of-life that supports the ramps at the main pavilion of the Ibirapuera complex.[19]

Niemeyer's single-family houses proposed informal living spaces opening onto a garden and sometimes the distant landscape. With Burle Marx he designed the Tremaine house (1948) in Montecito, California, as the ultimate beach retreat and a frame for the human body in motion. Revisiting archetypes was a more esoteric concern. To create Casa das Canoas (1951–53), his own house in Rio, he distorted a rectangular flat roof slab into a curvilinear U-shaped canopy and floated it over a larger platform in which a pool and an existing rock miniaturize nearby Botafogo Bay and Sugarloaf Mountain while also hiding the bedroom floor below. Whitewashed load-bearing masonry walls coexist with thin, irregularly spaced steel poles. In his Cavanelas country house (1954), four stone pillars support the roof and catenary steel trusses, forming a tent in a Burle Marx garden.

The most visible architect, after Niemeyer, was Reidy, largely thanks to his social-housing designs based on parallel slab buildings with an open *pilotis*, access galleries, and duplex apartments. Those built on steep hillsides allowed the buildings to increase in height without requiring elevators. In his plans for Pedregulho (1946–58) and Gávea (figs. 5, 6) Reidy bent slab buildings with spectacular results. He created sinuous ribbons with an intermediary open *pilotis* at sidewalk level, which echo the landscape and provide a foil for lower, straight, and shorter walk-ups, as well as for communal facilities differentiated by vaults, inclined roofs, and murals. On the outskirts of Rio, on another steep hillside, his small house (1950) seems a treetop platform on stilts with a U-shaped plan and a butterfly roof, the main wing opening toward the sea and closing toward the patio and the rainforest.

Reidy's Brazil-Paraguay school (figs. 7, 8), in Asunción, and Museu de Arte Moderna (MAM) (1953–67; page 128 and portfolio 4), in Rio, feature trapezoidal frames in raw concrete. The frames of the school refine those of the Hotel Tijuco, and the frames of the museum define its exhibition hall in an elaborate, colossal, symmetrical, three-story hybrid structure that includes a suspended mezzanine. The museum's near-transparent hall rises on landfill between Guanabara Bay and Avenida

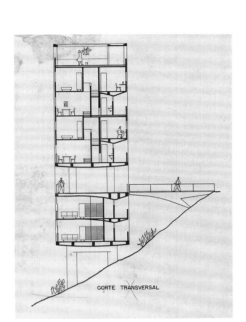

5. Gávea housing, Rio de Janeiro, 1952–57. Affonso Eduardo Reidy (Brazilian, born France. 1909–1964). Section of a housing block. 1952. Ink on paper, 9 7/16 x 7 1/16 in. (24 x 18 cm). Núcleo de Pesquisa e Documentação da Faculdade de Arquitetura e Urbanismo da Universidade Federal do Rio de Janeiro

6. Gávea housing, Rio de Janeiro. 1952–57. Affonso Eduardo Reidy (Brazilian, born France. 1909–1964). Photomontage with a photograph of the model, 6 5/16 x 8 11/16 in. (16 x 22 cm). Núcleo de Pesquisa e Documentação da Faculdade de Arquitetura e Urbanismo da Universidade Federal do Rio de Janeiro

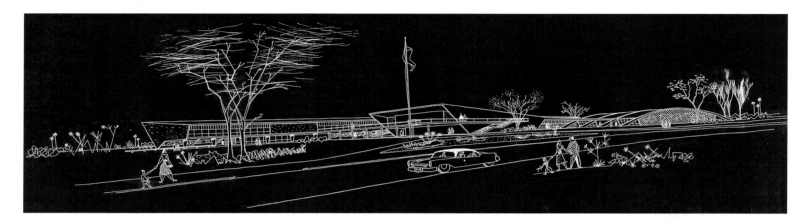

7. **Colegio Experimental Brasil-Paraguai, Asunción, Paraguay. 1952.** Affonso Eduardo Reidy (Brazilian, born France. 1909–1964). **Perspective study of the exterior. 1952.** Photomechanical transfer on photopositive paper. Núcleo de Pesquisa e Documentação da Faculdade de Arquitetura e Urbanismo da Universidade Federal do Rio de Janeiro

8. **Colegio Experimental Brasil-Paraguai, Asunción, Paraguay. 1952.** Affonso Eduardo Reidy (Brazilian, born France. 1909–1964). **Perspective study of the *pilotis*. 1952.** Photomechanical transfer on photopositive paper. Núcleo de Pesquisa e Documentação da Faculdade de Arquitetura e Urbanismo da Universidade Federal do Rio de Janeiro

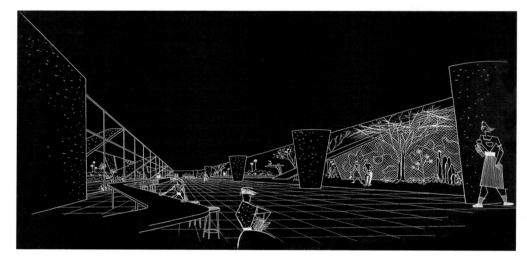

Beira-Mar, formerly the coastal avenue. An education wing at one end turns toward the sea, and a theater wing at the other turns toward the city. Burle Marx was enlisted to design two esplanades, which the museum both limits and bridges. The school wing has exposed-brick walls and a normal cantilevered structure, mixing cylindrical columns in the interiors with X-shaped steel posts in the covered walkways. The theater's open foyer features solid columns tapering toward the base. Reidy's exuberance matched Niemeyer's. The vast and porous entrance vestibule is an urban passage, following the example set at the Ministério da Educação. The underside of the first-story slab is shaped like a shallow vault, and the internal branches of the frames seem to prolong it, making it seem like a cave or big tent—impressions reinforced by a rug of stone mosaic in a traditional wavy pattern, set into a polished black granite field.

MAM's special structure was Reidy's primary means of programmatic characterization, as it was for Niemeyer in the Pampulha chapel. A normal structure would have been unassuming. A colossal colonnade would have been incongruous with a museum of modern art. The external trapezoidal frames could be related to both utilitarian and cultural buildings, suggesting a connection to the museum's focus on industrial design and the teaching of art. Big spans were thrilling engineering feats, associated with the sublime and with epics; they could be seen as emblems of technical development or a new kind of luxury, one whose symbolic value exceeded its cost-benefit. The museum's exoskeleton could be considered both a distortion of the frame of a normal structure or a more accurate and truthful expression of its structural behavior, clearly identifying the points of maximal bending, an ambivalence that corresponds to modern art's quest to defamiliarize and reveal.

Reidy's choice of materials also contributed to this characterization. Raw concrete was not new in modern architecture, as evidenced in Perret's church at Le Raincy, but the absence of facings connoted honesty, with building components shown in their original state, without postproduction corrections or additions—a move that could be called "brutalist," from the French word *brut* applied to Champagne: no sugar added.[20] The absence of facings also meant economy, a move that could be called minimalist, implying fewer and barer building components. It matched the big, clear span with fewer columns than would be expected. In Brazil, at that time, using raw concrete meant exposed concrete cast in a form made of wood planks, creating a rough, woolen tactility in contrast with the silky smoothness of polished stone. It reinforced the association with the utilitarian, as did the exposed hard brick used in factories built by the British in late-nineteenth-century Brazil. The roughness was offset by the polish of the black floors and the expanses of glass in the cool interiors. Inclusiveness had many dimensions.

Niemeyer and Reidy were not the only architects of distinctive works. Their own houses shared archetypal concerns with Bo Bardi's Casa de Vidro (Glass house) (1951–52), in which a transparent tree platform on thin steel poles abuts a grounded, U-shaped, cavelike wing containing a bedroom and kitchen. Bo Bardi's project for a museum in São Vicente (1951) is a box seemingly suspended from an exoskeleton made of orthogonal frames. Marcos Konder Netto and Helio Ribas Marinho, all of them Cariocas born in the late 1920s, designed the Monumento Nacional aos Mortos da Segunda Guerra Mundial (Monument to the dead of World War II) (figs. 9, 10) next to Reidy's museum in Rio. Its L-shaped viewing platform forms the rooftop for a half-sunk crypt; the platform is anchored at one side by large access stairs, and at the other side it seems to float as a cantilever on a single column. In the crypt, which affords an unusual perspective of Guanabara Bay, the columns are squat, solemn, interlocking pyramids with an anthropomorphic and sculptural *x* outline, an apt stylization of the fallen warriors. The Roberto brothers devised inventive solutions for mobile sunbreakers on faceted facades, the most spectacular example being the Marquês do Herval office building in Rio (1952–55). Helio Duarte, a Rio-trained contemporary of Costa, and Ernest Mange, a Paulista born in 1922, designed the Módulo E1 (1953–57) for the Escola de Engenharia da Universidade de São Paulo at São Carlos, a four-story slab building intended as a prototype integrating structure and ductwork. It has a central spine, made up of pairs of very close piers, and floor slabs resting on a grid of rectangular longitudinal beams and transverse beams tapering toward the edges of the building. The treelike section shows symmetrical hypercantilevers and inclined suspended ceilings made of gypsum. The academic *poché* is revived to hide ductwork and service rooms.

The criticism of the Carioca school began in 1948, after Costa equated grace with Brazilian and Niemeyerian architecture. Accusations of academism and social irresponsibility ensued. Costa replied, speaking for himself and his colleagues.[21] Some of the attacks were simply sectarian, citing formal exhaustion, praising in Reidy—or Aalto—the same forms being condemned in Niemeyer. Some were myopic, failing to link the vulgarization and misuse of the modern architectural vocabulary and syntax to its popularity. Other attacks were wishful, by critics who believed that architecture could bring about massive social change despite all the evidence pointing to the contrary; Brazilian modern architecture by itself could not lead to a brave new third world. And the attacks could be personal: Le Corbusier took Costa's graceful faceted design for the Casa do Brasil in Paris (1953–59) and transformed it into a heavy piece of rough tactility, Brutalist (insofar as it flaunted the original

9. **Monumento Nacional aos Mortos da Segunda Guerra Mundial, Rio de Janeiro. 1956–60.** Marcos Konder Netto (Brazilian, born 1927). View of the inaugural ceremony. 1960. Acervo do Monumento aos Mortos da Segunda Guerra Mundial, Rio de Janeiro

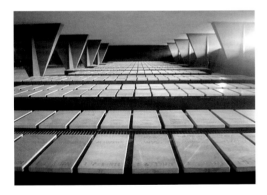

10. **Monumento Nacional aos Mortos da Segunda Guerra Mundial, Rio de Janeiro. 1956–60.** Marcos Konder Netto (Brazilian, born 1927). View of the crypt. c. 2014. Acervo do Monumento aos Mortos da Segunda Guerra Mundial, Rio de Janeiro

material condition of its structure and walls) and maximalist (insofar as it paraded thick structural members and multiplied formal episodes). Costa would disavow the work in 1959.[22]

The building of Casa do Brasil started about a month after the competition for the Pilot Plan for Brasília was announced by President Kubitschek, who had been sworn in at the beginning of 1956 with a promise to advance Brazil fifty years during the five years of his term. Most Brazilian architects applauded his declaration. All of them were progressivists, to use the historian Françoise Choay's useful label: they defended industrialization and the industrial society, even if with reservations.[23] They believed that socioeconomic development was tied to state or liberal capitalism and its large technobureaucracies. They endorsed mass production and advanced technology, which included engineering feats. They thought that tomorrow would be better and that one should not make small plans, that real transformation of the environment required a top-down approach even if it relied on support by the people.

Continuity

Inclusiveness achieves a larger scale in Costa's winning competition entry for Brasília (page 133).[24] He mixes *urbs* and *civitas*.[25] The ordinary city has a physical, curvilinear, asphalt spine and two mirror wings. The residential and business quarters extend from south to north and vice versa, succeeding each other along the opposite sides of a thoroughfare at once boulevard and highway, with two side roads and a sunken, six-lane central section whose southern extension leads to the airport. The monumental sector has a straight conceptual spine and two distinct, albeit related, sectors including verdant malls like those in Washington, D.C., and London. To the west, the railroad terminal and the municipal buildings abut a slope, with the freestanding Torre de TV (Television tower) (page 136) at its highest central point, a latter-day Eiffel Tower. To the east, federal buildings make up a grand composition on an esplanade and plaza raised using the earth excavated by building the curvilinear thoroughfare. The construction of Brasília would involve a cut-and-fill operation. Defining the ground is once more the first architectural act. The south and north wings and the east and west sectors are both separated and connected by a multilevel platform, part building and part roadway, including overpasses and an underpass, the entertainment center at the top, and the main bus station below it.

The ministries of justice and foreign affairs are singled out by their placement at the eastern extremities of the parallel rows of identical nine-story slab buildings proposed for the rectangular Esplanada dos Ministérios (page 136). The education ministry is singled out by being placed at the western extremity of the northern row, parallel to the theater farther away and perpendicular to the cathedral placed at the western extremity of the southern row. At the triangular Praça dos Três Poderes (Plaza of the three powers) (page 134), the twenty-eight-story Congresso Nacional (page 135 and portfolio 9) is a blocky landmark intended as a counterpart to the lacy television tower and as a contrast with the much lower presidential palace and supreme court building. Costa's project for the Universidade do Brasil is the immediate forerunner of the composition of the esplanade and the plaza.

The same concern with the repetition and variation of volumes in a dialogical relationship with program and situation is found in the alternation of residential *superquadras* with strips of one- or two-story shops and community facilities (page 139). The *superquadras* are informed by the Parque Guinle project, as they present only one point of access and egress for cars and are made up of six-story slab apartment buildings of similar length, each over an open ground-floor *pilotis* and resting in a lawn on a platform that is the roof of the underground garage. Costa's layout of parallel and perpendicular apartment buildings looks casual in comparison with the strict rows of ministries.

At the same time he insisted on enclosing each *superquadra* with two parallel rows of tall trees to create alleys and public green facades capable of masking differences in social status and architectural quality, recalling New York's tree-lined sidewalks between Central Park and Fifth Avenue. For the business quarters the plan eschews vegetation and adopts the standard solution of parallel slab buildings, no taller than the Congresso Nacional tower, on large two-story expanded bases crisscrossed by pedestrian routes, with garages underneath. Costa's diversified but orderly mass plan is a critique of both the cacophony of buildings of many heights packed cheek by jowl in Brazilian cities and Haussmannian homogenization.

The government asked Costa to revise the plan. Strips of inexpensive row houses and a suburban sector of single-family houses were added. Two shopping centers were substituted for the entertainment center, and the layout of buildings in the business quarters became more intricate. Costa agreed to these relatively minor alterations. He was not consulted, however, before the government decided to relocate construction workers to distant satellite cities, when they wished to remain in the federal district, and he cannot be blamed for the government failing to provide an efficient bus system that the linear layout would have easily accommodated. Costa felt that satellite cities should only have appeared when population of Brasília reached the five hundred thousand–person limit stipulated by the competition. Moreover, his scheme did not preclude the possibility of zoning changes. In fact the city's monofunctional zoning is deceptive, since many institutional buildings contain restaurants, shopping, and banks that are open to the public.

The basic symbolism of the plan is easily understood. It does not require much education to grasp its resemblance to a bird and an airplane, or its transformation of a cross, the sign of foundation, into a bow and arrow, the sign of propulsion. Yet the statements of lineage include references that a layperson would miss. The layout of the residential sectors combines the Ciudad Lineal (1882) of Spanish urban theorist Arturo Soria y Mata with the city in the park (1933) of the Congrès Internationaux d'Architecture Moderne (CIAM). The layout of the civic sectors monumentalizes the Corbusian Ville Radieuse (1930) in light of City Beautiful projects such as the McMillan plan for Washington, D.C. (1901), by Daniel Burnham and Charles McKim, and Alfred Agache's plan for Rio (1930). The central bus station is related to the central airport in Le Corbusier's Ville Contemporaine de Trois Millions d'Habitants (1922), which is in turn related to the railroad station in Antonio Sant'Elia's Città Nuova (1914). Such esoteric material does not contradict the more obvious references but sharpens, amplifies, and deepens them.

This double coding also appears in Niemeyer's palaces at Brasília. As glass boxes behind colossal peristyles, they suggest generic institutional monumentality and flirt with the advanced and reductive postwar work of Mies and offices such as Skidmore, Owings & Merrill, although the interiors still play with the autonomy of slabs, columns, and walls. The Palácio da Alvorada (1956–58, page 132), the presidential residence, rests on outer supports that Stamo Papadaki referred to as caryatids, perhaps because they suggest bulging, bellied, folding, static figures.[26] If that is so, in the Palácio do Planalto (1957–60), the presidential workplace, and the Supremo Tribunal (Supreme court) (1957–60), the flat outer supports are like lean and taut atlantes. The capitol complex provides compositional and representative balance, with the white domes of the assembly chambers as the scales, administrative towers as the scales' pivot, and the beam represented by a glazed entrance volume structured by a vast colonnade with classicizing overtones. The elegant Ministério das Relações Exteriores (Ministry of foreign affairs) (1959–70, portfolio 6) has sculptural arcades in minutely striped raw concrete, a delicate Brutalist touch spicing up the allusion to the old Neoclassical headquarters of the ministry in Rio. The muscular Ministério da Justiça (1957–72) has flat, round arches with a Romanesque flavor. Peristyles disappear in the special structures of the cathedral (1958–70) and the theater (1960–66). Both use full exoskeletons: the former as a transparent hyperboloid rising from the underground, the latter as a half-opaque truncated pyramid. It is a family, and it parades in pairs. The lightness that prevails in those designs underscores an antimonumental monumentality for many observers, suggesting the fragility of human institutions in the face of nature—or perhaps of underdeveloped countries in the face of the first world.[27] In the Praça dos Três Poderes, across from the Congresso, Niemeyer reiterates the balance motif in the small, near-opaque Museu da Cidade (1957–60), which contains a single room defined by two straightened C-shaped beams that rest off-center on a small square box containing vestibule and stairs. An oversized head of Kubitschek, crude but impressive, adds a figurative touch to the extreme cantilevering and structural *poché*, which prefigures Niemeyer's spectacular but unexecuted project for the Centro Musical da Guanabara (1968). Steel cables suspended from a mast were needed in the center to stabilize the symmetrically cantilevered beams, giving the design a special bridgelike quality quite different from that of the contemporary design by Louis I. Kahn and Auguste Kommendant for the Palazzo dei Congressi in Venice (1968).

Although Niemeyer used glass boxes in Brasília, he disagreed with Mies's ideas about universal character and universal space.[28] Niemeyer condemned repetition that makes "buildings lose the indispensable character that their purposes and programmatic conveniences command. Thus, public buildings, schools, theaters, museums, houses, etc. show identical aspects, despite their programs."[29] He would, however, create remarkable designs that make use of prefabricated elements of raw but not particularly rough concrete, including two schools at the Universidade de Brasília—the straight, block-length Instituto de Teologia (1962) and the long curved Instituto Central de Ciências (ICC) (1963–71, page 138), as well as the massive Quartel General do Exército (1967–72). The vertical thrust of these designs is consistent with Niemeyer's previous work in the new capital. Like the Ministério das Relações Exteriores, the Instituto de Teologia design features a colossal peristyle supporting a roof structure elevated like a canopy a few feet over an independent two-story box with a roof terrace. Yet its supports are amazingly svelte, like those of Costa's movie house and general store at Monlevade, and the arcades result from the roof structure being a succession of shallow, vaulted precast panels similar to those that make up the load-bearing walls of the box, appearing from the outside as convex elements separated by vertical strips of windows. The institute's chapel stands apart, like the chapel in the Palácio da Alvorada, and would have been built using cast-in-place panels with freer curves than the roof and wall panels. The military quarters are appropriately fortresslike, with concave load-bearing wall panels, a barrel-vaulted roof, and no peristyle. It is embellished with an entrance portico of an obelisk and asymmetrically arched plate, plus a civic plaza by Burle Marx. The contrasting Teatro Pedro Calmon (1973–76), to one side of the portico but slightly set back, reads like a tented variant of Niemeyer's unexecuted design for the Ministério do Educação auditorium (1948) and its crablike exoskeleton.

Lelé's work in Brasília also explored prefabrication's expressive possibilities. The apartment buildings for the Universidade de Brasília staff (1962–63) reinterpret the residential Carioca slab building in light of a different construction process. They feature wide-open *pilotis,* cantilevers, a differentiated crowning, and two long, opposing facades emphatically contrasting, but cast-in-place uncantilevered staircase modules provide bracing, and the prestressed ribbed slabs rest on prestressed U-beams. Concrete panels make up the end walls and the spandrels of one of the long facades; hollow screens fill the space between the slabs of the one opposite. The delicacy of the whole is really surprising. Two later projects feature precast structural floor-to-ceiling window boxes and other types of cast-in-place elements for bracing; they rise from the ground without cantilevers, and their facades achieve depth by integrating structure and sunlight control instead of relying on separate sunbreakers. Lelé's hospital at Taguatinga (1967–68), a satellite city, the first of a long series of health facilities, is a huge building with staggered floors and piers separating the window boxes. Each of his two Camargo Correa office towers (1974–75) comprises three volumes. The tower proper has a blank end wall and long, opposing facades featuring aligned window boxes; an equally blank service core with rounded extremities; and a symmetrical V-shaped slab that is the cantilevered roof of a glazed room for socializing and seems to float over the larger tower roof terrace. Joined by a covered walkway, the towers sit atop a common basement, facing each other with the service cores in inverted positions. The simple but dynamic composition is as striking as each of its crisp elements.

Brasília was not the only outlet for established Carioca architects. A building that looks more conservative than it is, and prefigures Lelé's window boxes, is Moreira's Faculdade de Arquitetura (1957–62) at the Universidade Federal do Rio de Janeiro. Is section coordinates structure and ductwork by using suspended ceilings and vertical shafts to create new *pochés* in a wholly orthogonal way, unlike Duarte and Mange's Módulo E1; the facade is a slightly cantilevered structural grid resting on colossal colonnades, and the expanded base includes workshops with sawtooth roofs. Costa's Jockey Club Brasileiro headquarters in Rio (1956–72), close to the Ministério da Educação, updates the City Beautiful perimeter block. Three narrow office wings stand over a base containing shops and public galleries. These wings occupy three contiguous sides of the block and surround a parking garage that fills the core. The club offices occupy the fourth side, across from the garage entrance, and the club's recreational facilities crown the block, including restaurants, ballroom, gym, sports courts, swimming pool, and terraces. The building exemplifies Costa's diverse approaches to the design of the modern urban block. His installation at the Milan Triennial in 1964 was a proud and ironic rebuttal of the idea of Brazilians as frivolous and lazy: it featured hammocks, guitars, photographs of Brasília and Brazilian people, and letters hung from the ceiling declaring "Riposatevi" (Relax). Niemeyer's headquarters for the Communist Party in Paris (1965–71), with Paul Chemetov, Jean Deroche, Jean Prouvé, and Luiz Pinho, demonstrates that the bent slab–building type had not been exhausted. The composite base, including the reception desk, gallery space, and auditorium, is sunk into the ground, and the undulating platform that forms its roof recreates the original topography of the site, embraces the rising dome that covers the auditorium, and accommodates the entrance through a straight flight of stairs. The body of the slab building rests on five central pillars. The open *pilotis* is reduced to a slit between the climbing platform and the underside of the thickened first floor slab inclining in the opposite direction. The pillars bifurcate in subsequent floors into a disguised version of tree columns; the big, apparent cantilevers also suggest a tree house.

Rio's biggest urban project of the 1960s was the linear Parque Brigadeiro Eduardo Gomes, better known as Parque do Flamengo (1961–65, page 130), by Burle Marx and Reidy, built over the Aterro do Flamengo (*aterro* means "landfill" in Portuguese), which dates back to 1922. The park design incorporates six high-speed traffic lanes, MAM, the World War II monument, and the Santos Dumont airport at one end, and the eighteenth-century church of Outeiro da Glória, one of the city's landmarks, at the other. As director of the Instituto do Patrimônio Histórico e Artístico Nacional, Costa played a major role in the landfill's history. Since 1943 he had promoted the demolition of the buildings hiding the hill atop which the church stands (*outeiro* means "hill"), and he helped define guidelines for the design of the landfill's curved shoreline. Parque do Flamengo was compensation for Rio's loss of status after the capital moved to Brasília, and a freer pendant to Brasília's axes. Burle Marx's magnificent esplanades around MAM and Reidy's elegant pedestrian bridge linking it to downtown Rio are among the highlights. Reidy's follies in raw concrete are suitably playful and light. Costa designed new ramps leading to the church and curving retaining walls to limit them (1965, page 131). Built with stones from the demolished Flamengo wharf, the walls seem ageless, a perfect foil for the church and the park's trees. Costa's monument to Rio's founder, Estácio de Sá (1973, page 131), is a later addition to the park, aligned with Sugarloaf Mountain. It comprises a square half-sunk base housing a small gallery and an obelisk with a triangular section, related to those found in the Passeio Público (1760)—Rio's first public garden, distanced from the sea by the Flamengo land-fill—but also to Costa's television tower in Brasília. Thus the consolidation of the park was both con-temporary and intertwined with the consolidation of the new capital. Niemeyer's Guanabara music center would also have stood in the park, next to MAM, but it was relocated to Barra da Tijuca, the southern expansion of Rio being planned by Costa the same year, before being abandoned.

Divergence

Opportunities for Paulista architects from the late 1950s to the early 1970s included state-sponsored schools, courts, bus terminals, and low-cost housing, as well as private clubs, single-family houses, and some office and apartment buildings in long and rather narrow plots once occupied by mansions and walk-ups; new legislation demanded lateral setbacks and expanded basements rather than expanded bases.

On the whole the exciting work in São Paulo combined rough tactility, a Brutalist attitude and strong minimalist impulses while giving primacy to the reinforced-concrete structure, with the help of engineers such as João Carlos Figueiredo Ferraz, Julio Kassoy, and Mario Franco. Cantileverless designs became as popular as mono- or bidirectional hypercantilevers, together with few and widely spaced supports, clear and big spans, ribbed and waffle slabs, and, on occasion, transfer beams between the building's body and base. Exterior walls and sunbreakers were confounded with the structure or subordinated to it; the ribs and coffers of roof slabs often framed skylights. Columns were sometimes treated sculpturally; cylindrical ones were infrequent and the colossal type even more so. Barrel-vaulted roofs and parabolic vaults rising from the ground appeared in low-rise projects. Compact boxes with straightforward plans were privileged over sprawling compositions. Curves were episodic and mostly regular. *Poché* was valued only in structural service cores, and exposed ducts were common. The reinforced-concrete formwork was generally made of wood planks and the result-ing surfaces left unpainted. Facings were despised, except for rough plaster on masonry walls.

Upper-middle class houses were considered architectural laboratories. Those of Mendes da Rocha and Millan were typically conceived as boxes on two to three pairs of columns, Rocha's with concrete end walls hanging from the roof slab, like blinders, and Millan's with end walls either of plastered masonry or light concrete panels contrasting with the darker tone of the slabs' borders. The open ground floor *pilotis* serves as reception, garage, playground; given the few and thin sup-ports, a person standing there cannot but feel that a weighty mass hangs overhead. Less minimalist than Mendes da Rocha, Millan designed also houses that are barrel-vaulted additive compositions. However, both add warmth to their gray concrete through the sheen of large hardwood floor planks or pastel-colored floor tiles in intricate nineteenth-century patterns or the sparkle of unframed panes of tempered glass.

Mendes da Rocha built only one tall structure before the 1980s: the Guaimbé apartment building (1962–65) on a typically narrow plot, with one unit per floor. He cut slits into its long concrete sidewalls and used inclined fins to mask the view of the neighboring apartment buildings; ribbon windows protected by a curved concrete awning run along the front facade. The bilevel floors add a

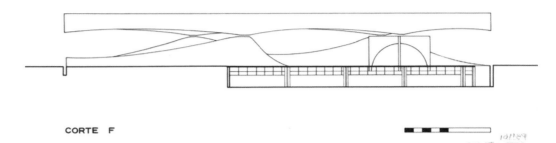

CORTE   F

11 . **Brazil Pavilion, Expo 70, Osaka. 1970.** Paulo
Mendes da Rocha (Brazilian, born 1928). Section.
Copy on vellum, 5 15/16 x 11 13/16 in. (15 x 30cm).
Acervo da Biblioteca da Faculdade de Arquitectura
e Urbanismo da Universidade de São Paulo

homely touch. The Gravatá (1964–71) and the Araucária (1965-72) apartments, by Levi, have external
frames filled with brick panels, concrete flaps shading living room windows, and transfer beams
over columns tapering toward the base in the open ground floor. Transfer beams reappear in the
maximalist Giselle apartments (1968–72), by Telesforo Cristofani, with a mixed-use ground floor
and projecting turrets for bathrooms and closets. The middle-range Gemini apartments (1968), by
Eduardo de Almeida, and the Modular apartments (1970, 1972), by Israel Sancovicz, were designed
to be replicated in different locations, the former with co-planar pillars and beams defining gridded
facades, the latter with projecting pillars defining vertically ribbed ones. The Quatiara building
(1972–73), by Ruy Ohtake, opposes the stark rationalism of the building's body with the expansive
curves of its base.

  Mendes da Rocha's Brazil Pavilion at Expo 70, in Osaka (fig. 11), occupied the width of a rectangular site, with a huge rectangular waffle slab of mostly glazed coffers between two prestressed
beams. The design of the beams reflected their bending moment, with indented lower borders delin-
eating a flattened scallop between overhanging half-scallops. The beams rested on four slightly
asymmetrical supports, three of them columns hidden by asphalt-covered hill-like volumes rising
out of a gently sloping ground, the fourth made up of two crossed planes with arched cutouts—a
virtual dome called the "coffee square." The scalloped edges of the beams echoed the curves of the
man-made hills, and the virtual dome of the arches was a negative, geometrically corrected image
of them. The pavilion reworked Niemeyer's artificial topography for the Communist Party headquarters and replied to Mies's design for the Bacardí building in Havana (1957), and it reinterpreted the
Carioca counterpoint between intermediary passages and lateral obstacles, curvilinear and straight
geometries, shade and sunlight. The solidity of the pavilion defied the ephemerality of the exhibition
while also rewriting archetypes with advanced engineering and artistic license: a real cave and an
imaginary dome in a complex relationship with a partially hidden trilith and an all-encompassing canopy. Penteado's clubhouse for the Sociedade Harmonia de Tênis (1964–70) is another freestanding
pavilion on uneven ground. The main space is a covered plaza on a half-sunk basement, with a roof
of a square waffle slab supported on twelve pillars slightly set back from the slab's perimeter. Giant
aluminum-frame awnings protect and enliven the elevations. Changes in floor level divide the interior
into different sectors, creating another kind of artificial topography.

Office buildings offer an array of interesting solutions. Millan's entry for the Jockey Club de São Paulo competition (1960), designed with Jorge Wilheim and Mauricio Tuck Schneider, was similar in program to Costa's Jockey Club Brasileiro, but the specified site was a block in the city's cramped old downtown. The proposed tower has prestressed floor slabs supported on two service cores and two huge piers only, and it starts four stories above a ground level occupied partly by a public plaza and partly by a two-story box with shops, entrances, and a roof terrace. Vertical sunbreakers on two adjacent sides protect the tower's curtain wall. Smooth tactility was combined with structural minimalism, as in the winning entry for the Peugeot building competition in Buenos Aires (1961–62), by Plínio Croce, Roberto Aflalo, and Gian Carlo Gasperini. Yet the Jockey Club's treelike volume suggests affinities with Wright's St. Mark's-in-the-Bouwerie Towers (1929), while the Peugeot winning entry is clearly attuned to the United States' postwar corporate approach to office buildings. The FIESP building by Cerqueira Cesar and Luiz Carvalho Franco (1969–79), for the Federação das Indústrias de São Paulo, is a different animal, a truncated dark-glass pyramid standing on a concrete tray that is held by giant frames and creates a covered public passage. The base is heavy sculptural Brutalism, the body suggests both a crystal and an obelisk; the whole feels maximally baroque. Jerônimo Bonilha Esteves's much smaller Morumbi building (1973), containing a variety of professional offices, occupies a steep hillside. The program and site are reflected in irregular excavations into a distorted rectangular prism with a normal structure. Irregular strata—created by the borders of the floor slabs, balconies, bands of vertical sunbreakers, and brick panels—are anchored by angled external service towers at the building's corner. Rodrigo Lefèvre, working for Hidroservice, a major Brazilian engineering firm, designed the headquarters for the Departamento Nacional de Estradas de Rodagem (1972–79) in Brasília, using modular coordination to rationalize construction and integrate its air-conditioning and electrical systems. Filling a whole block, the six-story building features a lushly landscaped central courtyard, a normal structure on a square grid, and a half-open ground floor containing a mezzanine and a protruding auditorium. Circular service towers disposed around the building in a pinwheel fashion contrast with the angled vertical sunbreakers running from floor to ceiling.

Mendes da Rocha's schools were a bigger version of his houses. Artigas enlivened his by using patios, paint, murals, and piers that tapered toward the base. In the single-story Itanhaem school (1959–60), the piers integrate transverse trapezoidal frames with intermediary triangular supports. At either end of the building, the intermediary support is set back, creating the illusion of a single big span; concrete gutters expose the edges of the frames, but their undersides prolong the flat ceiling created by cast-in-place lost-form slabs. At the Guarulhos school (1960–61), built over a natural hollow, a slightly off-center basketball court and an adjoining auditorium fit logically in the site. Most of the transverse frames feature a 66-foot (20-meter) span between two 33-foot (10-meter) spans. Two patios at either side of the building seem to result from suppressing the roof slab's central strip. The external and intermediary pillars fulfill the requirements of statics and sun control as well as of topography, creating, with their different shapes, richly textured facades and anthropomorphic overtones on the building's inside, where they look at once immaterial—simple colored trapezes between the floor and ceiling planes—and forceful—architectural devices keeping apart the slabs that create those planes. Structural virtuosity is even stronger in three sports facilities—the clubhouses for the São Paulo Futebol Clube (1961–70) and Anhembi Tênis Clube (1960–72), and the boathouse for the Santapaula late Clube (1961–64). By comparison, the XII de Outubro school (1962) looks sedate. It is Artigas's version of a midrise ordinary building. Its composite base uses the whole of a large lot made up of three joined frontages. Its slab building, with raw concrete end walls and glazed facades, has two similar parallel wings separated by a circulation spine with ramps. Below each wing, intermediary pillars cut through the base, and appear as a row of short trunks topped by trapezoidal capitals, comparable in flatness to Niemeyer's columns in the Palácio do Planalto; the capitals branch into two columns in the body of the building, prefiguring that of Niemeyer's Communist Party headquarters. Artigas's stylized figuration of natural forms is even more explicit in the tree columns with curving branches distinguishing the Jaú bus terminal (1973–76, page 142).

The dialogue with Niemeyer takes another turn in Artigas's Faculdade de Arquitetura at the Universidade de São Paulo (FAU-USP) (1961–69, page 146). It stands four stories and squarish in plan at the extremity of the humanities block. It develops, supported internally by a normal structure, in half-levels around a central void, lit from above, which is occupied partly by an exhibition and gathering space and partly by the foyer of the auditorium below it. The ramps at one side of the foyer allow dramatic vistas of the interior and propose a spiraling movement beneath the spectacular waffle-slab roof. Viewed from outside, the school looks stern and monumental: a one-storied blank concrete box resting on a peristyle of anthropomorphic columns that echo those at the crypt of the World War II monument. A latter-day temple of knowledge, it was definitely a match for Niemeyer's palaces in Brasília. Artigas designed variations on the type for the Jaú educational center (1968) and, with Penteado and Mendes da Rocha, the Escola Técnica de Santos (1968).

These Artigas buildings occupy an ambiguous territory where subdued monumentality and enhanced ordinariness meet. Ordinariness was inevitable in low-cost housing such as the CECAP- Guarulhos scheme (1967–72), by Artigas, Mendes da Rocha, and Penteado, a new urban sector with ten thousand dwellings units, half of which were eventually built. The repeating layout features parallel rows of long four-story boxes; the open ground-floor *pilotis* and bold patches of color in the facade panels relieve the monotony. Prefabricated using a normal structure with cantilevers, the boxes would make up four *freguesias* (from an old Portuguese word for "district") organized in a cruciform pattern and separated by green bands containing shops and other facilities.

In contrast with low-cost housing, even a modest stadium cannot help being a landmark. Mendes da Rocha's gymnasium for the Clube Atlético Paulistano (1958–61, page 143) is a circular roof structure lightly resting upon a square, half-underground, one-story base containing the sports court and dressing rooms. Visitors can enter the gymnasium directly from the street by a ramp or take a flight of stairs to the base's roof terrace. The metallic roof trusses rest on the inner border of a ring slab connecting six radial concrete pillars and hang from steel cables anchored in those pillars. It elegantly crowns a symmetrical composition that brings to mind the inverted dome and platform of Brasília's Congresso Nacional; the gymnasium is private property conceived as potential public amenity. With the Serra Dourada soccer stadium (1973–75) Mendes da Rocha smartly reworked the type. Two curved slab buildings on stilts replace the stands behind the goals; connected with the surrounding streets, they endow the stadium with visual porosity at both ends. The conventional marquee over the stands is expanded symmetrically on the street side to shelter a raised gallery with bars and other public amenities overlooking the city.

Various designs for cultural facilities were also monumental in aspiration, among them three by Penteado. His design for the Campinas cultural center (1967–76) reworks his competition entry for the Goiânia monument (fig. 12). Theaters and other facilities are disposed around an open-air arena, with roofs doubling as grandstands resembling thick washboards or faceted rock. His entry for the Teatro da Ópera de Campinas competition (1966) comprises two theaters of different size with an open-air amphitheater between them. The large theater is a volcanolike striped volume

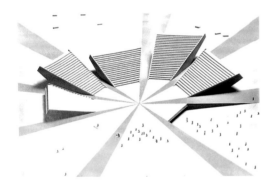

12. **Monumento comemorativo aos 30 anos de Goiânia. 1965.** Fábio Penteado (Brazilian, 1929–2011). View of a model

13. **House for Liliana Guedes, São Paulo. 1971.**
Joaquim Guedes (Brazilian, 1932–2008).
Exterior view

concealing the fly tower; roof slabs alternate between the tops and bottoms of obtuse-angled concrete ribs. The smaller theater follows a similar structural principle, recalling a peaked hill or the circus tent mentioned in Penteado's competition report.

Bo Bardi's Museu de Arte de São Paulo (MASP) (1957–68, page 144) uses the big span and the hybrid structure in a way at once perverse and marvelous. A glazed two-story box seems hung from a pair of prestressed concrete beams resting on four pillars at the box's narrow ends. It is a trick: the pillars support two additional beams, and from these hang the cables that secure the lower floor slab twenty-six feet (eight meters) above the ground. The covered plaza defined by that slab expands the sidewalk into a belvedere, constituting the rooftop for a T-shaped base inscribed into the sloping pentagonal site. To a person standing alone beneath it, the sensation of a weighty mass overhead is overwhelming. When the plaza is crowded, as it often is, standing beneath it is exhilarating. From the adjoining public garden, the museum is a treasure chest framing a portal. From an opposite and lower viewpoint, it levitates over a ziggurat enlivened with vegetation bands.

Guedes brought another dimension to Paulista architecture. He, too, thrived on hard tactility, few supports, and the primacy of structure. Four svelte pillars branching out like trees hold up his pioneering four-story Cunha Lima house (1958–63). Four columns carry his three-story house for Liliana Guedes (fig. 13), in which the impact of the daring cantilevers is intensified by the thin concrete flaps prolonging the ribbed slabs. But he privileged the picturesque, appreciated spatial complexity, multiplied planes and volumes; he was more eclectic in his choice of materials and experimented with different roof shapes. He could go almost vernacular with whitewashed walls, wood posts, and tiled roofs, as in the Itapira school (1960–61), or mix stepped asbestos-cement tiles with concrete frames and brick walls, as in the Francisco Landi house (1965). Tiled sawtooth roofs distinguish the classrooms of the Escola Técnica da Congregação Salesiana (1967) and superimpose a regular square pattern on its serrated volumes. For the Manuel da Nóbrega housing project (1974), he designed apartments with gallery access in angled, plastered four-story slab buildings without a *pilotis*. This was a smart variation of the parallel-slab layout, with two sizes of rectangular windows to enliven the facade, and it was a brave attempt to make the most of rigid economic constraints, all the while recognizing that open ground-floor *pilotis* did not come for free. But it failed at the ground floor too, by disregarding the need for privacy in the apartments there, something that architecturally unremarkable social-housing projects of the 1950s had dealt with competently.[30]

Nevertheless, Guedes was a progressivist showing culturalist tendencies, to borrow another Choay term. Culturalists suspected the industrial society, even if they made concessions to it. They viewed socioeconomic development with caution and thought it should be tailored to local conditions. They favored low technology and the rationalization of production: small was beautiful. Their outlook was retrospective: yesterday was often better than today in terms of human values and sense of community. Transformation of the environment, they felt, should follow a bottom-up approach that relied on popular participation. Guedes's position was timely. The Carioca school was already old-fashioned at the beginning of the Brazilian economic miracle in the late 1960s; when the economy started to slow in the mid-1970s, the Paulista school was suffering from vulgarization, as had the Carioca school in the mid-1950s.

Balance

Both the Carioca and the Paulista schools were progressivist, but they stood for different visions of Brazil. The Cariocas were optimistic (the country was rich; the issue was political autonomy); the Paulistas were pessimistic (the country was poor; the issue was economic autonomy). The Cariocas recalled the *inconfidentes*, the Brazilians who attempted to free the colony from Portugal in 1789; the Paulistas were more like the *bandeirantes*, those who had earlier gone into the hinterland looking for gold, diamonds, and Indian slaves. Cariocas and Paulistas clashed about the essential character of Brazilian modern architecture, and they had different conceptions of native genius, should it exist. Stoic severity challenged Epicurean grace. Although severity may be expressed under grace, as in the Teatro Nacional at Brasília, and grace may be expressed under severity, as in the Brazil Pavilion in Osaka, sensory impressions reveal differences between the two schools. Rio extending into Brasília favored smoothness, transparency, thinness, upward lightness, gloss, shallowness, and painterliness, even if it was not averse, on occasion, to the rustic. São Paulo was partial to rusticity and tended to cultivate roughness, opacity, thickness, downward heaviness and minimal supports, matte surfaces, depth, and sculptural effects. The elimination of facings and postproduction finish echoed the use of big clear spans, while tempered glass added sparkle to hardness. Compositionally stiffer than the Cariocas, the Paulistas gave expressive primacy to structure, often fusing it with external walls and fixed sunbreakers. In other words, structure and enclosure often merged.

Nevertheless, "pancakes on pins" did not disappear in São Paulo. It remained the normal structure for buildings of all heights, although the visual autonomy of the structure and walls was challenged and bent slab buildings almost vanished. The distinction between representative and ordinary buildings persisted. Special structures still corresponded to special programs, as in MASP, FAU-USP, the Brazil Pavilion in Osaka, Penteado's grandstands, and the inverted pyramid of Mendes da Rocha's design for the Museu de Arte Contemporânea of USP (1975). Special structures still were of two kinds; load-bearing masonry walls, wood posts, and tiled roofs appear in weekend houses by Millan, Mendes da Rocha and others. São Paulo did not abandon the idea of modern architecture as an inclusive and diverse formal system operating among three levels and offering multiple expressive possibilities. Characterization of program and situation still mattered, and thus relevant precedents and suitable ambiences did, too. Stylized figuration was explicit in the representative programs, and it made an appearance even in the domestic ones. Artigas explained, for example, that the concrete panels hanging from the floor slab of his Berquó house (1967) reinterpreted the roofline friezes of nineteenth-century chalets, and that he had added four real trees in the internal courtyard as a joke about primitivism and Roman roots.[30]

At the same time, there are correspondences between São Paulo and Brasília. Epicurean, in the proper sense of the word, means moderate, open, and balanced. It relates to an ethics, too. At its best, Rio balanced the Vitruvian triad of *firmitas*, *commoditas*, and *venustas*. Some aspects of *commoditas* were notoriously sacrificed to representation in São Paulo as in Brasília, although with different connotations. Comfort was considered bourgeois in São Paulo, and it may have taken second place, after speed of construction, in Brasília. In both cities exaggeration took command. And mutation took place in both cities. If São Paulo is not the full-fledged antithesis of the Carioca school, Brasília is not its simple extension, whether as apotheosis or twilight. The primacy of structure is as evident in the monumental buildings of Brasília as in São Paulo, and the merging of structure and enclosure clearly distinguish Niemeyer's Museu da Cidade.[31]

So the schools were genetically related in a complex way. They were family. Brilliant relatives included Le Corbusier, but it would be a mistake to overestimate his influence on the highly educated Brazilian architects. Corbusian references were important, but they were only one kind among many. Moreover, from the very beginning these multiple references included Brazilian work itself, past and present, erudite, vernacular, or utilitarian. It is difficult to tell, in Costa's houses at Monlevade, for example, which really came first: the Corbusian or the wattle-and-daub references. Both ways should be admitted.

The very continuity between the Carioca and the Paulista schools may be taken as an affirmation of national identity, but in light of their work it cannot be said that such an affirmation was the primary or exclusive concern of Brazilian modern architecture in Rio, São Paulo, or Brasília, just as it cannot be said that the primary concern of Miesian glass boxes was an affirmation of a US national identity, even if the rest of the world understood them that way. The exceptions are buildings whose programs required such national representation, such as the Ministério da Educação, the Brazil Pavilion at the New York World's Fair of 1939, Costa's installation at the Milan Triennial. The jury citation for the Brazil Pavilion at Expo 70, which praised the winning entry for being the most representative of Brazilianness, should be viewed in the context of what is appropriate to a fair pavilion rather than as some essence.[32]

It is easy to forget, too, amidst propositions for a modern international style, that the modern concept of the nation was the handmaiden of industrialization. The affirmation of national identity, a nineteenth-century idea, was not a difficult problem for academically trained architects. It did not require choosing a style as representative of the nation, as advocated by proponents of neocolonial style. And it needed not be modern. While Costa and his colleagues were promoting modern architecture in the 1930s, other academically trained architects were promoting Art Deco with indigenous ornament. For both groups it was a question of phenotype and genotype, individual and family traits, looks rather than selves, deliberate choice instead of ineffable inspiration.[32] Thus in Rio and Brasília the affirmation was made knowingly, in an international context. As it was with Paulista work, which was contemporary with comparable designs abroad, and thus part of a movement identified loosely as Brutalism, but which was rarely published abroad and thus spared the critique leveled against the other two.

14. Caraíba company town (now Pilar), Bahia. 1976–82. Joaquim Guedes (Brazilian, 1932–2008). View of an apartment building with row houses in the background

Extension

Niemeyer remained active and evolving, as did Costa, Lelé, and most of the leading Paulistas, but in the mid-1970s their work pursued distinctive individual character rather than collective expression. Another generation had entered the stage in the late 1960s, and it was critical of Brasília as a paradigm, opposed to the antistreet bias of Brazilian urban planning, and convinced that the favela was a solution instead of a problem, that urban structure mattered more than building form. These beliefs could be said to be culturalist, even antimodernist, but they were not without precedent in the work of older architects, including the Robertos' entry in the Brasília competition, with its cell-like urban districts, and Cajueiro Seco (1963, page 140), a very poor community in Recife, for which the Rio-trained architect Acácio Gil Borsoi, born in the 1920s, designed houses built with prefabricated panels of wattle and daub, still used locally, in a straightforward checkerboard urban plan. Carlos Nelson Ferreira dos Santos, born in the early 1940s, worked with the people of Brás de Pina (1969. page 140), a favela in Rio, to devise a new and improved street network and relocate those displaced by it in the same area. For Alagados (1973, page 141), in Salvador, a huge squatter's settlement filling Todos os Santos Bay, Mauricio Roberto and a young team proposed a system of cul-de-sacs and clusters. Bo Bardi, another progressivist showing culturalist overtones, designed the cooperative community of Camurupim (1975, page 141), a village for rural workers displaced by the construction of hydroelectric dams in the São Francisco River in northeastern Brazil. The communal facilities occupied a hilltop. The residential lots followed the topography and were large enough for subsistence agriculture. The simple houses of local materials could be built by the workers themselves. One particularly ingenious element is a combined toilet-shower.

In the end, progressivism or culturalism mattered less than the reality of more austere times. Designed in the late 1970s but inaugurated in the 1980s, a metropolitan transportation hub, a remote company town, and a megalopolitan social condenser exemplify the persistence of the modern tradition in Brazil.

Lelé designed the Lapa transportation center (1979–82, page 149) in Salvador to serve forty-nine lines. The structure combines precast and cast-in-place components. The access viaduct is supported by prestressed tie rods anchored to the top of a central mast. Precast slabs shelter the platforms. The main hall is a T-shaped platform suspended from cast-in-place hollow boxes that contain staircases, another example of structural *poché*; the hall connects to the grounds of an old convent, opening it to public use. The azulejo panels in the walls are both utilitarian and representative.

Guedes built the Caraíba company town (fig. 14), intended for fifteen thousand people, in a flat, semiarid region in the interior of Bahia. Like Brás de Pina, it is a critique of Brasília as a paradigm for the renewal and expansion of existing Brazilian cities. Like a typical northeastern small town, it has a checkerboard layout, with streets and squares defined by either aligned walk-ups with a public gallery and shops below apartments, or row houses with patios. Whole blocks were designated for freestanding communal facilities. The houses have load-bearing walls with tiled roofs; the apartment buildings are normal structures; and the communal facilities are a hybrid, with asbestos-cement roofs on wood trusses and posts in the bigger spaces, and load-bearing walls with tiled roofs elsewhere.

Bo Bardi's cultural center for SESC Pompéia (1977–86, page 152) rises from a flat, L-shaped parcel composed of a corner lot with an alley and two rows of sheds plus an adjoining through lot, with a creek running from one end to the other. The parti is straightforward. Bo Bardi recycled the sheds, so that the inner row became a canteen and storeroom and the outer row contains the center's administration, a theater, workshops, and a large covered plaza with a library and exhibition space.[33] A transversal passage in the outer row was roofed over to become the theater's foyer. The creek is covered by a boardwalk, and two raw concrete towers anchor one end. The lower tower contains four sports courts and a swimming pool; the floor and roof waffle slabs are prestressed and span 98 by 131 feet (30 by 40 meters)—no mean feat of engineering. The taller tower accommodates vertical circulation, a cafeteria, and exercise and locker rooms. Superimposed and diverging walkways link the towers to define a portal that is complemented by a svelte concrete reservoir featuring parallel scalloped bands, resembling an industrial chimney as well as a giant candle.

The design's straightforwardness increases its visual impact. The height and materials of the towers contrast with those of the recycled sheds, while unusual fenestration and other elements contrast with speculative apartment and office buildings nearby, of similar height and profile. Some walls are perforated by a regular grid of holes with irregular borders, recalling grotto entrances or bombed buildings, and others are punched by an irregular succession of near-square openings or corrugated by stacks of parallel balconies.[34] The rectangular prism of the shorter tower is fused to a smaller prism cut through with horizontal slits and indented by balconies with exposed metallic exhaust fans and water ducts. The taller tower has a pentagonal plan, articulating the inclination of the adjoining street to the orthogonal layout of the sheds. Its corner balconies suggest a domesticity belied by their irregular disposition, and its base widens, bringing to mind a medieval castle. The walkways, almost symmetrical in plan, fan out like refinery ducts, or like spears that transform the towers into warriors with armors bloodied by red pools (wooden trellises behind the holes), red streams (the external ducts), and red clots (the exhaust fans). The vindication of childhood innocence does not ignore its brutal and warlike component. The towers rise like fortresses watching over the boardwalk turned into a beach by virtue of the mural painted in the facing boundary wall. Yet there is openness inside, and abundant lateral lighting. Suddenly huge, the holes provide cutout frames of city, sky, trees, and mountains. The utilitarian interiors flirt with suburban kitsch: the women's toilets are painted pink and gold, the men's in blue and silver, and the murals in the cafeteria would not be out of place in a pub. And the columnless structure is quite special: there is nothing cozy about enormous waffle slabs.

Roughness and vulgarity are suitable for sports but not for cultural pursuits and social encounters. Bo Bardi replaced strips of clay roof tiles with translucent ones, so that the sheds become intimate shelters. The diffuse zenithal lighting underlines the elegance of the original concrete structure. The sweat and exploitation of factory work is gone, and the atmosphere exudes cultivated taste in details such as the wavy pond (after Niemeyer), or the Brutalist concrete (after Artigas) in the theater foyer. What was once formal audacity is now tamed by water and light, and accessible by trellised sliding doors that evoke Costa. The sheds are kept private, almost indistinguishable from the alley they create in a continuous and aligned neutral plane, indifferent to the diversity of functions they now accommodate. They are presented as ordinary components in an extended repeating fabric, while still contrasting in scale with the brick walls and roof tiles of the district's row houses. Meanwhile, viewed from close range, the towers, and their odd and dynamic play of volumes, celebrate difference, singularity, communication—at once portal, display, and lookout. The sheds exemplify mat building avant la lettre, now standing for gridded, timeless, functionally generic rationality; the towers break in, depending on the circumstances, as picturesque landmarks or monuments, always undisputed focal points for movement within the complex. Yet from afar the towers and recent construction merge, and only the void created by the boardwalk seems exceptional.

Bo Bardi's design defends continuity without shunning change, both evolutionary and radical. The space-time warp is built in. Given the embourgeoisement of the industrial sheds and alley, the hardship they once housed is appropriately and meaningfully recalled in the new sporting facilities—after all, hardship strengthens and, in due course, fades into soothing memory. Bo Bardi proclaims that urbanity requires both balm and blow: beauty is as inherent and relevant to the city as *terribilità*; appeasement is as important as provocation. Mellow or startling, her imagery is drawn from sources both within and without the conventional territory of architecture, from the work of cultivated, well-known artists, such as São Paulo's Concretists, and intuitive, often anonymous artisans, as well as from everyday objects both natural, like the *mandacarú* flower evoked in the parapet in one of the walkways, or man-made, like the candle and chimney evoked by the water tower.

Inclusiveness is given a temporal dimension at Bo Bardi's complex, with old and new interacting in many dimensions. Neither Guedes's company town nor Lelé's station is so rich in denotations and connotations. But Guedes correlated types of structure with types of program: the load-bearing walls of row houses and the concrete structure of walk-ups functioning as ground, and the hybrid structure of communal facilities functioning as figure. Lelé does a similar thing: the great hall announced by towering hollow boxes, singular tie rods, and hypercantilevers; the modest platforms announced by plain precast elements. Programmatic character is still a concern in all three cases, and characterization still resorts to the same generic strategies. The recalling of relevant precedents still matters, as much as the creation of suitable ambiences. Communicating with the people and the intelligentsia is still important. The double coding includes stylized figuration, so that like the works in Rio, Brasília, and São Paulo, these designs keep challenging the canonical association of modern architecture with abstract, nonobjective, and nonrepresentational art. Their intellectual and affective impact depends not only on intrinsic form but also, and explicitly, on narrative and representational content. At the same time, and maybe in different degrees, Lelé, Guedes, and Bo Bardi downplayed plastic exuberance and reaffirmed modern architecture's alliance with planarity and plainness, all the while insisting upon its foundation on structure. For them, iconography and tectonics did not part company, and both the immediate and the remote past remained a living presence. For better or worse, Brazilian modern architecture has a story of its own, and it is a long one.

1 For this essay the author relied primarily on Carlos Eduardo Comas, "Teoría académica, arquitectura moderna, corolario brasileño," *Anales del Instituto de Arte Americano e Investigaciones Estéticas Mario J. Buschiazzo* 26, (1988): 85–96; Comas, "Paulo Mendes da Rocha: O prumo dos 90," *AU Arquitetura e Urbanismo* 97 (2001): 102–09; Comas, "Précisions brésiliennes sur un état passé de l'architecture et de l'urbanisme modernes d'après les projets de Lucio Costa, Oscar Niemeyer, MMM Roberto, Affonso Reidy, Jorge Moreira et cie., 1936–45" (PhD diss., Université de Paris VIII, 2002); Comas, "Moderna 30–60," in Roberto Montezuma, ed., *Arquitetura Brasil 500 anos* (Recife: UFPe, 2002), pp. 182–238; Comas and Marcos Almeida, "Brasilia quadragenária: A paixão de uma monumentalidade nova" (paper presented at the IX Seminário da História da Cidade e do Urbanismo, São Paulo, September 4–6, 2006); Comas, "Niemeyer, el derecho a la diferencia," *A&V Monografías* 125 (2008): 14–21; Comas, "Lina 3x2," *ARQTEXTO (UFRGS)* 14, (2009): 14–34; and Ruth Verde Zein, "A arquitetura da escola Paulista Brutalista, 1953–1973" (PhD diss., PROPAR-UFRGS, 2005).

2 Costa, "Razões da nova arquitetura, "1934, and "Universidade do Brasil," 1936, republished in Costa, *Sobre arquitetura* (Porto Alegre, Brazil: CEUA, 1962), pp. 17–40, 67–85.

3 Julien Guadet, *Elements et théorie de l'architecture*, vol. 1 (Paris: Librairie de la construction moderne, 1904), p. 132.

4 See Costa's remarks on Filippo Brunelleschi, Le Corbusier, and the French Renaissance in *Sobre arquitetura*, pp. 24, 38. "Existing form" does not mean only architectural form or form already incorporated into the disciplinary tradition. See George Kubler, *The Shape of Time: Remarks on the History of Things* (New York: Yale University Press, 1962); and Alan Colquhoun, *Essays in Architectural Criticism: Modern Architecture and Historical Change* (Cambridge, Mass.: MIT Press, 1985), pp. 43–66.

5 Le Corbusier's five points were originally six, in *L'Architecture vivante*, Fall–Winter 1927, pp. 5–28, and they became eight in *Précisions sur un état present de l'architecture et de l'urbanisme* (Paris: G. Crès, 1930), pp. 55–56. His four compositions appear in *Le Corbusier: Oeuvre complète, 1910–29* (Zurich: Editions Girsberger, 1929), p. 189. On the Dom-ino structural scheme, see Colin Rowe, *The Mathematics of the Ideal Villa and Other Essays* (Cambridge, Mass: MIT Press, 1978), pp. 195–96; Kenneth Frampton, ed., *Oppositions* 15–16 (1979), a special issue dedicated to Le Corbusier; and Paulo F. Santos, *A arquitetura da sociedade industrial* (Belo Horizonte: Escola de Arquitetura da Universidade de Minas Gerais, 1961), pp. 160–82. The last book contains lectures given at the Faculdade de Arquitetura da Universidade do Brasil, later the Universidade Federal do Rio de Janeiro, and constitute a sophisticated survey of the evolution of structural systems in the nineteenth and twentieth centuries.

6 Costa, "Considerações sobre o ensino da arquitetura," 1945, in *Sobre arquitetura*, p. 113.

7 Rowe, *The Mathematics of the Ideal Villa*, p. 196.

8 Le Corbusier's project for the Universidade do Brasil was published in *Le Corbusier: Oeuvre complète, 1934–1938* (Zurich: Editions Girsberger, 1939), pp. 42–45. Costa's project is best presented in *Lucio Costa: Registro de uma vivência* (São Paulo: Empresa das artes, 1995), pp. 173–90.

9 Costa, *Sobre arquitetura*, pp. 82–83. The theme is further developed in "Considerações sobre o ensino da arquitetura," 1945, and "Considerações sobre arte contemporânea," 1952, both in *Sobre arquitetura*, pp. 111–17, 202–29.

10 Costa, "Vila Monlevade," 1936, in *Sobre arquitetura*, pp. 42–55.

11 Guadet, *Elements et théorie de l'architecture*, pp. 106–10.

12 See the entry on *caractère* in Antoine-Chrysôthome Quatremère de Quincy, *Encyclopédie méthodique* (Paris: Panckouke, 1788). A simplified version appears in his *Dictionnaire historique de l'architecture*, vol. 1 (Paris: Librairie d'Adrien le Clerc, 1832), p. 300. "Three … principal means … manifest the purpose of a building: by the forms of the plan and of the elevation; by the choice, the measure and the manner of ornament and decoration; through the massing and the kind of construction and materials." *The True, the Fictive and the Real: The Historical Dictionary of Quatremère de Quincy*, trans. Samir Younès (London: Andreas Papadakis, 1999), p. 107.

13 Costa, *Sobre arquitetura*, p. 72.

14 Arthur A. Drexler, ed., *The Architecture of the Ecole des Beaux-Arts* (New York: The Museum of Modern Art, 1977); and Robin Middleton, ed., *Beaux Arts and Nineteenth-Century French Architecture* (London: Thames and Hudson, 1984).

15 For Costa's comments about the Ionian and Doric in modern architecture see *Album comemorativo do Pavilhão Brasileiro de Nova York* (New York: H. K. Publishing, 1939); translated and with comments by the author and David Leatherbarrow, "Solving Problems, Making Art, Being Modern," *Journal of Architectural Education* 64 (2010): 65–68. Le Corbusier was a consultant for the Ministério da Educação, but he did not participate in the final design, as the correspondence between Le Corbusier and Costa corroborates. Cecilia Rodrigues dos Santos et al., *Le Corbusier e o Brasil* (São Paulo: Projeto/ Tessela, 1987).

16 On the opposition between *Neue Gemütlichkeit*, or the cozy International Cottage Style, and *Neue Sachlichkeit*, or the impersonal International Style, see Alfred H. Barr, Jr., "What Is Happening to Modern Architecture? A Symposium at The Museum of Modern Art," *The Museum of Modern Art Bulletin* 15 (Spring 1948): 8.

17 On the ideological conflicts among Brazilian architects in the 1950s, see Hugo Segawa, *Arquiteturas no Brasil, 1900–1990* (São Paulo: EDUSP, 1997), pp. 112–13, 143–44.

18 Costa's idea of grace first appears in a refutation to a Paulista critic's claiming that Brazilian modern architecture started with Warchavick, Costa, "Carta-depoimento," 1948, in *Sobre arquitetura*, pp. 119–28; and then in Costa's foreword to Stamo Papadaki, *The Work of Oscar Niemeyer* (New York: Reinhold, 1950); and later in "Imprévu et importance de la contribution des architectes brésiliens au développement de l'architecture contemporaine," *L'Architecture d'aujourd'hui*, nos. 42–43 (1952): 4–7.

19 Eugène Viollet-le-Duc, *Entretiens sur l'architecture* , vol. 1 (Paris: A. Morel et Cie, 1863), p. 450.

20 Brutalism is usually conceived as a style, and defined in terms of raw, rough, "as found" materials, primarily concrete. Yet concrete is a wholly artificial material, and the final

characteristics of its surfaces depend on formwork. This essay avoids that pitfall by defining it as an attitude instead of a style, in terms of building components instead of materials, while requiring additional information about tactility and number of elements for precision. For the different definitions of Brutalism, see Verde Zein, *Brutalist Connections* (São Paulo: Altamira, 2014).

21 Costa refuted the criticisms of Max Bill in "Oportunidade perdida," 1953, in *Sobre arquitetura*, pp. 252–59. Niemeyer's response was more generic, in "Forma e função na arquitetura," *Módulo* 4 (December 1960): 3–7, and he expanded the argument in *Minha experiência em Brasília* (Rio de Janeiro: Vitória, 1961), pp. 24–27.

22 Dos Santos et al., *Le Corbusier e o Brasil*, pp. 244–52, 266–83. See also Marcelo Puppi, "Unfinished Spaces: Le Corbusier, Lucio Costa, and Brazil House Saga, 1953–1956," *Arqtexto* (Porto Alegre) 12 (2007): 160–203.

23 Françoise Choay, *L'Urbanisme, utopies et réalités: Une Anthologie* (Paris: Seuil, 1965).

24 See Milton Braga, *O Concurso de Brasília* (São Paulo: Cosac Naify, 2010); and Alberto Xavier and Julio Katinsky, eds. *Brasilia: Antologia crítica* (São Paulo: Cosac Naify, 2012).

25 Costa, "Brasília," 1957, in *Sobre arquitetura*, pp. 264–78.

26 Papadaki, *Oscar Niemeyer* (New York: George Braziller, 1960), p. 29.

27 For some of the more perceptive comments, see Norma Evenson, *Two Brazilian Capitals: Architecture and Urbanism in Rio de Janeiro and Brasília* (New Haven, Conn.: Yale University Press, 1973).

28 Ludwig Mies van der Rohe, quoted in Peter Carter, *Mies van der Rohe at Work* (New York: Praeger Publishers, 1974), p. 61.

29 Niemeyer *Minha experiência em Brasília*, p. 27.

30 Rosa Camargo Artigas et al., eds., *Vilanova Artigas: Arquitetos brasileiros.* (São Paulo: Blau; Instituto Lina Bo e P. M. Bardi; Fundação Vilanova Artigas, 1997), pp. 138–39.

31 Oscar Niemeyer, "Depoimento," *Módulo* 9 (1958): 3-6.

32 For excerpts of the jury's report, see *Acrópole* 361 (May 1969): 13.

33 The recycling was suggested by the SESC directors who had visited Ghirardelli Square in San Francisco, a 1964 factory conversion by Halprin, Wurster, Bernardi & Emmons. Zeuler R. M. de A. Lima, *Lina Bo Bardi* (New Haven, Conn.: Yale University Press, 2013), pp. 158–59.

34 On the idea that the bombed buildings referred to Bo Bardi's experience of World War II, see Stanislaus von Moos, "L'Europe après la pluie ou le brutalisme face à l'histoire," in Jacques Sbriglio, ed., *Le Corbusier et la question du brutalisme.* (Paris: Editions Parenthèses, 2013), pp. 64–87.

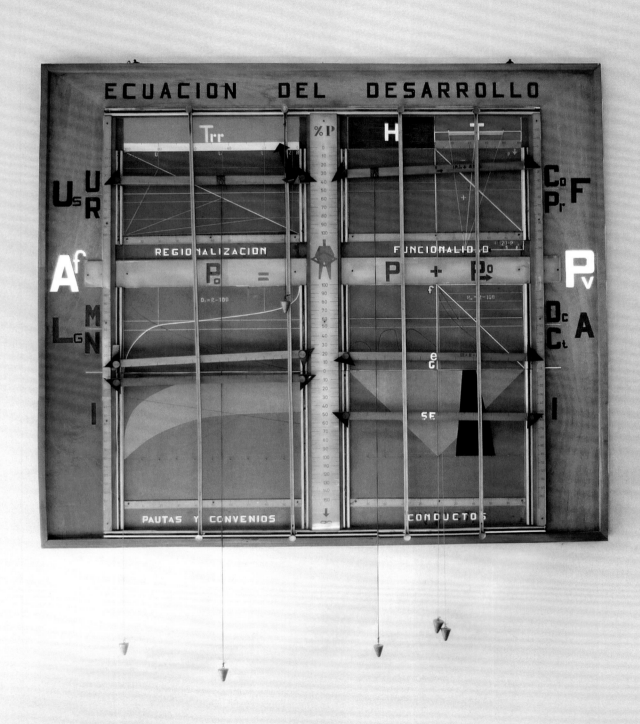

Ecuación del desarrollo (Development equation). 1960. Carlos Gómez Gavazzo
(Uruguayan, 1904–1987). A calculator for gauging the necessary level of development and
appropriate interventions for a region. Wood and metal, 66 15/16 × 63 in. (170 × 160 cm)

Architectures for Progress: Latin America, 1955–1980

Jorge Francisco Liernur

As in other parts of the world, the formative period of modernist positions in Latin America over the first three decades of the twentieth century was characterized by the search for a correlation between architecture and new general conditions of modernization—new production processes, materials, social sectors, means of transport, and bureaucratization. But after World War II it became clear that a structural gap separated Latin American countries from the great powers, and that no truly modern culture could be built without bridging it. And so in the 1950s and 1960s the celebration of the present that characterized the first half of the century gave way to an intense preoccupation with the construction of the future.

The historian Perry Anderson has argued that the most radical manifestations of modern culture were found in relatively tradition-bound societies, those in which processes of modernization had developed over long periods of great social and political turbulence, and during which different actors had to choose among the various, and frequently opposing, contending positions.[1] In this sense, it is not surprising that as postwar modernization spread from the United States to the rest of the world and was consolidated in Europe and Japan, architects discarded their avant-gardist banners and presented themselves as ideologically and politically neutral. In the thirty years after the war, the increasing tension known as the Cold War could also be characterized, broadly speaking, as opposition between two models for the progress of society, and this opposition had a profound influence on the direction taken by Latin American countries on the path to modernization. With a vigorous and still-unchallenged push toward modernization, these countries found themselves in conditions of extreme anxiety and creativity similar to those that, according to Anderson's hypothesis, had characterized earlier European modernisms.

Architects were forced to take sides, although the alternatives could in no way be reduced to a simple duality. On the contrary, there were a host of possible combinations, just as there were multiple nuances between the various factions and their respective centers. While there were those who believed the goal was to escape backward conditions and advance toward progress and development, others at the opposite end of the ideological spectrum believed that the path of development only brought about ever-greater dehumanization. Some thought that development could only be achieved through a revolutionary break with the Western model, while others believed that this very model was universally valid and that the history of the most advanced countries indicated the steps poorer nations would need to take in order to catch up.

The Question of Development

According to Heinz Wolfgang Arndt, the concept of economic development has a dual origin.[2] On the one hand, in the Hegelian genealogy, the concept can be traced to Karl Marx, and was later elaborated upon by Joseph Schumpeter in *Theorie der wirtschaftlichen Entwicklung* (*Theory of Economic Development*), originally published in 1911. In the Marxist tradition it implies an impersonal exchange process created by the forces that compose a society. The idea of change is central to this interpretation; for Schumpeter, if in an economy only "the data change and . . . the economy continuously adapts itself to them, then we should say that there is *no* economic development."[3] For Arndt, the Marxist interpretation is derived from using the verb "to develop" in its intransitive sense. On the other hand, the verb was used in the transitive sense for the first time by Alfred Milner in the second decade of the twentieth century, to describe the course of action the British Empire should take in order to maximize exploitation of the natural resources of its colonies and dominions. In this case, natural resources were an object to be modified (developed) by a specific agent: the colonial administration.

In neither of these senses, particularly in the second, is the idea of economic development directly related to improving the material well-being of the populace of the territories concerned. Likewise, in none of these cases was backwardness necessarily associated with the countries of non-European regions. As the British historian Eric Hobsbawm observed, the problem of economic backwardness with respect to different nations had been attentively studied before the post–World War II period, with the goal of understanding not only the behavior of those nations that began the process of industrialization relatively late but also the different levels of development found in different regions of the same nation.[4]

Before World War II, the elites of industrialized countries believed that the populations of territories under colonial or semicolonial control were incapable of carrying out independent processes of—as Milner understood it—development; for the Marxist vanguard of the Third International, the distinction was between "oppressor" and "oppressed" nations, or between "backward" and "advanced."

In 1922 Sun Yat-sen, the first president of modern China, appears to have been the first to formulate the idea of rescuing his country from a state of poverty and relative backwardness through a development plan supported by international capital. But it would not be until 1939 that Eugene Stanley, in a publication issued by the Council on Foreign Relations, presented the first initiative for a world-development program; three years later, at the International Labor Organization, Wilfred Benson spoke for the first time of underdeveloped areas, followed in 1944 by Paul Rosenstein-Rodan's study of the problem of the "international development of economically backward areas."[5]

The issue gained momentum after the creation of the United Nations in 1945. The idea of a Development Bank, already implemented without success by the US-appointed governor Rexford Tugwell in Puerto Rico in 1942, was taken up by the International Bank of Reconstruction and Development, created in December 1945 to contribute to the reconstruction of European countries after the war. In the fourth session of the Economic and Social Council in 1947, deliberation began over the development of countries with minor incomes that had suffered the consequences of the war, and in 1948 various Latin American delegates proposed the creation of the Comisión Económica para América Latina (CEPAL), which would be similar to commissions already created for Europe and Asia. Consolidated in 1951, CEPAL was significant because it applied the concept of development to a region not directly affected by World War II. But the critical stimulus for the international extension and implementation of the concept was Harry Truman's second inaugural address, known as the "Four Point Speech," delivered on January 20, 1949. What he called the "improvement and growth of underdeveloped areas" became a foreign-policy objective of the United States and thus a priority of international bodies.[6]

And yet within the new framework of the Cold War, the administration of Dwight D. Eisenhower, upon its inauguration in 1953, gave priority to military cooperation and stimulating private economic affairs. At the beginning of 1958 Vice President Richard Nixon was greeted with particularly virulent protests while on a Latin American tour. Shortly after, with the conviction that US policy needed reappraisal, the president of Brazil, Juscelino Kubitschek, sent a proposal for what he envisioned as a Pan-American venture. Seduced by the ideas of CEPAL, both the Brazilian president and his Argentine counterpart, Arturo Frondizi, believed that cooperation should be oriented toward encouraging *desarrollismo*, or developmentalism, in the countries of the south by emphasizing the expansion of heavy industry. Thanks to influential North American intellectuals such as Walter Rostow and world leaders such as Kwame Nkrumah of Ghana, the concept of development had been adopted on the international level, and in January 1961, following a proposal of the recently sworn-in US president John F. Kennedy, the United Nations declared the 1960s the "Decade of Development." In March of that year, Kennedy proposed to advance the plan previously outlined by Kubitschek, and in August the Organization of American States (OAS) approved the creation of the Alliance for Progress (ALPRO).

Metropolis and Territory

Postwar Latin America was characterized by an explosion in population and urbanization, as Barry Bergdoll has noted in his essay for this volume. For the architectural discipline this phenomenon had contradictory implications. On the one hand, some cities were enriched by new functions, new technologies, the reorganization of old city quarters, and the development of larger-scaled modernist structures than those built in the preceding decades. But informal cities also grew, constructed in a marginal and precarious manner by their inhabitants and increasingly occupying greater areas of urban space. Nonetheless, buildings of an unknown scale and complexity, capable of housing new combined functions, began to emerge.

Perhaps the most emblematic structure of this large-scale, multiuse type is Oscar Niemeyer's COPAN building (1952–66, page 40) in São Paulo, which was designed to incorporate, in a single great building, apartments, an enormous hotel, event spaces, restaurants, a cinema, a theater, parking garages, and a shopping mall. In its scale and its relation to its urban context, the COPAN building opened the door to a new type of multifunctional architectural and urban intervention. Since then, São Paulo has been the venue for numerous buildings that can only be understood as elements of this new urban scale, and it is in this sense that one should consider the Museu de Arte de São Paulo (MASP) (1957–68, page 144), designed by Lina Bo Bardi, a covered plaza and urban lookout capable not only of housing a collection of objects but also of functioning as a civic gathering space.

Likewise, the facilities demanded by the new transportation networks transcended prior limits of engineering, and the results were complex urban nodes that articulated cultural, commercial, service, and transport uses, creating unprecedented public spaces—such as the Rodoviaria de Jaú bus station, by João Batista Vilanova Artigas (1973–76, page 142); the main bus station in Brasília, designed by Lucio Costa to be located at the crossing of the city's two main axes; or the Centro Cultural de São Paulo (fig. 1), by Eurico Prado Lopes and Luiz de Castro Telles.

In Buenos Aires, an urban ensemble of particularly high quality was constructed over much of the period in question: the Teatro and Centro Cultural San Martín (1953–60 and 1960–70, page 112), designed by Mario Roberto Álvarez y Asociados. The complex overlays three different theaters and forms a new typology, with covered plazas and interior streets that traverse the traditional city block and constitute a new kind of public space.

1. **Centro Cultural de São Paulo, 1976–82.** Eurico Prado Lopes (Brazilian, 1939–1985), Luiz Benedito de Castro Telles (Brazilian, 1943–2014). View of the main exhibition spaces. 2012. Photograph by Cristiano Mascaro

Latin America saw a dramatic increase in the number of skyscrapers, a type of building and real estate instrument rarely used before then. The event with perhaps the greatest impact was the international competition for the Peugeot headquarters in Buenos Aires (1961–62, page 96), which attracted an extraordinary collection of entries from around the world; although the proposed megabuilding was never built, the competition advanced the conversation about skyscrapers by several decades. In a neighboring area of the city, a renewal project known as Catalinas Norte (1956–61) gained momentum. Its aim was to contain the advance of such large-scale office buildings on the urban fabric, and among the new towers built there were the building for the Unión Industrial Argentina (UIA) (1969–73, page 115) and the Conurban building (1973, page 115), both of which proposed architectural and structural variants (in the former a continuous glazed surface on the curtain wall; in the latter the use of brick masonry in the west wall facing the sun) and organizational variants (in the former the displacement of the circulation core to one side; in the latter a sawtooth plan) that make these buildings singular among skyscrapers.

The covered shopping mall had singular manifestations in Chile in Santiago's so-called *caracoles* (snails, or spirals) (fig. 2), which were reminiscent of Frank Lloyd Wright's Guggenheim Museum, or in the mulitilevel shopping centers that had been built in Mexico City and Caracas. But the boldest and most surprising private enterprise was undertaken at the very outset of this period with the construction of El Helicoide de la Roca Tarpeya in Caracas (1958–61, page 282), designed by Jorge Romero Gutiérrez, Dirk Bornhorst, and Pedro Neuberger as an open-air shopping mall based on a continuous system of ramps for vehicular traffic around an existing hill.

In parallel to these particular private or public initiatives, and inspired by the postulates of the Congrès Internationaux d'Architecture Moderne (CIAM) and the postwar achievements in the United States, governments began to consider wide-ranging urban reforms for the central areas of some of the largest cities. The renewal of Santiago's central neighborhood of San Borja (1966–73; page 159, fig. 4) was one of the most significant. In the spirit of President Eduardo Frei's slogan "Revolution in liberty," the Corporación de Mejoramiento Urbano (Corporation for urban improvement), created in 1965, was charged with designing and building new residential towers covering an area of 53,500 acres, a density that would free central city land for other uses.

Two urban settlements of exceptional quality had been undertaken earlier in Caracas, as an outgrowth of the oil boom, and were promoted by the dictatorship of General Marcos Pérez Jiménez. The first, the Centro Simón Bolívar (1949; page 278, fig. 2), designed by Cipriano Domínguez and placed at the intersection of the city's main avenues, featured twin office towers of thirty-two floors each, joined in a complex architectural section at the lower stories, with a variety of commercial and recreational services, as well as parking. The second, adjacent to the city, was the Hotel Humboldt (1956, page 280), an elegant project by Tomás José Sanabria situated 4,068 feet (1,240 meters) above the city on the summit of Cerro El Ávila. As important as the hotel was the construction of a cable car system that linked the installations with, on one side, the coast, which provided access to tourists arriving at the port of La Guaira, and, on the other side, the city center. In recent years there has been renewed interest in this form of transportation, in efforts to integrate informal and burgeoning settlements into the city.

In Mexico, President Adolfo López Mateos opened another large urban residential project, the Nonoalco-Tlatelolco housing complex (1960–64, page 242), covering an area of 240 acres and sited a little less than eight minutes' walk from the Zócalo, the city's historic central plaza. The project relocated more than seven thousand inhabitants previously occupying informal dwellings to 102 housing blocks and additionally comprised shopping centers, parking lots, schools, hospitals, athletic centers,

2. Caracol Ñuñoa Centro, Santiago. 1979.
Sergio Larraín García-Moreno (Chilean, born 1917), Carlos Bolton (Chilean, born 1917), Luis Prieto (Chilean, born 1918), Armando Lorca (Chilean, born 1923). View of the interior atrium. 2012. From Cristobal Palma, *Espacio continuo: Registro tipológico de los caracoles comerciales de Santiago, 1974–1983* (Santiago: Ediciones Daga, 2012)

administrative office buildings, theaters, and cinemas. Equally massive and ambitious was the Parque Central complex in Caracas (1969–79, page 294), which was built on the initiative of President Rómulo Betancourt and combined eight buildings for residential use with two commercial and office towers of fifty-nine floors each, to which were added, beyond the typical services, cinemas and large-scale cultural programs such as the Museo de Arte Contemporáneo and the Museo de los Niños (Children's museum).

But euphoric metropolitanization was not the only reaction to the phenomenon of urban growth. Many supported the idea that this kind of growth was abnormal and in some way monstrous. For those on the political left, it was deemed a product of a development process distorted by dependency, to be combated through social revolution. For others, by contrast, it was a process that could and should be corrected, since, unlike cities in the United States and Europe, Latin American cities were experiencing growth without the accompaniment of consistent national processes of industrialization.[7] This growth, they postulated, resulted from the obsolescence of agrarian economic structures and the displacement of rural populaces to the cities, which functioned as poles of attraction. For this reason, they favored an integrated development, promoted by nation-states through the creation of multiple "poles of development" that would contribute to spatial balance within the national territory.

In the case of Venezuela the plans for such poles involved explicit policies for the containment of urban growth. The new urban nucleus of Ciudad Guayana—developed by the Orinoco Mining Company and the Corporación Venezolana de Guayana (CVG) beginning in 1961, to support an ambitious steel-production enterprise—was the most prominent expression of this policy. The city's magnificent administration building for CVG (1967–68; page 288 and portfolio 1), designed by Jesús Tenreiro-Degwitz, was able to organize, through skillful volumetric expression and form, the otherwise desolate space of the new settlement.

In Argentina, poles of development formed part of the program of the military dictatorships of the 1960s and early 1970s, in major projects such as a large aluminum plant for Aluar in Puerto Madryn, on the Patagonian coast. The firm Manteola, Sánchez Gómez, Santos, Solsona, Viñoly constructed a unique dwelling complex for the company's workers (1974, page 120) in which circulation paths protected inhabitants from the site's strong winds, and a small but well-scaled urban landscape formed a contrast with the severe surroundings. The years 1977 to 1979 also witnessed the creation of the city of Federación, by the firm Pasinato, Soler, Viarenghi y Asociados, the result of the construction of one of the region's largest dams. The creation of the Argentine province of La Pampa and the construction of its civic center (1955–63, page 100) in its capital, Santa Rosa, was an early step in the same direction.

In Peru, on the other hand, access to the country's vast Amazonian region from the eastern side of the Andes was the paramount goal. For this reason, President Fernando Belaunde Terry initiated another of the great projects of territorial expansion with the construction of the Peruvian section of the Carretera Marginal de la Selva (fig. 3), a highway project extending to Bolivia, Ecuador, and Colombia.

But the most salient occupation and reorganization of the territory in the region was the creation of Brasília—discussed at length by Carlos Eduardo Comas in this volume—which was cast as the primary symbol of Latin American developmentalism. Brasília was not, however, an isolated event among Brazil's territorial policies. Beginning in the mid-1960s, the military dictatorship in Brazil promoted policies defending the country's physical and interior frontiers, which encouraged such development. These interior frontiers were topics of discussion in military academies all over Latin

3. "Road to New Lands." 1963. Fernando Belaunde Terry (Peruvian, 1912–2002). Article on the Carretera Marginal de la Selva, Peru. From a publication of the Organization of American States, reprinted in *El arquitecto peruano*, 1960

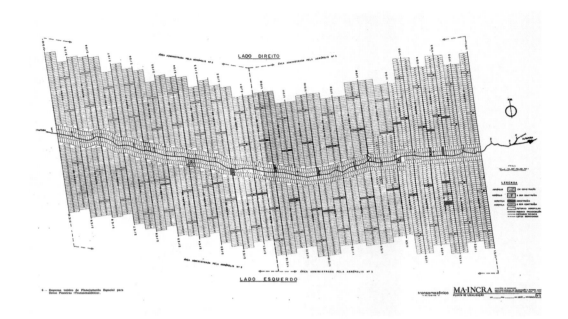

4. Instituto Nacional de Colonização e Reforma Agrária. 1971. José Geraldo Camargo (Brazilian, born 1925). Map showing planned Amazon deforestation for the development of new urban settlements. Instituto Nacional de Colonização e Reforma Agrária (INCRA), Brazil

America—under the rubric of national security doctrine during the Cold War—in response to the increase in guerrilla movements. In the case of Brazil, the goal of colonizing the vast expanse of the Amazon rainforest would find expression in the Plano de Integração Nacional (1971), which established a network of land and river communications and a series of poles of development and urban centers. This plan emerged out of previous experiences in the region, such as the project for Serra do Navio (1955), developed by Oswaldo Bratke for a mining concern directed by multiple companies including Bethlehem Steel and Icomi. In 1970 the architect José Geraldo Camargo, director of the office of planning of the Instituto Nacional de Colonização e Reforma Agrária, developed a system of colonization along the Rodovia Transamazônica, establishing growth in herringbone-shaped extensions perpendicular to the main road (fig. 4). Joaquim Guedes designed the new cities of Caraíba, in the state of Bahia, and Carajás, Marabá, and Bacarena, all in the state of Pará, and all outside the Amazon region and intended to foster exploitation of mining resources.

Finally, antiurbanism provided an alternative approach to development. If, according to urban sociologists, metropolization entailed the dissolution of family bonds, the loss of identity, a crisis of values, and weakened defenses against corporations and international powers, the antiurbanists sought to reconstitute those bonds and reinforce traditional values and characteristics through the construction of alternative communities. Among such projects, the work of the Mexican architect and developer Luis Barragán in El Pedregal de San Ángel in the 1940s, is among the most emblematic. Barragán also created compelling images of pacific environments in the residential developments Las Arboledas (1957–61, page 222) and Los Clubes (1964), on the outskirts of Mexico City. The architectural forms of these small-scale developments—with thick-textured walls, fountains, old pieces of timber, brick floors, among other resources—refer to quiet, traditional rural retreats in contrast to metropolitan chaos.

The same intentions were embodied by the small complex of El Jacarandá (1965, page 110), a community in Reconquista, Argentina, conceived as a Catholic spiritual retreat and designed and built by Claudio Caveri. This project was not an isolated case in Caveri's career; his passionate opposition to the canonical forms of urbanization and the architecture of development was already clear in his design for the construction of the church of Nuestra Señora de Fátima in Martínez (1957), designed with Eduardo Ellis, and, later, Comunidad Tierra in Trujuí (1958–75) for an alternative community based on Christian values.

No collective initiative is more representative of such opposition than that launched by the Escuela de Valparaíso, led by Alberto Cruz and Godofredo Iommi. The Ciudad Abierta (Open city) in Ritoque (pages 169–71) was built by the school's students and faculty during the tensest period of recent Chilean history, during the Unidad Popular government and its tragic end, when General Augusto Pinochet came to power. Inspired by sources as diverse as the Surrealist movement and the philosophies of Jacques Maritain and Martin Heidegger, the Ciudad Abierta is a large-scale cultural project realized in precarious materials; its spontaneous and largely ephemeral appearance expresses the fragility of the modern condition and constitutes a sophisticated reflection about the relationship between architecture and nature.

Revisiting the International Style

International Style was the preferred idiom for those sectors that imagined that the future of Latin America should look like the first-world present. The application of this set of norms and forms to Latin American buildings produced, along with quite a homogeneous landscape, an ensemble of works of remarkable quality that later historians scarcely recognized.

The Panamericano building in Montevideo (1958–64, page 270), by Raúl Sichero, for example, contains elements that a historian might identify as Miesian and Corbusian, but it utterly surpasses simple imitation thanks to its distinct proportions, subtle siting, and careful execution. The application of International Style in Latin America no longer replicated the work of the European modernist masters; rather, it adopted a system whose process of collective codification, dismissed by some as the architecture of corporations, had been mainly produced in the United States since the end of the war. Indeed, US universities were attracting as many students from Latin America as those in Europe were, perhaps even more.

It is evident that Miguel Rodrigo Mazuré, in his Casa Chávez (1958, page 253) in Lima, tried to put into practice the very style that he had admired in the United States, where he had worked in the office of Skidmore, Owings & Merrill, the International Style's major proponents. The work of Mario Roberto Álvarez in Buenos Aires, from his early projects in the 1940s to those in the 1970s, consistently reflects a similar allegiance, including his annex for the Buenos Aires stock exchange (1971–77) and a high-rise for the Club Alemán (German club) and Instituto Goethe (1970–72), both realized with elegance and an obsessive attention to design and construction. The work of Augusto H. Álvarez in Mexico is similarly impressive for its careful and precise execution in line with the tenets of International Style; this is true of both his single-family houses, such as the one designed for Arturo Quintana (fig. 5) or for Leandro Rovirosa Wade in El Pedregal (1962), and his office buildings such as the Jaysour building (1961–64, page 226) or the building for the Banco del Valle de México (1958, page 227). During the postwar Mexican economic boom, there were many examples of wonderful houses of this kind in El Pedregal, such as the Fernández house (1956), by Francisco Artigas, and the Perezcano house (1968), by José María Buendía.

In Cuba the sober Seguro Médico building in Havana (1956–58, page 200) is the most polished of such creative adoptions of the modernist system, a trend that houses constructed by Quintana and Mario Romañach manifest as well.

5. **Casa Arturo Quintana, Jardines del Pedregal, Mexico City. 1965.** Augusto H. Álvarez (Mexican, 1914–1995). View of the garden facade. Archivo de Arquitectos Mexicanos, Facultad de Arquitectura, Universidad Nacional Autónoma de México

Colombia produced a rich vein of internationalist works in those years and in the following decades, although it was later ignored by critics who focused instead on Colombian architects' use of exposed brickwork, an aesthetic that soon came to stand for the country's architecture as a whole. Buildings such as the El Dorado airport (1955–58), by the firm Cuéllar Serrano Gómez, with its advanced functional design and its bold structure; the Abbott laboratories (1963), by the firm Esguerra Sáenz & Samper; the Banco de Bogotá (1960), by Ignacio Martínez Cárdenas; and the skyscraper headquarters for Avianca, the Colombian airline (1963–69), by the firm Esguerra Sáenz Urdaneta Samper & Cía, persuasively demonstrate the flexibility of internationalist design and its potential to relate to the built or natural environment without stridency or exhibitionism.

Rino Levi was one of the main proponents of this approach in Brazil. A pioneer of Brazilian modernism who had practiced architecture since the 1920s, Levi distinguished his designs with subtle manipulations of internationalist norms, as in the Hospital Israelita Albert Einstein in São Paulo (1958) and the Castor Delgado Perez house (1958) in the São Paulo neighborhood of Jardim Europa. His case was not isolated, although it is part of a category of usually forgotten works. Costa's extraordinary stance toward neutral reproducibility is implicit in his decision to make the ministries flanking Brasília's monumental axis all practically equal in stature.

Somewhat dwarfed by the ambitions of its two huge neighbors, and without visible monuments of pre-Columbian cultures, Uruguay developed a secular, cosmopolitan character and came to be the most urbanized country of the region, with an extensive and cultivated middle class. It is therefore not unexpected that a good part of its urban landscape has been constructed with a relatively neutral international character. This is reflected in the trajectory of Guillermo Gómez Platero, with works such as the Edificio del Puerto, in Punta del Este (1957), or the La Caldera (1966), Son Pura (1960), and Poyo Roc (1960) houses (pages 274, 275), all three in Punta del Este and built with Rodolfo López Rey, who also designed the noteworthy Casa Ahel (page 275). The same preference for a sober but highly elaborated use of the norms can also be seen in the work of Walter Pintos Risso, including the Il Campanile building in Pine Beach (1960) and the Hyde Park building in Montevideo (1958); as well as in the work of Luis García Pardo, such as the Positano building in Montevideo (1957–63, page 271), with its synthetic central structure of two H-shaped pillars.

The Housing Question

Some examples are elucidative. The population of the villas miséria *in Lima represented 9 percent of its population in 1957, 21 percent in 1961 and 36 percent in 1969. . . . Between 1947 and 1961 it began to represent . . . from 14 to 46 percent of the population of Mexico City . . . between 1961 and 1964 from 21 to 35 percent of the population in Caracas. The* villas miséria *represented 41 percent of the population of Brasília in 1962 and 46 percent of Ciudad Guayana in 1966. . . . There are dramatic cases in all the countries. 80 percent of the population of Buenaventura (Colombia) . . . in 1964 lived in informal slum housing, as well as 49 percent of the 730,000 inhabitants of Guayaquil.*[8]

Jorge Enrique Hardoy's 1975 account of poverty in Latin America is heartrending, and the figures he cited kept growing into the 1980s. The nature of the policies intended to resolve these problems depended on the diagnosis. For some analysts, it was a transitional situation brought on, among other causes, by the incapacity of construction industries to produce sufficient dwellings to meet demand. The solutions, in this case, were strongly influenced by the ideas of mass housing that emerged from CIAM during the first half of the century, led by Le Corbusier and Walter Gropius. One such proponent was the Peruvian president-architect Belaunde, who was a founding member of the group Espacio, which was associated with CIAM. He was convinced that technological modernization and industrialization would lift his country out of poverty. With 1,600 dwellings, the San Felipe residential complex in Lima (1962–69, page 254) is a good example of that policy.

In Venezuela, under the dictatorship of General Pérez Jiménez, petroleum revenue enabled the Banco Obrero to build neighborhoods such as the 2 de Diciembre (today the 23 de Enero) residential area (1955–57, page 290) and the Simón Rodríguez development (1956) in Caracas, designed by a team led by Carlos Raúl Villanueva. In Bogotá the Antonio Nariño urban center, by the firm Esguerra Sáenz Urdaneta Suárez & Cía, with Néstor Gutiérrez, was constructed in 1957, and in 1961, with the support of ALPRO, the Ciudad Kennedy was built to house two hundred thousand inhabitants. Also aligned with the tenets of CIAM were the *superquadras* of Brasília (page 139), designed by Costa and composed of six-story apartment blocks, each set above an open ground floor and organized into small neighborhood units around landscaped spaces free of cars; and the residential complex Zezinho Magalhães Prado in Guarulhos, São Paulo (1967), by Vilanova Artigas, Paulo Mendes da Rocha, and Fábio Penteado.

Critiques of CIAM doctrine's schematic nature were aligned with a search for different architectural and urban values, according to the schismatic Team X group: greater attention paid to personal experience, such as everyday encounters between residents; the importance of circulation patterns; and greater volumetric and spatial complexity. To achieve this, the Portales neighborhood in Santiago (1955–68, page 164) featured open corridors on upper-level floors, an idea that Mario Pani had powerfully deployed during the previous decade in the Centro Urbano Presidente Alemán, a multifamily apartment complex in Mexico City. In the Chilean example, the complex combines apartments in longitudinal bars of six levels, with single-family houses placed in the spaces between the bars. The most original feature is the continuation of the open-air corridors as raised passerelles, which create a circulation grid that passes right over the houses and connects to the six-story structures at the opposite side of the site. The use of pedestrian streets as organizing axes for residential complexes was fundamental in numerous projects. In Brazil Guedes applied it to an entire ensemble of blocks in the case of the Padre Manoel da Nobrega housing project in Campinas (1974). Central circulation, interwoven with a sort of communal linear park, was also essential in the Cafundá housing complex in Rio de Janeiro (1977–82), designed by MBPP Arquitetos Asociados.

Many Argentine projects contributed to the larger regional debate on mass housing. In Buenos Aires the immense complex Lugano I–II (1969–73), designed by a municipal team, employs a cluster system: corridors in upper-level floors accommodating commercial and service spaces along a central spine. Numerous projects, especially in the late 1960s and early 1970s, introduced creative designs for residential units and, especially, in systems of circulation and social encounter. The most expressive of these works is the Rioja housing complex (1969, page 116) by MPSGSSV, a sort of city in space with unprecedented spatial, structural, and expressive qualities. And the architectural office Estudio Staff—whose enormous production includes the Ciudadela (1970–73, page 122), Soldati (1972–75), and Florencio Varela (1973) housing complexes, among others—was also a laboratory of new typological, structural, and graphic solutions.

Meanwhile, in Cuba, the state-promoted urbanization of La Habana del Este, and particularly Unidad No. 1 (1959–61, page 201), constituted a large-scale test of new organizational systems, dwelling units, and industrialized structural systems. In Uruguay the action of cooperative forms of property and construction absorbed a significant proportion of social housing, from modest working-class houses to middle- and lower-middle-class apartments. The most remarkable achievement in terms of scale and complexity is the Bulevar Artigas complex in Montevideo (1971–74; page 272 and portfolio 11).

In frank opposition to these developmentalist ideas was a conception, promoted by experts from the United States, that defended self-help methods, the employment of simple technologies, and the recovery of community, and that thus converged in some ways with the approaches of the Catholic, anarchist, and Guevaran sectors. To put forward these ideas, the Centro Interamericano de Vivienda (CINVA) was created in Bogotá in 1951, as a result of an agreement between the OAS and the government of Colombia, with guidance from technical experts, including Leonard Currie and Anatole Solow, and the influence of Jacob Crane, the assistant director of the Federal Housing Administration in the United States. CINVA considered the housing shortage impossible to resolve with industrialization and grand plans, given the economic conditions of most Latin American countries, but the gravity of the problem made it essential to test alternative responses, otherwise the growing demand would be capitalized on by groups promoting revolutionary solutions. One of the most important outcomes of its research was the CINVA Ram machine, developed by the Chilean architect Raúl Ramírez, which made compact blocks of sand and cement (fig. 6); some of the projects developed by CINVA in Colombia were the Quiroga neighborhood in Bogotá (1954), interventions in the settlements of Siloé and Las Colinas (1956–73), the remarkable high-density projects for La Fragua (1960, page 183), by Germán Samper, and the Centro Urbano Antonio Nariño.

Similar premises were applied in the Chilean prefabricated timber house known as the *mediagua*, influenced by the ideas of the Jesuit priest Alberto Hurtado. Conceptual support also came from the Centro para el Desarrollo Económico y Social de América Latina (DESAL), directed by the Belgian Jesuit Roger Vekemans. Vekemans and DESAL warned the government about the structural marginalization of the slums' inhabitants, and advocated modernization through education and self-help methods. In Argentina the progressive Catholic architect Horacio Berreta also worked with slum communities, trying to improve them by using technical solutions he had investigated as the director of Centro Experimental de la Vivienda Económica.

The housing ideas of John Turner, an English architect with anarchic sympathies, influenced both architects and politicians. Turner understood that informal settlements were not a problem; rather they were a solution provided by the users themselves, and with this idea he mounted a powerful offensive against policies of industrialization and large-scale interventions.

6. A demonstration of a CINVA Ram machine making bricks in Bucaramanga, Colombia. 1961. Photographic Collection of the International Basic Economy Corporation, Rockefeller Archive Center

The most significant creation of alternative dwellings made with the participation of the users occurred in the competition for the Proyecto Experimental de Vivienda (PREVI) in Lima (pages 256–59), initiated in 1966 as a pilot project for new urbanization and housing; it was led by the British architect Peter Land and supported after 1968 by the United Nations Development Program. Other self-constructed complexes of single-family homes include the project for Alagados in Salvador de Bahia (1973, page 141), Brás de Pina in Rio de Janeiro (1969, page 140), and the project for the Barrio Justo Suárez in Buenos Aires (1971–74).

Developmentalism and Brutalism

The adoption of an internationalist model constituted, for many architects and critics, an unacceptable sign of insensitivity to local reality. If simply "being modern" had been the slogan of the first part of the twentieth century, the theme of difference, or identity, would dominate the period after 1955. But how could the consciousness of difference be made explicit without at the same time rejecting outright the path to progress? That the problem of housing should be the focus of Latin American architects was a programmatic response to this question but not an ideological one; instead, the critical reflections focused on experiments in materiality. Lessons from Le Corbusier's Unité d'Habitation in Marseille (1946–52)—including the communicative possibilities of raw materials—stimulated the search for solutions that would allow the particular identity of Latin American architecture to be revealed without appealing to conservative forms of regionalism.

Reinforced concrete, directly expressed without any finish, was the highlight of this experimentation. It was not a novelty: in Brazil, Mexico, and Argentina it was a tradition that began in the nineteenth century, with the pioneering activities of European companies such as Hennebique and Siemens-Bauunion and local firms such as Tolteca. In Argentina the government buildings of La Pampa, the Manuel Belgrano school in Córdoba (1960–71, page 111), and the Escuela Normal in Leandro N. Alem (fig. 7) reinterpreted Corbusian Brutalist approaches with variations in scale and proportion.

The most original use of exposed concrete is in the building for the Banco de Londres y América del Sur in Buenos Aires (1959–66; page 102 and portfolio 12), designed by SEPRA with Clorindo

7. Escuela Normal No. 1 Domingo Faustino Sarmiento, Leandro N. Alem. 1957–63. Mario Soto (Argentine, 1928–1982), Raúl Rivarola (Argentine, born 1928). Exterior view. c. 1957

8. **Iglesia de Soca. 1960.** Antoni Bonet (Spanish, 1913–1989). Exterior view. 2012. Photograph by Andres Cardinal

Testa. Although the building is usually considered Brutalist, it paradoxically did not make use of materials just "as found." Instead, with its slabs hanging from a giant roof plate, sophisticated air-conditioning system, and special concrete derived from large-scale infrastructure projects, it represents quite the opposite: a complex attempt to push forward a contradictory local context midway between development and underdevelopment. Its structure, composed of external portals and an interior space organized around open office spaces on hanging trays, relied on a stunning precedent: the Museu de Arte Moderna in Rio de Janeiro (1953–67; page 128 and portfolio 4), by Affonso Eduardo Reidy, a building of extraordinary power that visually organizes the Parque do Flamengo (1962–65, page 131), designed by Reidy and landscaped by Roberto Burle Marx. The Palacio Municipal de Iribarren in Barquisimeto, Venezuela (1966–68), by Tenreiro, is a disjointed yet restrained ensemble of cubic pieces that shows a similar care for the finish of the exposed concrete and also bears some relation to the Banco de Londres in its use of natural light, especially in the deliberation room. The building for the Colegio de México (1974–76, page 244) has a rich and extended spatiality, the design of which follows a poetics of the materials' structural abilities: exposed concrete with diverse additions and a bush-hammer finish would be the architects' signature feature from then on. In Uruguay Antoni Bonet's design for the Iglesia de Soca (fig. 8) uses the triangle as a simple module, maximally and fractally multiplied, in a small building that can be perceived as a total whole; Nelson Bayardo, in imagining a container capable of sheltering human remains for eternity, for the columbarium of the Cementerio del Norte of Montevideo (1960–62, page 268), radicalized the use of rough reinforced concrete—which might be considered grim in this context—by conceiving it as pure stone shaping a simple but dramatic enclosure.

The square plan, central courtyard as an organizing space, and elevation of a building's body above the ground, all deployed by Bayardo, are also the main features of another of the emblematic buildings of this era: Emilio Duhart's CEPAL building in Santiago (1960–66, page 162), which is a clear expression of the developmentalist ideas for which CEPAL was a major intellectual nucleus. Duhart's rustic use of materials and of a patio—a typical form of the colonial heritage—and allusions to pre-Hispanic monuments explicitly essayed an architecture to be placed between local traditions and the most advanced positions of contemporary architectural debate.

In projects with less (or nonexistent) rhetorical content, the expressive potential of reinforced concrete led to the articulation of the supporting structures as the building's main organizing principle, visible in the IBM building in Buenos Aires (1978–83), by Mario Roberto Álvarez; the SENA building in Bogotá (1960, page 179); and the CIESPAL building in Quito, Ecuador (fig. 9), by Milton Barragán. Instead of emphasizing the tectonic effect, Juan Sordo Madaleno proposed the contrary in the Palmas building in Mexico City (fig. 10 and portfolio 7), one of his last works. In it, the different levels of the tower are treated as solid plates of concrete in discontinuous positions, avoiding the repetition of equal bands of glazed surfaces and generating a disturbing feeling of instability in a city frequently rocked by tremors and earthquakes.

The idea of national industrial development—a part of the attempt to maintain relative autonomy from international powers—inclined regional architects toward a project's technical aspects. This tendency produced works inspired by alternative or experimental uses of materials, such as the headquarters for SOMISA (1971–78, page 119), the national steel-manufacturing company in Argentina, by Mario Roberto Álvarez. It is built entirely of steel in a city where this material had not regularly been used; as a result its exceptional character became emblematic. To take advantage of the prow shape of the intersection where the site is located, Álvarez designed the building as a triangular plan divided into two parts, the larger of which uses a system of large perimeter supports that eliminates the need for interior columns. Amancio Williams's unbuilt project for an office tower with

9. **El Centro Internacional de Estudios Superiores de Comunicación para América Latina (CIESPAL), Quito, Ecuador. 1976.** Milton Barragán (Ecuadorian, born 1934), Ovidio Wappenstein (Ecuadorian, born 1938). View from Calle Almagro

10. **Edificio Palmas 555, Mexico City. 1975.** Juan Sordo Madaleno (Mexican, 1916–1985). Exterior view. 1975. Photograph by Guillermo Zamora. The Museum of Modern Art, New York. Gift of Javier Sordo Madaleno Bringas

offices hung from the uppermost floor (1946) inspired other works that attempted to put this structural concept into practice. García Pardo's El Pilar building in Montevideo (1957–59, page 271) is contained within a plot of modest size but with a splendid location at a beachfront overlooking the Río de la Plata; the building is organized around a cylinder for vertical circulation that supports the cantilever from which the lower levels hang. Ricardo Legorreta, with the engineer Leonardo Zeevaert, developed the same type of structural system, albeit with a different exterior expression, in his astonishing design for the Celanese Mexicana company (1968, page 239), one of his earliest works.

Thin shell roofs were also explored in various projects, including the advanced works of Eladio Dieste, which I will discuss later in the essay. In Venzuela Fruto Vivas, with the Spanish engineer Eduardo Torroja, carried out the design and construction of the Club Táchira in Caracas (1954) with a very elegant shell roof, 197 feet (60 meters) long and 131 feet (40 meters) wide, the largest Torroja would ever design. The roof of the restaurant of the Hotel La Concha in San Juan, Puerto Rico (1958), by the firm Toro & Ferrer, alludes to the shell of a Caribbean crustacean; it was made in very thin reinforced concrete, curved at regular intervals to introduce a rhythmic factor. In Argentina Williams researched shell vaults over several decades, and he achieved a subtle 2-inch (5-centimeter)-thick warped surface of reinforced concrete, square in plan, standing at the top of a a single circular column. Williams included his vaults in designs for hospitals, private homes, service stations, and museums, although they were only realized in an exhibition pavilion built in 1966 (page 108).

The Seduction of the Second World

The way out of underdevelopment demanded some kind of planning, and no other realization of the ideology of the Plan—an ethos of the architecural avant-garde, as laid out by Manfredo Tafuri—could compare with the process of transformation undertaken in the Soviet Union.[9] It is true that the authoritarianism of a communist regime was unacceptable to some, but it is no less accurate to say that for perhaps a major sector of Latin American society during that period the values of freedom and democracy were not a priority. The main concern was getting millions of people out of misery, for which a rational organization of production was required, and there were more than a few architects and politicians seduced by Soviet achievements.

For those who had not fully endorsed the academism and Socialist Realism of the Communist Party, certain transformations after Joseph Stalin's death opened a door for reconciliation. Nikita Khrushchev, his successor, advocated industrialization and prefabrication in order to overcome the Soviet Union's tremendous housing shortage. In addition, the 20th Congress of the Communist Party, in 1956, paved the way for what would later be called "peaceful coexistence," an international policy that (in theory) would allow the Soviet Union to demonstrate the technical and political superiority of socialism over capitalism, socialism's more expansive and efficient approach to the scientific and technical revolution, and its productive strengths—already demonstrated by its outpacing of the United States in the first episodes of the space race. The Cuban Revolution of 1959 introduced socialism into the Latin American architectural debates. In 1963 the congress of the International Union of Architects, held in Havana, focused on "Architecture in Developing Countries"; at the same time the first Encuentro Internacional de Estudiantes de Arquitectura was taking place. Fidel Castro gave the closing speech to the congress, and Che Guevara to the students.

Marxist theories on the city range from Marx's own appreciation of the metropolis as one of the greatest of human accomplishments to Engels's negative view of it and their proposals for recovering the balance between countryside and city. Cuban as well as Chinese communists promoted what was basically a rural agenda, which in Cuba was incorporated in the laws of the Reforma

Urbana; these included the expropriation of bourgeois properties and their redistribution to those in need of a dwelling. This, together with a national concentration of effort on expanding sugar production, led to Havana's neglect and gradual physical deterioration.

The socialist government of the Unidad Popular alliance in Chile, from 1970 to 1973, advanced a very different position, focusing on the necessities of the urban working class. In 1972 this led to a competition for the renovation of the city center of Santiago, to create housing for eighty thousand people, including the former settlers of the area and the working people living in shantytowns in the city and in the encampments at its outskirts. Construction of the winning entry, an ambitious urban network influenced by the ideas of Team X, was interrupted, however, by the military coup of September 11, 1973, which brought to an abrupt end both the government and the life of President Salvador Allende.

The pro-Soviet factions in many countries maintained that the only way to solve the problem of housing shortages was to employ prefabricated building systems adjusted to ever-larger production. To this end, the Soviet Union gave Cuba a concrete-panel factory in 1965. The system, cleverly adapted to local conditions by Cuban architects, was used for the first time in the José Martí district in Santiago de Cuba, and then in the construction of new neighborhoods at the edges of other Cuban cities. In 1972 a process using sliding molds of Hungarian origin was added to the system, as was Yugoslavian IMS technology. A panel factory was also installed in Chile during the period of the socialist government, but production was ended by the military coup.

The Cuban architect Fernando Salinas managed to put prefabricated systems into practice in a flexible way and with great formal potential. This is apparent in his contribution to the building for the Ciudad Universitaria José Antonio Echeverría (1960–64, page 195) in Havana, designed with Humberto Alonso and others, which was constructed with a lift slab of Canadian origin, another prefabricated system. Other international companies, such as Outinord or Coignet, from France, tried to set up shop in Argentina, and other countries promoted prefabrication. Some buildings reached a formal expressiveness of high quality, as in the case of the Instituto Central de Ciências at the Universidade de Brasília (1963–71, page 138), by Niemeyer and João Filgueiras Lima, and the Las Ruinas restaurant in Havana (1969–72, page 213), by Joaquín Galván.

So-called Paulista Brutalism, associated with the São Paulo group of Brazilian architects, represented an important development in the Marxist debates about architectural expression. Although the use of exposed, reinforced concrete is characteristic of designs by the school's two leaders, Vilanova Artigas and Mendes da Rocha, the most notable aspect of each architect's work is that they operated on a large scale with apparent simplicity and the objectivity of engineering. This is evident in the housing projects they designed together, as well as their individual projects: Artigas's changing rooms for the São Paulo Futebol Clube (1962), his Faculdade de Arquitetura e Urbanismo at the Universidade de São Paulo (1961–69, page 146), and gymnasium at Guarulhos (1960); and in Mendes da Rocha's Clube Atlético Paulistano (1958–61, page 143), Brazil Pavilion for Expo 70 in Osaka, and the jockey club in Goias (1962). Neither of them reached this position arbitrarily: it is worth noting Marx and Engels's clear devotion, in the *Communist Manifesto*, to engineering as the technical lever for the true transformation of the world.

After the Council

The Roman Catholic sectors in Latin America—accustomed to criticizing both capitalism and socialism and backed by new theoretical conceptions, such as those of Jacques Maritain, and by the spirit
of the reforms of the Second Vatican Council—found their own political expression in the Christian
Democratic parties. Their contributions to the search for alternatives to social housing, in some
cases inspired by the movement known as "liberation theology," have been discussed earlier in this
essay. But their influence also extended to the language of expression, most obviously visible in new
churches but extending to other programs as well.

The works of the Uruguayans Dieste and Mario Payssé Reyes represent two very different
interpretations of Christianity. Payssé Reyes believed in the manifestation of divinity through the universe's exact order, which in architectural terms was translated into a faith in proportional harmonic
systems and the integration of art in building designs. Among other ideas, the search for this kind of
order guided the construction of one of his main works, the Seminario Arquidiocesano of Montevideo
(1952–56, page 265), which is characterized by the use of surprising supergraphics rendered in brickwork, which seem to aspire to the "carved Bible" ethos of medieval churches. Dieste, on the other
hand, thought that the relationship with divinity could only be reached through communal work and
the honest employment of materials, particularly in a frank symbiosis of materials and structural
form, something possible for him only with a rational approach. Richness in techniques, money, and
materials did not matter to him: Brutalist in his own way, he thought it possible to extract extraordinary results from a simple material, such as brick, by understanding the infinite possibilities contained in its apparent modesty. With these convictions he created his most celebrated projects, the
churches of Cristo Obrero, in the small village of Atlántida (1958–60, page 266), and San Pedro, in
the inland crossroads town of Durazno (1967; page 267 and portfolio 2). This ideology was also behind
his many utilitarian buildings produced for other programs, from communication towers to markets
and warehouses.

The disavowal of consumer society through Christian inspiration was explicit in the formal
and constructive austerity of Luis Barragán's work in Mexico, although his impulse was less toward
material authenticity than toward a relationship with the divine, fostered by spaces of maximum
introspective and mystical intensity. His Capilla del Calvario in Guadalajara (1955) and, more important, the Capilla de las Capuchinas Sacramentarias in Mexico City (1960) are *boîtes-à-miracles*
conceived to provoke, or at least to house, such introspection in a phenomenological way, through
spatial, luminous, and textural effects that also permeate his nonreligious projects.

It is important to note the similar interpretations of Barragán and Caveri. But it is also necessary to realize that although Caveri differed from Dieste about rationalism—Caveri having less confi-
dence than Dieste in its potential to understand the world as a precise creation of God—they shared
an interest in constructive experimentation and an appreciation for communal creation, both absent
in Barragán's approach.

It is also worth mentioning the profound Catholic basis of the school of architecture at the
Universidad Católica de Valparaíso, whose designs for churches represented meaningful reflections
on the relationship between form, matter, place, and human behavior. The school's foundational
project was the church for Los Pajaritos in Maipu (1952–53), by Alberto Cruz, a white cube that would
serve as a neutral container for the richly unpredictable interior vitality that the community would
develop. Later churches such as Curanilahue and La Florida (1960–65), Puerto Montt (1960–64), and
Nuestra Señora de la Candelaria (1960) share a preference for local and so-called poor materials with
Dieste, Caveri, and Barragán, but the buildings by the school push the formal employment of those

materials past their usual possibilities. The chapel for the Benedictine monastery on Cerro Los Piques in Santiago (1963–64; page 166 and portfolio 3), designed by the monk-architects Gabriel Guarda and Martín Correa, was in a sense a consequence of the Los Pajaritos church: a white cube of exposed concrete, but here achieving remarkable effects of light and spatial dynamism.

Critical Realisms

The search for ethical intermediate positions between development and the rejection of it crossed the tense period covered by this exhibition and publication. Some nonreligious sectors, often disenchanted by more radical positions, resolved it with a sort of secular humanism, drawing upon existentialism or phenomenology. Rogelio Salmona, on his return to Bogotá after his experience with Le Corbusier (and with Marxist thought) in France, began an uninterrupted search for such a position, one that would sensitively respond to the demands of his society. His Torres del Parque (1964–70, page 184), one of the most extraordinary architectural works of the twentieth century, reaches it majesty precisely for its ability to synthetize the various dimensions of that search. The towers are anchored to their site by their formal echo of the bullring they are built around, as well as of the surrounding mountains, and by the local building traditions expressed in the use of brick.

Using a similar premise, Horacio Baliero, another influential humanist, with his partner and associate Carmen Córdova, realized another outstanding work, the Argentine student housing at the Ciudad Universitaria de Madrid (1968–71, page 114), a brick building organized on multiple stepped levels around a small central pit. Baliero and Córdova later established a fruitful association with Ernesto Katzenstein and Alberto Casares Ocampo, with whom they designed the headquarters for an industrial park in Oks (1977–79). By using brick, the team was able to respond to the functional, expressive, and financial requirements of the program while also obviating the need to experiment with the kinds of sophisticated technical solutions that frequently resulted in costly deterioration. While it was thus possible to defend a rhetoric of austerity—as in examples such as the El Polo residential complex (1960–63, page 186) by Salmona and Guillermo Bermúdez, and in the Calderón, Santos, and Wilkie houses (1962–63, page 180), by Fernando Martínez Sanabria and Guillermo Avedaño— in other cases the search for virtuosity in brickwork led to rather baroque experiments, such as those in the Escuelas Nacionales de Arte in Cuba (pages 206–10), the work of Carlos Mijares in México, some late works by Salmona, and those of José Ignacio Díaz in Córdoba and Jorge Scrimaglio in Rosario, Argentina.

The Crazy Years

The positions discussed so far in this essay revolve around the core idea of development and various interpretations of it based on social or political conviction. The climate of international and generational rebellion against the establishment (including political parties and systems) that characterized the 1960s and 1970s also led to architectural explorations fed by popular culture, as it did in the Western world. The proponents of such experimentation were fascinated by the possibilities offered by materials such as aluminum or plastic and by advertising and space-travel imaginaries.

Many of the most challenging ideas were embodied in architectural works produced in the language of art. Between 1966 and 1971 the Venezuelan architect Jorge Rigamonti created compelling collages that alternated between fascination with the new technological world (in the *Fluídica urbana* [Urban fluidity] series) and terror at the prospect of its unlimited expansion (in *Caution Radiation Area*, *Nuclear City*). In 1966 the Argentine architect Mario Gandelsonas created clear antifunctionalist proclamations in buildings imagined in conjunction with the artist Marta Minujín, such as the *Transformador*

11. **Casa Bola, São Paulo. 1979.** Eduardo Longo (Brazilian, born 1942). **Exterior view. 2009.** Photograph by Chico Prestes Maia

12. **Casa Bola, São Paulo. 1979.** Eduardo Longo (Brazilian, born 1942). **Plans and sections.** Nankin ink and pencil on paper

de cuerpos (Transformer of bodies) (page 98). In 1978 the Chilean Surrealist Roberto Matta constructed, in collaboration with Bruno Elisei, his *Auto-apocalipsis*, a habitat built out of pieces of cars. Architectural projects such as Mazuré's design for a hotel in Machu Picchu (1969, page 249), with its strident presence and daring structural plays; a municipal auditorium for Buenos Aires (1972), by the Baudizzone-Lestard firm, with its moon-base appearance; and the excessive proposal for the Urbanización El Conde (1965) in Caracas, the precursor to the city's Parque Central complex, seemed to celebrate an unlimited technological availability of resources that was far from the reality of Latin America.

Pavilions built for international exhibitions, being ephemeral and a sort of spectacle-oriented installation, often featured similar experimentation. The Cuba Pavilion for Expo 70 in Osaka, by Emilio Escobar, Oscar Hernández, and Humberto Ramírez, was remarkable for its spatial steel-mesh structure, much like Cedric Price's Fun Palace (1961); at Expo 67, in Montreal, Cuba's pavilion had been a molded metallic structure of steel, aluminum, and plastic (page 214), by Sergio Baroni, Vittorio Garatti, and Hugo D'Acosta, which alluded to the possibility of an industrialized and creative constructed space. The Mexico Pavilion at the Milan Triennial in 1968 (page 217), by Eduardo Terrazas, was part of a system for publicizing the Olympic Games in Mexico City that year; its forceful use of Op art was intended to promote an image of a young, renovated culture.

Experimentation with capsules, supergraphics, and plug-in pieces was also common, in tune with the vibrant, visual world of the period. Many of these experiments took place in Cuba, in the cultural climate of the first decade after the Cuban Revolution, where D'Acosta and Mercedes Álvarez designed and constructed an asbestos cement housing system (1964–68, page 202) and where Salinas constructed a complex of dwellings with the Multiflex modular system (1965–70, page 203), integrated with rather small pieces that could be built in and were easily assembled by the user. Along the same lines, Jorge Castillo designed the Casa Mara (1970–77, page 294) in Caracas, with sections with different functional features, and Eduardo Longo designed the extravagant Casa Bola in São Paulo (figs. 11, 12), as a new type of habitat—literally a sphere conceived as a reproducible module.

The spirit of experimentation and carefree, youthful rebellion also informed the activities of architects confronting programs or requirements that were more limited by market or administrative demands. The Centro Cultural de São Paulo, already noted for its complex metropolitan program, is equally remarkable for its daring formal, spatial, and structural profile, which is difficult to compare with preexisting models. Gorka Dorronsoro managed to give up the principle of formal continuity that characterized the work of his mentor Villanueva by relying on metallic elements for the Facultad de Ingeniería Sanitaria (School of sanitary engineering) (1967–78) and for an administrative building for the engineering department (1978–84) at the Ciudad Universitaria of Caracas, thus generating a new architecture of junctions and additions. Tenreiro and Castillo also tried to find new paths not already covered under the shadow cast by the great Villanueva. Tenreiro's CVG building in Ciudad Guayana, mentioned earlier, links the technology of steel with the tradition of brick in an unprecedented and spectacular way. In addition to designing the aforementioned Mara house, Castillo also designed the Instituto Valenciano de Arte Moderno in Valencia (1963–84), where the rooms are metal containers above an open ground floor that creates a visual relationship with the surrounding park.

For the central headquarters and branch offices of the Banco de la Ciudad de Buenos Aires (1969, page 106), the studio MPSGSSV was given a program largely free of formal or structural preconceptions. The objective was first and foremost one of public relations: to construct a friendly profile for the bank. Unlike other financial organizations, this bank would not try to impress the consumer with an image of solidity and consistency but would instead offer an image of transparency, accessibility, and reform, more like a boutique than a bank. By using colored glass bricks contained in metal

13. Hospital Naval Central, Buenos Aires. 1970–81.
Clorindo Testa (Argentine, born Italy. 1923–2013),
Héctor Lacarra (Argentine, 1935–1981), Juan Genoud
(Argentine), Eduardo Bompadre (Argentine). **Exterior
view. 2006. Photograph by Daniela Mac Adden**

frames, the architects gave to all the buildings a unique image that was enormously effective from a marketing standpoint.

While in the Argentine banks the pop character of the intervention was clearly linked to the rise of advertising culture, in the work of Bo Bardi, in Brazil, or Testa, in Argentina, it is more appropriate to invoke the populist roots analyzed by Hobsbawm.[10] The fascination with pop culture was shared by the European avant-garde, and the popular manifestations in antisystemic code apparent in the work of Bo Bardi came from her experience in Italy, but it was also stimulated by the vast universe of Brazilian underground culture. Bo Bardi's work became more explicit in that sense—from MASP, conceived to contain the unpredictable vitality of the crowds on the ground floor rather than to house the works of art in the interior, to the small island of popular celebration housed by SESC Pompéia (1977–86, page 152), in which the towers lodge a protest against "official" architectural culture, and ending with a primitivist mode in her later works in Salvador de Bahia. At the end of the 1960s Testa began increasingly to question the established certainties of architecture. His liberated attitude was expressed in eclectic pop works such as the naval hospital in Buenos Aires (fig. 13), designed with Héctor Lacarra and Juan Genoud, which suggests water with its colored tiles and represents almost literally a ship, including portholes. But like Bo Bardi, Testa also attempted to locate touchstones in so-called vulgar experiences: he recovered the structure of popular houses in the Río de la Plata, in works such as the Di Tella house (1967) and a house in Núñez (1972).

Interior Escape: Utopias and Formalisms

Some architects—perhaps to defend themselves against the harsh tensions in the architectural world during this period—preferred to focus on themes internal to the discipline. Williams, moved by the theological conception of beauty as the most perfect, dense, and unique conjunction of the various levels of existence, tried to create buildings that resolved the varied programs of modernism in an extremely precise manner. This drive toward beauty as an expression of absolute reason led him to imagine, in the last phase of his career, what he called *La ciudad que necesita la humanidad* (The city that humanity needs) (1974–89, page 109), a theoretical project adaptable to any place on the planet, in which all the problems of collective inhabitation, as well as those of mankind's relationship with the natural environment, would be resolved. In a similar theoretical, almost abstract vein, in *La primera ciudad en Antártida* (First city in Antarctica) (1980–83, page 109), he designed habitation for the least urbanized territory on the planet.

Levi's proposal for Brasília, in its dependence on an absolute and centralized power, can also be considered a way of imagining a utopian alternative, albeit one that left no room for the nuances or mediations of reality. This critical awareness also led Vivas to imagine *La ciudad del futuro* (1980), a kind of city-forest based on the idea of trees to live in, and Sergio Bernardes's project for *O Rio do futuro* (fig. 14), with its vertical helicoid neighborhoods.

Formalism was another way to elude the dilemmas of the era. Niemeyer's interpretation of Marxism, for example, looked ahead to an architecture truly adjusted to the needs of men and women at a future (communist) time; he posited that until then the only possible architectural forms were free, poetic, and not necessarily subordinated to any kind of instrumental reason. After the harsh critiques he received at the Bienal de São Paulo in 1953, Niemeyer responded with Brasília, a rich terrain of experimentation whose first large-scale structures can be understood as a compound of prisms that represent their author through expressive but arbitrary calligraphy.

At the core of Niemeyerian production are the works he built abroad during a period of political exile, from 1966 to 1985. The spherical domes of Brasília reappeared in the headquarters for the

14. Project for *O Rio do Futuro*. 1965. Sérgio
Bernardes (Brazilian, 1919–2002). Cover of
Manchete magazine, April 1965

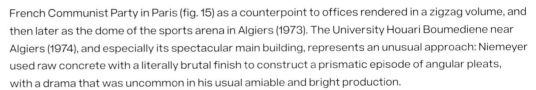

15. **Headquarters for the Communist Party, Paris. 1967–81.** Oscar Niemeyer (Brazilian, 1907–2012). View of the back of the building. 1972. Photograph by Michel Moch. Architecture & Design Study Center, The Museum of Modern Art, New York

16. **Auditorium for the Conservatorio Nacional de Música, Guatemala City. 1962–78.** Efraín Recinos (Guatemalan, 1928–2011). Exterior view. 1978

French Communist Party in Paris (fig. 15) as a counterpoint to offices rendered in a zigzag volume, and then later as the dome of the sports arena in Algiers (1973). The University Houari Boumediene near Algiers (1974), and especially its spectacular main building, represents an unusual approach: Niemeyer used raw concrete with a literally brutal finish to construct a prismatic episode of angular pleats, with a drama that was uncommon in his usual amiable and bright production.

Not even Cuba was spared the period's tendency toward formalism. The 1959 project of transforming an expropriated country club into a community for artists has been widely written about; the resulting Escuelas Nacionales de Arte, based entirely, even obsessively, on circles, express a new world of possibilities and creative freedom released by the revolution, as well as the potential for an Afro-Caribbean language in architecture. But formalism was not restricted to the schools. The circular form—perhaps as a manifestation of liberation from the orthogonal tradition of architecture—was applied to very different programs, such as the Coppelia ice cream parlor (1966, page 212), designed by Mario Girona; the round houses designed by Nicolas de la Cova (1963); and a school in Nuevo Vedado (1963) by Rafael Mirabal. Outside Cuba the circular plan was also adopted in the Arcobaleno complex in Uruguay (1960, page 272) and the Hotel Tropical Tambaú in Brazil (1966).

More extreme manifestations of architects' obsessions can be found in works of the Valparaíso school, such as the Cruz house (1959–61), by Fabio Cruz, and the Peña house (1982), by Miguel Eyquem. Efraín Recinos's formalism, by contrast, a product of his long experience as a sculptor, is applied with a jump in scale to his design for the auditorium of the Conservatorio Nacional de Música in Guatemala City (fig. 16).

It was perhaps the Mexican architects Pedro Ramírez Vázquez and Agustín Hernández who most openly opted for uninhibited formal grandiosity, in many cases as a response to political demands for rhetorical effects. Ramírez Vázquez's Museo Nacional de Antropología (1964, page 232), in Mexico City, has been broadly recognized as his greatest achievement; while this project is marked by a discreet

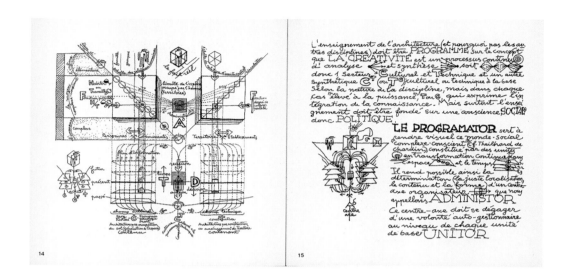

17. *Le Programmator*. **1981**. Justino Serralta
(Uruguayan, 1919–2011). From Serralta, *L'Unitor*
(Paris, 1981)

half-covered interior courtyard—and other works, such as the stadiums of Cuauhtémoc in Puebla (1968) or Azteca in Mexico City (1966), by the control of an eminently engineered structure—the architect achieved monumental excess in works such as the Centro Cultural Tijuana (1982) and the art museums in Ciudad Juárez (1964, page 229) and Mexico City (1964, page 233). Hernández's formal search, on the other hand, made an appeal to Mexico's pre-Hispanic cultures. With vigorous changes in scale, from small to large and the other way around, and assembled using a quasi-mechanical technique, the indigenous references he preferred come together in a kind of futuristic scenography; this has been true in designs including the Escuela de Ballet Folklórico (1968), his own studio (1973–75, page 246), and the Heroico Colegio Militar (1971–76, page 247) in Mexico City.

Some architects, in response to the aggressive economic, political, and social forces of the time, thought it possible to restore order and a sense of purpose to their profession by constructing wholly theoretical systems. The most influential was the Mexican architect José Villagrán García, the author of *Teoría de la arquitectura* (1964), *La esencia de la arquitectura* (1964) and *Introducción a una morfología arquitectónica* (1976). Enrico Tedeschi, an Italian architect, wrote his own *Teoría de la arquitectura* (1963), in which he tries to reorder the practice of architecture around the axes of nature and art, after he came to Argentina.

But it was the Uruguayan Justino Serralta and the Chilean Juan Borchers who made the most original attempts at rigorous systematization. Serralta worked with Le Corbusier on the Modulor scale of proportions, and he later developed a system for organizing the entire architectural process, from early creative procedures to the final articulation of the works and then to the entire universe. In numerous investigations into complex mathematical systems and grids of relationships, all expressed in his book *L'Unitor* (fig. 17), he outlined what he considered a synthesis of useful instruments not only for architects but also for administrators, clients, and users.

Borchers elaborated on the genesis of form in numerous writings, some of which were published in his books *Institución Arquitectónica* (1968) and *Meta-Arquitecta* (1975). His ideas led to projects including a small headquarters building for the Cooperativa Eléctrica of Chillán, or COPELEC (1960–64, page 160). He, too, drew on Le Corbusier's ideas and made obsessive analyses of the human figure, buildings, musical scores, and natural elements. In the COPELEC building, Borchers took pieces taken from the Corbusian repertoire and experimented with deploying them in the limited space of a relatively small box of reinforced concrete.

Isolated in his office near the southern tip of the world, Borchers was, without knowing it, taking an important leap. By consciously experimenting with Corbusian signifiers but depriving them of their signifieds, he entered a new stage of discovery, in which forms produced according to modernist postulates became a language that did not need to appeal to ethical foundations in order to continue its development. He was also entering a new phase in the history of architectural culture, at the threshold of which our period of investigation ends. Certainly his work did not fit the mold of any other response to the developmentist imperative. Nor would it need to: in the second half of the 1970s the economic and political conditions in Latin America would radically change.

None of the economic proposals tested over the years covered by this exhibition achieved successful results, and by the late 1970s the reality of underdevelopment seemed endemic. The political situation seemed equally dire: since the mid-1960s, democracy had been controlled either by repression, as it was in Mexico, or replaced by military regimes, as it was in Chile, Uruguay, and Brazil, presaging the barbarity that would settle in Argentina in 1976. The ideas about the future and progress that had motivated projects since World War II were replaced by the pragmatism of neoliberalism; the overwhelming modernist task of designing a different and better world fell victim to an ideology of the end of history, and to the ephemeral but devastating postmodernist wave in architectural style.

But history did not end, and the future still lies in the open hope of the many, that the construction of Latin America is ver far from being finished.

1 "European modernism . . . arose at the intersection between a semi-aristocratic ruling order, a semi-industrialized capitalist economy, and a semi-emergent, or -insurgent, labour movement." Perry Anderson, "Modernity and Revolution," *New Left Review* 1, no. 144 (March–April 1984): 105.

2 Heinz Wolfgang Arndt, *Economic Development: The History of an Idea* (Chicago: University of Chicago Press, 1987).

3 Joseph Schumpeter, *The Theory of Economic Development: An Inquiry into Profits. Capital, Credit, Interest and the Business Cycle*, trans. Redvers Opie, reprint, ed. (1934; New Brunswick, N.J.: Transaction Publishers, 2011), p. 63. Originally published as *Theorie der wirtschaftlichen Entwicklung* (Leipzig: Duncker & Humblot, 1911).

4 Eric Hobsbawm, "First comers y second comers," in Miguel Bilbatúa et al., *Industrialización y desarrollo* (Madrid: Alberto Corazón Editor, 1974), p. 74.

5 Arndt, *Economic Development*, pp. 46–47.

6 Harry S. Truman, in Joint Congressional Committee on Inaugural Ceremonies, *Inaugural Addresses of the Presidents of the United States* (New York: Cosimo, 1989), pp. 285–92.

7 This was particularly true of CEPAL.

8 Jorge E. Hardoy, "Las áreas metropolitanas," in Roberto Segre, ed., *América Latina en su arquitectura* (Mexico City: Siglo XXI Editores, 1975), p. 71.

9 Manfredo Tafuri, *Progetto e utopia: Architettura e sviluppo capitalistico* (Bari, Italy: Guis. Laterza & Figli, 1973).

10 Hobsbawm, "La revolución cultural," in *Historia del siglo XX* (Buenos Aires: Grupo Editorial Planeta, 2005), pp. 322–45. Originally published in *The Age of Extremes: The Short Twentieth Century, 1914–1991* (New York: Vintage Books, 1994).

Latin America

Ciudad Juárez

Mexico

San Juan
de los Lagos
Guadalajara • Cuautitlan
Izcalli
Mexico City •
Ixtapa •
Acapulco

Havana
Pinar del Rio •

Cuba
Siboney •

**Dominican
Republic**
San Juan •
Santo Domingo • **Puerto Rico**

Belize
Honduras
Guatemala
El Salvador
Nicaragua
Costa Rica
Panama

Cartagena •

Caracas •
Ciudad Bolívar
Ciudad Guayana
Venezuela
Guyana
Suriname
French Guiana

Bogotá •
Colombia

Ecuador

Peru

Brazil
Propriá •
Salvador •

Lima •
Callao •
Machu
Picchu •
Brasília •

Arica •

Bolivia

Antofagasta •
Chile
Paraguay
Jaú • Tietê •
São Paulo • Rio de Janeiro •

Corrientes •
Leandro N. Alem •
Reconquista •
Porto Alegre •

Ritoque
Viña del Mar
Valparaíso
Santiago •
Córdoba •
Mendoza •
Uruguay
Durazno •
Toledo • Manantiales
Buenos Aires • Punta del Este
Atlántida
Montevideo

Chillán •
Santa Rosa •
Mar del Plata

Argentina

Puerto Madryn •

These plates offer a visual encyclopedia of the major documents assembled for the exhibition *Latin America in Construction*. Whenever possible we have preferred to keep terms in either Spanish or Portuguese for major building types, in particular for the publically funded housing projects of the period, which are referred to by a number of terms such as *unidad vecinal*, *unidad habitacional*, *vivienda*, *conjunto residencial*, or *conjunto urbano*, all of which can be translated, with few nuanced distinctions, as "housing project" or "housing estate." Otherwise we have provided translations where necessary, except for common or easily understood terms such as *edificio* or *edifício* (building), *escuela* or *escola* (school), *cine* (cinema), *teatro* (theater, in both languages), *iglesia* or *igreja* (church), and *barrio* or *bairro* (neighborhood or district).

Although we have included all major collaborators on architectural projects wherever possible, we have not included the names of engineers unless they are acknowledged as having played a significant role in shaping the design. In many cases there are sources that indicate further collaborators, but our attributions are meant to indicate a work's principal team of designers.

Unless otherwise noted, the images reproduced here were provided by the offices or estates of the architects, and all photographic rights are listed on page 318 of this volume.

To the extent that we have been able to establish the full chronological scope of a project, we have opted for the range of years that represent a building's design from conception to completion. We have provided the dates, materials, and dimensions for documents and the names of photographers whenever they were available.

The authors of the short texts, identified by their initials, are Barry Bergdoll, Carlos Eduardo Comas, Jorge Francisco Liernur, and Patricio del Real.

The explosive growth of Argentina's export economy in the late nineteenth and early twentieth century made Buenos Aires one of the great cosmopolitan centers in Latin America and a site of significant architectural activity. Modern architects such as Alberto Prebisch, Wladimiro Acosta, Antonio Vilar, and the firm Birabén & Lacalle Alonso (fig. 1) confronted an established and conservative culture entrenched in European academicism, but the sustained growth of Buenos Aires included a vertical thrust, which populated the city with skyscrapers such as Alfredo Joselevich and Enrique Douillet's Comega building (1932) and Gregorio Sánchez, Ernesto Lagos, and Luis María de la Torre's elegant Kavanagh building (1934–36), as well as a new scale of building, such as in Prebisch's Cine Gran Rex (fig. 2). The creation of the Avenida 9 de Julio, which runs across the city from north to south, made radically clear the need for new models and ideas. A collective conversation about the production and roles of architecture began with the formation, in 1938, of the Grupo Austral, which proposed a formal, materials-oriented paradigm embodied in the ateliers by Antoni Bonet, Jorge Ferrari Hardoy, and Juan Kurchan, on the corner of Calle Suipacha in downtown Buenos Aires (fig. 3). The intense metropolization that followed the beginnings of industrialization in the 1940s gave rise to a nostalgic construction of a past rural identity in both architects and clients, which provided counterweight and texture to modern proposals such as the plan for the Universidad de Tucumán (1943–52), by Horacio Caminos, Eduardo Sacriste, and Jorge Vivanco.

World War II broke the Eurocentric grip on Argentine culture and provided a renewed opportunity for the country to industrialize and end its dependency on an export economy. Architecture was enlisted by the state in pursuit of this new independence. The administration of Juan Perón and the first Plan Quinquenal (Five-year plan) called for the hiring of modern architects in the state planning offices, although significant works were awarded directly to preselected independent firms, as were the headquarters for Buenos Aires's town hall (1948), by Oscar Crivelli and Jorge Heinzmann, and the Teatro San Martín (1953–60), by Mario Roberto Álvarez y Asociados. The compulsory party affiliation required by *Peronismo* meant that many architects were removed from the state technical ranks. But in 1947 the Facultad de Arquitectura y Urbanismo of the Universidad de Buenos Aires remained, by government policy, autonomous, and in 1949 the Ley de Propiedad Horizontal (Condominium law), facilitated the development of tall residential buildings, as well as engaging the expertise of civil engineers and architects.

Headquarters for the Banco de Londres y América del Sur, Buenos Aires. 1959–66. SEPRA Arquitectos (Argentina, est. 1936), Clorindo Testa (Argentine, born Italy. 1923–2013). **Exterior view at night. 1965. Photograph by Manuel Gómez Piñeiro. Archivo Manuel Gómez Piñeiro**

Also in 1949, the Consejo Profesional de Arquitectura y Urbanismo was organized and subsequently developed regulations for professional practice that favored sponsoring competitions to determine commissions, as was done for the Centro Cívico de Santa Rosa in 1955, with the winning entry by Boris Dabinovic, Augusto Gaido, Francisco Rossi, and Clorindo Testa. Most of the contests meant opportunities for participation by new, younger architects and for refreshed theoretical debate, which the Peronist cultural policies had suppressed; they were also such rare opportunities for creativity that the distance between the winning designs and their effective material feasibility was great indeed and had to be stubbornly resolved using available techniques. The employment of local materials and techniques to configure modern design, understood as regionalism—which points to the impact of Alfred Roth's *La Nouvelle Architecture* (1939)—had a local variant, in which so-called rustic resources and æsthetics were imported into the metropolitan context. This style came to be known among architects as *casas blancas*, for the predominant use of white stucco surfaces, and is seen in the chapel for Nuestra Señora de Fátima, in Martínez (1957), by Claudio Caveri and Eduardo Ellis.

Brutalism would offer its own particular nuance to the tension between the rustic and the technological. The implementation, without fanfare, of an artisanal workforce with simple methods could be justified as fidelity to *art brut* rather than a reaction to the aesthetics and methods promoted by the Congrès Internationaux d'Architecture Moderne (CIAM). The impact of Le Corbusier's Unité d'Habitation in Marseille (1947–52), and its adaptability for commercial and administrative projects, was confirmed in the SEPRA firm's headquarters for ENTEL (1951), and Raúl Rivarola and Mario Soto's *hosterías* in the Misiones province (fig. 4) or their Hotel de Turismo de Posadas (1957–58). Amancio Williams's project *La ciudad que necesita la humanidad* (The city that humanity needs) (1974–89) also drew upon Le Corbusier's communitarian proposals, in a megastructural concretist utopia running free along the pampas. Francisco Bullrich, Alicia Cazzaniga, and Testa's winning design for the new Biblioteca Nacional

(1962–92) no longer partook of any regional tendencies; the design evinced a formal current somewhere between Japanese Metabolism and North American institutional monumentalism.

Argentina's development policies from 1957 onward, supported by the Comisión Económica para América Latina (CEPAL), mandated large-scale infrastructure and industrial projects that demanded modern building techniques and programs. These new projects took the form of private commissions, assigned or awarded through competitions, which at times called for expertise imported mostly from the United States. The firms ASLAN y EZCURRA and SEPRA became specialists in the field, as evidenced by the latter's factory designs for Talleres Perdriel (1956) and Laboratorios Abott (1958). Encouraged by the sculptural and resistant possibilities of reinforced concrete, architects and engineers turned toward formalism, with integrated techniques, services, and spaces, as in the design by the firm Manteola, Sánchez Gómez, Santos, Solsona, Viñoly (MSGSSV) for the Papel Prensa factory in 1975. With the IGGAM factory, in the province of Córdoba (1962), Williams proposed a structure whose manufacturing processes were made transparent by its glass walls, so that machines in action constituted the building's aesthetic.

The development of prismatic towers—the truest expression of modernity—followed the increased amount of foreign capital in Argentina and the administration it required. Such towers were considered unique moments, based in creativity and exception, rather than indicating knowledge accumulated over time. These projects, and the technicians necessary to bring them about, should have been supported by appropriate regulations, but the decree for freestanding buildings known as "edificios de iluminación total" authorized their development with more technical imagination than support, as finally laid out in the master plan for Buenos Aires (1958–65). Modernist aesthetics appeared in financial institutions, such as in the headquarters of the Banco de Londres y América del Sur (1959–66, portfolio 12), by SEPRA working with Testa, and the Banco de la Ciudad de Buenos Aires (1969), by the firm then known as Manteola, Petchersky, Sánchez Gómez, Santos, Solsona, Viñoly (MPSGSSV).

1. **Edificio Uruguay, Buenos Aires. 1934.** Jorge Birabén (Argentine, 1895–1954), Ernesto Lacalle Alonso (Argentine, 1893–1948). **Exterior view.** Archivo Francisco Bullrich, Universidad Torcuato Di Tella

2. **Cine Gran Rex, Buenos Aires. 1937.** Alberto Prebisch (Argentine, 1899–1970). **Interior view.** Archivo Francisco Bullrich, Universidad Torcuato Di Tella

3. **Artist studios at the corner of calles Paraguay and Suipacha, Buenos Aires. 1938**. Antoni Bonet (Spanish, 1913–1989), Jorge Ferrari Hardoy (Argentine, 1914–1977), Juan Kurchan (Argentine, 1913–1975). View from Calle Suipacha. Fons Bonet, Colegio de Arquitectos de Catalunya, Barcelona

The works of Louis I. Kahn and James Stirling, visited abroad by young Argentine graduates and seen in Latin American magazines, gave formal and theoretical shape to local work. The SOMISA headquarters (1971–78) in Buenos Aires, by Álvarez y Asociados with Javier Sánchez Gómez, is a fine example of a systemic arrangement of technological modernization. More recent designs attempted to organize forms and spaces according to metaphors of consumption—of pop culture, of industrial adaptability—in revolt against accepted notions of modern architecture. Such subversion of the canon was a marked contrast with the harmony invoked in apathetic long-term urban plans, in monumental and ludic high-tech solutions such as those in a project for an auditorium (1972) by the Baudizzone-Lestard firm, although it failed to establish an alternative to what was, by then, an exhausted modernist tradition. Only the impact of Nordic pragmatism, mainly the work of Alvar Aalto (filtered, somehow, through Stirling), offered a realistic leap forward, by involving landscape, nature, and available techniques with simple, rational design. Horacio Baliero, in the Colegio Nuestra Señora de Luján, in Madrid (1968–71), and Ernesto Katzenstein, in his Conurban building (1969–73), in Buenos Aires, swung between the radical and the nostalgic, between the technical and the cultural.

At the beginning of the 1970s, an era of intensely politicized ideals, the debate about form reemerged as a kind of defensive maneuver with which architectural discourse might protect itself from becoming a tool of the establishment. Architectural projects were designed in a manner independent of technical, social, or functional determinants, thus recuperating their autonomous formal and theoretical content. At the end of the decade, for a few brief years, the architecture program known as La Escuelita (The small workshop), founded in 1977 by Justo Solsona, Rafael Viñoly, and Antonio Díaz, with Katzenstein and the Laboratorios de Arquitectura, and organized by Alberto Varas at the Centro de Arte y Comunicación, explored theoretical constructions drawing on language, typologies, and the architectural history and culture of cities. Architects and intellectuals alike were attracted to these alternative practices, including Aldo Rossi, Manfredo Tafuri, and Tomás Maldonado.

The state continued to link architects and commissions in housing and infrastructure. Industrialization and large-scale construction provided the scope for the construction of mass public-housing construction from 1960 to 1980, necessitating a quantitative confrontation with the problem of quality housing. Between the Rioja complex (1969) by MPSGSSV, with its radical proposal for a city in the air, with suspended, elevated streets and alleyways, and the Barrio Centenario in Santa Fe (1976), by Baudizzone, Diaz, Lestard, Varas, which returned to traditional city blocks integrated in the city's existing forms, is amply demonstrated the tension between innovation and architectural response to the problem of metropolitan housing.

4. **Hostería, San Javier. 1957–58**. Mario Soto (Argentine, 1928–1982), Raúl Rivarola (Argentine, born 1928). Exterior view

Roberto Aflalo (Brazilian, 1926–1992)
Plínio Croce (Brazilian, 1921–1984)
Gian Carlo Gasperini (Italian, born 1926)

Cover of *Habitat* magazine showing the model for the winning entry. 1967

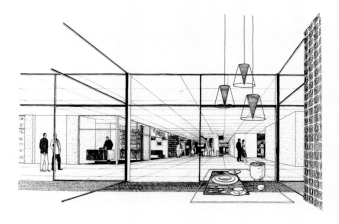

Perspective views of the interior, showing restaurant (above), and gallery (below). 1962. Ink and pen on paper, 22 ¹³⁄₁₆ x 17 ¹⁵⁄₁₆ in. (58 x 45.5 cm)

In 1958 the government of President Arturo Frondizi decided to push a second phase of national industrial development and to encourage foreign investment. In 1961 the Foreign Building and Investment Company decided to erect a sixty-story skyscraper with the French car manufacturer Peugeot as its lead tenant. The international competition to design the building that, at 680 feet (207 meters) tall, would be Latin America's tallest skyscraper, surpassing the Torre Latinoamericana in Mexico City, drew 226 projects from more than fifty-five countries. Representing the International Union of

Architects on the jury were Marcel Breuer and Affonso Eduardo Reidy, and for the investment company, the architects Martín Noel and Alberto Prebisch, the latter the brother of the development theorist and economist Raúl Prebisch. Although different entries were widely published, including in the inaugural issue of the magazine *Summa*, the tower was never built, and many critics found the winning project (by the Brazilian firm Croce, Aflalo, Gasperini) to be conventional. Still, the competition entries constitute a landmark in new thinking about skyscrapers.   BB/JFL

1. Competition entry no. 170. (Uruguay)
2. Competition entry no. 3 (Brazil, honorable mention)
3. Competition entry no. 154 (Japan)
4. Competition entry no. 138 (Japan)
5. Competition entry no. 20. (Uruguay)
6. Competition entry no. 101 (Japan)
7. Competition entry no. 206 (Spain)
8. Competition entry no. 44 (Brazil)
9. Competition entry no. 163 (Italy, honorable mention)

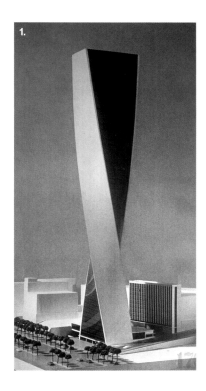

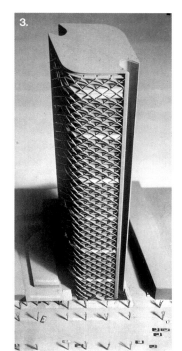

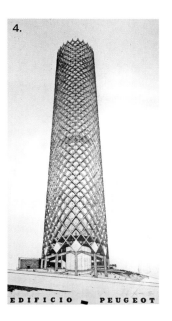

EDIFICIO PEUGEOT

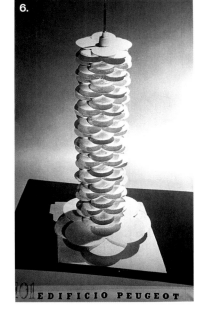

EDIFICIO PEUGEOT

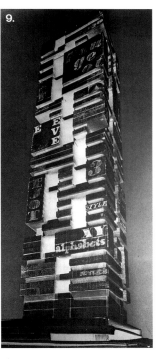

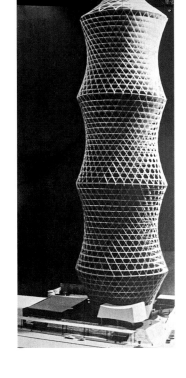

Argentina Oro Azul company pavilion for Signo Mas,
Feria Anual de la Industria Argentina, Buenos Aires. 1969
Mario Gandelsonas (US, born Argentina, 1938)
Diana Agrest (US, born Argentina, 1945)
Project for *Transformador de cuerpos*, Buenos Aires. 1966
Mario Gandelsonas (US, born Argentina, 1938)
Marta Minujín (Argentine, born 1943)

View of the Oro Azul installation. 1969. The Museum of Modern Art, New York. Gift of the architects

Exterior view of the pavilion. 1969. The Museum of Modern Art, New York. Gift of the architects

Pencil and ink on paper, 28 ½ × 42 in. (72.4 × 106.7 cm). The Museum of Modern Art, New York. Gift of the architects

The architectural theorist Mario Gandelsonas created a series of seminal projects while in Paris with his partner, Diana Agrest, between 1967 and 1969. Earlier, with the artist Marta Minujín, he imagined what he called a *transformador de cuerpos* (body transformer), which reflected new French structuralist thinking about the relationship of architecture to regimes of power, a project he would further elaborate when he established himself in New York in the 1970s. Shortly before leaving Buenos Aires, Gandelsonas designed the Oro Azul pavilion for an industrial fair, with a scaffold for information, advertisements, and activities, anticipating Renzo Piano and Richard Rogers's winning project in the 1971 competition to design the Centre Pompidou.   BB

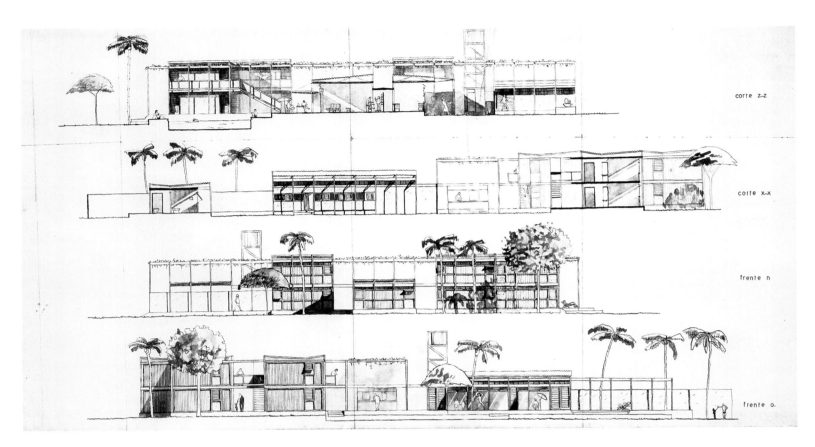

Composite elevations of the guesthouse. 1957. Ink on paper,
39 ⅜ x 27 ⁹⁄₁₆ in. (100 x 70 cm)

View of a school corridor. c. 1963

Argentina Centro Cívico, Santa Rosa. 1955–63
Boris Dabinovic (Argentine, 1920–1994)
Augusto Gaido (Argentine, 1920–2007)
Francisco Rossi (Argentine, 1922–2007)
Clorindo Testa (Argentine, born Italy. 1923–2013)

View of the main facade during construction. c. 1960. Archivo Museo de la Cámara de Diputados de La Pampa, Santa Rosa

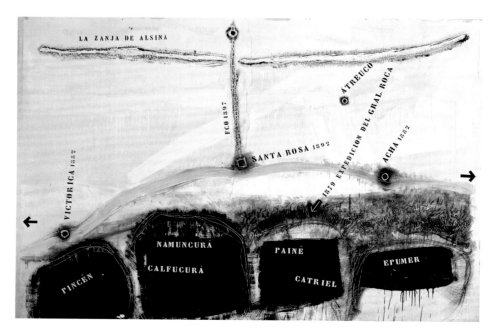

Línea de fronteras (Frontier line), by Clorindo Testa. Mural in the executive meeting room, depicting *la conquista del desierto* (the conquering of the desert), the event that preceded the founding of Santa Rosa, in 1892. 6 ft. 10 in. x 13 ft. 1 in. (210 x 400 cm). Archivo Museo de la Cámara de Diputados de La Pampa, Santa Rosa

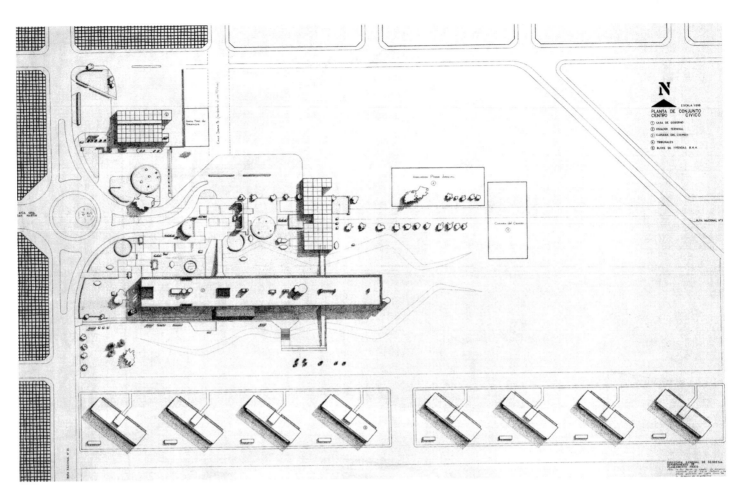

Site plan. 1956. Ink on tracing paper, 27 ¹⁵⁄₁₆ x 39 ³⁄₈ in. (71 x 100 cm).
Archivo Museo de la Cámara de Diputados de La Pampa, Santa Rosa

Exterior view at night. 1965. Photograph by Manuel Docal. Archivo Museo de la Cámara de Diputados de La Pampa, Santa Rosa

View of covered walkway and front entrance. 1972. Photograph by Paolo Gasparini

Headquarters for the Banco de Londres y
América del Sur, Buenos Aires. 1959–66
SEPRA Arquitectos (Argentina, est. 1936)
Clorindo Testa (Argentine, born Italy. 1923–2013)

View of the main lobby. 2013. Photograph by Daniela Mac Adden

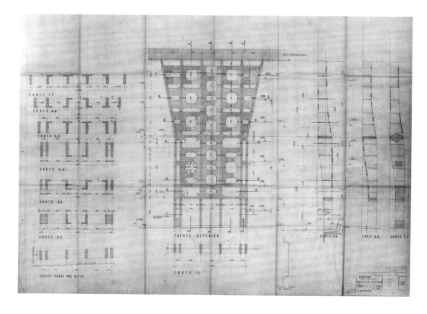

Structural drawing of the facade. c. 1960. Ink on paper,
33 ⅛ x 33 ⅛ in. (84.1 x 84.1 cm)

Sketch of the street as seen through the hung facade, drawn by Clorindo Testa. c. 1990. Ink on paper, 12 9/16 x 8 7/8 in. (31.9 x 22.5 cm)

Sketch of a worm's-eye view of the intersection of calles Reconquista and Bartolomé Mitre, drawn by Clorindo Testa. c. 1990. Ink on paper, 12 5/8 x 8 5/8 in. (32.1 x 21.9 cm)

View of the central staircase and atrium. 2013. Photograph by Daniela Mac Adden

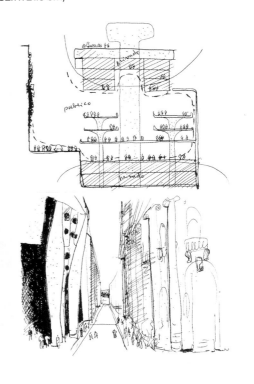

Sketch of section (above) and perspective view of urban setting (below), drawn by Clorindo Testa. c. 1970

Biblioteca Nacional, Buenos Aires. 1962–92
Clorindo Testa (Argentine, born Italy. 1923–2013)
Francisco Bullrich (Argentine, 1929–2011)
Alicia Cazzaniga (Argentine, 1928–1968)

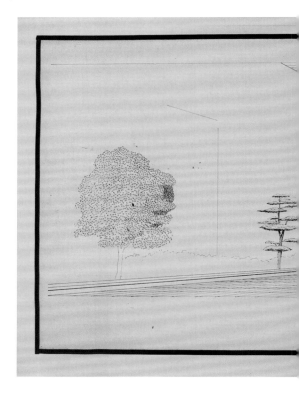

Exterior view during construction, seen from Calle Guido. c. 1980

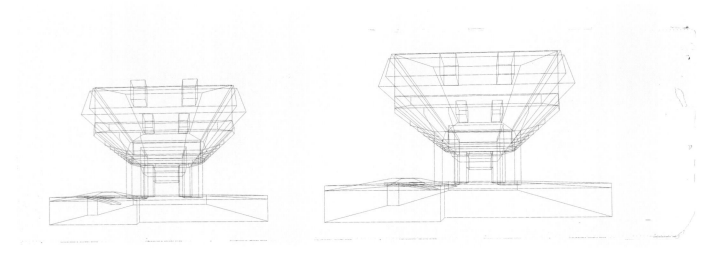

Wire-frame perspective from street level, drawn by computer with early plotter. c. 1965.
Digital print, 31 in. x 8 ft. 1 ½ in. (78.7 x 247.7 cm)

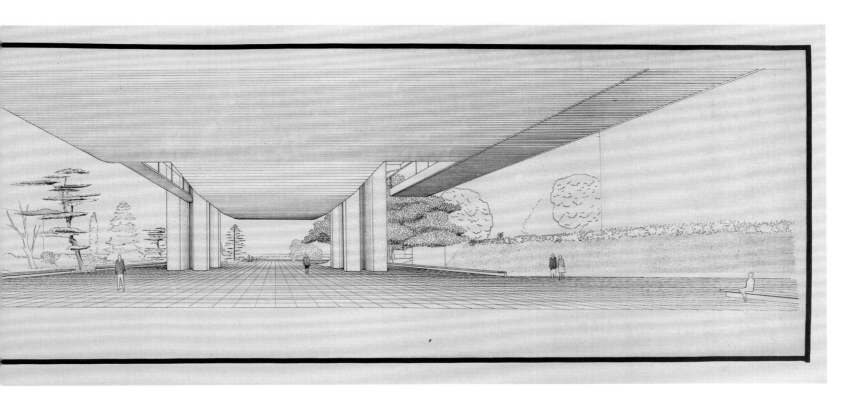

Perspective of the plaza at ground level. c. 1965. Ink on paper, 15 ¾ x 47 ¼ in. (40 x 120 cm).
Archivo Francisco Bullrich, Universidad Torcuato Di Tella

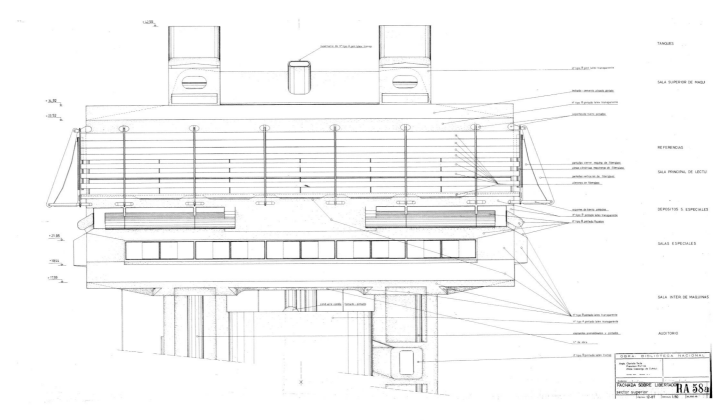

Structural drawing of the facade. c. 1965. Ink on paper, 29 ¾ x 51 ⅜ in. (75.6 x 130.5 cm)

Exterior view from Calle Florida. Photograph by Mignone Izquierdo

In 1967 the Banco de la Ciudad de Buenos Aires decided to pursue an ambitious plan: to renew its public image as an institution, to overcome the stereotype of the bank as an imposing temple of money, and to conceive a new type of architectural interface that would bring bankers closer to customers and foster a more shoplike atmosphere, attractive and accessible. The plan encompassed the redesigning of the bank's graphics and logo, the remodeling of its headquarters and neighborhood branches, and the construction of several new branches. The architectural firm of Manteola, Petchersky, Sánchez Gómez, Santos, Solsona, Viñoly studied the project and proposed a total design program that included custom-made furniture.

The architects developed a highly creative approach using colored glass blocks—a system that proved adaptable enough, in different colors, to unify the bank across renovations, new structures, and downtown and peripheral locations. The renovation of the headquarters was the most complex and impressive undertaking, in which the turn-of-the-century building was opened up, exposing parts of its Beaux Arts–style facades and adding transparent bridges, not only making transparent to passersby the bank's operations— including its monumental vault—but also making passersby into part of the décor, seen through the building's vibrant reddish-orange glass bricks.   JFL

Exterior view of the bank's Retiro branch (1970)
from Avenida Leandro N. Alem. c. 1971

View of the lobby. Photograph by Mignone Izquierdo

View of the lobby, looking toward Calle Sarmiento.
Photograph by Mignone Izquierdo

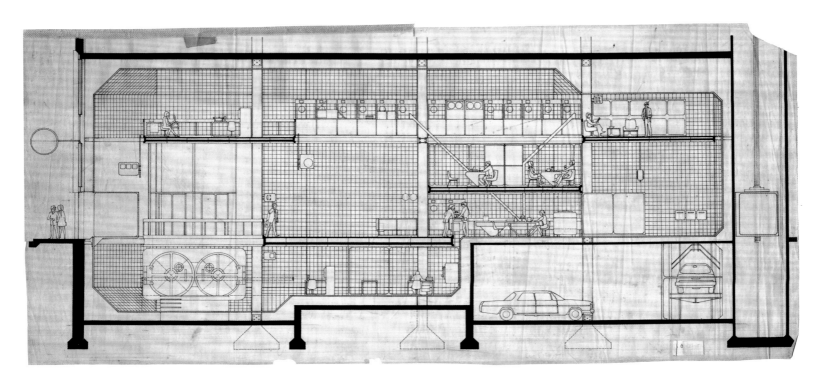

Longitudinal section. 1969. Ink on paper, 13 ¾ x 17 ¹¹⁄₁₆ in. (35 x 45 cm)

Argentina Hospital, Corrientes. 1948–53
House, Lomas de San Isidro, Buenos Aires. 1969
Pavilion for Bunge y Born at the
Sociedad Rural de Palermo, Buenos Aires. 1966
Amancio Williams (Argentine, 1913–1989)

Perspective view of the hospital. 1948. Oil on paper, 25 9/16 x 37 5/8 in. (65 x 95.5 cm)

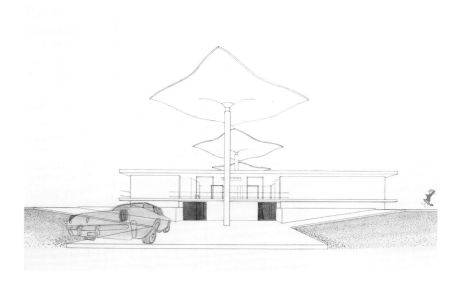

Perspective of the house in Lomas de San Isidro. 1969. Ink on tracing paper, 19 5/16 x 14 3/16 in. (49 x 36 cm)

View of the pavilion, showing shell-vaulted canopies. 1966.
Photograph by Amancio Williams

Project for *La ciudad que necesita la humanidad*. 1974–89   **Argentina**   109
(The city that humanity needs)
Project for *La primera ciudad en la Antártida*. 1980–83
(The first city in Antarctica)

Diagram of *La ciudad que necesita la humanidad*, showing differentiated functions by level. Ink and pastel on paper, 28 ⅛ x 47 ¼ in. (71.5 x 120 cm)

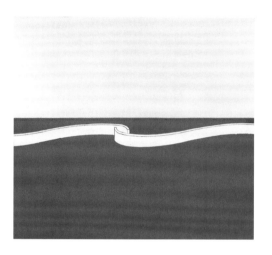

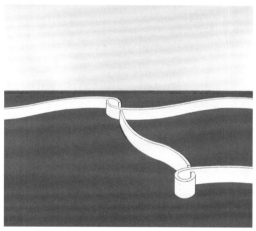

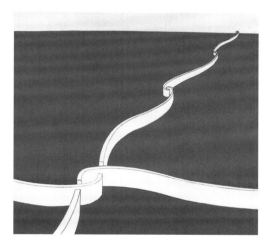

Studies of knots for different crossings for *La ciudad que necesita la humanidad*. 1982.
Collage with colored papers, each: 12 ⅝ x 15 ¾ in. (32 x 40 cm)

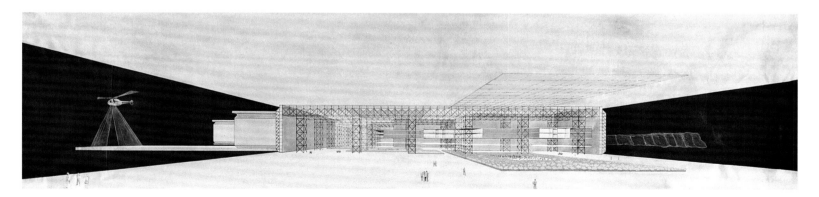

Perspective of *La primera ciudad en la Antartida*. 1981. Ink and pastel on paper, 39 in. x 8 ft. 9 ½ in. (99 x 268 cm)

Postcard of an exterior view. 1966

Sections. 1964. Ink on tracing paper, 19 5/16 x 26 15/16 in. (49 x 68.5 cm)

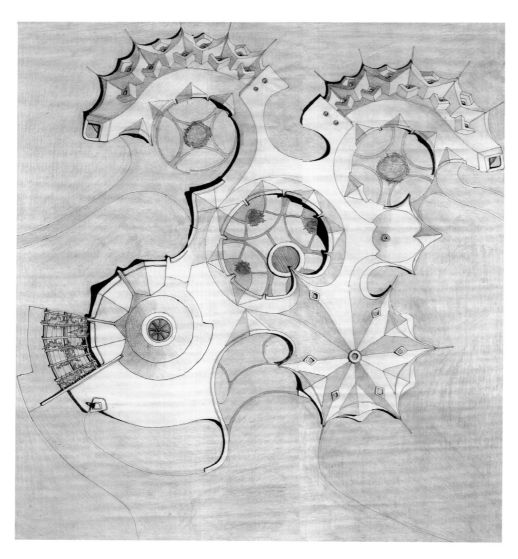

Roof plan. 1964. Ink and pencil on tracing paper,
18 7/8 x 21 1/4 in. (48 x 54 cm)

Osvaldo Bidinost, (Argentine, 1926–2003)
Martín Meyer (Argentine, born 1933)
José Gassó (Argentine, born 1932)
Mabel Lapacó (Argentine, born 1930)

View of the main atrium. 2009. Photograph by Fabio Grementieri

Perspective view from the plaza. 1962. Ink on paper, 33 ⅛ x 46 ¹³⁄₁₆ in. (84.1 x 118.9 cm)

View of students on an atrium walkway

Exterior view. c. 1964

View of the mezzanine. c. 1970

View of the main lobby. c. 1970

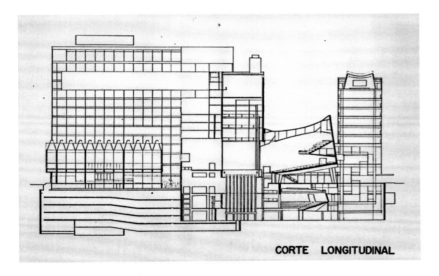

CORTE LONGITUDINAL

Longitudinal section

View of the auditorium. c. 1970

The Teatro San Martín, a large multipurpose theater complex of more than 323,000 square feet (30,000 square meters), was designed in 1953, by Mario Roberto Álvarez, and inaugurated in 1960. It contains a theater, a chamber theater, and a cinema, as well as a large hall and space for behind-the-scenes services. In 1960 a cultural center was added, also designed by Álvarez, in a connected building with spaces for conferences and exhibitions. Exquisitely built and soberly detailed, the complex penetrates its city block, with facades on two major Buenos Aires avenues, while also integrating itself with the greatest respect and care into the urban environment. JFL

Horacio Baliero (Argentine, 1927–2004)
Carmen Córdova (Argentine, died 2011)

Plan. Ink on tracing paper, 28 ⅜ x 40 ¾ in. (72 x 103.5 cm). Dirección de Archivos de Arquitectura y Diseño Argentinos, Facultad de Arquitectura, Diseño y Urbanismo, Universidad de Buenos Aires

View of terraces from the garden. c. 1971

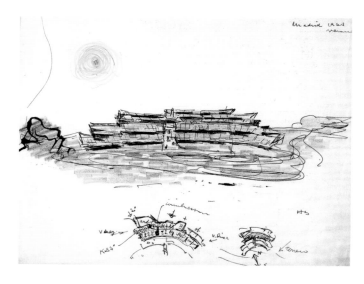

Sketches of plans and elevation of a terraced garden, drawn by Horacio Baliero. 1971. Watercolor and ink on paper, 7 ⅞ x 13 in. (20 x 33 cm). Collection Arch. Nestor Otero

(Unión Industrial Argentina)
Manteola, Petchersky, Sánchez Gómez,
Santos, Solsona, Viñoly (Argentina, est. 1966)
Edificio Conurban, Buenos Aires. 1969–73
Ernesto Katzenstein (Argentine, 1932–1995)
Estanislao Kocourek (Argentine, born 1930)
Carlos Llorens (Argentine)

Exterior view of the UIA (left) and Conurban (right) buildings

Perspective, drawn by Ernesto Katzenstein. Pencil on paper, 11 ¹³⁄₁₆ x 8 ¼ in. (30 x 21 cm)

Exterior perspective of the UIA building, drawn by Rafael Viñoly. 1969. Ink and watercolor on paper, 39 ³⁄₈ x 27 ⁹⁄₁₆ in. (100 x 70 cm)

Conjunto Habitacional Rioja, Buenos Aires. 1969
Manteola, Petchersky, Sánchez Gómez, Santos, Solsona, Viñoly
(Argentina, est. 1966)

Above: View in urban setting. c. 1970

Left: Exterior view toward an interior courtyard. c. 1970

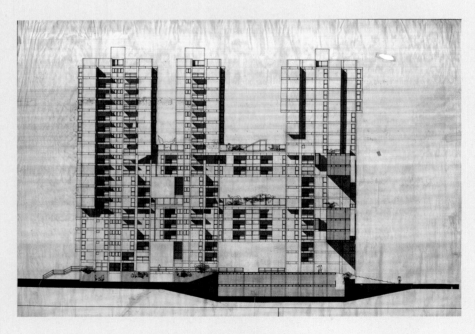

Elevation of the northeastern facade. 1969. Ink on paper,
27 5/8 x 39 9/16 in. (70.2 x 100.5 cm)

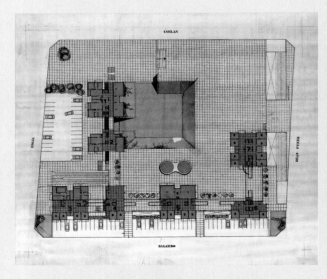

Site plan. 1969. Ink on paper, 29 15/16 x 36 9/16 in. (76 x 92.8 cm)

Manteola, Sánchez Gómez, Santos, Solsona, Viñoly (Argentina, est. 1966)
Carlos Sallaberry (Argentine, born 1943)
Felipe Tarsitano (Argentine, born 1943)

Perspective. 1976. Ink on paper, 23 ¼ x 16 ⁹⁄₁₆ in. (59 x 42 cm)

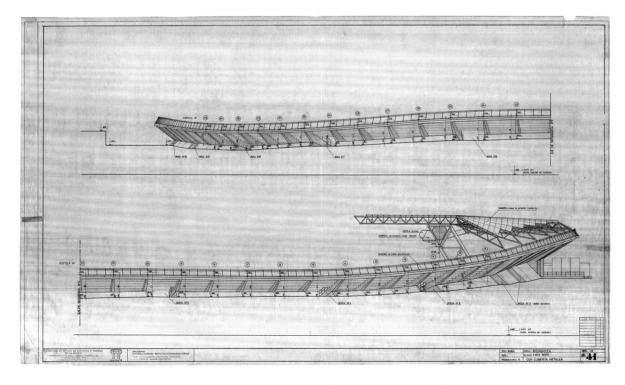

Construction drawing of northern elevations. 1976. Ink on paper, 51 ³⁄₁₆ x 31 ½ in. (130 x 80 cm)

Enrico Tedeschi (Italian, 1910–1978)

View of main facade. 1964. Lydia Ozsi Archives

View of a corridor behind the facade. 1964. Lydia Ozsi Archives

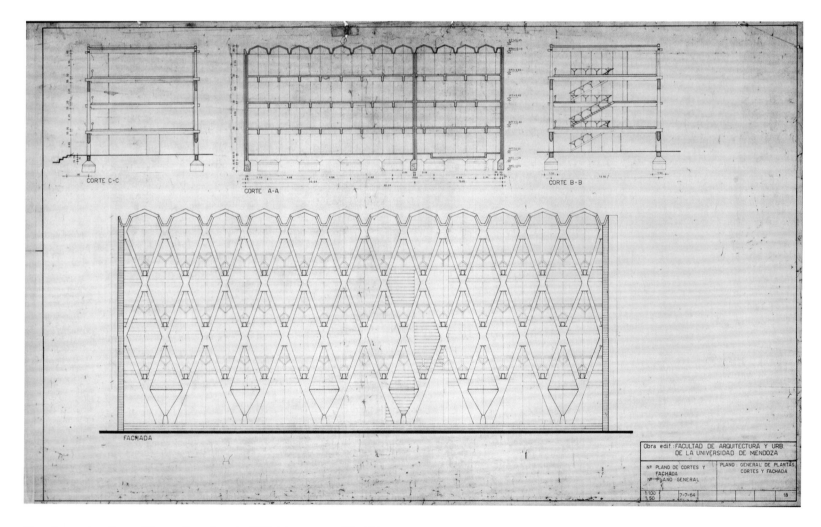

Elevation and sections of the northern facade. 1960. Ink on paper, 35 x 23 in.
(88.9 x 58.4 cm). Archivo Universidad de Mendoza

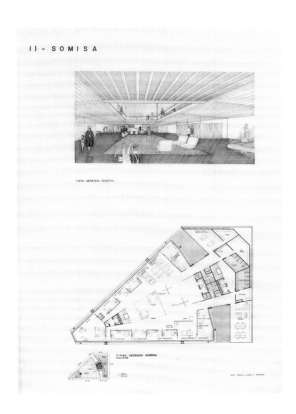

Interior perspective (above) and first-floor plan (below). Ink, pencil, and colored pen on tracing paper, 33 ⅛ x 23 ⅜ in. (84.1 x 59.4 cm). Musée National d'Art Moderne, Centre de Création Industrielle, Centre Pompidou, Paris. Gift of the architect

View of the lower level. c. 1978

Exterior view. 2014. Photograph by Daniela Mac Adden

Barrio Aluar, Puerto Madryn. 1974
Manteola, Sánchez Gómez, Santos,
Solsona, Viñoly (Argentina, est. 1966)
Carlos Sallaberry (Argentine, born 1943)
Felipe Tarsitano (Argentine, born 1943)

View of housing from the courtyard. c. 1975

Exterior view. 1975

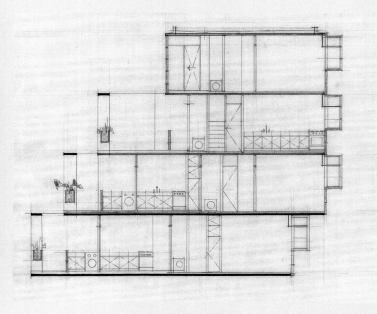

Section of apartments. 1973. Pencil on paper, 15 3/8 x 12 3/16 in. (39 x 31 cm)

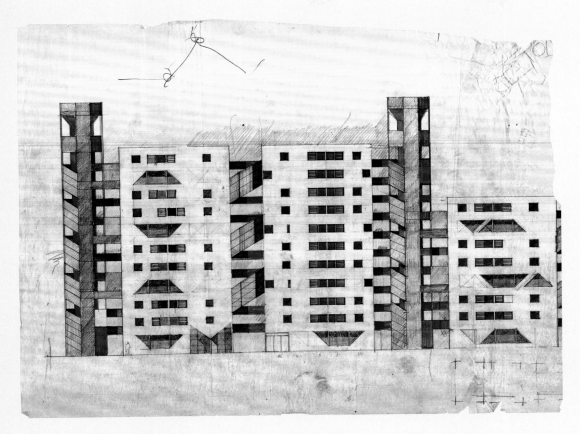

**Barrio Comandante Luis Piedrabuena,
Buenos Aires. 1975–78**
Manteola, Sánchez Gómez, Santos,
Solsona, Viñoly (Argentina, est. 1966)
Carlos Sallaberry (Argentine, born 1943)
Felipe Tarsitano (Argentine, born 1943)

Elevation of the housing. 1974. Pencil and
crayon on paper, 27 9/16 x 39 3/8 in. (70 x 100 cm)

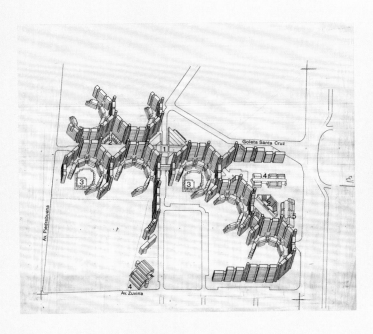

Axonometric aerial view. 1974. Ink on paper, 27 9/16 x 39 3/8 in. (70 x 100 cm)

View of the circulation towers during construction. c. 1974

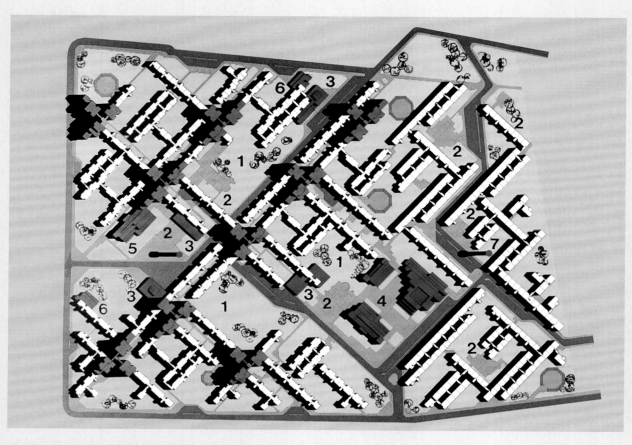

Conjunto Habitacional Ciudadela, Buenos Aires, 1970–73
Estudio Staff (Argentina, est. 1964)

Site plan. 1970. Ink on mylar with adhesive colors,
6 ft. 6 ¾ in. x 55 ⅛ in. (200 x 140 cm)

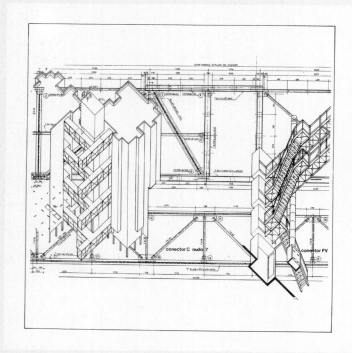

Structural drawing showing walkways. 1973. Ink on mylar, 59 1/16 x 59 1/16 in.
(150 x 150 cm)

Exterior view. 1973

**Conjunto Habitacional Villa Soldati,
Buenos Aires. 1972–75**
Estudio Staff (Argentina, est. 1964)

Exterior view. 1975

Aerial view. 1975

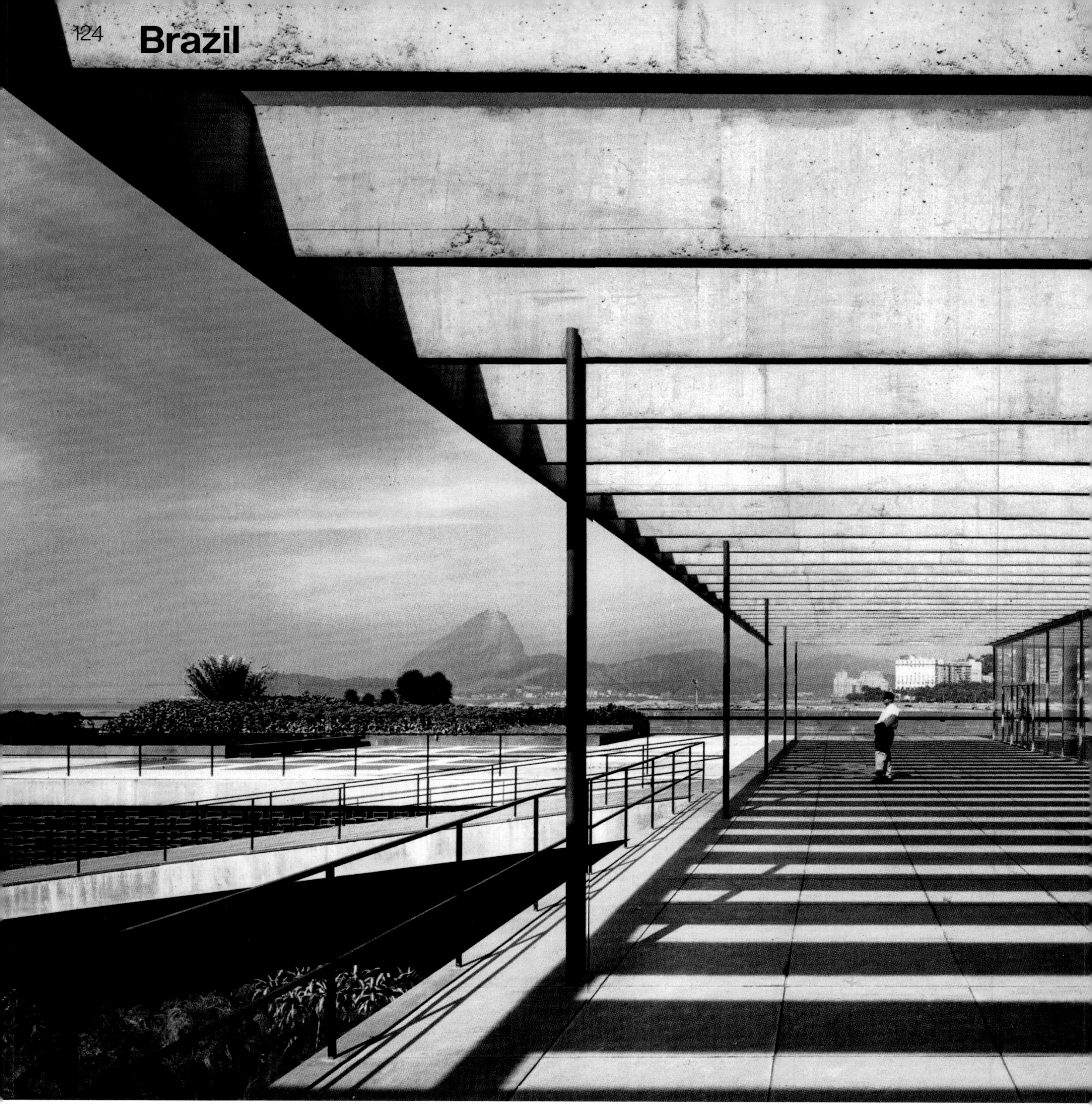

In 1943 a selection of Baroque architecture milestones, early São Paulo houses by Gregori Warchavchik (fig. 1), and masterly examples of modern architecture by the Carioca school of Rio de Janeiro of the 1930s and early 1940s went on view in the exhibition *Brazil Builds*, organized by The Museum of Modern Art, New York. The modernist examples included the classical monumentality of the headquarters of the Ministério da Educação e Saúde (Ministry of education and health) in Rio, by Lucio Costa's team (1936–45), along with such sober functional cases as the IRB headquarters (1936–38), by the firm MM Roberto, and such sensual innovative approaches as the Pampulha complex (1940–55), by Oscar Niemeyer. This timely triumph was followed by widespread international recognition of Brazilian architects; the school's authority at home was established by these works plus those by the Cariocan masters outside Rio, and their influence was felt in Brazilian architecture in other regions and through the following decades.

With such a magnificent foundation laid down, it is not unusual that the first historical view of modern Brazilian architecture—established in the 1950s, consolidated in the 1960s—conceived of it as a cohesive fact, a notion encouraged by the strategic clarity of masters such as Costa. However realistic, this historical attitude delayed the perception of other trends, but in 1952–53 it was already possible to notice some changes, some generational and regional divergences. The 1950s were an interesting period for fermentation and differences, with various paths emerging that would be followed by many young architects. New programmatic challenges, new materials, and pioneering structural and construction techniques suggested and stimulated different architectural possibilities.

São Paulo's architectural culture gained momentum during this period. After 1951 its art and architecture biennials were the site of the earliest critical debates about the achievements of the modern Carioca school, and at the same time, other architectural possibilities began to emerge. Providing a counterpoint to the more hedonistic Cariocan modernity, the Paulista architects, by training and temperament, tended to be more functionally strict, with structures informed by their deep knowledge of engineering.

The post-1950s works of some Carioca masters evince some similar formal and constructive changes that distinguish them from the propositions of the 1930s and '40s. The Parque Ibirapuera pavilions in São Paulo (fig. 2), connected by an epic canopy, were a turning point in Niemeyer's career, which from then on was illuminated by the pursuit of unity and clarity, further developed in his Brasília buildings and beyond. Affonso Eduardo

Museu de Arte Moderna (MAM), Rio de Janeiro. 1953–67. Affonso Eduardo Reidy (Brazilian, born France. 1909–1964). View of the roof terrace looking south, toward Sugarloaf Mountain. 1958. Núcleo de Pesquisa e Documentação da Faculdade de Arquitetura e Urbanismo da Universidade Federal do Rio de Janeiro

1. **House, Rua Bahia, São Paulo. 1930.** Gregori Warchavchik (Brazilian, born Ukraine. 1896–1972). Exterior view. c. 1930. Acervo Gregori Warchavchik/ Biblioteca da Faculdade de Arquitetura e Urbanismo da Universidade de São Paulo

Reidy's smooth and sinuous urban-scale housing at Pedregulho and Gávea were followed by masterly experiments in Brutalism, as in the Colegio Experimental Paraguay-Brasil in Asunción (1951) and the Museu de Arte Moderna in Rio (1953–67). Some rising stars of the Paulista school, such as Lina Bo Bardi and João Batista Vilanova Artigas, interpreted the lessons of the Carioca school and the binuclear house with a tropical approach, using enclosed and covered patios that progress, in the case of Artigas, from a white and transparent architecture to a gray and compact one.

At the end of the decade the Paulista architects adopted a Brutalist sensibility that marked many of the buildings designed in São Paulo after 1957. Although the discourses of the Paulista architects were still aligned with the those of the Carioca school, their buildings adopted a denser,

heavier, rougher appearance, and they show a fondness for exposing innovative structural solutions—such as the plastic possibilities of reinforced and post-tensioned concrete—in a didactic, almost exhibitionist way. Unlike the Carioca school, which was illuminated by Costa's tolerant cosmopolitanism, the Paulista architects did not claim membership in any international movement, nor did they ever accept the epithet "brutalist" to describe their work. Nevertheless, the term may be legitimately used to understand those works in correlation with other international Brutalist connections, sharing similar constructive, sculptural, and technological aspects and contributing some memorable works, such as the gymnasium for the Clube Atlético Paulistano (1958–61), by Paulo Mendes da Rocha and João de Gennaro; the boathouse for the Santapaula Iate Clube (1961), by Vilanova Artigas; or the Museu de Arte de São Paulo (1957–68), by Bo Bardi.

In the same period there was the significant achievement of the planning and construction of Brasília, with a plan by Costa and government buildings by Niemeyer. In a vibrant, triumphal fashion, Brasília crystallized the paradigms of modern city planning: functionalist in design and monumental aspirations, reverberating with the symbolic plasticity of its buildings. Its example heralded the great and expansive infrastructural, urban, social, and housing projects of the 1960s and '70s. Yet Brasília cannot just be regarded as sign of other things: it is also a real modern city, peculiar in certain aspects and ordinary in others. At the time of its inauguration it elicited a storm of criticism, not always well informed; much vilified and insufficiently studied, the city and its qualities and challenges have for some time merited wider recognition.

The main achievements of Brazilian architecture in the 1950s and '60s make up a dense and multilayered panorama. The influence of the Carioca school persisted through the 1960s and was not abrogated by the rise of the Paulistas. Brasília marks neither an end of Carioca modernism nor a beginning of Paulista Brutalism, but it is certainly a hinge between a previously rural and now urbanized country. Despite its widespread influence through the 1970s, Paulista Brutalism had masters but no coherent architectural discourse, which had been replaced by a cluster of leftist

2. **Palácio das Indústrias, Parque Ibirapuera, São Paulo. 1951–54.** Oscar Niemeyer (Brazilian, 1907–2012). Interior view of the pavilion with tree-of-life column and ramps. 2007. Photograph by Leonardo Finotti

political aspirations. And other regions were already developing their own peculiar narratives and architectural experiences, which have only recently begun to be studied.

In any case, it was variety rather than hegemony that typified the next decades, and a cross-section of Brazilian architecture in the early 1970s reveals simultaneous and not necessarily cohesive propositions. The themes of industrialization and constructive repetition were in vogue, although they were difficult to put into practice for economic and practical reasons. The most successful examples of Brazilian architecture based on industrialized components, in terms both of manufacturing and aesthetic

3. **Workers' housing, Rua Gamboa, Rio de Janeiro. 1932–33.** Gregori Warchavchik (Brazilian, born Ukraine. 1896–1972), Lucio Costa (Brazilian, born France. 1902–1998). Exterior view. c. 1933. Acervo Gregori Warchavchik/Biblioteca da Faculdade de Arquitectura e Urbanismo da Universidade de São Paulo

results, are found in the work of João Filgueiras Lima (known as Lelé), from schools to bus stops to hospitals. On the other hand, traditional materials, such as wood and brick, once again aroused the interest of those architects who sought to reconcile technological advancement with local traditions; the Cajueiro Seco housing complex (1963), by Acácio Gil Borsoi, Gildo Guerra, and Geraldo Gomes is an early example. The ideas of context and identity encouraged experiments with the restoration and recycling of urban buildings and environments, from traditional to contemporary; Costa's example will always remain a seminal one, but Bo Bardi, too, explored radical creative possibilities of great force and presence, from her work in Bahia (the museum at Solar do Unhão [1959], for example) to her distinctive SESC Pompéia cultural center (1977–86). The immense and urgent infrastructural needs, created by the explosive growth of Brazilian cities after the 1960s, made the construction of a better future an urgent matter; in balance, there arose an increased awareness of the need to preserve the past. The works that combine the two ranged from new cities, as in Joaquim Guedes's design for Caraíba (1976), to revitalized historical centers, social housing, and public spaces in peripheral neighborhoods.

In the 1980s Brazilian architecture rediscovered its modern past and both revised historical discourses and renewed contemporary practices. The Carioca modernity of the 1930s and '40s—such as the workers' housing in Rua Gamboa (fig. 3) designed by Warchavchik and Costa, and the Aeroporto Santos Dumont, by the Roberto brothers (fig. 4)—has continued to inspire academic research and deep reflections. The Brutalist tradition of the 1950s and '60s has remained partially alive and in close contact with the work of new generations of architects. The diversity and tolerance of the 1970s and '80s has set the tone for the variety of contemporary output. Brazilian architecture has once again opened itself to an active international dialogue without losing sight of its strong and beautiful modern tradition.

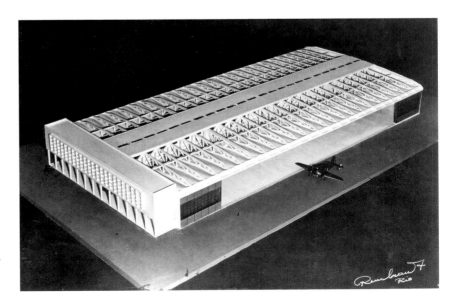

4. **Hangar at Aeroporto Santos Dumont, Rio de Janeiro. 1938–40.** Marcelo Roberto (Brazilian, 1908–1964), Milton Roberto (Brazilian, 1914–1953), Paulo R. Fragoso (Brazilian, 1904–1991). **Model (now lost).** Architecture & Design Study Center, The Museum of Modern Art, New York

Affonso Eduardo Reidy (Brazilian, born France. 1909–1964)

Exterior view from the pergola. 1967. Núcleo de Pesquisa e Documentação da Faculdade de Arquitetura e
Urbanismo da Universidade Federal do Rio de Janeiro

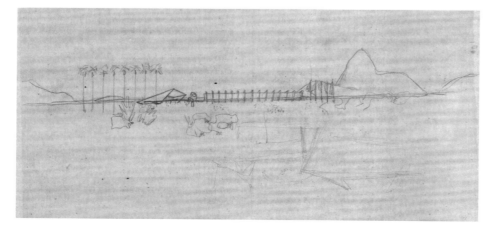

Perspective drawing of the museum in context. 1953. Pencil on tracing paper, 14 15/16 x 27 9/16 in.
(38 x 70 cm). Núcleo de Pesquisa e Documentação da Faculdade de Arquitetura e Urbanismo da
Universidade Federal do Rio de Janeiro

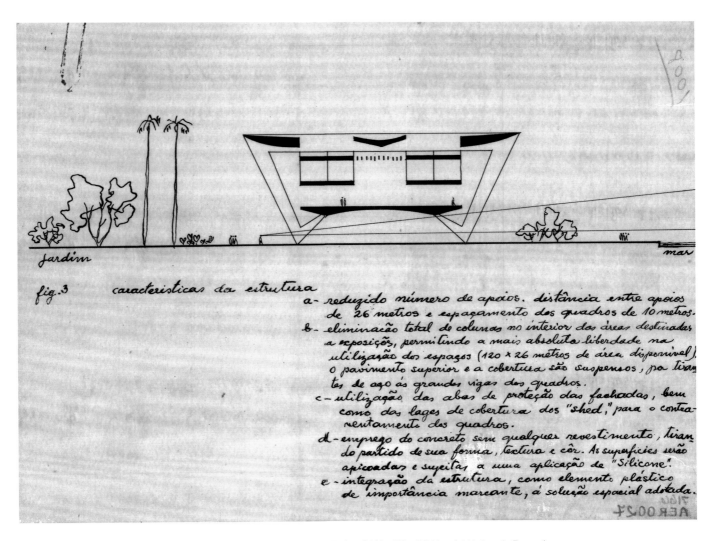

Sectional sketch with notes by the architect. 1953. Ink on vellum, 7 1⁄16 x 9 1⁄4 in. (18 x 23.5 cm). Núcleo de Pesquisa e Documentação da Faculdade de Arquitetura e Urbanismo da Universidade Federal do Rio de Janeiro

Interior view during construction. 1965. Núcleo de Pesquisa e Documentação da Faculdade de Arquitetura e Urbanismo da Universidade Federal do Rio de Janeiro

View of the exhibition pavilion's central staircase during construction. 1965. Núcleo de Pesquisa e Documentação da Faculdade de Arquitetura e Urbanismo da Universidade Federal do Rio de Janeiro

Roberto Burle Marx (Brazilian, 1909–1994)
Affonso Eduardo Reidy (Brazilian, born France. 1909–1964)

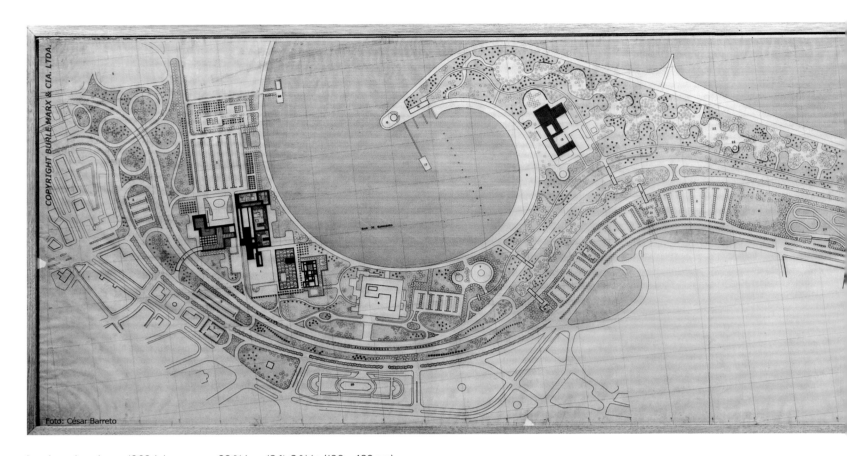

Landscaping plan. c. 1962. Ink on paper, 39 ⅜ in. × 13 ft. 9 ⅜ in. (100 × 420 cm)

Aerial view. c. 1960. Núcleo de Pesquisa e Documentação da Faculdade de Arquitetura e Urbanismo da Universidade Federal do Rio de Janeiro

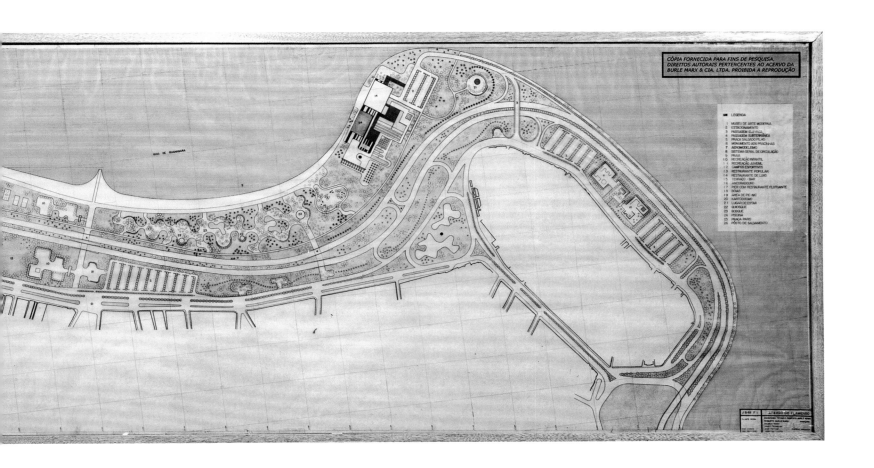

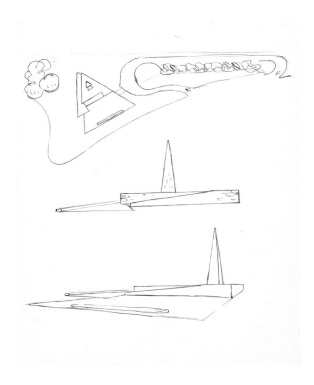

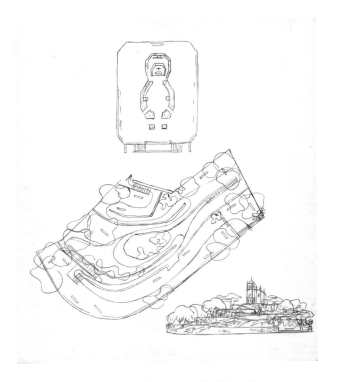

Monument to Estácio de Sá, Parque do Flamengo, Rio de Janeiro. **1973.** Lucio Costa (Brazilian, born France. 1902–1998). Site plan and two perspective views. c. 1973. Ink on paper, 11 x 8 9/16 in. (27.9 x 21.8 cm). Casa de Lucio Costa

Church of Nossa Senhora do Outeiro da Glória, Rio de Janeiro. **1960–69.** Lucio Costa. Sketch of the layout of ramps leading through the park to the church. 1965. Ink on paper, 11 x 9 3/16 in. (27.9 x 23.4 cm). Casa de Lucio Costa

Aerial view. c. 1960. Photograph by Mário Fontenelle. Arquivo Público do Distrito Federal

The idea of moving the capital from Rio de Janeiro to the savanna of the central plateau was born in colonial times, but the Distrito Federal was not demarcated until a few years after the republic was created, in 1889, and the site of the city was proposed and defined in 1954–55, during the presidency of João Café Filho. During the administration of Juscelino Kubitschek, from 1955 to 1960, industrial development and Brasília's construction were prioritized; Kubitschek created the Companhia de Urbanização da Nova Capital (NOVACAP) in 1956 and appointed Oscar Niemeyer its director of architecture and urbanism. Niemeyer announced a national competition to plan a city for an eventual five hundred thousand inhabitants, although he designed the Palácio da Alvorada, the presidential residence by

Paranoá Lake, in 1957, before the competition was judged that year.

From twenty-six entries, the international jury selected Lucio Costa's plan, citing its adaptation to the topography, density, integration among urban components, regional connections, formal composition, and appropriate expression of a national capital's civic character. Costa's imaginatively pragmatic design combined multiple references in a quasi-symmetrical plan; to build its two main axes he sank an arced highway among the residential *superquadras* (urban residential superblocks) and used the dug-up earth to raise a rectilinear platform for the monumental sector, where the main government buildings would be built. A bus terminal was placed at the crossing of the axes, to be surrounded by commercial,

recreational, and cultural sectors. Brasília was to be monumental, domestic, bucolic, gregarious, middle-class and car oriented, and responsive to the automotive and telecommunications industries promoted by Kubitschek.

NOVACAP asked Costa to move the city closer to the lake and add a row of *superquadras* to the east, strips of row houses to the west, and plots for single-family houses around the lake. Niemeyer's buildings would develop along the lines set out by Costa, with slight, significant changes: the esplanade would be widened to manifest externally the bicameral nature of the Congresso, and the articulation between the esplanade and the Praça dos Três Poderes would be simplified. Although far from complete, Brasília was an irreversible reality at its inauguration in 1960.　CEC

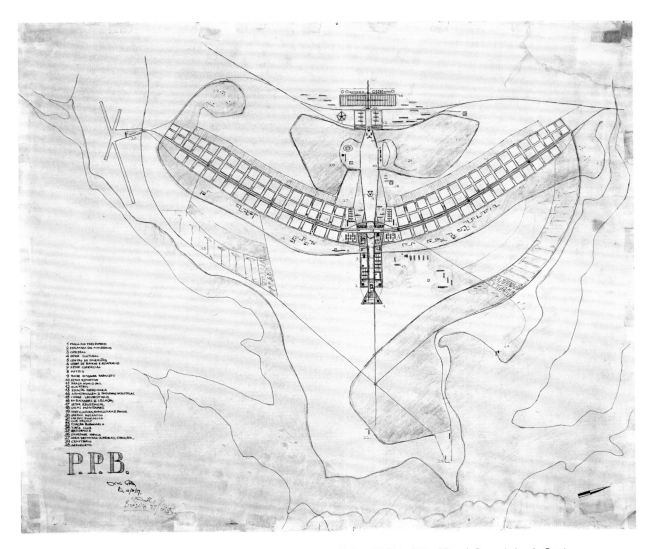

Competition entry. 1957. Ink and colored pencil on drafting paper, 22 7/16 x 26 3/8 in. (57 x 67 cm). Casa de Lucio Costa

Aerial view showing the crossing of the plan's axes before construction. 1957. Photograph by Mário Fontenelle. Aquivo Público do Distrito Federal, Brasília

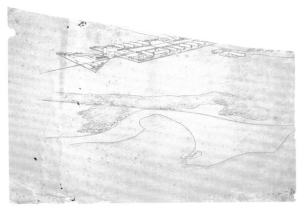

Bird's-eye perspective of the monumental axis and proposed lake. 1957. Ink and colored pencil on paper, 19 7/8 x 14 1/8 in. (50.5 x 36 cm) (irreg.). Casa de Lucio Costa

Brazil Praça dos Três Poderes, Brasília. 1958–60
(Plaza of the three powers)
Lucio Costa (Brazilian, born France. 1902–1998)
Oscar Niemeyer (Brazilian, 1907–2012)

Left: Aerial view showing the Supremo Tribunal, Palácio do Planalto, and Congresso Nacional. c. 1960. Photograph by Marcel André Félix Gautherot. Instituto Moreira Salles Collection

Below: View of the Palácio do Planalto. c. 1959. Photograph by Marcel André Félix Gautherot. Instituto Moreira Salles Collection

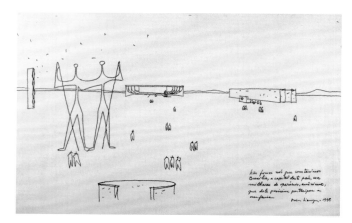

Above: Sketch of the plaza showing the Supremo Tribunal (center) and the Museu da Cidade (right). c. 1960. Ink on paper. Fundação Oscar Niemeyer

Right: View of the Praça dos Três Poderes and the Supremo Tribunal from the Palácio do Planalto. c. 1961. Photograph by Marcel André Félix Gautherot. Instituto Moreira Salles Collection

Left: Exterior view. c. 1960. Photograph by Marcel André Félix Gautherot. Instituto Moreira Salles Collection

Below: View of ramps. c. 1960. Photograph by Marcel André Félix Gautherot. Instituto Moreira Salles Collection

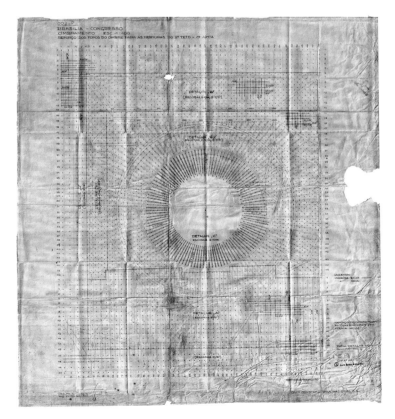

Above: View of the inverted dome structure during construction. c. 1958. Photograph by Marcel André Félix Gautherot. Instituto Moreira Salles Collection

Left: Construction drawing for the inverted dome structure. 1958. Ink on paper, 51 3/16 x 58 1/4 in. (130 x 148 cm). DETEC Departamento Técnico da Câmara dos Deputados

Esplanada dos Ministérios, Brasília. 1958–60
Lucio Costa (Brazilian, born France. 1902–1998)
Oscar Niemeyer (Brazilian, 1907–2012)

Exterior view during construction. 1958. Photograph by Mário Fontenelle. Arquivo Público do Distrito Federal, Brasília

Lightness pervades Oscar Niemeyer's buildings in Brasília's monumental sector. Delicacy and internal simplicity create a modern monumentality, which is as controversial as the emptiness of the Praça dos Três Poderes and the Esplanada dos Ministérios. Critics of the buildings find that they lack gravitas, the solemn physiognomy associated with ancient monuments; critics of the urban composition see as waste what others think is space legitimately reserved for the rare manifestation of collective joy or anger, protest rally or presidential inauguration. The out-of-the-ordinary spectacle leaves no one indifferent, although the casual observer might miss how it complements the straightforward bus terminal and commercial facilities that have developed perpendicular to it.

In 1970 the monumental sector was largely complete according to Lucio Costa's 1960 plan, and the visual tension between the man-made artifact and the natural landscape reached a peak. The military dictatorship installed in 1964 had not yet disfigured the sector and its surroundings by multiplying annexes to the ministries and erecting a giant flagpole in front of the Praça dos Três Poderes. The reinstallation of a democratic government in 1985 did not halt the expansion of bureaucracy, and subterranean passages have proliferated, along with new annexes and memorials. Events take place regularly in the esplanade. The emptiness of the monumental sector has become more apparent than real.
CEC

View of the Torre de TV, designed by Lucio Costa, Paulo R. Fragoso, and Joaquim Cardozo. c. 1967. Arquivo Público do Distrito Federal, Brasília

Aerial view, taken from the TV tower, of the bus station platform, ministries, and Eixo Monumental (Monumental axis). 1970–79. Casa de Lucio Costa

Exterior view during construction, seen from the cathedral. 1959. Photograph by Gabriel Gondim. Gabriel Gondim Archive, Brasília

Exterior view of the Ministério das Relações Exteriores, with the sculpture *O meteoro* (The meteor), by Bruno Giorgi. c. 1970. Photograph by Marcel André Félix Gautherot. Instituto Moreira Salles Collection

View of a colonnade, pergola, garden, and gallery. c. 1975. Arquivo Central, Universidade de Brasília

The Instituto Central de Ciências at the University of Brasília accommodates most of its functions in a curving 2,300-foot (700-meter)-long mega-structure that exemplifies Oscar Niemeyer's use of prefabrication. Two-story-high precast concrete frames and slabs define a series of pavilions, with pedestrian colonnades flanking a central garden. Narrower single-story frames and slabs, also precast, are inserted in the pavilions providing flexible, column-free space for classrooms above and below. Circulation takes place in the two-story-high galleries alongside the garden and the one-story-high continuous upper balcony looking into them, creating an experience of moving that is at once dynamic and intimate.   CEC

Aerial view of the campus during construction. 1960.
Arquivo Central, Universidade de Brasília

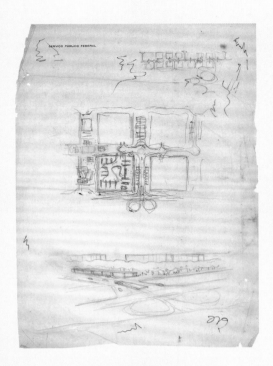

Above: Plan for a residential sector with four *super-quadras* and perspective sketch of a tree-lined block. Ink on paper, 8 7/16 x 11 in. (21.5 x 28 cm). Casa de Lucio Costa

Right: View of a playground. c. 1961. Arquivo Público do Distrito Federal, Brasília

Above: View of a road through a commercial strip. c. 1960. Photograph by Gabriel Gondim. Gabriel Gondim Archive, Brasília

Right: Aerial view of residential sectors. Photograph by Silvio Cavalcante. Casa de Lucio Costa

**Taipa prefabricated housing system,
Cajueiro Seco. 1963**
Acácio Gil Borsoi (Brazilian, 1924–2009)

View of a prefabricated wattle panel, before
the daub coating. 1963. The Museum of Modern
Art, New York. Gift of Carlos Eduardo Comas

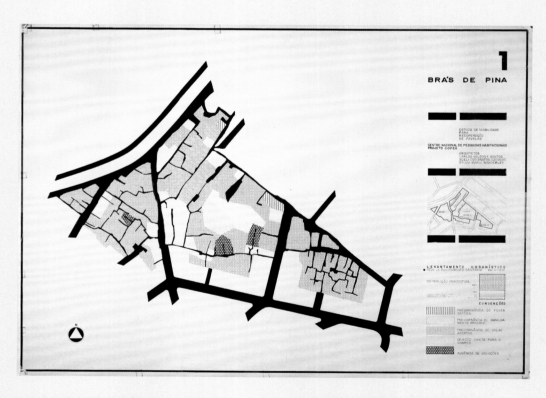

Plan for Brás de Pina, Rio de Janeiro. 1969
Carlos Nelson Ferreira dos Santos (Brazilian,
1943–1989)

Master plan for the favela. 1969. Ink on paper,
28 ¼ x 40 ³⁄₁₆ in. (71.7 x 102 cm). Museu de Arte do
Rio (MAR Rio)

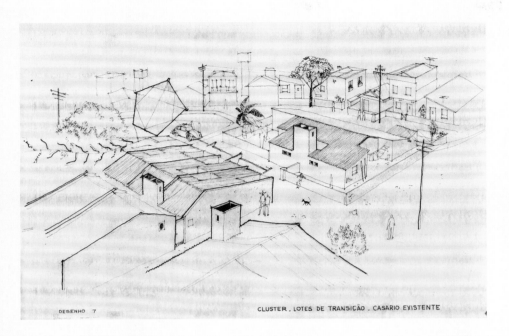

Alagados, Salvador. 1973
Mauricio Roberto (Brazilian, 1921–1996)
Marcio Roberto (Brazilian, born 1945)

Perspective view of a cluster. 1973. Ink on paper, 8 ¹/₁₆ x 11 ⅝ in. (20.5 x 29.5 cm). Núcleo de Pesquisa e Documentação da Faculdade de Arquitetura e Urbanismo da Universidade Federal do Rio de Janeiro

Axonometric view of a cluster. 1973. Ink on paper, 9 ⁷/₁₆ x 7 ⁵/₁₆ in. (24 x 18.5 cm). Núcleo de Pesquisa e Documentação da Faculdade de Arquitetura e Urbanismo da Universidade Federal do Rio de Janeiro

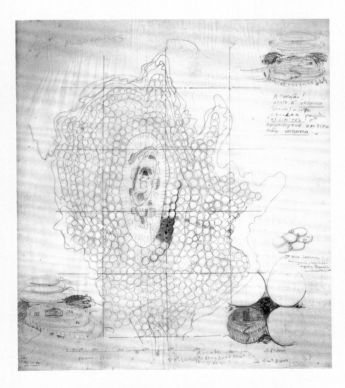

Project for a cooperative community, Camurupim. 1975
Lina Bo Bardi (Brazilian, born Italy. 1914–1992)

Site plan. 1975. Watercolor, hydrographic, pencil, and ink on off-set paper, 22 ⁷/₁₆ x 19 ½ in. (57 x 49.5 cm). Instituto Lina Bo e Pietro Maria Bardi

Perspective. 1975. Watercolor, hydrographic, pencil, and ink on offset paper, 11 ⅞ x 8 ¹¹/₁₆ in. (30.1 x 22 cm). Instituto Lina Bo e Pietro Maria Bardi

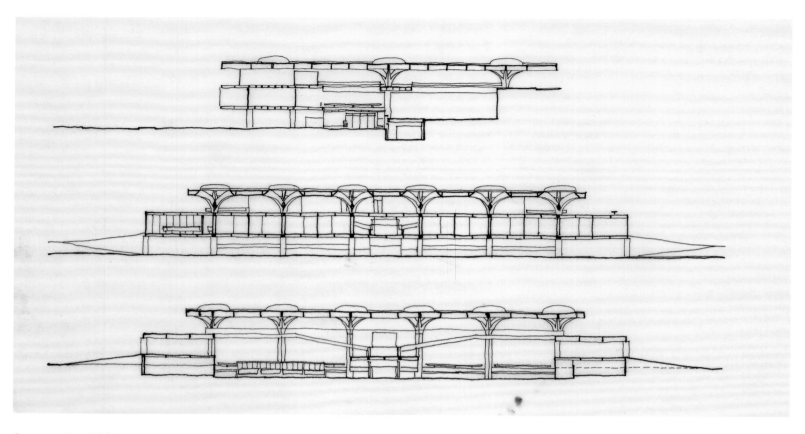

Cross-section. 1983. Ink on paper, 6 ⁵⁄₁₆ x 13 ¾ in. (16 x 35 cm). Musée National d'Art Moderne, Centre de Création Industrielle,
Centre Pompidou, Paris. Gift of Rosa Artigas and Julio Camargo Artigas

Exterior view. 1973. Acervo da Biblioteca da Faculdade de Arquitectura e
Urbanismo da Universidade de São Paulo

Interior view. 1997. Photograph by Nelson Kon

Exterior view. Photograph by José Moscardi

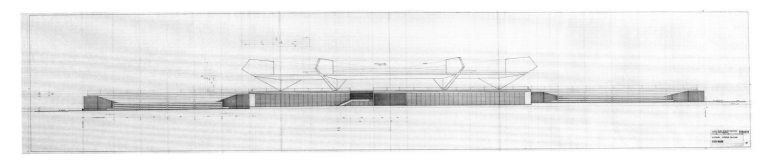

Front elevation. 1960. Ink and red ink on tracing paper, 25 ⁹⁄₁₆ in. x 10 ft. 6 ¾ in. (65 x 322 cm). Musée National d'Art Moderne, Centre de Création Industrielle, Centre Pompidou, Paris. Gift of Paulo Mendes da Rocha

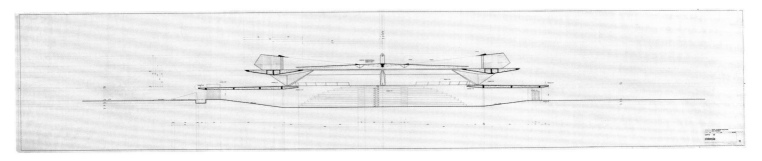

Section. 1960. Ink and red ink on tracing paper, 25 ⁹⁄₁₆ in. x 10 ft. 6 ¾ in. (65 x 322 cm). Musée National d'Art Moderne, Centre de Création Industrielle, Centre Pompidou, Paris. Gift of Paulo Mendes da Rocha

View from Parque Trianon. 1969. Instituto Lina Bo e Pietro Maria Bardi

View from Avenida Paulista during construction. 1968. Photograph by Hans Günter Flieg. Instituto Moreira Salles Collection

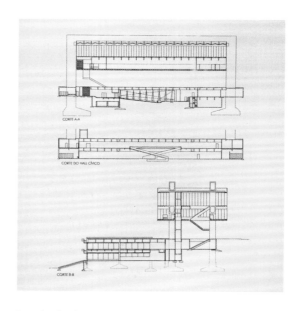

Longitudinal section (above) and lateral section (below). Instituto Lina Bo e Pietro Maria Bardi

Interior view of the main gallery with the original display system. c. 1971.
Photograph by Paolo Gasparini. Instituto Lina Bo e Pietro Maria Bardi

Perspective view of the plaza underneath the museum. India ink, pencil, and collage on
paper, 18 9/16 x 27 ½ in. (47.2 x 69.8 cm). Instituto Lina Bo e Pietro Maria Bardi

Faculdade de Arquitetura e Urbanismo, Universidade de São Paulo. 1961–69
João Batista Vilanova Artigas (Brazilian, 1915–1985)
Carlos Cascaldi (Brazilian, 1918–2010)

Interior view of the atrium c. 1968. Photograph by José Moscardi. Acervo da Biblioteca da Faculdade de Arquitectura e Urbanismo da Universidade de São Paulo

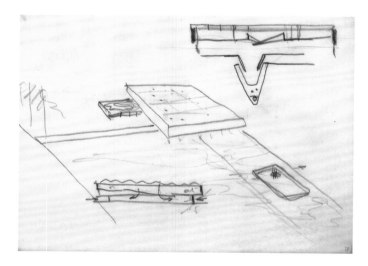

Sketch with aerial view, section, and column structure. 1961. Pencil on tracing paper, 9 1/16 x 11 13/16 in. (30 x 23 cm). Acervo da Biblioteca da Faculdade de Arquitectura e Urbanismo da Universidade de São Paulo

Sketch of the atrium. 1961. Ballpoint pen on paper, 9 1/16 x 11 13/16 in. (30 x 23 cm). Acervo da Biblioteca da Faculdade de Arquitectura e Urbanismo da Universidade de São Paulo

Exterior view during construction. c. 1968. Photograph by José Moscardi. Acervo da Biblioteca da Faculdade de Arquitectura e Urbanismo da Universidade de São Paulo

Above: View of the atrium during a school assembly. 1979. Photograph by Raul Garcez Pereira. Acervo da Biblioteca da Faculdade de Arquitectura e Urbanismo da Universidade de São Paulo

Left: Exterior view. c. 1968. Photograph by José Moscardi. Acervo da Biblioteca da Faculdade de Arquitectura e Urbanismo da Universidade de São Paulo

João Filgueiras Lima (Lelé) (Brazilian, 1931–2014)

Exterior view. c. 1980

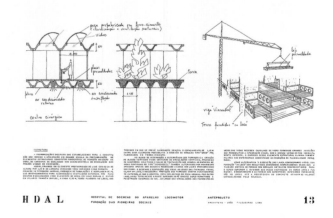

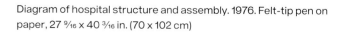

Diagram of hospital structure and assembly. 1976. Felt-tip pen on paper, 27 9/16 x 40 3/16 in. (70 x 102 cm)

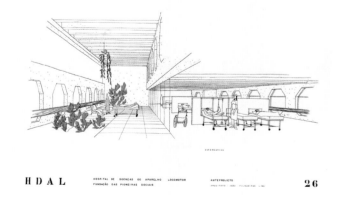

Interior perspective. 1976. Felt-tip pen on paper, 27 9/16 x 40 3/16 in. (70 x 102 cm)

PREFEITURA DE SALVADOR - RENURB
ESTAÇÃO DE TRANSBORDO DA LAPA   JFL   ETL

Aerial perspective of the bus station. 1979. Felt-tip on paper, 26 ³⁄₁₆ x 38 in. (66.5 x 96.5 cm)

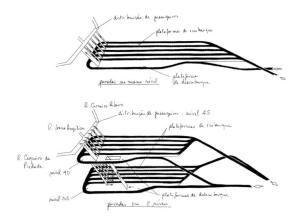

Diagram showing circulation in the bus station. 1979. Felt-tip pen
on tracing paper, 26 ³⁄₁₆ x 38 in. (66.5 x 96.5 cm)

Exterior view. c. 1979

Paulo Mendes da Rocha (Brazilian, born 1928)

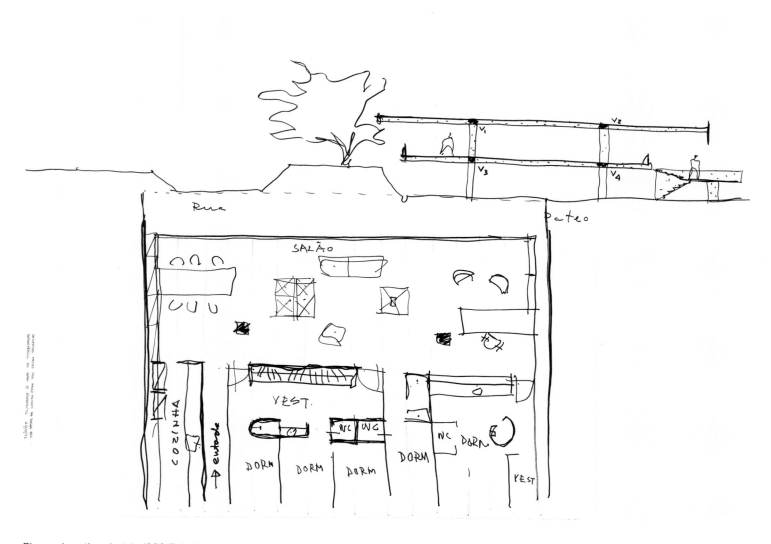

Plan and section sketch. 1992. Felt-tip pen on paper, 26 x 37 ¾ in. (66 x 95.9 cm). Acervo da
Biblioteca da Faculdade de Arquitectura e Urbanismo da Universidade de São Paulo

View of the entrance. 2001. Photograph by Nelson Kon

View of the living room. 2001. Photograph by Nelson Kon

Marcos de Azevedo Acayaba (Brazilian, born 1944)

Bird's-eye perspective. c. 1975. Ink on tracing paper, 11 $^{13}/_{16}$ x 11 in.
(30 x 28 cm). Musée National d'Art Moderne, Centre de Création
Industrielle, Centre Pompidou, Paris. Gift of the architect

View of the house and pool. 1975. Photograph by Jorge Hirata

SESC Pompéia, São Paulo. 1977–86
(Serviço Social do Comércio)
Lina Bo Bardi (Brazilian, born Italy. 1914–1992)

Above: View of towers, walkways, and sun deck.
Photograph by Romulo Faldini. Instituto Lina Bo e
Pietro Maria Bardi

Above right: Perspective sketch of the towers in their
urban setting. 1983. Hydrographic and reprographics
on offset paper, 13 ⅞ x 19 ¹¹⁄₁₆ in. (35.2 x 50 cm).
Instituto Lina Bo e Pietro Maria Bardi

View of activities center. Photograph by Sérgio Gicovante.
Instituto Lina Bo e Pietro Maria Bardi

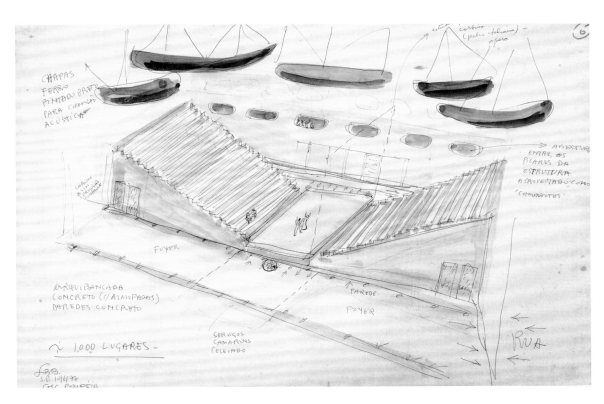

Perspective sketch of the auditorium. 1977. Watercolor and ballpoint pen on cardboard, 14 ¾ x 22 ⁹⁄₁₆ in. (37.5 x 57.3 cm). Instituto Lina Bo e Pietro Maria Bardi

Collage showing various programs and activities for children. 1977. Ink, pencil, and mixed mediums on cardboard, 15 ⅜ x 22 ⁵⁄₁₆ in. (39 x 56.6 cm). Instituto Lina Bo e Pietro Maria Bardi

Feria de la Paz, Santo Domingo. 1955
Carles Buïgas (Spanish, 1898–1979)
Guillermo González Sánchez
(Dominican, 1900–1970)

Night view. 1955. Photograph by Max Pou. Colección Eduardo León Jimenes de Artes Visuales

Staged to celebrate the twenty-fifth anniversary of the coming to power of the Dominican dictator Rafael Trujillo, the Feria de la Paz y Confraternidad del Mundo Libre (Fair of peace and brotherhood of the free world) created a monumental new administrative and cultural district for the capital, Santo Domingo, then called Ciudad Trujillo. Planned in haste and inaugurated with great bombast when construction was far from complete, on December 20, 1955, the fairgrounds were intended to assert the nation's claim to a place on the world stage. A new city hall and national congress, both designed by Guillermo González Sánchez, were among the most important of the more than seventy permanent structures built on a tract of land at the western edge of the capital, facing the Caribbean Sea.   BB

Map produced by the Esso Standard Oil Company (detail). 1955. Miguel D. Mena Collection

Henry Klumb (US, born Germany. 1905–1984)

Exterior view. c. 1965. Photograph by Pedro Martínez. Henry Klumb Collection, Archivo Arquitectura y Construcción, Universidad de Puerto Rico, San Juan

The German-born and -trained architect Henry Klumb immigrated to the United States as a young man and apprenticed himself to Frank Lloyd Wright, who would remain an influence throughout his career, even as he developed his own practice. Klumb had an equally decisive relationship with Rexford Tugwell, an economist who was part of the brain trust assembled by Franklin Delano Roosevelt to formulate the policies of the New Deal. After Tugwell was appointed governor of Puerto Rico in 1941, he called on Klumb to be his architect; Klumb arrived on the island in 1944 and remained there for the rest of his life.

In addition to his master plan for the Universidad de Puerto Rico, Río Pedras, Klumb left a legacy of innovative modernist churches. For the municipality of Cataño, adjacent to San Juan, he designed a centralized space in inexpensive concrete, with porous lateral walls to accommodate the Caribbean climate and a dome admitting zenithal light. Originally planned with the engineer August Komendant as a prefabricated piece to be shipped to the island, in the end the church was executed using simpler concrete techniques.   BB

Interior view of the sanctuary. c. 1965. Henry Klumb Collection, Archivo Arquitectura y Construcción, Universidad de Puerto Rico, San Juan

Chile

On Wednesday, June 18, 1924, in the newspaper *La nación*, the Chilean writer and artist Juan Emar published "Ideas sueltas sobre arquitectura" (Various ideas about architecture), in which he reviewed Le Corbusier's *Vers une architecture* (*Toward an Architecture*), published in Paris the previous year.[1] Emar had been introduced to the work of Le Corbusier by the poet Vicente Huidobro. Thus new architectural ideas arrived in Chile through literary and poetic means.

Europe continued to exert an influence in the early twentieth century. Many Chilean artists and architects traveled there to experience the avant-garde movements taking place around 1930. Juan Martínez, a promising architect, won the competition to design the Chile Pavilion for the Exposición Iberamericano in Seville in 1929 and traveled to Spain to direct the construction process. Sergio Larraín García-Moreno, after graduating from the architecture school at the Universidad Católica in Santiago in 1928, made a series of visits to some of the central figures of the European avant-garde, including Le Corbusier. When he returned, the studio he shared with Jorge Arteaga, which had previously designed more traditional buildings, began producing modernist designs, including the Oberpauer (fig. 1) and Santa Lucía (1932) buildings.

During his studies in Vienna in 1927–29, Rodulfo Oyarzún Philippi had met the urban planner Karl Brunner, who shared Werner Hegemann's ideas about the evolutionary modernization of cities. In 1929 Oyarzún brought Brunner to Chile, where he founded one of the first seminars on urbanism in Latin America. Roberto Dávila Carson, who would later become a professor in the architecture school at the Universidad de Chile, studied in Europe from 1931 to 1934 at the Akademie der bildenden Künste Wien, where he connected with the artists Theo van Doesburg and Georges Vantongerloo and worked for several months with Le Corbusier on his Plan Obus projects for Algiers (1932). When he returned to Chile, he designed the Restaurant Cap Ducal in Viña del Mar (fig. 2), inspired by naval motifs. But the most extraordinary of these European experiences was the three-year tour, starting in 1929, of twenty-six professors from the Escuela de Bellas Artes, sponsored by the government of Carlos Ibáñez.

The expansion of modern architecture and urbanism was hastened by two events: on December 25, 1938, Pedro Aguirre Cerda, of the Frente Popular (Popular front), became president of the republic, and on January 24, 1939, an earthquake devastated the city of Chillán and the surrounding area, causing nearly thirty thousand deaths. The rebuilding after the earthquake forced the quick modernization of both architecture and engineering.[2]

Escuela Naval, Valparaíso. 1956–57. Francisco Méndez Labbé (Chilean, born 1922), Escuela de Arquitectura, Universidad Católica de Valparaíso (Chile, est. 1952). Competition entry. Photocollage, 22 ⁷⁄₁₆ x 14 ¾ in. (57 x 37.5 cm). Archivo Histórico José Vial Armstrong, Pontificia Universidad Católica de Valparaíso

In response to the disaster, Aguirre Cerda's government created the Corporación de Reconstrucción y Auxilio (Corporation for reconstruction and aid), which organized rebuilding activities and, later, promoted social housing programs. The Corporación de Fomento a la Producción (Corporation for the encouragement of production), was founded to promote industrialization and planning in the country as a whole. Disagreement about the new city plan pitted Brunner's followers against those who supported the radical views of Le Corbusier, who had been proposed, but not hired, as the reconstruction's planner.

The architects who finished their studies in the late 1930s and early 1940s became central figures in the renewal of the following decades, among them Jorge Aguirre, Emilio Duhart, Alberto Cruz, Héctor Valdés, Fernando Castillo, and Mario Pérez de Arce. The curriculum reforms at the Universidad de Chile, in 1945, and the Universidad Católica, in 1949, shifted architectural culture in the country, in both teaching and practice. This culminated in 1952 in the refounding of the architecture school at the Universidad Católica in Valparaíso, initiating one of the most radical pedagogical experiments in Latin America, in which students would travel and observe the city as a starting point for projects nurtured by a poetic vision of reality.

The 1950s were marked by a developing professionalism, in works such as the Portales housing complex in Santiago (1955–68), by the firm Bresciani Valdés Castillo Huidobro. The same firm designed a remarkable collection of projects in the northern city of Arica, among them the Chinchorro (1955–56) and Estadio (1956–57) complexes—the former composed of housing units set around courtyards, the latter a combination of apartment blocks and low-rise houses. The Salar del Carmen housing complex in Antofagasta (fig. 3) is another notable project in the northern region, designed by Pérez de Arce and Jaime Besa, who very carefully inserted the complex into the desert landscape. The government of Ibáñez encouraged the development of these outer regions, and in 1953 it created the Corporación de la Vivienda (Housing corporation), which absorbed the Corporación de Reconstrucción y Auxilio and the Caja de la Habitación Popular (Popular housing fund) in order to modernize them.

2. **Restaurant Cap Ducal, Viña del Mar. 1936.** Roberto Dávila Carson (Chilean, 1889–1971). **Exterior view**

In the 1950s Chilean architecture matured recognizably, but it was in the following decade that some of the canonical works appeared. Many international organizations had chosen Santiago for their headquarters, and the 1960 competition for the design of a United Nations branch in Santiago drew the most important architects in the country, who were attracted by the spectacular location and the international and symbolic relevance of the commission. The winning project, designed by Duhart with Christian de Groote, Roberto Goycoolea, and Oscar Santelices, was inaugurated in 1966 and given over to the Comisión Económica para América Latina (CEPAL), whose model of economic development would dominate the region for decades to come. The building's powerful design and technological advancement make it the height of midcentury Chilean architecture.

Alternative modes of architectural practice also emerged, combining theory and practice, favoring experimentation, and eschewing conventional offices. Juan Borchers, Isidro Suárez, and Jesús Bermejo were known for their theoretical work in books such as Borchers's *Institución*

1. **Edificio Oberpauer, Santiago. 1929.** Sergio Larraín García-Moreno (Chilean, 1905–1999), Jorge Arteaga (Chilean, died 1967). **Exterior view from Calle Huérfanos**

arquitectónica (1968) and *Meta-arquitectura* (1975), elements of which were made incarnate in their building for the Cooperativa de Servicios Eléctricos (COPELEC) in Chillán, completed in 1964. The Valparaíso school, already a decade old, also managed to build some of its projects, including the dense, complex Cruz house in Santiago (1958–62); a competition entry for the naval schol in Valparaíso (1956–57), focused primarily on manipulating the wind at the site, did not win the commission. Architects associated with the school built a number of churches in the country's southern region after another earthquake, in 1960; Gabriel Guarda and Martín Correa, two then-unknown architects who were also Benedictine monks, designed and built a church for their monastery in Las Condes, Santiago, in 1963–64 (portfolio 3). They made natural light the protagonist of their structure, following the reforms of the Liturgical Movement, and the brilliance of their ascetic—albeit rich and intense—design was immediately recognized both nationally and internationally.

The need for social housing became increasingly acute. Large housing projects, which began under the government of Jorge Alessandri, from 1958 to 1962, were prolonged through the administrations of Eduardo Frei, from 1964 to 1970, and Salvador Allende, from 1970 to 1973. Despite these efforts, which made use of both on-site construction and extensive prefabrication, the deficit in urban housing continued to grow because of the vast number of people migrating from rural areas. The 1958 Plan Regulador Intercomunal de Santiago laid out a master plan for the city facing the challenges of metropolization. In 1965 the Corporación de Mejoramiento Urbano (Corporation for urban improvement) was created to propose large-scale projects of urban renovation, which included the remodeling of San Borja (fig. 4), which replaced an old downtown hospital, and the San Luis complex (1970–73) in a rural plot in the city's eastern area.

But the radical politics and economic difficulties of the late 1960s and early 1970s did not favor building activity. Significant public competitions and private commissions dramatically decreased, with only a few exceptions, including the structure built for the third United Nations Conference on Trade and Development (1971–72), by José Covacevich, Hugo Gaggero, Juan Echeñique, José Medina, and Sergio González. The building, a monumentalized version of standard podium and tower design with the work of visual artists integrated into it, precipitated a series of renewal projects in the neighborhood, which in turn generated interstitial public spaces. VIEXPO, an international housing exhibition held in 1972, and the competition the same year for the renovation of the west-central area of Santiago were both efforts to generate discussion about the greatest architectural and urban challenges of the moment, including how to make modern urbanism compatible with the historic grid of colonial cities.

The first architecture biennial, organized by the Colegio de Arquitectos de Chile (Association of Chilean architects), was inaugurated in August of 1977, providing a rare breath of fresh air for architects: an opportunity for discussions and encounters within the rarefied cultural environment ushered in by the coup d'état of September 1973. The exhibitions, however, signaled the end of a general agreement about the social and aesthetic meaning of modern architecture and urban planning. A gaze toward history and context—one not exempt from nostalgia— would dominate Chilean architecture for at least the next decade.

1 The author would like to thank CEDEUS for the support it provided in writing this article through the FONDAP 15110020 project.

2 The Frente Popular was a political alliance that included the radical, socialist, and communist parties.

3. **Salar del Carmen housing complex, Antofagasta. 1960.** Mario Pérez de Arce (Chilean, 1917–2010), Jaime Besa (Chilean, 1920–1975). **Panoramic view. 1964.** Archivo de Originales, Pontificia Universidad Católica de Chile

4. **Plan for remodeling San Borja, Santiago. 1966–73.** Corporación de Mejoramiento Urbano (Chile, active 1965–1976). **Photograph of model. 1969.** From *Revista AVCA*, no. 16. Ministerio de Vivienda y Urbanismo (MINVU)

Juan Borchers (Chilean, 1910–1975)
Isidro Suárez (Chilean, 1918–1986)
Jesús Bermejo (Spanish, born 1928)

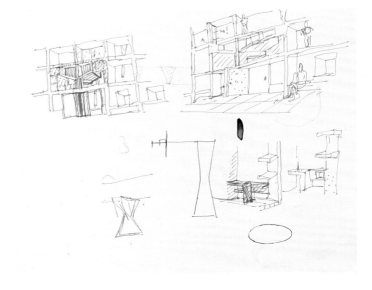

Above: Interior view. 1966. Photograph by Patricio Guzmán.
Archivo de Originales, Pontificia Universidad Católica de Chile

Top right: Sketches. c. 1960. Ink on paper, 8 ½ x 11 in. (21.7 x 27.2 cm).
Archivo de Originales, Pontificia Universidad Católica de Chile

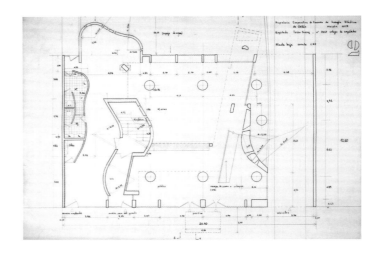

Plan of the first floor. c. 1960. 14 ⅝ x 21 ⅝ in. (37.3 x 54.2 cm).
Archivo de Originales, Pontificia Universidad Católica de Chile

(United Nations Conference on Trade and Development)
José Covacevich (Chilean, born 1934)
Juan Echeñique G. (Chilean, 1919–2000)
Hugo Gaggero (Chilean, born 1928)
Sergio González (Chilean, born Poland. 1938–2012)
José Medina (Chilean, died 2012)

View of the delegates' room during the UNCTAD III conference, with a lighting project by the architects with Bernardo Trumper and a mural by Mario Toral. 1972

In 1972, as Chile prepared to host the third meeting of the United Nations Conference on Trade and Development (UNCTAD), hundreds of Chileans participated in creating a venue for the event. Built in a remarkable 275 days, the complex comprises a horizontal bar for a convention center and a twenty-two-story tower, both built on-site with prefabricated metal components. President Salvador Allende hoped the complex would eventually become a cultural center, but this only happened after years of use by the military dictatorship and a reconstruction after a fire in 2006.   BB/JFL

CEPAL, Santiago. 1960–66
(Comisión Económica para América Latina)
Emilio Duhart (Chilean, 1917–2006)

Exterior view over the pond. c. 1966. Archivo de Originales,
Pontificia Universidad Católica de Chile

The United Nations' decision in 1959 to build a branch in Santiago, which would later house the Comisión Económica para América Latina (CEPAL), extended the organization's role in a conversation about monumentality and symbolism in postwar architecture that had begun with the UN headquarters in New York (1947) and the UNESCO building in Paris (1952). Emilio Duhart won the competition in 1960 with a design both specific to the majestic site and in dialogue with the powerful Andean topography and, later, with a park designed by Roberto Burle Marx. Duhart had worked with Le Corbusier on the new Punjab capital at Chandigarh, a project recalled here in the distinctive conical form of CEPAL's assembly hall, which rises above the roofline of the open rectangular frame of offices, creates skylighting for an inward-looking meeting room, and offers a public observatory on the roof. The structure rests on powerful piers above the landscape, which flows under the building to join an interior courtyard. Burle Marx imagined the gardens, which were never completed, as a continuation of Santiago's park system and a series of interlocking courtyard spaces. The roof, reached via a gently curving spiral ramp, looks over the site and gives visitors a chance to read the pre-Columbian–style pictograms cast in the concrete surface. BB

View of the courtyard during construction. c. 1966.
Archivo de Originales, Pontificia Universidad
Católica de Chile

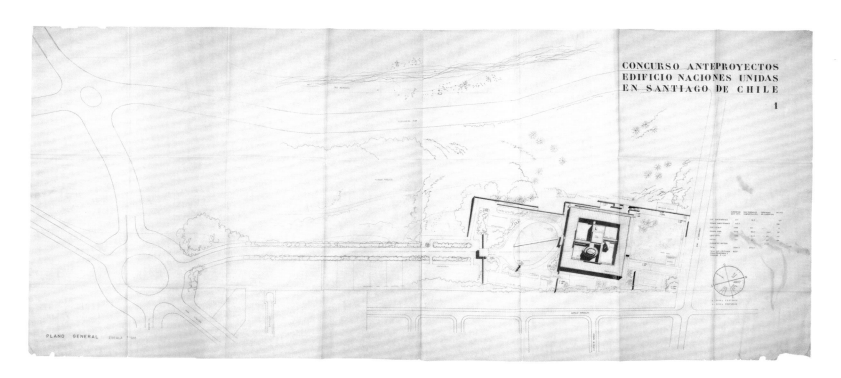

Above: Master plan for the site's landscaping. 1960. Ink on paper, 41 ⁵⁄₁₆ in. x 7 ft. 10 ½ in. (105 x 240 cm). Archivo de Originales, Pontificia Universidad Católica de Chile

Right: View of the assembly room in session. c. 1966. Photograph by Heliodoro Torrente. Archivo de Originales, Pontificia Universidad Católica de Chile

Unidad Vecinal Portales, Santiago. 1955–68
Bresciani Valdés Castillo Huidobro (Chile, est. 1955)

Exterior view of housing block and gardens. c. 1965.
Photograph by René Combeau Trillat. Archivo de
Originales, Pontificia Universidad Católica de Chile

Exterior view of housing block and ramp. c. 1965.
Photograph by René Combeau Trillat. Archivo de
Originales, Pontificia Universidad Católica de Chile

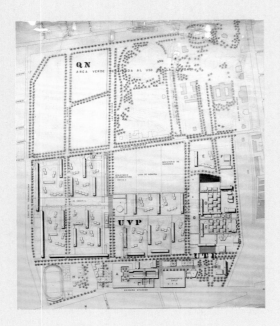

Site plan. c. 1960. Ink on paper, 35 x 25 ½ in.
(89 x 65 cm). Archivo de Originales, Pontificia
Universidad Católica de Chile

Since passing the Ley de Habitaciones Obreras
(Law for workers' housing) in 1906, Chile had
been one of the the most active countries in the
Americas in creating government-supported
housing. The institutions created during the
1950s and 1960s, such as the Caja de Habitación
Popular (Popular housing fund), the Corporación
de la Vivienda, and, in particular, the Ministerio de
Vivienda, were critical to this effort. Operación
Sitio, born during the presidency of Eduardo Frei,
encouraged self-construction with economic
assistance from the United States–backed
Alliance for Progress. Heavy prefabrication, by
contrast, inspired by methods being utilized in
the Soviet Union, were favored during the presidency of Salvador Allende.

Architects made vital experiments with
new housing types and methods of grouping them, in settlements such as Portales in
Santiago and Chinchorro in Arica. A daring project of urban transformation in the city center,
with a focus on housing, is equally noteworthy
but was interrupted by the military coup of
November 9, 1973.   JFL

Conjunto Habitacional Chinchorro, Arica. 1955–56
Bresciani Valdés Castillo Huidobro (Chile, active 1955–1969)

View of rear facade and roof shade. c. 1955. Photograph by René Combeau Trillat. Archivo de Originales, Pontificia Universidad Católica de Chile

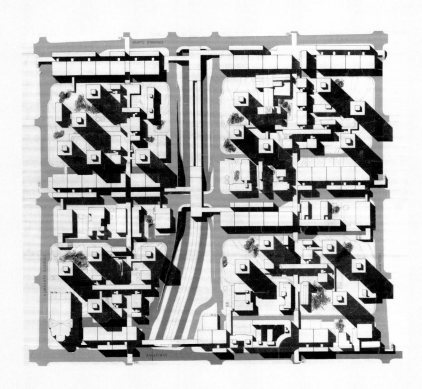

Plan for remodeling the Santiago city center. 1972
Enrique D. Bares (Argentine, born 1942)
Santiago F. Bo (Argentine, born 1942)
Tomás O. García (Argentine, born 1942)
Roberto S. Germani (Argentine, born 1940)
Emilio T. Sessa (Argentine, born 1947)
Rodolfo Morzilli (Argentine, 1942–2004)
Inés Rubio (Argentine, born 1938)
Carlos Ucar (Argentine, born 1942)
Jaime Lande (Argentine, born 1934)

Competition entry. Ink on paper, 33 ⅛ x 46 ¹³⁄₁₆ in. (84.1 x 118.9 cm)

Chile Church for the Benedictine monastery of
Santísima Trinidad de Las Condes, Santiago. 1963–64
Hermano Martín Correa (Chilean, born 1928)
Hermano Gabriel Guarda (Chilean, born 1928)

Exterior view. c. 1990. Photograph by Juan Purcell Mena. Archivo de
Originales, Pontificia Universidad Católica de Chile

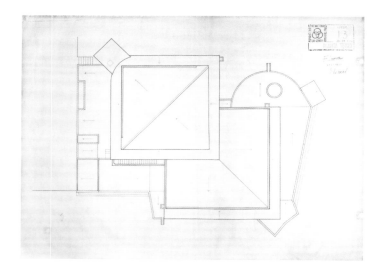

Roof plan. 1964. Ink on paper, 26 ½ x 36 ¼ in. (67.5 x 92 cm). Archivo de
Originales, Pontificia Universidad Católica de Chile

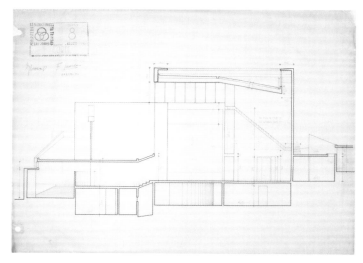

Section. 1964. Ink on paper, 20 ⁷⁄₁₆ x 27 ⅞ in. (51.9 x 70.8 cm). Archivo de
Originales, Pontificia Universidad Católica de Chile

Proposal for the Benedictine monastery and church. 1960. Alberto Cruz (Chilean, 1917–2003),
Escuela de Architectura, Universidad Católica de Valparaíso (Chile, est. 1952). **Perspective.**
Watercolor, ink, and pencil on paper. Archivo Histórico José Vial Armstrong, Pontificia
Universidad Católica de Valparaíso

Interior view from the entrance ramp.
c. 1990. Photograph by Juan Purcell Mena.
Archivo de Originales, Pontificia
Universidad Católica de Chile

View of the entrance. c. 1990. Photograph by Juan Purcell Mena. Archivo
de Originales, Pontificia Universidad
Católica de Chile

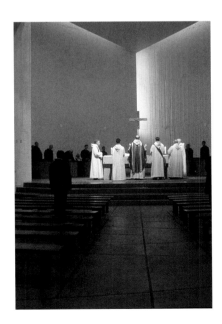

View of the altar during liturgy. c. 1990.
Photograph by Juan Purcell Mena. Archivo
de Originales, Pontificia Universidad
Católica de Chile

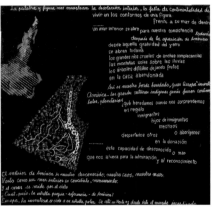

Above: Project for Avenida del Mar, Valparaíso. 1969. View of the site model at an exhibition.
Archivo Histórico José Vial Armstrong, Pontificia Universidad Católica de Valparaíso

Right: Presentation on the school's philosophy for *Exposición de los 20 años de La Escuela de Arquitectura de la Universidad Católica de Valparaíso*. 1972. Four chalkboards, each: 59 x 59 in. (150 x 150 cm). Archivo Histórico José Vial Armstrong, Pontificia Universidad Católica de Valparaíso

Cooperativa Amereida (Chile, est. 1970)
Escuela de Arquitectura,
Universidad Católica de Valparaíso (Chile, est. 1952)

Phalène los espectros (Ghosts). 1979. Poetic act. Archivo Histórico José Vial Armstrong, Pontificia Universidad Católica de Valparaíso

Apertura de los terrenos (Opening of the terrain). 1971. Founding meeting of the Ciudad Abierta. Archivo Histórico José Vial Armstrong, Pontificia Universidad Católica de Valparaíso

Cortejo (Courtship). 1975. Tournament for a course on the culture of the body. Archivo Histórico José Vial Armstrong, Pontificia Universidad Católica de Valparaíso

Guante nocturno (Nocturnal glove). 1978. Tournament for a course on the culture of the body. Archivo Histórico José Vial Armstrong, Pontificia Universidad Católica de Valparaíso

In 1970 a group of architects, poets, designers, and artists gathered in the dunes of Ritoque, north of Valparaíso, to found the Ciudad Abierta (Open city), an experimental community linked to the architecture school of the Universidad Católica de Valparaíso. Led by the architect Alberto Cruz and the poet Godofredo Iommi, the school has taught architecture as a practice in the service of poetry since 1952, and it has developed the relationship between scientific research, technology, and architecture through such projects as the Escuela Naval (1956–57) and the Avenida del Mar proposal for the Valparaíso–Viña del Mar oceanfront highway. In 1960 a catastrophic earthquake in the Concepción region propelled the school to southern Chile to rebuild a series of damaged and destroyed churches, and these endeavors prepared the way for the Ciudad Abierta and its experimental building practices. In 1965 Cruz and Iommi organized and carried out a journey from Punta Arenas, at the very tip of the continent, to Santa Cruz de la Sierra, in Bolivia—which they declared the "poetic capital" of the Americas. The Amereida journey, as they called it, synthesized the research produced by the school, projected its mission throughout South America, and focused its work on the question of inhabitation. The school continues to employ language as a tool to complement scientific inquiry and challenge the status of technology and industry as the sole creators of the modern world. PdR

Chile **Ciudad Abierta, Ritoque. 1971–present**
Cooperativa Amereida (Chile, est. 1970), Escuela de Arquitectura,
Universidad Católica de Valparaíso (Chile, est. 1952)

Cemetery. 1974–present. View toward the northern gate. c. 1977. Photograph by Juan Ignacio Baixas

Water tower. 1974. Exterior view. 1980. Archivo Histórico José Vial
Armstrong, Pontificia Universidad Católica de Valparaíso

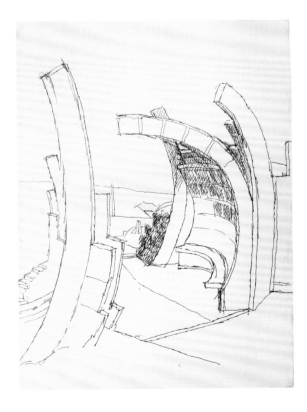

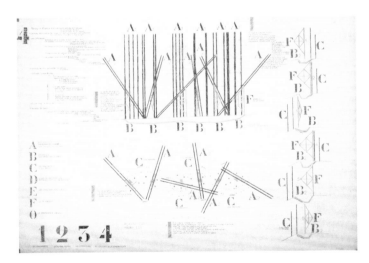

Above: Drawing of the water tower's structural elements. Pencil and
ink on paper, 43 5/16 x 35 7/16 in. (110 x 90 cm). Archivo Histórico José Vial
Armstrong, Pontificia Universidad Católica de Valparaíso

Left: Sketch of *arcos falsos* (freestanding arch structures) at the
entrance of the cemetery). Pencil on paper, 15 1/4 x 11 in. (38.7 x 27.9 cm).
The Museum of Modern Art, New York. Gift of Juan Ignacio Baixas

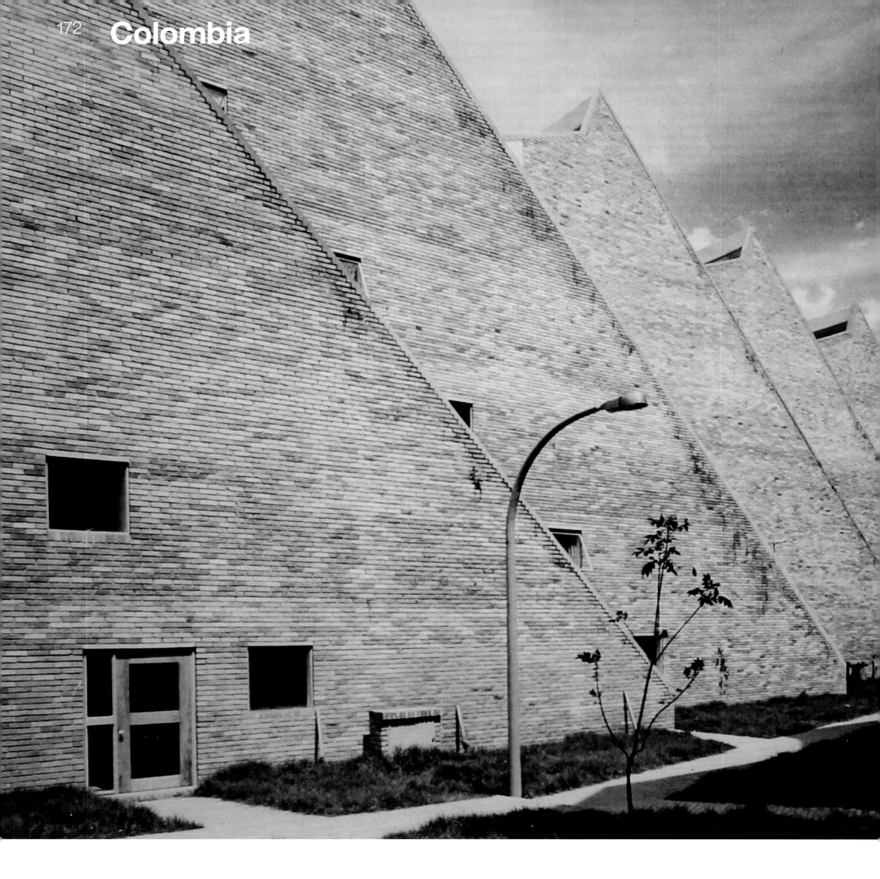

Modern architecture in Colombia reached its peak between 1945 and 1960—a paradox, given the era's climate of violence and intolerance. The liberal modernization of the country, from 1930 to 1946, was interrupted by a conservative backlash, during which many political and social reforms were abolished. The period known as La Violencia continued with the assassination of the populist leader Jorge Eliécer Gaitán on April 9, 1948, and the bloodshed escalated through the 1950s, under the dictatorship of Gustavo Rojas Pinilla, from 1953 to 1957. Nonetheless, architecture continued to develop in many important works and projects, by master architects and others, and in retrospect we can understand the time to have been a golden age for architecture, if not also for urban planning.

Modern architecture arrived late in Colombia, via magazines, the arrival of foreign architects, and Colombians who studied abroad. The idea took root through the activities of the Ministerio de Obras Públicas; the architecture department at the Universidad Nacional, created in 1936; and the magazine *PROA*, established in 1946, with the support of the Sociedad Colombiana de Arquitectos, created in 1934. In *Arquitectura en Colombia*, published in 1951 by *PROA*, Carlos Martínez and Jorge Arango summed up the magnificent modernist architectural production so far, in a list of works of astonishing quality and number.

For the purposes of brevity, the panorama of Colombian architecture can be reduced to two main axes of rational functionalism and organic regionalism. The reality is, of course, more complex: architects existed within both modalities and created works employing elements of both currents. Magnificent buildings such as the baseball stadium in Cartagena (1947) or the market building in Girardot (1947), the printing press at the Universidad Nacional (1946), the churches of Juvenal Moya (1950s), or many of Guillermo Bermúdez's works, among others, cannot be classified in just one category.

The first sign of functionalism appeared in 1939, when Gabriel Serrano published Walter Gropius's proposal for functional architecture in *Ingeniería y arquitectura*; Serrano supported Gropius's idea that architecture should be an expression of the technologies of the new industrialized civilization.[1] That same year, Serrano visited the World's Fair in New York, where he contemplated a range of pavilions built according to these ideas, including Brazil's, designed by Oscar Niemeyer and Lucio Costa, although he was unaware of Alvar Aalto's pavilion for Finland. In his scant writings and numerous designs, he advocated an essential architecture that would respect functionalist parameters. This conception was also notable in the work of firms including Esguerra Sáenz & Samper and Pizano, Pradilla &

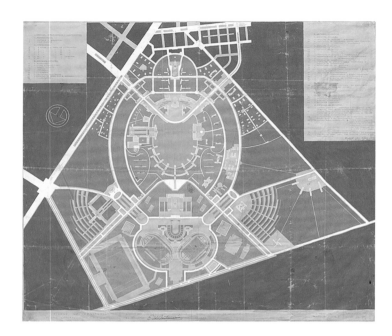

1. **Plan for the Ciudad Universitaria de Bogotá, Universidad Nacional de Colombia. 1937–45.** Leopold Rother (Colombian, born Germany. 1894–1978). Gouache on blueprint paper, 32 ¹¹/₁₆ x 36 ¼ in. (89 x 92 cm). Museo de Arquitectura Leopoldo Rother

Caro, in Bogotá; Lago & Sáenz and Borrero Zamorano & Giovanelli, in Cali; or Vieira Vásquez & Dothé, in Medellín. The hallmarks of functionalism also appeared in the plan for the Ciudad Universitaria de Bogotá (Bogotá campus) (fig. 1), by Leopoldo Rother for the Ministerio de Obras Públicas (Ministry of public works), and the prismatic buildings on the university campus, including the materials-testing laboratory and engineering department (both 1940).

Along Bogotá's Carrera Décima, which culminates at the Centro Internacional (fig. 2), from the Tequendama Hotel (1952), by Cuéllar Serrano Gómez, to the Bavaria housing project (1964), by Obregón & Valenzuela, are

many magnificent buildings that demonstrate how architects responded to the growth of capitalism in Colombia, as both national and international businesses increasingly required headquarters in the capital city, as well as in Colombia's regional capitals. The momentum of modernization required more housing for the growing populaton, creating exemplary neighborhoods in Bogotá and all over the country: the Instituto de Crédito Territorial and the Banco Central Hipotecario (Central mortgage bank) backed the development of projects in Bogotá including Quiroga (1954), Alcázares (1956), El Polo (1960–63), Ciudad Kennedy (1961), and Niza (1970); each comprising either clusters of houses set among pedestrian paths, promenades, and playgrounds; or multifamily buildings constructed around green spaces, all aimed at creating healthy urban conditions.

Urban planning in Colombia first took its cue from the proposals of the Austrian planner Karl Brunner, starting in 1933, for various cities including Bogotá, Barranquilla, Cali, and Medellín. Brunner's designs were marked by nineteenth-century urban form; his work was later rejected by young modernists, although it is highly appreciated today. In 1950 Le Corbusier formulated his plan for Bogotá (fig. 3), which followed the functionalist parameters laid out by the Congrès Internationaux d'Architecture Moderne (CIAM)— although Rojas Pinilla opted to take the city in a different direction—and he welcomed into his studio the Colombian architects Germán Samper and Rogelio Salmona. Samper went on to employ Corbusian elements in his practice, but Salmona criticized his teacher's ubiquitiousness and abstract purity. He would become a fundamental advocate for an architecture of place.

The notion of organicism soon came to the fore among advocates for architecture of place, or topological architecture, who rejected the planting of ubiquitous prismatic volumes into any site, climate, or social context. Instead they encouraged consideration of a project's specific site in order to shape the space, using forms distinct from orthogonal prisms, with sensual vernacular materials that invited touch. Such rejection of International Style had its foundations in the work of Frank Lloyd Wright and the Scandinavians, above all Aalto; many Colombian architects

2. **Centro Internacional de Bogotá. 1950–82.** Cuéllar Serrano Gómez (Colombia, est. 1933)

admired the town hall of Säynätsalo, Finland (1949–52), designed by Aalto, for its employment of brick, the material that would become the core of Colombian architecture in notable contributions from Fernando Martínez Sanabria, Salmona, and others.

The opposition between functionalism and organicism became clear in the competition entries for the Emilio Cifuentes school (1959). The project that won was rational and correct but insignificant; the most remarkable design to come out of the competition was by Martínez Sanabria, whose dynamic and innovative shapes proposed a topological relationship to the monumental stones at the front of the school. At the first Colombian architecture biennial, in 1962, Martínez's design for the school was recognized as the best unbuilt project, while the national prize was given to the Ecopetrol building, by Cuéllar Serrano Gómez, and the best residential project to the house Bermúdez designed for himself (fig. 4).

The debate continued at the second biennial, in 1964, when the jury was unable to decide on a recipient for the prize, although honorable mentions were given to the Bravo house by Bermúdez and an affordable housing complex by Hans Drews.[2] Among the entries that year was one of the best projects of that era, or of any time: the El Polo complex, by Bermúdez and Salmona, notable for its terraced trapezoidal plan, its sculptural stairways, the playful disposition of its windows, and the rich expression of its brick facade. But the judges dismissed it, citing the risks posed by the whims of the architects, the difficult formalism, and the lack of standardization in responding to the needs of the masses. Among the projects that did follow these concerns was Salmona's Torres del Parque (1964–70), a masterful work that combined artisanal techniques such as brickwork with industrialized methods such as concrete in buildings of fifteen and twenty-five stories. The towers were not arranged as simple shapes but rather as impressively curved and richly plastic fans.

Some excellent private houses were constructed in this period, many of them made out of brick, inside as well as on the exterior, with designs that adhered to the topography of the site and whose visual elements poetically enriched the landscape. The works of Martínez Sanabria

and Bermúdez stand out in particular. These qualities appeared in multifamily buildings by Arturo Robledo, Arango, Hernán Vieco, and many others.

Toward the end of 1960s and the Frente Nacional—a pact between the two political parties to take turns controlling the government, from 1958 to 1974—the quality of Colombian architecture declined. The biggest studios continued to be active, although their efficient skyscraper projects, such as the Avianca, in Bogotá (1968–79), or Coltejer, in Medellín (1968–72), lacked the character of previous works. A few projects maintained the tradition of austerity and good craft, above all in brickwork; among them are Alto Los Pinos (1977), and the Casa de Huéspedes in Cartagena (1979), by Salmona; Los Eucaliptos (1978), by Dicken Castro and Alberto Saldarriaga; and the Los Virreyes building (1980), by Enrique Triana Uribe. Aníbal Moreno's Facultad de Enfermería (Nursing school) at the Universidad Javeriana (1965–67) is one of the rare innovative buildings of this period: an experiment with concrete and the laws of statics that goes beyond the conventional use of columns and reticulate beams.

We might wonder about the reasons for this decline, after such a peak of postwar achievement. No response is offered; the question remains unresolved, although the dominance of real estate promoters and speculative interests, the proliferation of architecture schools, the failure to teach either architectural or political history, and the precariousness of criticism and research must have contributed to the fall. Nevertheless, the period between 1955 and 1980 presents many fine examples of the consistency and quality of modern architecture in Colombia. These projects are not limited to a language of abstract cubes but respond to the specifics of climate and various geographies, reaching a level of poetic achievement. Having taken in European and North American lessons of modernism, the architects of Colombia implemented them with imagination and rigor.

1   Walter Gropius, "Arquitectura funcional," trans. Darío Achury, *Ingeniería y arquitectura*, no. 1 (1939): 27–29.

2   The judges were Colombian architects, with the predominant voices being those of Gabriel Serrano and Serge Chermayeff; the latter was acting as an outside judge.

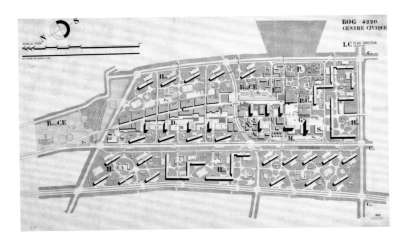

3. **Plan for Bogotá. 1947–51.** Le Corbusier (French, born Switzerland. 1887–1965). Master plan in three dimensions, showing buildings, neighborhood planning, circulation, and access. 1950. Ink on paper, 37 7/16 x 61 13/16 in. (95 x 157 cm). Fondation Le Corbusier, Paris

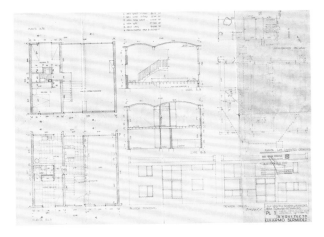

4. **Casa Bermúdez, Bogotá. 1953.** Guillermo Bermúdez (Colombian, 1924–1995). Blueprint, 33 1/8 x 46 13/16 in. (84.1 x 118.9 cm). The Museum of Modern Art, New York. Gift of Daniel Bermúdez

Obregón & Valenzuela (Colombia, active 1943–1976)

View from the garden. 1957. Photograph by Paul Beer

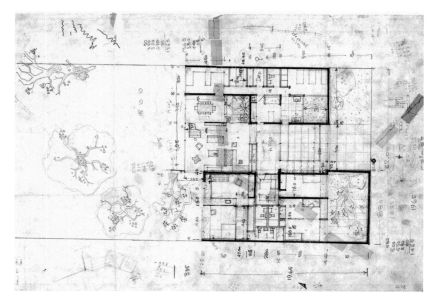

Plan of the main floor. Ink and pencil on tracing paper. 11 9/16 x 15 15/16 in. (29.4 x 40.5 cm). Archivo Rafael Obregón Herrera

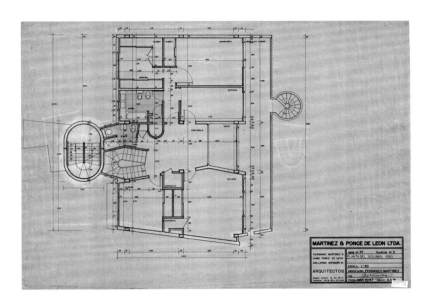

Plan of the second floor of the Martínez house. Ink on paper, 26 ¼ x 34 ½ in. (66.7 x 87.6 cm). Museo de Arquitectura Leopoldo Rother

Exterior view of the Martínez house. 1958. Photograph by Paul Beer

View of the Triana house from the southwest. 1966

View of the living room of the Triana house. 1966

Germán Samper (Colombian, born 1924)

View of upper-level stadium seating and cantilevered canopy. 1956. Photograph by Paul Beer

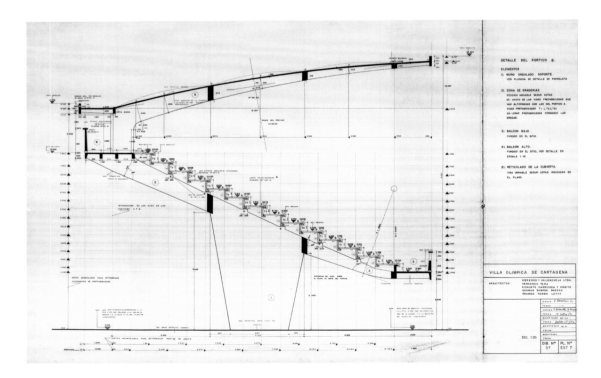

Detail of a cantilevered canopy. 1956. Ink on paper, 47¼ x 30⅞ in. (120 x 78.5 cm). Archivo de Bogotá

Above: Exterior view. 1966. Photograph by
Paul Beer

Left: View of piers during construction. 1960.
Photograph by Paul Beer

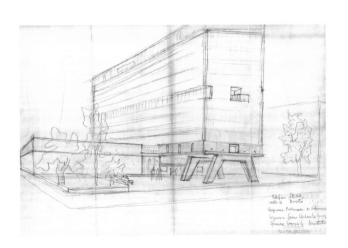

Preliminary perspective. c. 1960. Ink on paper, 27½ x 19¾ in.
(69.8 x 50.3 cm). Archivo de Bogotá

Perspective study. 1960. Pencil, ink, and color on paper, 27½ x 22¼ in.
(69.8 x 56.5 cm). Archivo de Bogotá

Fernando Martínez Sanabria (Colombian, born Spain. 1925–1991)
Guillermo Avendaño (Colombian)

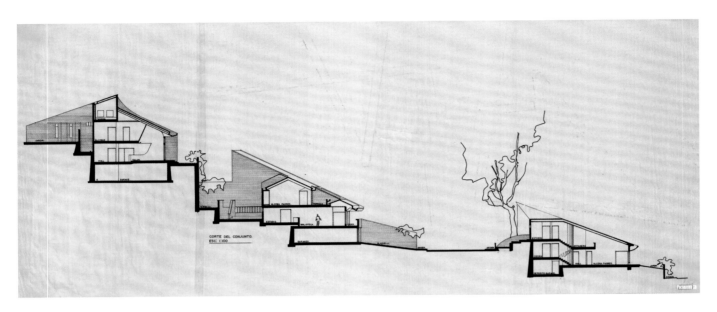

Section of the site, showing (left to right) the Wilkie, Santos, and Calderón houses. c. 1963.
Ink on paper, 16 ½ x 39 ½ in. (41.9 x 100.3 cm). Museo de Arquitectura Leopoldo Rother

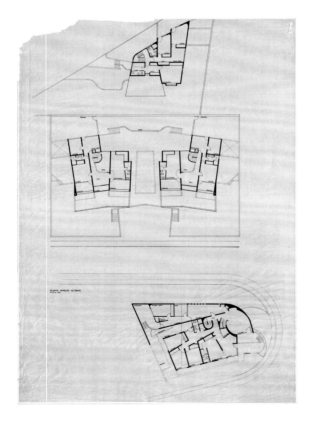

Fernando Martínez Sanabria, one of the most
highly respected and influential architects in
Colombia, was at the height of his career when
he received the commissions for four houses on
adjacent lots on a steep slope in northern Bogotá.
He conceived of them as a continuous building
and landscape project made up of two freestanding houses and one mirror-paired set. The result
is a brilliantly choreographed sequence of spaces
that flow within and among the houses, creating
dramatic diagonals on individual floors and from
one level to the next as the houses respond to
one another in echoing lines. The structures are
oriented to command views of both east and
west, of the mountains and the savanna, and their
expressive brick walls evince the increased admi-
ration on the part of Colombian architects for
the organicism of Alvar Aalto and the work of the
Spanish architect Josep Antoni Coderch.   BB

Plans showing (top to bottom) the Wilkie, twin Santos, and
Calderón houses. c. 1963. Ink on tracing paper, 39 ½ x 27 ¾ in.
(100.3 x 70.5 cm). Museo de Arquitectura Leopoldo Rother

View of the northern facade of the Wilkie house.
c. 1963. Photograph by Ludwig Glaeser. Museo de
Arquitectura Leopoldo Rother

Exterior view of the twin Santos houses. 1963. Photograph by
Ludwig Glaeser. Museo de Arquitectura Leopoldo Rother

View of the entrance to the Calderón house. 1973. Photograph by Germán Téllez

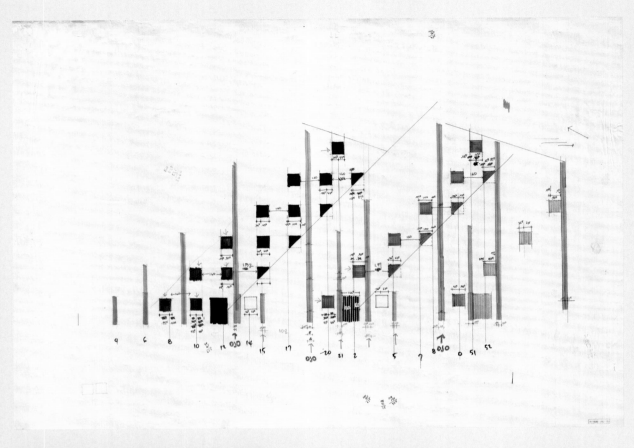

Fundación Cristiana de la Vivienda San Cristóbal, Bogotá. 1963–66
Rogelio Salmona (Colombian, born France. 1929–2007)
Hernán Vieco (Colombian, 1924–2012)

Elevation study. c. 1963. Pencil and markers on tracing paper, 23 ⅜ x 33 ⅛ in. (59.4 x 84.1 cm). Fundación Rogelio Salmona

Exterior view with a sports field. 1973. Photograph by Paolo Gasparini. Fundación Rogelio Salmona

Interior view of an apartment. 1972. Photograph by Paolo Gasparini. Fundación Rogelio Salmona

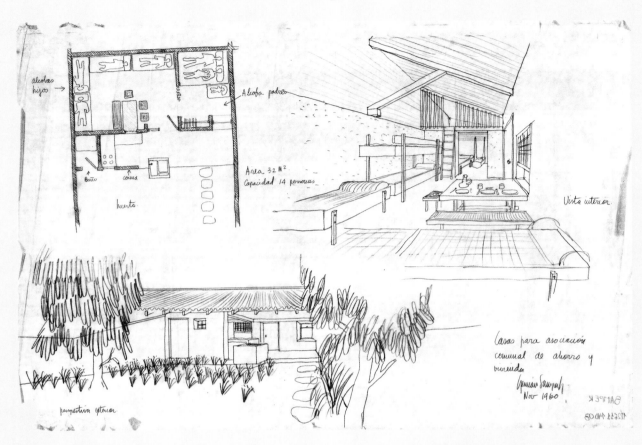

Barrio La Fragua, Bogotá. 1960
Germán Samper (Colombian, born 1924)
Yolanda Martínez de Samper (Colombian)

Perspective studies and plan. Pencil on paper,
27 9/16 x 39 3/8 in. (70 x 100 cm). Archivo de Bogotá

**Apartamentos Calle 26, for the Banco Central
Hipotecario, Bogotá. 1962**
Arturo Robledo (Colombian, 1930–2007)

View of a courtyard between apartment
blocks. 1968. Photograph by Germán Téllez

Residencias El Parque (Torres del Parque), Bogotá. 1964–70
Rogelio Salmona (Colombian, born France. 1929–2007)

Aerial view looking west. 1973. Photograph by
Paolo Gasparini. Fundación Rogelio Salmona

Preliminary model (now lost). 1964. Photograph by Germán Téllez.
Fundación Rogelio Salmona

Site plan. 1969. Ink and charcoal pencil on tracing paper, 33 ⅛ x 46 ¹³⁄₁₆ in.
(84.1 x 118.9 cm). Fundación Rogelio Salmona

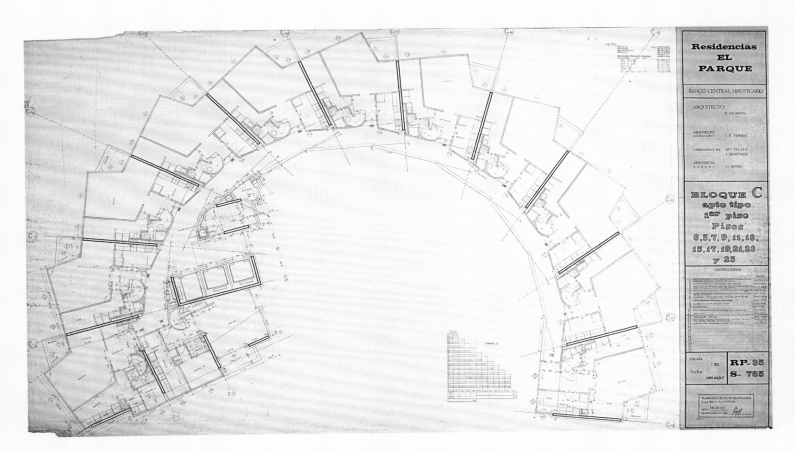

Plan of the first floor of apartment tower C. 1969. Ink and pencil on tracing paper, 27 ⁹⁄₁₆ x 39 ⅜ in.
(70 x 100 cm). Fundación Rogelio Salmona

Residencias El Polo, Bogotá. 1960–63
Rogelio Salmona (Colombian, born France. 1929–2007)
Guillermo Bermúdez (Colombian, 1924–1995)

View of the facade facing the street. 1973. Photograph by
Paolo Gasparini. Fundación Rogelio Salmona

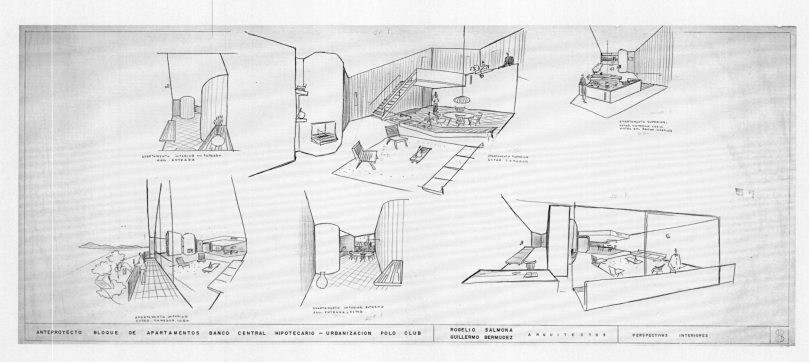

Interior perspectives. c. 1959. Pencil and ink on tracing paper,
23 ⅝ x 59 in. (60 x 150 cm). Fundación Rogelio Salmona

View of the interior garden. c. 1977. Fundación Rogelio Salmona

Interior view of an apartment. 1973. Photograph by Paolo Gasparini. Fundación Rogelio Salmona

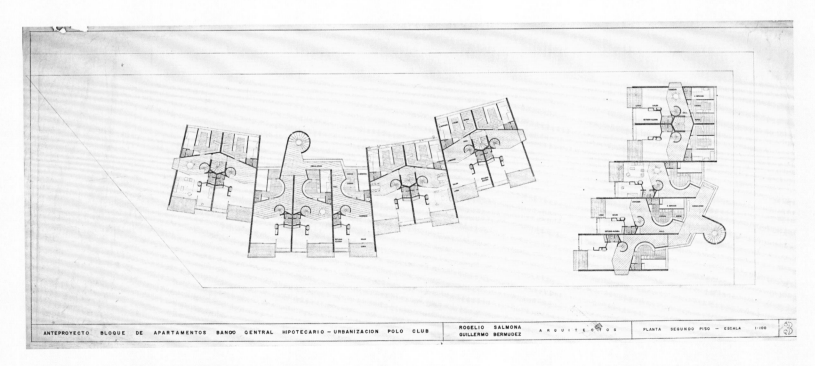

Plan of the third floor. c. 1959. Pencil and ink on tracing paper, 23 ⅝ x 59 in. (60 x 150 cm). Fundación Rogelio Salmona

Biblioteca Luis Ángel Arango, Bogotá. 1956–59
Esguerra Saénz Urdaneta & Suárez (Colombia, est. 1954)
Germán Samper (Colombian, born 1924)

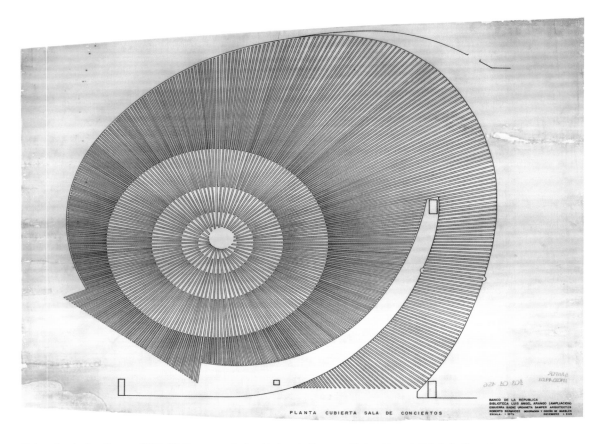

Extension to the library. 1962–65. Esguerra Saénz Urdaneta Samper (Colombia est. 1954). Ceiling plan
of the concert hall, drawn by Gérman Samper. 1965. Ink on tracing paper, 32 ¹¹⁄₁₆ x 39 ⅜ in. (83 x 100 cm).
Archivo de Bogotá

Above: Interior view of the library. 1971. Photograph by
Paul Beer

Left: Interior view of the concert hall. 1957. Photograph by
Paul Beer

Museo de Ciencias Naturales, Universidad Nacional de Colombia, Bogotá. 1969–71
Elsa Mahecha (Colombian, born 1940)

Facultad de Enfermería, Universidad Javeriana, Bogotá. 1965–67
Aníbal Moreno (Colombian, born 1925)

Exterior view of the museum. 1972 . Photograph by Paul Beer

Above: View of the interior courtyard of the nursing school. 1967

Left: Perspective sketch of the nursing school. 1965. Ink and pastel on paper, 8¼ x 11 in. (21 x 28 cm)

Modern Cuban architecture is the most visible outcome of the accelerated changes and sustained development that began with the republic in 1902. Alongside political independence came a wave of advanced modernity that would manifest itself in all aspects of life and particularly in architecture and would be renewed in successive processes of assimilation, adaptation, and reformulation until the 1960s. The process that corresponded to the modern movement began around 1925, with the arrival of French and German ideas about architectural rationalism and with an increase in exchanges of all types brought about by the recently achieved freedom. Cuban architects quickly incorporated new ideas into local idioms, as compensation for the backwardness of having been a Spanish colony for four hundred years.

The most remarkable architectural vocabularies in the colonial period had been Baroque, in the eighteenth century, and Neoclassical, in the nineteenth; their steady stylistic sequence functioned as an expression of slow economic development. In the first decades of the new century, however, the rate of change in Cuban cities accelerated noticeably. Streets were paved, buildings reached new heights, and the quality of materials and construction greatly improved. Reinforced concrete was used in residential projects, and steel structures in public and commercial ones, swiftly replacing colonial construction materials and techniques. Existing cities expanded, and many new districts were created. The new architecture employed neo-Gothic and neo-Baroque elements, among the many revival trends of the eclecticism that was replaced by Art Deco in the second half of the 1920s. In opposition to Art Nouveau's naturalistic emphasis and eclectic decorative approach, Art Deco's apparent lack of historical references and sternly defined geometrical conception were easily identified with a new and even more advanced wave of modernity.

In the mid-1920s the magazine of the Colegio de Arquitectos de La Habana (Architects' association of Havana) began to publish texts and works by the most outstanding European modern architects, which were then assimilated, although not without controversy. The architecture school at the Universidad de La Habana, founded in 1900, was late to join the reform process, but the demands for an upgraded curriculum—which reached an apex in 1947, with students burning copies of the Italian Mannerist Giacomo Barozzi da Vignola's classical treatise on architecture on the patio of the school—produced the hoped-for results: two years later, the school invited Walter Gropius to Cuba to give a series of lectures. His presence, and that of other renowned foreign architects, strengthened the

Cuba Pavilion, Congress of the Union Internationale des Architectes, Havana. 1963. Juan Campos (Cuban, 1930–2007). View of the main hall from the lateral courtyard. 1963. Eduardo Luis Rodríguez Archive

acceptance and facilitated the dissemination of a vocabulary that sought to be of universal value and that would be integrated with functional, technical, and expressive local solutions.

The austere rationalist language of compact layouts, smooth facades, and flat roofs was critical for the initial assimilation of the modern movement, but it soon became clear that it did not fully respond to the needs of the tropical region, nor to the exuberance of the local character. The relatively lengthy survival of this language, through the beginning of the 1940s, was to some extent due to its appropriateness in the era of economic difficulties suffered as a result of the North American financial crisis of 1929. Its use in residential architecture was recurring, and thus examples of it were produced that were as remarkable as Manuel Copado's Solimar apartment building (fig. 1), whose sequence of semicircular balconies makes reference to the ocean waves nearby. This link to the figurative and the symbolic would be used frequently, and it would culminate in the Arcos de Cristal hall of the Cabaret Tropicana (fig. 2), by Max Borges Recio, which expresses, through slender vaults integrated into dense existing vegetation, the intense, radiating sensuality associated with Cuba.

This period of exceptional creativity was sustained by two basic ideas: the full acceptance of modern codes, particularly those of the International Style, and the functional and expressive convenience of considering physical and cultural contexts, which together encouraged the emergence of the modern regionalism that marks many of the most important designs of the era. This integration as an expression of the most advanced architectural modernity originated at the end of the 1930s, in part thanks to the thinking of Eugenio Batista, and reached significant levels of quality at the end of the 1940s and during the 1950s, as seen in the works of some of the most renowned Cuban modern architects including Mario Romañach (fig. 3) and Aquiles Capablanca (fig. 4). Despite the political instability of the 1950s, many of the best examples of twentieth-century Cuban architecture were created during that decade, thanks not just to postwar economic prosperity but also to the solid level of maturity and profound technical and artistic knowledge Cuban architects had achieved and to

2. **Salón Arcos de Cristal, Cabaret Tropicana, Havana. 1951.** Max Borges Recio (Cuban, 1918–2009). View toward the stage. 1952. Photograph by Muñiz. Architecture & Design Study Center, The Museum of Modern Art, New York

an atmosphere of creative freedom. But the impending period of superior architectural achievement that all these factors seemed to announce was interrupted by the triumph of the Cuban Revolution in 1959, the year that would mark a drastic division between "before" and "after."

Thus began a different stage for architects in Cuba, a moment of unusual intensity marked by its epic nature, demands for sacrifice, measure of anxiety, and double impact—of deeply appreciated benefit for some and irreparable loss for others. This moment is often called the "heroic period" of the revolution, when the new government felt obliged to demonstrate its superiority over the preceding one. It did so through grandiloquent gestures, accompanied by an optimism that was frequently outsized in relation to

1. **Edificio Solimar, Havana. 1944.** Manual Copado (Cuban, 1902–1983). Exterior view. 1947. Eduardo Luis Rodríguez Archive

the country's economic reality, and also by inexperience, which leaders attempted to overcome with the vehemence of their proposals.

The radical definitions established by the new government would lay the foundations for the suppression of the previously held conception of architecture as art, and for the emergence of a new type of revolutionary technician, working exclusively in service of the people. The politics of the new government in relation to culture were defined by its leader, Fidel Castro, in his 1961 speech known as "Palabras a los intelectuales" (Words to intellectuals): "Within the Revolution, everything; against the Revolution, nothing"—a demand that many found impossible to accept. The new rules dictated architectural practice, tacitly suppressing private practice and provoking massive dissent among the ranks of the most prestigious Cuban architects, many of whom went into exile. This schism, which occurred among all Cuban intellectuals, had all the elements of a cultural tragedy and was a loss of great proportions.

The architecture of the 1960s was largely defined by three aspects: the re-creation of familiar forms and solutions taken to an unprecedented scale; the popular character of urban and architectural endeavors; and the extreme politicization of professional practice. The major achievements of the period did not occur in conceptual terms but in formal ones: never before had Cuban architecture experienced such a boom in formal exploration and innovation, nor such inclusive programmatic diversity. Plans of extraordinary dimensions were implemented in housing, health, education and culture, gastronomic and commercial services, national tourism, recreation and sports, and industry, and nearly all of them produced outstanding architectural achievements.

This was a convulsive and contradictory era for the country. Important decisions and epic triumphs were frequently accompanied by significant errors in conception, perspective, planning, and execution. At the same time that extraordinary construction plans were being developed and works of excellent quality were being built in a timely fashion, the primary foundations were being laid for the dullness of design and construction that would be imposed the following decade, an architecture marked by reductionist pragmatism, simplification, and an exaggerated institutionalization that eliminated alternatives and, in particular, the creative freedom that had flourished during the first half of the 1960s.

The heroic optimism of the 1960s gave way, in the 1970s, to overbearing technocracy, a situation advanced by various factors: the irregular publication of the magazine *Arquitectura*, which in a nationalist gesture had changed its title to *Arquitectura Cuba*; the establishment of professional exchange with the Soviet Union and other socialist countries to replace those with the United States and Western Europe; the closing of the Colegio de Arquitectos in 1967, excising the heart of the professional class; the failure to complete highly symbolic works such as the Escuelas Nacionales de Arte; the inconceivable move, in 1964, of the architecture school from the main campus of the university, in the Vedado neighborhood, to the new school of technology under construction on the outskirts of the city; and the extreme centralization of all decisions related to architecture in the Ministerio de la Construcción. These facts marked the premature end of the 1960s and the arrival of a period in which quantity was only occasionally accompanied by quality, quite the opposite of the previous decade.

Nonetheless, even in the 1970s some valuable works were constructed, completing the panorama of an era marked by deficiencies that were compensated for by ingenious and unprecedented exuberance and some extraordinary formal achievements—all of it part of an attempt to materialize a utopia believed to be within reach.

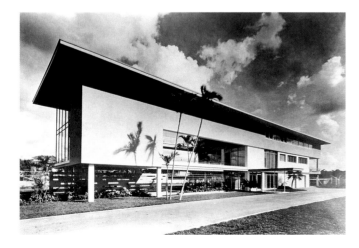

3. **House for José Noval Cueto, Havana. 1949.** Mario Romañach (Cuban, 1917–1984), Silverio Bosch (Cuban 1918–2005). **Exterior view. 1949.** Eduardo Luis Rodríguez Archive

4. **Tribunal de Cuentas (Office of the comptroller), Havana. 1953.** Aquiles Capablanca (Cuban, 1907–1962). **Exterior view. 1953.** Photograph by Constantino Arias

**Electrical and mechanical engineering workshops,
Universidad Católica de Santo Tomás de Villanueva, Havana. 1959**
Manuel R. Gutiérrez (Cuban, 1925–2006)

Above: View of the main facade. 1959. Eduardo Luis Rodríguez Archive

Right: View of the stairs. 1959. Eduardo Luis Rodríguez Archive

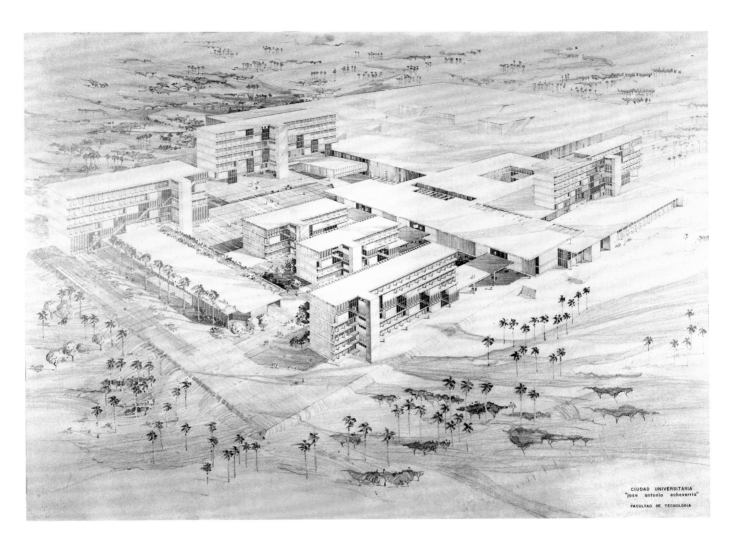

Aerial perspective of the campus. 1960. Pencil and ink on illustration board,
8 x 10 in. (20.3 x 25.4 cm). Eduardo Luis Rodríguez Archive

View of the Facultad de Ingeniería Civil. Eduardo Luis Rodríguez
Archive

View of a courtyard. 1964. Eduardo Luis Rodríguez Archive

Cuba Cabanas, Jibacoa. 1959
Antonio Quintana (Cuban, 1919–1993)
Residencial Yacht Club, Varadero. 1957
Nicolás Quintana (Cuban, 1925–2011)

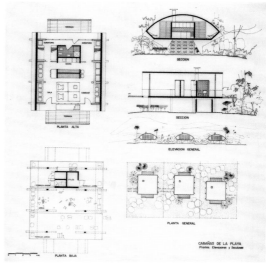

Above: Plans of the cabanas, sections and elevation of a single unit, and the site plan. Ink on paper, 23 ⅜ x 33 ⅛ in. (59.4 x 84.1 cm). 1959. Eduardo Luis Rodríguez Archive

Left: View from the beach. 1959. Eduardo Luis Rodríguez Archive

Aerial view of the yacht club. Eduardo Luis Rodríguez Archive

View of a gazebo and the main building at Santa Lucía. Eduardo Luis Rodríguez Archive

Perspective. Ink on paper, 20 x 30 in. (50.8 x 81.3 cm).
Eduardo Luis Rodríguez Archive

House for Timothy J. Ennis, Havana. 1957   Exterior view. 1957. Eduardo Luis Rodríguez Archive
Ricardo Porro (Cuban, 1925–2014)

House for Ana Carolina Font, Havana. 1956   Exterior view. 1957. Eduardo Luis Rodríguez
Mario Romañach (Cuban, 1917–1984)   **Archive**

Apartment building for Evangelina Aristigueta de Vidaña, Havana. 1956
Mario Romañach (Cuban, 1917–1984)

Exterior view. 1956. Eduardo Luis Rodríguez Archive

Apartment building for Isabel and Olga Pérez Farfante, Havana. 1955
Frank Martínez (Cuban, 1923–2011)

Exterior view. 1955. Photograph by Muñiz

Building for Seguro Médico, Havana. 1956–58 Exterior view. 1958. Eduardo Luis Rodríguez Archive
Antonio Quintana (Cuban, 1919–1993)

Unidad No. 1, La Habana del Este, Havana. 1959–61
Hugo D'Acosta (Cuban, 1932–2010)
Mario González (Cuban, 1931–2008)
with Julio Baldarón, Enrique Enríquez, Mercedes
Álvarez, Ana Vega, Héctor Carrillo Miyares, Eradia

Hurtado de Mendoza, Reynaldo Estévez, Eduardo
Rodríguez, Roberto Carranza, and others
Exterior view of the day care center and low- and
high-rise apartment buildings. 1961. Eduardo Luis
Rodríguez Archive

Among the many transformations brought about
by the Cuban Revolution, one of the most significant was a new and intense commitment to
social housing. Before 1959 government efforts
to house the less-well-off population were modest and infrequent, while interesting projects
in the tourist sector thrived, especially in the
Vedado neighborhood of Havana. Nevertheless,
some housing of superb quality was built before
the revolution, including Antonio Quintana's
building at the corner of calles 23 and 26 and the
FOCSA building by Ernesto Gómez Sampera.
The revolution provided the impetus to look into
large-scale solutions for the problem of housing,
and one of the most spectacular expressions
of this is the new urban quarter La Habana del
Este, on the eastern side of the harbor. This was
largely traditional in construction, but noteworthy experimental approaches to housing types
and construction methods, such as the prefabricated Multiflex system, were used in other
projects.   JFL

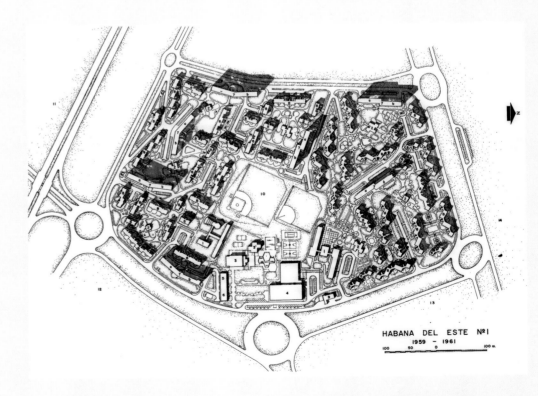

Site plan. 1959. Ink on paper, 23 ⅜ x 33 ⅛ in.
(59.4 x 84.1 cm). Eduardo Luis Rodríguez Archive

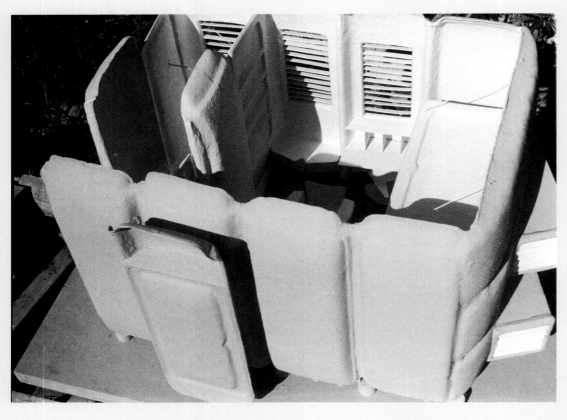

**Asbestos-cement housing module, various locations.
1964–68**
Hugo D'Acosta (Cuban, 1932–2010)
Mercedes Álvarez (Cuban, born 1931)

Prototype model. Plaster, wood, cardboard, and thread,
16 x 24 x 16 in (40.6 x 61 x 40.6 cm). Eduardo Luis
Rodríguez Archive

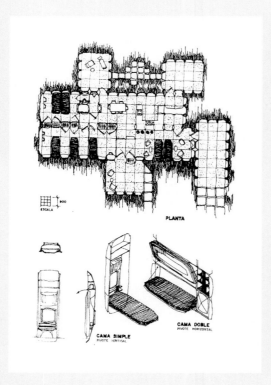

Far left: Plan of modular assembly with
built-in furniture. Ink on paper, 33 ⅛ x 23 ⅜ in.
(84.1 x 59.4 cm). Eduardo Luis Rodríguez
Archive

Left: Interior view. 1968. Eduardo Luis
Rodríguez Archive

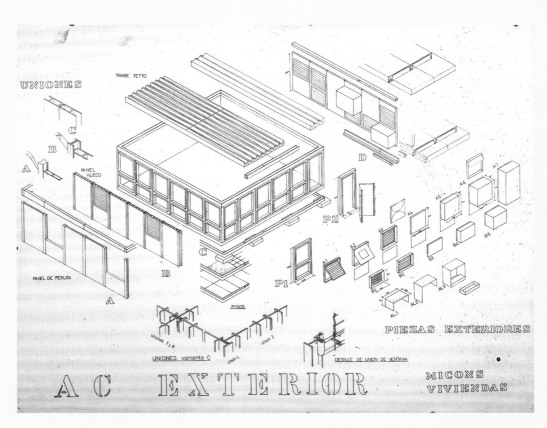

Multiflex system, Havana. 1965–70
Fernando Salinas (Cuban, 1930–1992)

Exploded axonometric diagram of prefabricated components and assembly. Ink on paper, 23 ⅜ x 33 ⅛ in. (59.4 x 84.1 cm). Eduardo Luis Rodríguez Archive

View from a courtyard. c. 1972. Photograph by Paolo Gasparini

Las Terrazas community, Sierra del Rosario, Pinar del Río. 1968–75

Mario Girona (Cuban, 1924–2008)

Osmany Cienfuegos (Cuban, born 1931)

Top left and right: Views from the lake. 1975. Eduardo Luis Rodríguez Archive

Above: Aerial view. 1975. Eduardo Luis Rodríguez Archive

Ángel Macías (Cuban)
Escuela Primaria Gustavo Pozo, Havana. 1963
Rafael Mirabal (Cuban, born 1931)

Exterior view of the kindergarten. 1959. Eduardo Luis Rodríguez Archive

Aerial view of circular primary-school classrooms and the central amphitheater. 1963.
Eduardo Luis Rodríguez Archive

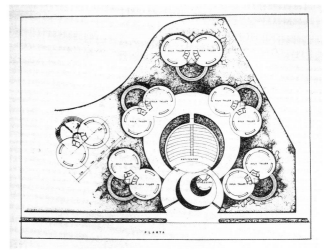

Site plan of the primary school. Eduardo Luis Rodríguez Archive

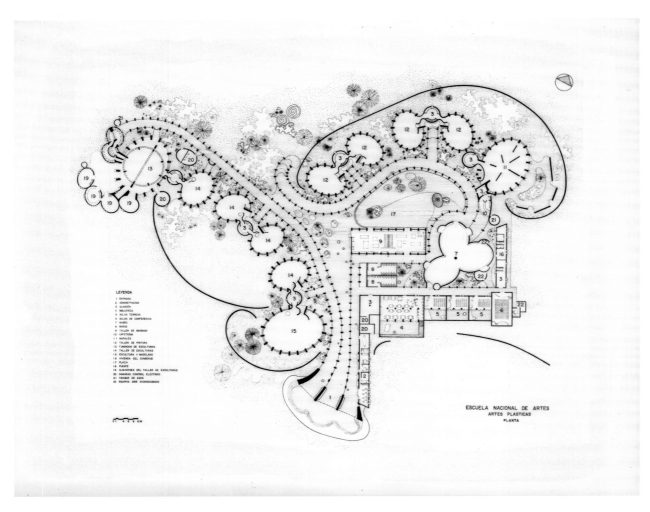

Plan. Ink on paper, 11 x 14 in. (27.9 x 35.6 cm). Eduardo Luis Rodríguez Archive

Aerial view. Vittorio Garatti Archive

View from the colonnade into the central courtyard. 1965.
Eduardo Luis Rodríguez Archive

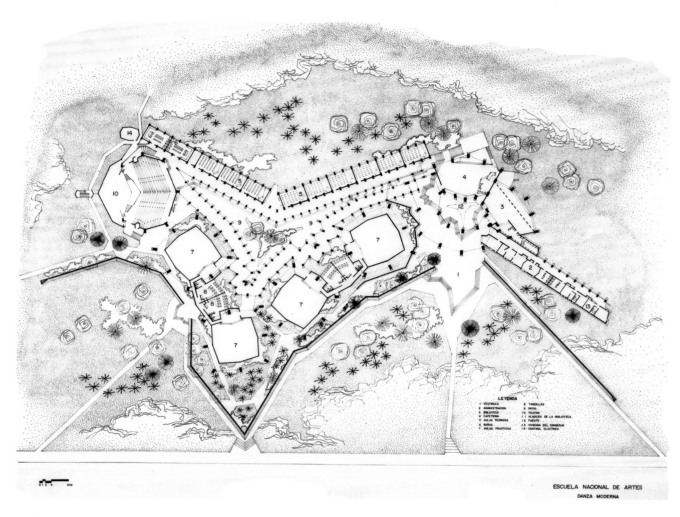

Plan. Ink on paper, 14 x 11 in. (35.6 x 27.9 cm). Eduardo Luis Rodríguez Archive

Aerial view of the school and surroundings. 1965. Eduardo Luis Rodríguez Archive

View of an interior courtyard. 1961. Photograph by Jorge Rigamonti

Site plan. Ink on paper, 23 ⅜ x 33 ⅛ in. (59.4 x 84.1 cm). Eduardo Luis Rodríguez Archive

Aerial view of the school and surroundings. 1965

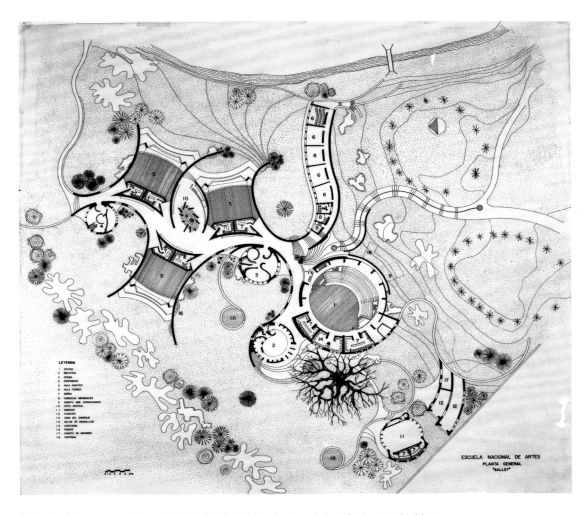

Site plan. Ink on paper, 23 ⅜ x 33 ⅛ in. (59.4 x 84.1 cm). Eduardo Luis Rodríguez Archive

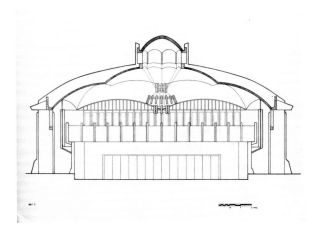

Section. Archive of Jorge Rigamonti

Detail of a dome. 1965

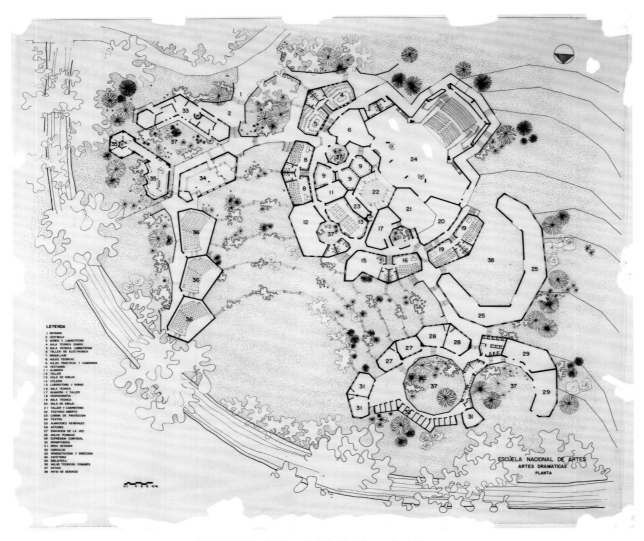

LEYENDA

1 ENTRADA
2 VESTÍBULO
3 SONIDO Y LUMINOTECNIA
4 AULA TEÓRICA SONIDO
5 AULA TEÓRICA LUMINOTECNIA
6 TALLER DE ELECTRÓNICA
7 MAQUILLAJE
8 AULAS TEÓRICAS
9 AULAS PRÁCTICAS Y CAMERINOS
10 VESTUARIO
11 ALMACÉN
12 TALLER
13 AULA DE DIBUJO
14 UTILERÍA
15 LABORATORIO Y HORNO
16 AULA TEÓRICA
17 ALMACÉN Y TALLER
18 ESCENOGRAFÍA
19 AULA TEÓRICA
20 AULA DE DIBUJO
21 TALLER Y CARPINTERÍA
22 TEATRINO ABIERTO
23 CABINA DE PROYECCIÓN
24 TEATRO
25 ALMACENES GENERALES
26 ACTORES
27 EDUCACIÓN DE LA VOZ
28 AULAS TEÓRICAS
29 EXPRESIÓN CORPORAL
30 DRAMATURGO
31 MESA REDONDA
32 CURRÍCULUM
33 ADMINISTRACIÓN Y DIRECCIÓN
34 CAFETERÍA
35 BIBLIOTECA
36 AULAS TEÓRICAS COMUNES
37 PATIOS
38 PATIO DE SERVICIO

ESCUELA NACIONAL DE ARTES
ARTES DRAMATICAS
PLANTA

Site plan. Ink on paper, 23 ⅜ x 33 ⅛ in. (59.4 x 84.1 cm). Eduardo Luis Rodríguez Archive

View of the school roofs. 1964. Eduardo Luis Rodríguez Archive

Parque de los Mártires Universitarios, Havana. 1967 **Cuba** 211

Emilio Escobar (Cuban, born Peru. 1934–2008)
Mario Coyula (Cuban, 1935–2014)
Sonia Domínguez (Cuban, born 1935)
Armando Hernández (Cuban, 1933–1998)

View of the park from a neighboring building. Eduardo Luis Rodríguez Archive

Emilio Escobar and Mario Coyula's monument to the university martyrs, one of the first monuments constructed after Fidel Castro came to power, commemorates, among other lives, those of the students who confronted the Batista regime's army on March 13, 1957. Inaugurated on the tenth anniversary of the uprising, the monument is at once an urban design project and an element that constructs the heroic history of the revolution. The brilliant design, poised between abstraction and representation, merges sculpture and landscape in a work that evokes both acropolis and ceremonial frieze. The walls of various heights—sometimes jagged, sometimes undulating—create a free-form plaza set beneath a plantation of trees; they are formed of poured concrete, with surfaces textured by the addition of jute sacks and empty paper bags to evoke the clothes of the students.   BB

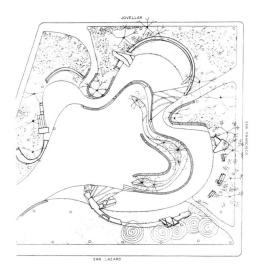

Right: Site plan. Ink on paper, 33 ⅛ x 23 ⅜ in.
(84.1 x 59.4 cm). Eduardo Luis Rodríguez Archive

View from the intersection of Calle L and Avenida 23. 1966. Eduardo Luis Rodríguez Archive

Interior view. 1966. Eduardo Luis Rodríguez Archive

Exterior view. Eduardo Luis Rodríguez Archive

View of the main entrance. Eduardo Luis Rodríguez Archive

Exterior view, 1968

Cuba's first major international representation of itself after the revolution was a pavilion at Expo 67 in Montreal, tellingly set on the fairgrounds within view of both the Soviet and the US pavilions. The design by Sergio Baroni and Vittorio Garatti, chosen in a national competition in 1965, was interpreted by the press as both Cubist work of architecture and evidence of Cuba's growing interest in prefabrication. The structure was a hybrid of steel frame and vinyl-coated aluminum panels, with highlights picked out in brightly colored elements including blue Perspex portholes and triangular skylights. Inside, the pavilion provided a dynamic scaffold for large-scale photographs of the revolution's progress and posters, designed by Enrique Fuentes, celebrating Cuban advances and vilifying American imperialism. Musicians and artists—including the team of Soviet and Cuban filmmakers who made *Soy Cuba* (*I Am Cuba*), (1967)—collaborated on an interior every bit as hip and psychedelic as anything the capitalist West had to offer. In addition to exhibitions on Cuban economy, industry, education, medical care, and social welfare, visitors were invited to a canalside Cuban café featuring rum, cigars, fresh Cuban fish, and Cuban music. The pavilion was heavily criticized by anti-Castro forces in Canada, but it was nevertheless one of the exhibition's most popular installations.   BB

View of the exhibition. 1967

Exterior view at night. 1967

Interior view. 1967

Display of political posters. 1967

Throughout the history of Mexico, and particularly in the twentieth century, architects have sought forms with which to express the nation's character. The construction boom of the *paz porfiriana*, a period of stability and growth during the long presidency of Porfirio Díaz, from 1876 to 1910, ended abruptly in 1910 with the start of the revolution, and building largely came to a halt. This rupture, however, helped to make a break with historical models, and what emerged was a social movement that favored a full entry into modernity. In both design and pedagogy the ideas of José Villagrán García, who is widely held to be the father of contemporary Mexican architecture, were paramount.[1] Villagrán García became a professor at the architecture school at the Universidad Nacional Autónoma de México (UNAM), in Mexico City, in 1924, and he designed the Granja Sanitaria de Popotla (Institute of hygiene), Mexico's first modern building, in 1925.

Among Villagrán's first students were Enrique del Moral, Juan O'Gorman, Juan Legarreta, and Enrique Yáñez, who with Villagrán constituted the vanguard of functionalism and sought to address the principal shortages in society—housing, education, and health care—with a sense of responsibility and a desire for innovation. O'Gorman and Legarreta, in particular, proposed a radical socially engaged architecture, which they outlined in the lecture series known as the "Pláticas sobre arquitectura del 1933."[2] Although O'Gorman was known for his functionalist houses for Diego Rivera and Frida Kahlo in San Ángel (fig. 1), his significant finished projects include many schools, and both he and Legarreta built workers' housing complexes. In this same period, buildings for both government agencies and emerging bourgeoisie were designed in a local variant of Art Deco, in which neoindigenism coexisted with contemporary neocolonial, although the precepts of functionalism were never fully abandoned. Among the architects who gained prominence in this era were Carlos Obregón Santacilia, Juan Segura, and Francisco Serrano, as well as Manuel Amábilis and Federico Mariscal.

In 1940, with Mexico's economy strengthened by the nationalization of oil and the growth of industry, architects began to favor industrially produced materials at the same time as the general public became interested in modern architecture. Several key works from this period significantly changed the profile of Mexico's principal cities. State-sponsored building programs for schools and hospitals emerged, with the Comité Administrador del Programa Federal de Construcción de Escuelas and the Plan de Construcción de Hospitales.[3] The first housing complexes were also built around this time, among them Mario Pani's Centros Urbanos Presidente Miguel Alemán and Benito Juárez, in Mexico City, both of them

Mexico Pavilion, XIV Triennale di Milano. 1968. Eduardo Terrazas (Mexican, born 1936). Interior view with design based on Olympic logo by Lance Wyman and printed matter by Beatrice Trueblood. 1968

characterized by their suitable combination of International Style with a Mexican way of life (fig. 2).[4]

The International Style provided the template for some of the most innovative Mexican architecture of the 1950s. Augusto H. Álvarez, with his Latinoamericana de Seguros tower in Mexico City (fig. 3), and Juan Sordo Madaleno, with a variety of hotels, have the distinction of being its earliest adopters, followed by Ramón Torres, Héctor Velázquez, Enrique Carral, Ricardo de Robina, and Francisco Artigas.[5] Reinaldo Pérez Rayón proposed an architecture that relied on prefabricated elements. The Celanese Mexicana building (1966–68), by Ricardo Legorreta, is distinguished by a hanging structure that made use of advanced technologies. And the Casa Torres (1960), by Torres and Velázquez, is but one example of how modernism redefined Mexican domestic architecture.

A group of architects began to explore technical and design solutions in their responses to this international tendency, among them Pani, del Moral, Enrique de la Mora, Pedro Ramírez Vázquez, Alejandro Prieto, Héctor Mestre, and Jorge González Reyna. In their works from the 1950s and '60s they employed different modes of expression to overcome the impersonal aspect of international architecture. One such mode was *integración plástica* (integration of the arts), which united buildings with works by important visual artists; one of the most significant examples was perhaps that of UNAM's main campus (1947–54), which, following Pani and del Moral's master plan, united many architects and artists in a plurality of specific expressions.[6] This magnum opus marked a decisive moment in the history of Mexican architecture, representing the pinnacle of one style of construction and the beginning of another.

Other projects that employed *integración plástica* are the Museo Nacional de Antropología (1964), in Mexico City, by Ramírez Vázquez with Jorge Campuzano and Rafael Mijares, which combines archeological richness with contemporary art, and the Centro Médico Nacional (1961), for which Yáñez directed a team of architects and artists. The works proposed by Pani and his Taller de Urbanismo (Urban-planning workshop) show an adequate relationship between architecture and urban planning; these

2. **Centro Urbano Presidente Alemán, Mexico City. 1947–49.** Mario Pani (Mexican, 1911–1993), Salvador Ortega (Mexican, 1920–1972), Bernardo Quintana (Mexican, 1919–1984). Aerial view. 1949. Photograph by Compañía Mexicana Aerofoto, S.A. Archivo histórico Compañía Mexicana Aerofoto (FICA)

projects ranged from large-scale housing complexes, such as the Conjunto Urbano Nonoalco-Tlatelolco (1960–64), to plans for Mexican cities on the US border, through the Programa Nacional Fronterizo (National border program).

The second mode of counteracting the impersonality of modernist architecture is typified in the thin shell roof developed by the Spanish émigré Félix Candela, who arrived with many European architects displaced by the Spanish Civil War and World War II. This type of structure is an example of an element that created novel and unique forms within modernist structures, in both industrial buildings, such as his bottling plant for Bacardí (fig. 4) and churches such as Nuestra Señora de la Soledad (1955–56), San Antonio de

1. **Casa Estudio Diego Rivera y Frida Kahlo, Mexico City. 1931.** Juan O'Gorman (Mexican, 1905–1982). View of the northern facade. 1932. Photograph by César Flores. Architecture & Design Study Center, The Museum of Modern Art, New York

las Huertas (1956), and La Virgen de la Medalla Milagrosa de San Vicente de Paúl (1960), all three of them collaborations with de la Mora. One of Candela's last projects, designed with Enrique Castañeda Tamborrel and Antonio Peyri, is the Palacio de los Deportes (Sports palace), built for the 1968 Olympics, which has a copper geodesic roof that was ahead of its time.

The third mode of expression seeks national identity through the values of traditional Mexican architecture. Luis Barragán and some of his contemporaries who in the 1940s proposed that a refinement of popular architecture could be combined with great simplicity.[7] Barragán's houses and his chapel for the Capuchinas Sacramentarias (1955) are excellent examples of his expressive style; his contributions to landscape architecture, in urban developments such as the Jardines del Pedregal (1945–50) and other residential subdivisions such as Las Arboledas (1958), are original statements.

In the atmosphere of the student uprisings and Tlatelolco massacre of 1968, and of these events' concurrence with the Olympics, various new architectural themes came to the fore. The common denominator for the projects of this era is a privileging of the particularities of site and user, while nonetheless producing a distinctive language. Some works signaled this new, engaged approach, including the Colegio de México (1974–76), by Teodoro González de León and Abraham Zabludovsky; the Hotel Camino Real (1968), by Legorreta Arquitectos; brick religious buildings by Carlos Mijares; and houses by José Antonio Attolini Lack. Agustín Hernández's firm, with its interest in advanced technologies and a formalism inspired by the pre-Hispanic, is notable for works like the Heroico Colegio Militar (1971–76), designed in collaboration with Manuel González Rul, as well as some of the proposals of Juan José Díaz Infante and Castañeda Tamborrel.

It is possible to appreciate the richness and originality of the works throughout the twentieth century of Mexican architects who have, in the majority of cases, sought a singular expression. A diverse range of designers was capable of responding to the necessities of both sites and their inhabitants, with appropriate material and aesthetic solutions, while always keeping an open door on their creativity.

1   See various articles by José Villagrán García titled "Apuntes para un estudio," in *Arquitectura/México*, July 1939 and subsequent dates. Reprinted in *Teoría de la arquitectura* (Mexico City: INBA, 1963).

2   *Pláticas sobre arquitectura*, reprint ed. (1934; Mexico City: INBA, 2001).

3   CAPFCE was founded in 1942, under the leadership of Villagrán, José Luis Cuevas, Mario Pani, and Enrique Yáñez. In that same year Villagrán and Dr. Salvador Zubirán established the Seminario de Estudios Hospitalarios. See Comité Administrador del Programa Federal de Construcción de Escuelas, *Memoria* (Mexico City: SEP, c. 1947); and *Arquitectura/México*, no. 15 (1944).

4   Pani, *Los multifamiliares de pensiones* (Mexico City: Editorial Arquitectura, 1952).

5   For a long time this was the tallest building in Mexico City, with a foundation design and antiseismic structure engineered by Adolfo and Leonardo Zeevart.

6   Pani and Enrique del Moral, *La construcción de la Ciudad Universitaria del Pedregal* (Mexico City: UNAM, 1979).

7   UNESCO has designated Casa Barragán (1950) and the Ciudad Universitaria at UNAM (1952) World Heritage sites.

Factory for Barcardí, Mexico City. 1960. Félix Candela (Mexican, born Spain. 1910–1997). View of the factory floor

3. **Torre Latinoamericana de Seguros, Mexico City. 1946–56.** Augusto H. Álvarez (Mexican, 1914–1995). Perspective, drawn by Luis González. 1952. Watercolor on cardboard, 40 3/16 × 29 15/16 in. (102 × 76 cm). Colección Torre Latinoamericana

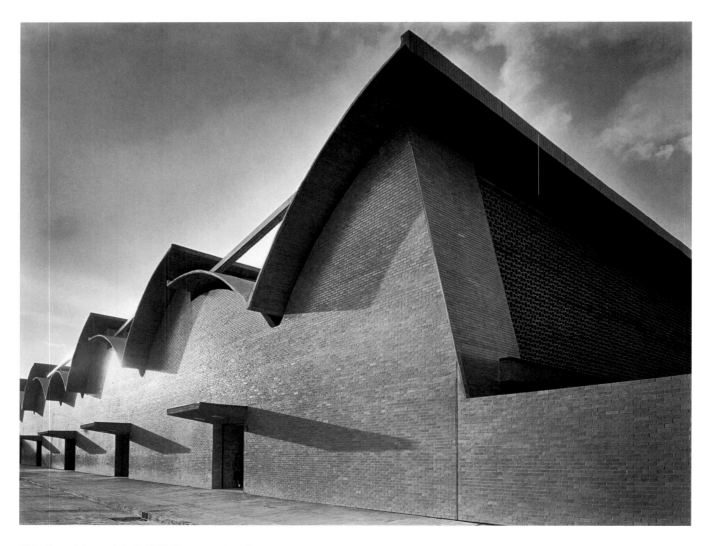

Side view of the main hall. 1957. Photograph by Guillermo Zamora. Archivo Enrique del Moral. DACPAI, INBA

View of the main hall's central axis. 1957. Photograph by Guillermo Zamora

View of the main hall from the west, showing openwork masonry of hollow bricks. c. 1957. Photograph by Armando Salas Portugal. Fundación Salas Portugal, Mexico

Alejandro Zohn (Mexican, born Austria. 1930–2000)
Mercado Municipal, San Juan de los Lagos. 1967–68
Salvador de Alba (Mexican, 1926–1998)

View of the Mercado Libertad from Avenida Juárez-Mina. 1958

Interior view of the Mercado Libertad. 1958

Interior view of the Mercado Municipal. 1968

Aerial view of Las Arboledas and Los Clubes. c. 1957. Cut-and-pasted paper and ink on black-and-white print, 10 x 13 ³⁄₁₆ in. (25.4 x 33.5 cm). Barragan Foundation, Switzerland

Study for freeway access to the development. Watercolor, ink, and colored pencil on cardboard, 30 x 23 ³⁄₈ in. (76 x 59.4 cm). Barragan Foundation, Switzerland

View of the Fuente del Bebedero (Fountain of the trough). Photograph by Armando Salas Portugal. Armando Salas Portugal Collection, Barragan Foundation, Switzerland

Study for the Muro Rojo (Red wall). Ink and colored pencil on transparent paper, 11 ⅞ x 17 ¾ in. (30 x 45 cm).
Barragan Foundation, Switzerland

View of the Muro Rojo. 1958. Photograph by Armando Salas Portugal.
Armando Salas Portugal Collection, Barragan Foundation, Switzerland

Perspective view of El Ziggurat. Cut-and-pasted paper on cardboard, 23 ⅝ x 20 in. (60 x 50.8 cm). Barragan Foundation, Switzerland

Louis I. Kahn, after seeing Luis Barragán's garden work at El Pedregal in Elizabeth Kassler's 1964 book *Modern Gardens and the Landscape*, invited Barragán to consult on the outdoor spaces of his Salk Institute in La Jolla, then nearing completion. Barragán famously met Kahn and Jonas Salk at the construction site and, to Kahn's proposal for rows of trees flanking a central strip of water, responded, "I would not put a tree or blade of grass in this space. This should be plaza of stone, not a garden." He went on to say, "If you make this a plaza, you will gain a facade—a facade to the sky."   BB

Perspective sketch of the Salk Institute courtyard. Pencil and felt-tip pen on paper, 12 x 18 in. (30.3 x 45.8 cm). Barragan Foundation, Switzerland

Perspective sketch of El Palomar's dovecote tower. Pencil
and colored pencil on cardboard, 16 x 11 in. (40.8 x 28 cm).
Barragan Foundation, Switzerland

Perspective view of the Torres de Satélite. Chalk on cardboard,
28 ¼ x 28 ¾ in. (71.9 x 73 cm). Barragan Foundation, Switzerland

Aerial view of the Torres de Satélite. c. 1958. Photograph by
Compañía Mexicana Aerofoto, S.A. Fototeca Tecnológico de
Monterrey

View of the facade. c. 1964. Photograph by Guillermo Zamora. Archivo de Arquitectos Mexicanos, Facultad de Arquitectura, Universidad Nacional Autónoma de México

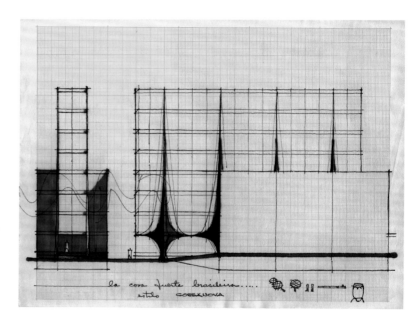

Alternative elevation. 1961. Ink on graph paper, 8 ⁷⁄₁₆ × 11 in. (21.5 × 28 cm). Archivo de Arquitectos Mexicanos, Fondo Augusto H. Álvarez, Facultad de Arquitectura, Universidad Nacional Autónoma de México

The Jaysour building, a veritable symbol of Augusto H. Álvarez's fidelity to the principles of International Style, is widely recognized as one of the finest works of his long career. Álvarez first established his credentials as an architect of high-rises with the Torre Latinoamericana (1946–56), at the time the tallest building in Latin America. Jaysour, by contrast, is of modest height but of far greater refinement, with Mexican architecture's first large-scale curtain wall, created with fine aluminum sections. The building's composition of two separate volumes—a four-story, L-shaped block and a nineteen-story tower without setbacks—which define an urban plaza along the prestigious Paseo de la Reforma, has often been compared to Ludwig Mies van der Rohe's Seagram Building in New York (1958), although in the Jaysour building the aesthetic is crystalline rather than tectonic. In one drawing Álvarez imagines what the building would look like if executed in the new inverted-column style of Oscar Niemeyer's Palácio da Alvorada (1956–58), in Brasília.   BB

Office and commercial building, Mexico City. 1958–59 **Mexico** 227
Augusto H. Álvarez (Mexican, 1914–1995)
Germán Herrasti (Mexican)
Building for the Banco del Valle de México, Mexico City. 1958
Augusto H. Álvarez (Mexican, 1914–1995)

Perspective of the office building, drawn by Ricardo Flores Villasana.
1958–59. Mixed mediums on paper, 17 15/16 x 23 15/16 in. (45.6 x 60.8 cm).
Archivo de Arquitectos Mexicanos, Facultad de Arquitectura, Fondo
Augusto H. Álvarez, Universidad Nacional Autónoma de México

Exterior view of the bank at night. 1958. Photograph by Guillermo Zamora.
Archivo de Arquitectos Mexicanos, Facultad de Arquitectura, Fondo
Augusto H. Álvarez, Universidad Nacional Autónoma de México

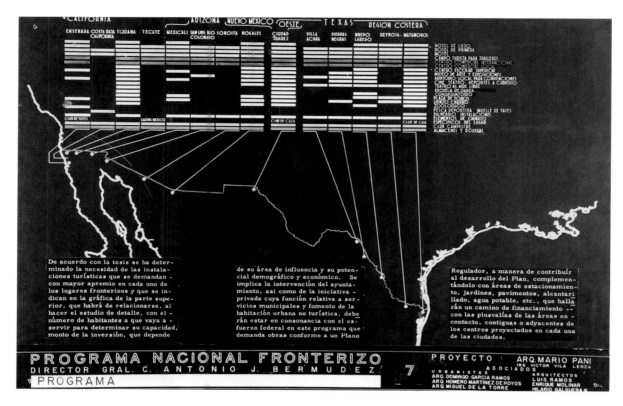

Presentation board. 1961. 8 ½ x 11 ½ in. (21.5 x 29 cm). Fototeca Tecnológico de Monterrey

In 1961 the Mexican President Adolfo López Mateos launched the ambitious Programa Nacional Fronterizo (National border program) to reinvigorate the northern region along the border of the United States. US labor policies during World War II had drawn many Mexicans northward, leading to housing shortages and spectacular population growth. Directed by the architect Mario Pani and the Taller de Urbanismo, the program was meant to extend at a regional scale the lessons of integrated development that had been applied in the 1950s in such large projects as the Universidad Nacional Autónoma de México (National autonomous university of Mexico). To create jobs as well as an enhanced sense of national culture, PRONAF provided funds for cultural and entertainment centers along the border, focusing its efforts on such important cities as Piedras Negras, Mexicali, Tijuana, Nuevo Laredo, Matamoros, and Ciudad Juárez. Pedro Ramírez Vázquez designed several key buildings. In the 1960s he emerged as a major architect of Mexican cultural institutions, in the renowned Museo Nacional de Antropología and Museo de Arte Moderno in Mexico City, and, in collaboration with Rafael Mijares, the dramatic convention center and adjacent museum in Ciudad Juárez. Here, as in Mexico City's museum, the whole complex was placed under a dome of experimental translucent plastic, 92 feet (28 meters) in diameter. The border itself was reconceived to provide a more positive image of Mexico, notably the great vaulted gateway at Nogales–Sonora, on the Arizona border, designed by Pani.   BB

Convention center, Ciudad Juárez. 1961–63. Mario Pani (Mexican, 1911–1993), Luis Ramos Cunningham (Mexican, 1948–1973). Exterior view. Fototeca Tecnológico de Monterrey

Museo de Arte de Ciudad Juárez. 1964. Pedro Ramírez Vázquez (Mexican, 1919–2013). Exterior view. Photograph by Armando Salas Portugal

Customs and immigration building, Nogales. 1963. Mario Pani (Mexican, 1911–1993), Hilario Galguera (Mexican, 1948–1965). Exterior view. Fototeca Tecnológico de Monterrey

José Antonio Attolini Lack (Mexican, 1931–2012)

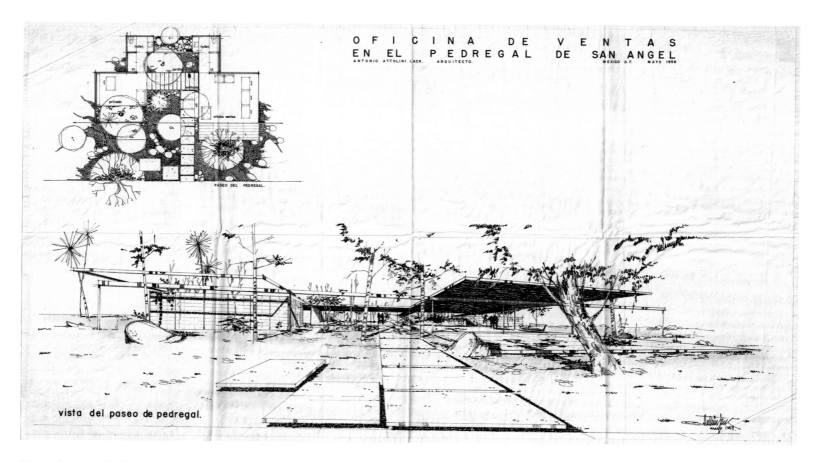

Plan and perspective from Paseo del Pedregal. Ink on paper, 20 1/16 × 35 7/16 in. (51 × 90 cm).
The Museum of Modern Art, New York. Gift of Carmen Pesqueira de Attolini

Exterior view. 1958. Photograph by Roberto Luna

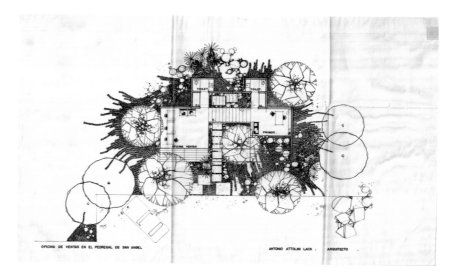

Site plan. 1958. Ink on paper, 14 15/16 × 24 3/16 in. (38 × 61.5 cm). The Museum
of Modern Art, New York. Gift of Carmen Pesqueira de Attolini

Exterior view. 1958. Photograph by Roberto Luna

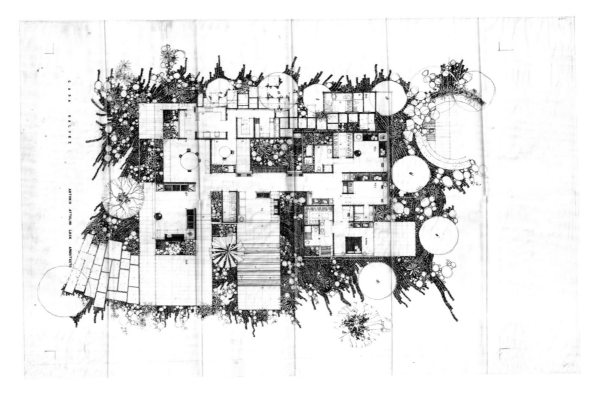

Site plan. Ink on paper, 23 ¹³⁄₁₆ × 35 ¹⁄₁₆ in. (60.5 × 89 cm). The Museum of Modern Art, New York. Gift of Carmen Pesqueira de Attolini

Pedro Ramírez Vázquez (Mexican, 1919–2013)
Rafael Mijares (Mexican, born 1924)
Jorge Campuzano (Mexican, born 1931)

View of the courtyard and fountain. 1964. Photograph by Armando Salas Portugal. Fundación Salas Portugal, México

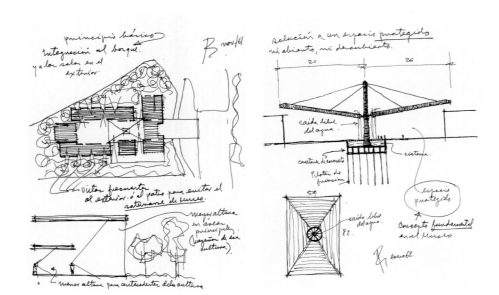

Sketches of the site plan and monumental canopy. 1961–62.
Ink on two pieces of paper, overall: 13 ½ x 21 in. (34.3 x 53.3 cm)

Perspective, showing the facade. 1963. Colored ink on paper, 9 × 24 in. (22.9 × 61 cm)

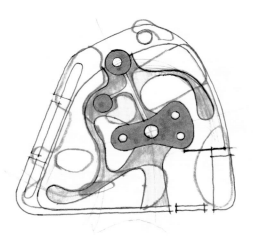

Early study for the site plan (detail). 1963. Ink on tracing paper, 9 × 12 in. (22.9 × 30.5 cm)

View from the garden. 1964. Photograph by Armando Salas Portugal. Fundación Salas Portugal, México

Pedro Ramírez Vázquez (Mexican, 1919–2013)

Presentation board for the XII Triennale di Milano, with photographs by Nacho López. 1960.
Ink and photographs on paper, 18 ⅛ x 18 ⅛ in (46.1 x 46.1 cm)

Jaime Torres Bodet, the secretary of education during the presidency of Adolfo López Mateos, launched a program to reverse dramatically the illiteracy of the rural population, which was estimated to be more than seventy-five percent among Mexico's indigenous peoples. Central to the program's success was a lightweight prefabricated *aula-casa*, a building that would house a large classroom and adjacent teacher's dwelling under a single roof, which would become the hallmark of the Comité Federal de Escuelas. Conceived by Pedro Ramírez Vázquez with Ramiro González del Sordo and the engineer Elias Macotela García, the building consisted of a prefabricated metallic armature weighing less than 110 pounds (50 kilograms), which could be adapted to different regions and climates by accepting exterior walls and interior panels of locally available materials. In the first years of the program more than 35,000 schools were built in the most impoverished regions of Mexico, and the project was displayed at the Milan Triennial in 1960, where it was awarded the Gran Premio. In the following years more than 150,000 units were sold in some seventeen countries, not only in Latin America but also to India, Indonesia, Italy, and Yugoslavia.   BB

Promotional flyer for a rural schoolhouse in Tabaso, with photographs by Nacho López. 1958–60

View of a rural schoolhouse, Narayana Villas, Vadodara, India. 1964

View of a rural schoolhouse, Tlaxcala. 1960. Photograph by Nacho López

Nuevo Club de Yates de Acapulco. 1955
Mario Pani (Mexican, 1911–1993)
Salvador Ortega (Mexican, 1920–1972)
Chapel of Nuestra Señora de la Soledad (El Altillo), Mexico City. 1955–56
Enrique de la Mora (Mexican, 1907–1978)
Félix Candela (Mexican, born Spain. 1910–1997)

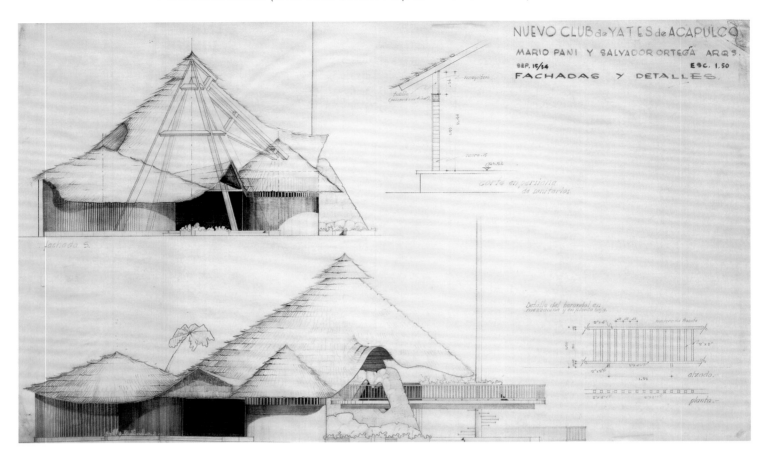

Elevations and sectional detail of the construction system for the yacht club. 1955. Pencil on vellum, 20 ¹³⁄₁₆ × 34 ¹³⁄₁₆ in. (52.9 × 88.5 cm). Archivo de Arquitectos Mexicanos, Fondo Mario Pani, Facultad de Arquitectura, Universidad Nacional Autónoma de México

Exterior view of the chapel. 1956. Archivo de Arquitectos Mexicanos, Facultad de Arquitectura, Universidad Nacional Autónoma de México

View of the chapel's roof during construction. 1955. Archivo de Arquitectos Mexicanos, Facultad de Arquitectura, Universidad Nacional Autónoma de México

Félix Candela (Mexican, born Spain. 1910–1997)
Enrique Casteñeda (Mexican, 1917–1977)
Antonio Peyri (Mexican)

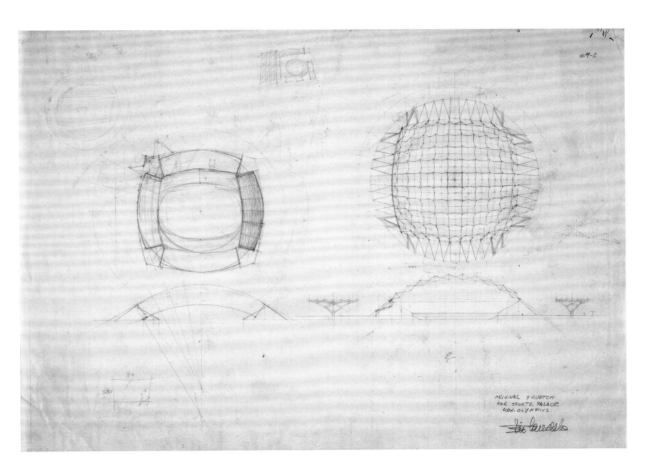

Floor plan, roof plan, and sections. Ink on paper, 16 ¼ x 22 ½ in. (41.9 x 58.4 cm).
Avery Architectural and Fine Arts Library, Columbia University, New York

Aerial view. 1968. Photograph by Armando Salas Portugal. Fundación Salas
Portugal, México

Hotel Camino Real, Mexico City. 1968
Hotel Camino Real, Ixtapa. 1981
Ricardo Legorreta (Mexican, 1931–2011)

View of the entrance and patio, Mexico City. 1968. Photograph by Armando Salas Portugal. Fundación Salas Portugal, México

View of the front gate designed by Mathias Goeritz, Mexico City. 1968. Photograph by Armando Salas Portugal. Fundación Salas Portugal, México

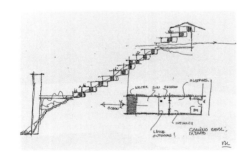

View of the hotel from the beach, Ixtapa. 1981. Photograph by Armando Salas Portugal. Fundación Salas Portugal, México

Top: Section sketch of the Ixtapa hotel. 1981. Ink on paper, 11 11/16 x 16 9/16 in. (29.7 x 42 cm)

Above: Aerial view of hotel balconies, Ixtapa. 1981

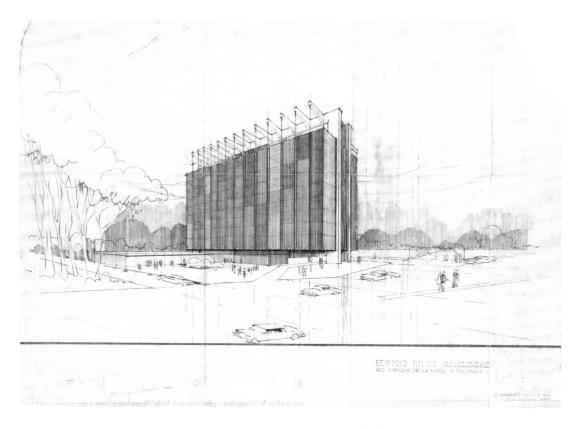

Perspective of Edificio Elite. Pencil and sanguine on paper, 18 x 24 in. (45.2 x 61.1 cm). Archivo de Arquitectos Mexicanos, Facultad de Arquitectura, Universidad Nacional Autónoma de México

Three views of the Celanese Mexicana building during construction and one view of the completed exterior. 1968. Photographs by Kati Horna

Unidad Habitacional La Patera. 1969
Abraham Zabludovsky (Mexican, born Poland.
1924–2003)

Exterior view. Archivo de Arquitectos Mexicanos,
Facultad de Arquitectura, Universidad Nacional
Autónoma de México

Villa Olímpica, Mexico City. 1968
Héctor Velázquez-Moreno (Mexican, 1922–2006)
Ramón Torres Martínez (Mexican, born 1924)
Agustín Hernández (Mexican, born 1924)
Manuel González Rul (Mexican, 1923–1985)
Carlos Ortega Flores (Mexican)

Exterior view. 1973. Photograph by Julius Shulman
for the *Los Angeles Times*. Julius Shulman
Photography Archive, Research Library at the Getty
Research Institute, Los Angeles

Unidad Habitacional El Rosario, Mexico City. 1976

Ricardo Legorreta (Mexican, 1931–2011)

Left and above: Two views of the courtyard. 1975. Photograph by Julius Shulman for the *Los Angeles Times*. Julius Shulman Photography Archive, Research Library at the Getty Research Institute, Los Angeles

Flores Magón community-built housing, Guadalajara. 1976

Alejandro Zohn (Mexican, born Austria. 1930–2000)

View of an internal walkway. c. 1976

**Conjunto Urbano Nonoalco-Tlatelolco, Mexico City.
1960–64**

Mario Pani (Mexican, 1911–1993)
Luis Ramos Cunningham (Mexican, 1948–1973)

View of the Plaza de las Tres Culturas. 1964.
Photograph by Armando Salas Portugal
Fundación Salas Portugal, México

View of the archeological zone, church of Santiago
de Tlatelolco, and Plaza de las Tres Culturas. 1964.
Fototeca Tecnológico de Monterrey

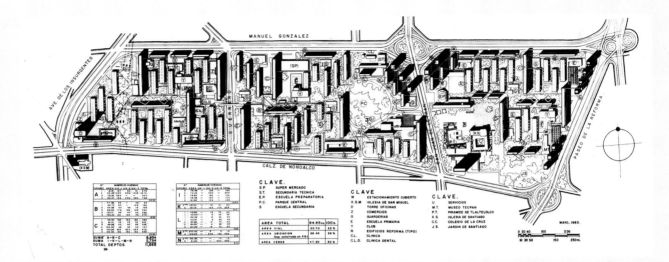

Site plan. 1964. Ink on paper, 3 15/16 x 9 ¾ in. (10 x 24.8 cm). Fototeca Tecnológico de Monterrey

View of a covered corridor. c. 1964. Photograph by Guillermo Zamora. Fototeca Tecnológico de Monterrey

Guadalupe Victoria housing block. 1964. Photograph by Guillermo Zamora. Fototeca Tecnológico de Monterrey

In the late 1950s and early 1960s, the Dirección General de Pensiones Civiles developed a series of housing estates of exceptional scale and quality, designed by Mario Pani. Along with other national and municipal institutions, it sought solutions for the population's urgent housing needs, one of the promises of the Mexican Revolution. Precedents for low-cost housing included the projects of Juan O'Gorman and Juan Legarreta for Mexico City from the 1930s and '40s, but it wasn't until the Fondo de Operación y Financiamiento Bancario de la Vivienda was created, in 1963, that an institution was dedicated solely to this purpose. In 1972 the influential Institutio del Fondo Nacional de la Vivienda was created to the same end.

Among the period's noteworthy efforts is the housing built for the 1968 Olympic Games in Mexico City, which includes twenty-nine midrise towers with 905 apartments for athletes and other visitors. Another is the El Rosario housing complex, with more than 10,000 dwellings on an 865-acre site. The Nonoalco-Tlatelolco complex has more than 11,000 units and also includes shopping and other services for a self-sufficient community. The design incorporates colonial and pre-Columbian monuments that were already on the site, including the base of a stepped pyramid and a large sixteenth-century church; the area with the monuments (plus an administrative tower) was renamed the Plaza de las Tres Culturas, which became the infamous site of the violent suppression of a student uprising in the months before the opening of the 1968 Olympics.   JFL

View of a courtyard. 1977. Photograph by Julius Shulman. Julius Shulman Photography
Archive, Research Library at the Getty Research Institute, Los Angeles

Above: View of the main entrance. 1981. Photograph by Julius Shulman. Julius Shulman Photography Archive, Research Library at the Getty Research Institute, Los Angeles

Above right: View from Chapultepec Park. 1981. Photograph by Julius Shulman. Julius Shulman Photography Archive, Research Library at the Getty Research Institute, Los Angeles

View of the central hall and atrium. 1981. Photograph by Julius Shulman. Julius Shulman Photography Archive, Research Library at the Getty Research Institute, Los Angeles

Agustín Hernández (Mexican, born 1924)

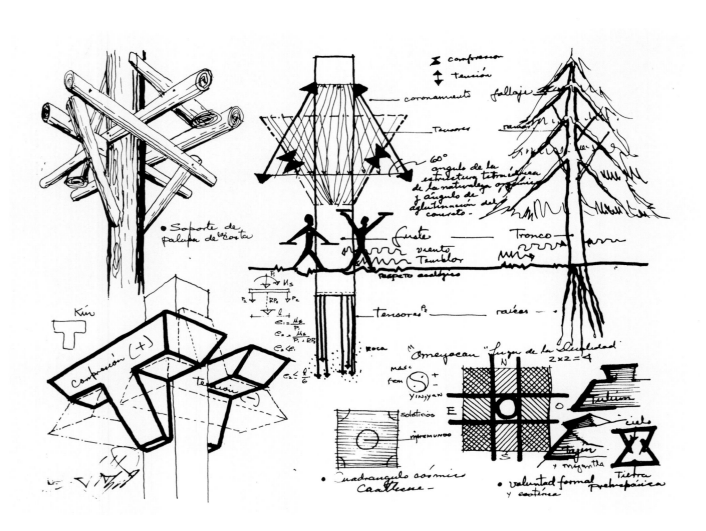

Conceptual sketches. 1973–75. Ink on paper, 8 ¼ x 11 ¹¹⁄₁₆ in. (21 x 29.7 cm).
Musée National d'Art Moderne, Centre de Création Industrielle, Centre
Pompidou, Paris. Gift of the architect

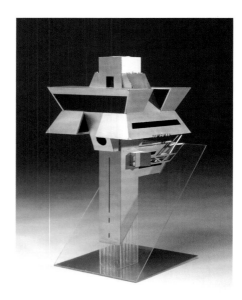

Model. 1975. Mat board, paper, and balsa wood with acrylic
silver paint, 27 x 17 x 13 in. (69 x 44 x 33.2 cm). Musée National
d'Art Moderne, Centre de Création Industrielle, Centre Pompidou,
Paris. Gift of the architect

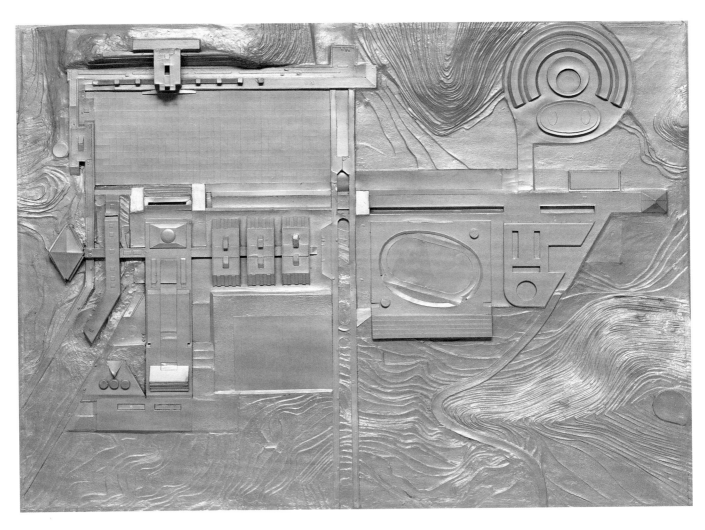

Model. 1976. Mat board, paper, and balsa wood with acrylic silver paint,
5 ⅞ × 35 ⁷⁄₁₆ × 47 ¼ in. (15 × 90 × 120 cm). The Museum of Modern Art, New York.
Gift of the the architect

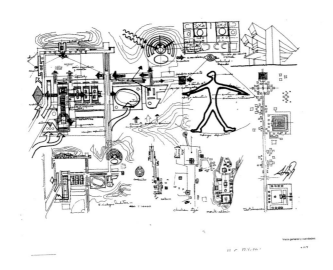

Conceptual sketches. c. 1971. Ink on paper,
8 ¼ x 11 ¹¹⁄₁₆ in. (21 x 29.7 cm)

View of the administration building from the main courtyard. 1976.
Fundación Ingenieros Civiles Asociados

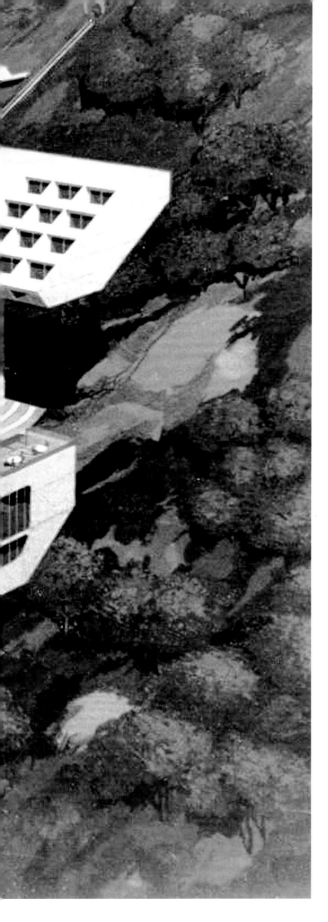

The period between 1955 and 1980 in Peru was characterized by a close relationship between politics and modern architecture, both of which were driven by and intensely reflected the profound social and economic changes of the time. In this context, modern architecture played two different roles, initially functioning as a true instrument of social transformation—through urban planning, programs for workers' housing, and educational and health facilities—and then becoming a tool for the economic and political aspirations of the military dictatorship that ruled Peru from 1968 to 1980. It was during this regime that architecture—and politics—found itself paralyzed by the rapid growth of Peruvian cities and the resulting overflow in population. During the 1980s the state was no longer able to control or plan urban growth, and architecture lost its privileged status as an agent of modernization.

The government's efforts to plan Lima's growth had begun in the 1930s, when housing and health care were provided to low-income laborers and workers as a form of social compensation. At the same time, architects were developing and promoting their discipline. The Sociedad de Arquitectos was founded in 1937, followed immediately by the first issue of *El arquitecto peruano*, both of which made a case for the role of architects in urban interventions and city planning. These actions created an early link between social progress and modern architecture. A relevant project from this period is the La Victoria workers' neighborhood (1937), by Alfredo Dammert, which shows the influence of interwar German rationalism.

During the decade that followed, modern ideas about housing and urban planning gained currency. The Instituto de Urbanismo was founded in 1944, through the vision and effort of the architects Fernando Belaunde Terry, Luis Dórich, Luis Ortiz de Zevallos, and Carlos Morales Macchiavello, and it would go on to lay out a framework for the development of Peruvian cities up to the 1970s. The Corporación Nacional de la Vivienda (CNV) and the Oficina Nacional de Planeamiento y Urbanismo (ONPU), both created in 1946 and based on the ideals outlined by Le Corbusier in his Athens Charter of 1942, inspired some outstanding urban developments, including the Unidad Vecinal 3 (Neighborhood unit 3) (1946), by the CNV; the Pilot Plan for Lima (1949), by the ONPU; and the Plan de Chimbote (1948), by the American firm formed by José Luis Sert and Paul Lester Wiener. The manifesto "Expresión de principios," published in 1947 by Agrupación Espacio, staked a claim for both political legitimacy and intellectual and professional acceptance of modern architecture.

The 1950s saw the largest and most innovative projects to date in housing, health, and institutional building in Peru, largely thanks to economic

Project for a hotel, Machu Picchu. 1969. Miguel Rodrigo Mazuré (Peruvian, 1926–2014). Perspective (now lost). 1968. Water-based paint on cardboard, 19 ¹¹/₁₆ x 31 ½ in. (50 x 80 cm)

support flowing from the United States as a result of the Inter-American Treaty of Reciprocal Assistance (also known as the Rio Treaty) of 1947, as well as the sale of raw materials such as copper and other mining resources, to the United States during the Korean War. These economic conditions made possible the construction of big housing complexes, such as the Matute, Rímac, and Mirones neighborhoods of Lima, and the Centro Vocacional de Huampaní (fig. 1), all designed by Santiago Agurto at CNV between 1951 and 1955; the Ministerio de Educación, designed by Enrique Seoane in 1954; and the Hospital del Empleado, designed by the American firm led by Edward Durell Stone (1954). These projects developed and adapted a Corbusian language to local conditions and promoted the idea of progress through modernist public buildings. The school of architecture at the Universidad Nacional de Ingeniería, built at the beginning of the 1950s by the Italian architect Mario Bianco with Peruvian Juan Benítez, was a breeding ground for architects who would later participate in different political movements and work on state-sponsored projects.

In the mid-1950s, a new professional middle class began to emerge, one that identified with modern forms and ideals. Many prosperous families, as well as private businesses and institutions, opted for the exploration of forms and spaces practiced by the new generation of architects. Influenced by the modern masters, these new structures deployed large overhangs, shaded spaces, and expressive formal freedom. Among them are the Atlas building (1953), by Walter Weberhofer Quintana and José Álvarez-Calderón; the Hotel Savoy (1957), by Bianco; the El Pacífico building (1957), by Fernando de Osma; the Neptuno building (1958), by Alberto Menacho; the Chávez and Rodrigo houses (both 1958), by Miguel Rodrigo Mazuré; and the houses in Ancón (1961–62), by Seoane.

This new middle class became the most powerful voting population in the 1960s, progressively replacing the aristocracy and significantly changing the political landscape. The new government focused on development, with a sustained and organic increase in prosperity for Peruvian society as a whole. In 1963 Belaunde, the architect, became Peru's president, and it was during his administration that modern architecture

2. **Conjunto Habitacional Palomino, Lima. 1964–67.** Luis Miró Quesada Garland (Peruvian, 1914–1994), Fernando Correa (Peruvian, born 1928), Fernando Sánchez-Griñan (Peruvian, 1923–1998), Santiago Agurto (Peruvian 1921–2010). **View from the courtyard. 1967.** From *El arquitecto peruano* (January–February 1967)

1. **Centro Vocacional de Huampaní, Lima. 1955.** Santiago Agurto (Peruvian, 1921–2010), Corporación Nacional de la Vivienda (Peru, est. 1946). **Aerial view. 1955.** Servicio Aerofotográfico Nacional

transformed both the scale of Peruvian cities and rural areas through planning. These projects were driven by a strong desire for modernization as well for social progress; monumentality and formal expression were important to the country's construction of a new identity.

The most important projects of those years were high-density collective housing complexes, including, in Lima, the San Felipe residential complex (1962–69), by Enrique Ciriani, Mario Bernuy, Victor Smirnoff and Luis Vásquez; the Palomino housing complex (fig. 2), by Luis Miró Quesada, Agurto, Fernando Correa, and Fernando Sánchez-Griñán; and the second phase of Matute, Rímac, and Mirones neighborhood units (1963), by Jacques Crousse and Ciriani. Similar projects elsewhere in Peru—such as the Nicolas de Piérola housing complex in Arequipa (1965), by Adolfo Córdova and Carlos Williams, and the Mariscal Gamarra complex in Cusco (1965)—were principally developed by the Junta Nacional de Vivienda (National housing board). Among those built to contribute to the image of the new state are the civic centers in Lima (1966) and Huancayo (1962), the Jorge Chávez airport in Lima (fig. 3), the Marginal de la Selva freeway (1964), and many other large infrastructure projects related to transit, energy, water supply, and social services.

The 1960s also saw an enormous increase in citizen participation in housing construction, through government-supported self-help programs created to solve the housing crises in several Peruvian cities. One remarkable project that emerged from these programs is the Ciudad Satélite in Ventanilla (1961), designed by Luis Marcial through the Instituto Nacional de Vivienda, in which small housing units, set in a pedestrian zone with green spaces, could be progressively expanded by the residents themselves. Beginning in 1966 the Proyecto Experimental de Vivienda (PREVI) offered the developing world a new vision of social housing based on innovative prefabricated building systems adapted to poverty conditions. The project was organized by Belaunde's government and supported by the United Nations Development Program under the direction of Peter Land; the model, developed by such prominent international architects as James Stirling, Atelier 5, Christopher Alexander, and Charles Correa, used prefabrication as a means toward self-help construction and promoted public spaces and plazas for social interaction.

Although the coup d'état of 1968 did not completely interrupt PREVI's development, the military regime rejected this model to address the need for new low-income housing, and the project of social development dissolved into organized squatter settlements and self-built housing.

The new priorities of the military regime, such as the extraction of natural resources, were not accompanied by the industrial and social development it had promised, and the great buildings that were meant to represent progress instead became monuments to cultural, political, and economic independence from the West. Among the most outstanding projects of this decade were the Ministerio de Pesquería (Ministry of fishing), by Rodrigo Mazuré, Miguel Cruchaga Belaunde, and Emilio Soyer Nash (fig. 4); the Ministerio de Guerra (Ministry of war) (1972), by Hector Tanaka, Alberto Chueca, and Walter Mesía; the Petroperú headquarters (1969), by Weberhofer and Daniel Arana; the headquarters of the Acuerdo de Cartagena (1971), by the firm of Arana-Orrego-Torres; and the Centro de Esparcimiento de las Fuerzas Policiales (Police force recreation center) (1969), by Rodrigo Mazuré. Each embodied the yearning for absolute power within a Brutalist language, in forms of structural boldness and forceful tectonics.

The return to democracy in 1980—and the return of the architect Belaunde to power—did not mean a return to the alliance between modernity and development. Despite the government's efforts to reinvigorate housing, infrastructure, and development programs, the economic crisis caused by a decade of dictatorship could not be overcome by the joined forces of architecture and politics. Government institutions had lost control over the growth of the cities, particularly Lima, and in the absence of planning policies, informal housing solutions took over. By 1980 Lima had nearly five million inhabitants, and almost thirty percent of the city was made up of squatter settlements that made incursions onto public and private lands. It would not be until the twenty-first century that the ethnic, cultural, and social expressions produced by internal migration would begin to generate a new society, in which architecture could play a new, unexpected, singular role.

3. **Aeropuerto Internacional Jorge Chávez, Lima. 1961–65.** Arana-Orrego-Torres (Peru, est. 1958), Luis Vásquez (Peruvian, 1922–2010), Luis Bao (Peruvian, 1924–2012). View of the main terminal. 1966. Antenor Orrego Archive

4. **Ministerio de Pesquería, Lima. 1970–72.** Miguel Rodrigo Mazuré (Peruvian, 1926–2014), Emilio Soyer Nash (Peruvian, born 1936), Miguel Cruchaga Belaunde (Peruvian, born 1940). **Exterior view.** 1971

Walter Weberhofer Quintana (Peruvian, 1923–2003)

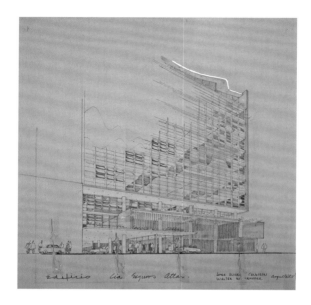

Perspective. c. 1955. India ink and watercolor on card
stock, 19 ⅞ × 19 ½ in. (50.5 × 49.5 cm)

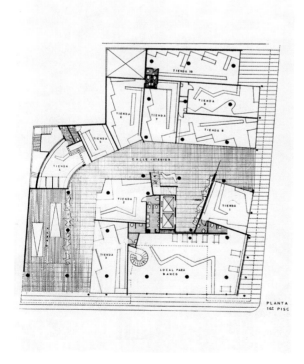

View through the colonnade of Portales de San Agustín. c. 1955

Plan. 1953. Blueprint, 19 ⅞ × 19 ½ in. (50.5 × 49.5 cm)

Miguel Rodrigo Mazuré (Peruvian, 1926–2014)
House, Ancón, Lima. 1961–62
Enrique Seoane (Peruvian, 1915–1980)

Exterior view of the Chávez house. 1960. Photograph by José Casals

Perspective drawing of the house in Ancón. Ink and watercolor on vellum, 11 13/16 × 15 3/4 in. (28.5 × 46.5 cm). Universidad de Piura

Conjunto Residencial San Felipe, Lima. 1962–69
Enrique Ciriani (Peruvian, born 1936)
Mario Bernuy (Peruvian, 1929–2013)
Luis Vázquez (Peruvian, 1922–1996)
Victor Smirnoff (Peruvian, born 1933)

Project for phase two, model by Jacques Crousse and Oswaldo Núñez. Wood, base: 35 ⁷⁄₁₆ x 23 ⁵⁄₈ in. (90 x 60 cm)

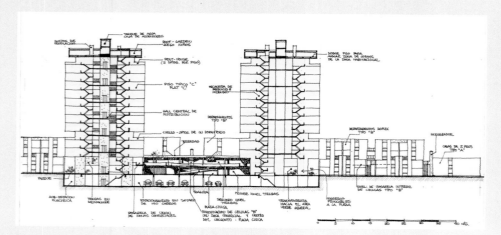

Sectional diagram of phase one towers, drawn by Enrique Ciriani (detail). Ink on paper, 8 ½ x 11 ¹¹⁄₁₆ in. (21.6 x 29.7 cm)

Aerial view of phase three. 1969
Servicio Aerofotográfico Nacional

Social housing, Callao. 1971–74
Miguel Rodrigo Mazuré (Peruvian, 1926–2014)
Emilio Soyer Nash (Peruvian, born 1936)
Miguel Cruchaga Belaunde (Peruvian, born 1940)

Exterior view. 1972

View of a staircase. 1972

View of a courtyard. 1972

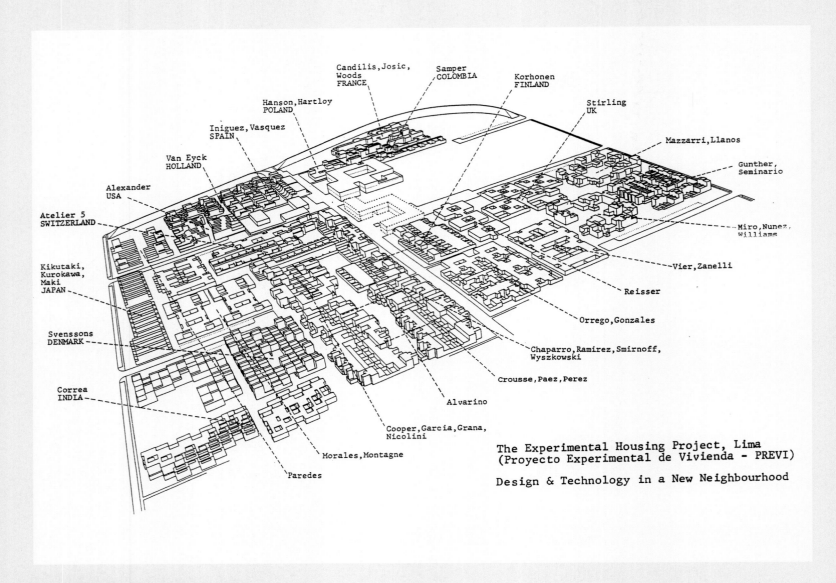

Candilis, Josic,
Woods
FRANCE

Samper
COLOMBIA

Korhonen
FINLAND

Stirling
UK

Hanson, Hartloy
POLAND

Mazzarri, Llanos

Iniguez, Vasquez
SPAIN

Gunther,
Seminario

Van Eyck
HOLLAND

Alexander
USA

Miro, Nunez,
williams

Atelier 5
SWITZERLAND

Vier, Zanelli

Reisser

Kikutaki,
Kurokawa,
Maki
JAPAN

Orrego, Gonzales

Svenssons
DENMARK

Chaparro, Ramirez, Smirnoff,
Wyszkowski

Crousse, Paez, Perez

Correa
INDIA

Alvarino

Cooper, Garcia, Grana,
Nicolini

Morales, Montagne

Paredes

The Experimental Housing Project, Lima
(Proyecto Experimental de Vivienda - PREVI)

Design & Technology in a New Neighbourhood

Site plan showing participating architects
Peter Land (British)

The Proyecto Experimental de Vivienda (PREVI), a neighborhood of low-cost experimental social housing, was conceived in 1966 by the British architect and planner Peter Land in response to the desire of Peruvian president Fernando Belaunde Terry, himself an architect, to tackle the growth of *barriadas*, or informal settlements, in Lima. With the support of Belaunde's administration, Luis Ortiz de Zevallos (then the architect-director of the Banco de la Vivienda del Perú), and the United Nations Development Program, Land developed four different pilot plans for PREVI, each for a different site, from urban to rural. The first plan was an international competition for a new neighborhood of 1,500 houses along the Carretera Panamericana at the outskirts of Lima. In 1969 Land invited twenty-six architects and teams, half of them Peruvian and half from countries representing the economic and geographical range of UN membership, to design proposals for individual clusters of houses. PREVI sought to radically change the way social housing was being addressed in Peru and, by extension, in the developing world. Until PREVI, the production of social housing had been dominated by the *unidad vecinal*, or superblock model, in successful projects such as the Conjunto Residencial San Felipe in Lima. Such developments pursued a set of fixed formal and spatial relationships for residents to adapt to; PREVI, instead, proposed an open, unfinished form governed by guidelines to be followed—or disregarded—by its inhabitants. PREVI's architects advanced a synthesis of *vivienda popular* (popularly produced housing, using traditional and ad hoc methods) and industrially produced structures to navigate the volatile housing market in a politically unstable country.   PdR

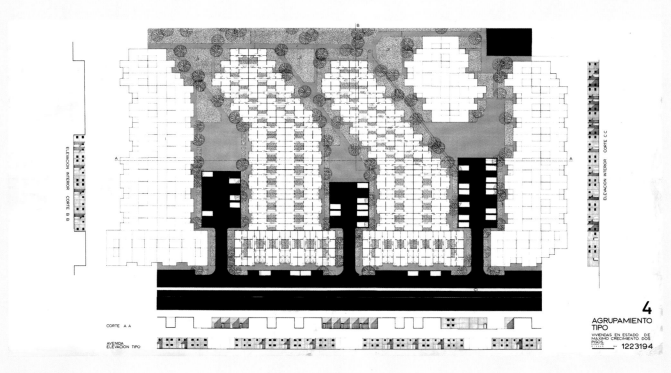

PREVI housing

Cooper Graña Nicolini Arquitectos (Peru, est. 1966)

Site plan. Ink on paper, 25 ½ × 47 ⅜ in. (64.7 × 120.3 cm). The Museum of Modern Art, New York. Gift of the architects

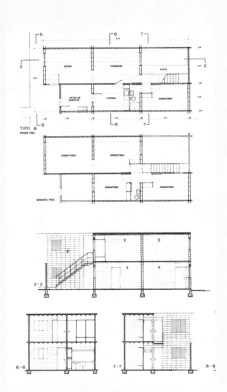

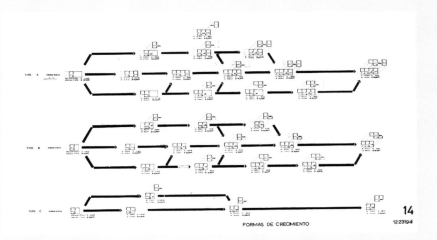

Left: Unit plans (detail). Ink on paper, 31 ⅞ × 49 ¹³⁄₁₆ in. (81 × 120.3 cm). The Museum of Modern Art, New York. Gift of the architects

Above: Diagram showing strategies for growth. Ink on paper, 26 ⅝ × 47 ⅜ in. (67.6 × 120.3 cm). The Museum of Modern Art, New York. Gift of the architects

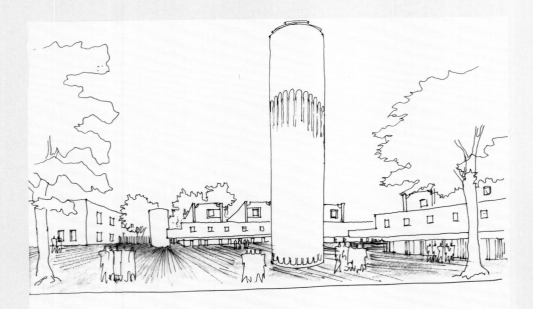

PREVI housing
Germán Samper (Colombian, born 1924)

Perspective (detail). Ink and pencil on paper,
39 ⅜ × 27 ⁹⁄₁₆ in. (100 × 70 cm). Archivo de Bogotá

PREVI housing
Oskar N. Hansen (Polish, born Finland. 1922–2005)

View of model (detail). Zofia & Oskar Hansen
Foundation, Warsaw

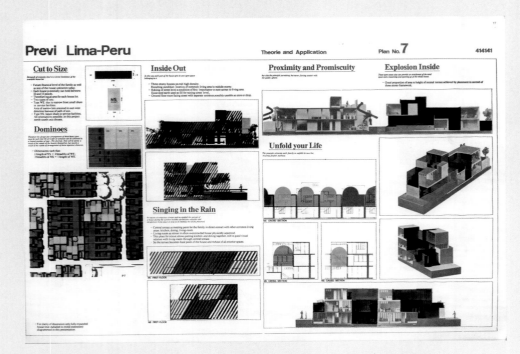

PREVI housing
Atelier 5 (Switzerland, est. 1955)

From *International Competition for an
Experimental Housing Project (PREVI), Lima, Peru*
Department of Architecture & Design Study
Center, The Museum of Modern Art, New York.
Gift of the architects

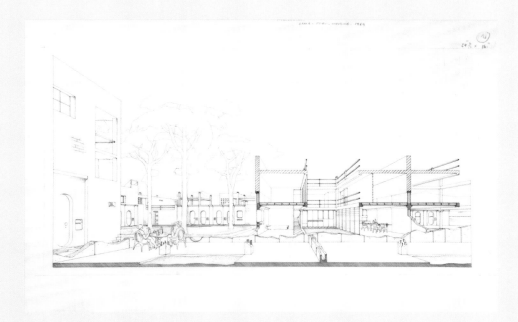

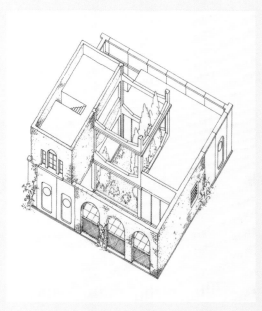

PREVI housing
James Stirling (British, born Scotland. 1926–1992)

Perspective section. Ink and pencil on tracing paper, 20 ¾ x 32 ¼ in. (53 x 82.1 cm). James Stirling/Michael Wilford fonds, Collection Centre Canadien d'Architecture/Canadian Centre for Architecture, Montreal

Axonometric section. Ink and pencil on tracing paper, 10 ⁵⁄₁₆ x 8 ³⁄₁₆ in. (26.2 x 20.8 cm). James Stirling/Michael Wilford fonds, Collection Centre Canadien d'Architecture/Canadian Centre for Architecture, Montreal

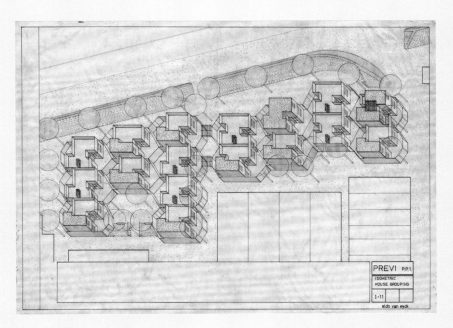

PREVI housing
Aldo van Eyck (Dutch, 1918–1999)

Ink on tracing paper, 16 ⁹⁄₁₆ × 23 ³⁄₈ in. (42 x 59.4 cm). Aldo van Eyck Archive

Throughout the twentieth century, the qualities of Uruguayan modern architecture—among them the wise articulation of buildings and urban issues, syn-
chronicity with international debates and projects, competent and accurate
execution of projects, and rapid spread throughout the country—gave shape
to a voice all its own. This voice, however, was expressed only discreetly, at low
volume, so that few works and names have achieved international recognition.
Still, Uruguayan architecture has produced very interesting works (if remote
from the mainstream), from its swift affiliation with modernity at the beginning
of the century through the political turmoil of the 1970s.

By the 1920s modernism had taken hold in Uruguay, and it soon
became the preferred option for public and private initiatives: the first major
transformation of Uruguayan architecture had begun. Academy-trained
young architects translated International Style into their own idiom, and
the result was favorably received by the public. Uruguay was experiencing
a period of prosperity, optimism, and social equilibrium, without significant
income disparity; the country's liberal, secular, republican ideology was
grounded in *batllismo*—named for José Batlle y Ordóñez, the president
between 1903 and 1907 and again between 1911 and 1915, who encouraged
development through broad government regulations. The architecture of
the period was a natural and timely reflection of the reigning spirit of modernity and progress.

Real estate investments tended to be small in scale. One- and two-
story houses proliferated in cities all over the country, mainly in Montevideo,
resulting in low-density expansion. New architectural modes were accepted
readily, for their ability to organize space as well as for their aesthetics. The
1928 Ley de Higiene de la Vivienda (Law of sanitary housing) was a favorable
stimulus; the law's mandate that all housing be built with decent amounts
of light and ventilation threw the inward-looking structures of the past into
crisis. In the domestic as well as the institutional sphere, the transition to
modernist forms of housing was rapid and smooth.

During the 1920s there were few urban plans, with the sole—and
highly relevant—exception of La Rambla, the large-scale project that put a
promenade along the coast of Montevideo, changing the structure and ambi-
ence of the city. Even without an urban plan, large sections of Montevideo
achieved a kind of cohesion through new modern buildings designed
with an implicit awareness of urban construction: consistency grew out of
the wisdom of collecting little things. Nor were architects writing much in
this period, with the possible exception of Mauricio Cravotto and Leopoldo
Artucio. *Arquitectura*, a magazine published by the Sociedad de Arquitectos

Iglesia de Cristo Obrero (Church of Christ the worker), Atlántida. 1958–60.
Eladio Dieste (Uruguayan, 1917–2000). Exterior view. 1967. Photograph by
Julius Shulman. Julius Shulman Photography Archive, Research Library
at the Getty Research Institute, Los Angeles

del Uruguay, was created in 1914 and published regularly, with monthly issues between 1922 and 1931; the Uruguayan response to the avalanche of manifestos and theoretical discourses of the era was offered principally by architects who were immersed in its praxis and were teaching at the architecture school at the Universidad de la República. It was in the humanist and relaxed atmosphere of the school (created in 1915, although studies of architecture had begun nearly thirty years earlier) where a solid and lasting project-based tradition was established, and it was there that the features that characterize Uruguayan architecture were forged: rigorous practice, urban consciousness, and—in particular through the work of Julio Vilamajó (fig. 1)—a marked awareness of space. The significant works that came out of this period include the Facultad de Ingeniería (1938), Casa Vilamajó (1929), Villa Serrana (1946–47), and the Juncal (1936) and Moncault (1947) buildings, by Vilamajó; the Palacio Municipal (1935) and the architect's own house (fig. 2), by Cravotto; the Estadio Centenario (1930) and Escuela Experimental (1929), by Juan Antonio Scasso; the Centenario building (1930), by Octavio de los Campos; and the Hospital de Clínicas (fig. 3), by Carlos A. Surraco (these are all in Montevideo except Villa Serrana, which is in Lavalleja).

The second stage of evolution in Uruguayan architecture arrived at midcentury, as film, television, and the mass media brought about the dawning of mass culture, and the world of architecture witnessed the expansion of International Style. The distribution of income became increasingly asymmetrical, changing the country's social structure. Its economic resources were more concentrated, with companies and individuals looking for new forms of investment and willing to take on the risks of large construction projects and commercialization processes. These conditions, along with a general public that seemed willing to shift its cultural preferences, made it possible for undertakings at a larger scale. Investors and clients focused on high-rise housing and sought zones where it could be built. Once again, regulations helped things along, in this case, the 1946 Ley de Propiedad Horizontal (Condominium law). The conditions were ripe for architectural transformation; what remained was for the public to move toward creative ownership, and a new generation of architects was ready.

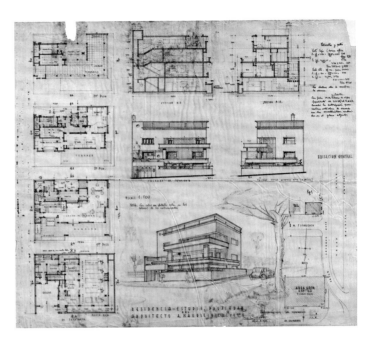

2. **House for Mauricio Cravotto, Montevideo. 1932–33.** Mauricio Cravotto (Uruguayan, 1893–1962). Composite with plans, sections, and perspective. c. 1932. Pencil on tracing paper, 28 ¾ x 23 ⅝ in. (73 x 60 cm). Fundación Cravotto, Montevideo

Some of the pioneers from the first half of the century played a role in this era, but it was primarily their students who turned an attentive gaze to the international debate and to the possibilities for local interpretation of it, and who produced architecture with a wholly new style. The effects were felt across the country in extremely diverse public and private projects, by such outstanding figures as Raúl Sichero and Luis García Pardo, both of them rigorous and imaginative in integrating form and technology; Mario Payssé Reyes, who incorporated the conceptions of the artist Joaquín Torres García into his architecture of subtle spatial transitions; and Eladio Dieste, whose inventions in structural terra-cotta brick were

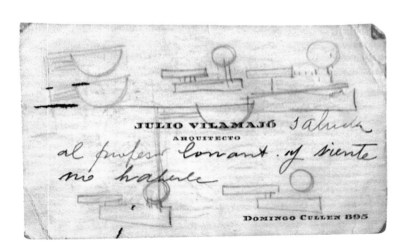

1. **United Nations Headquarters, New York. 1947–49.** Julio Vilamajó (Uruguayan, 1894–1948). Sketch studies on the architect's business card. Instituto de Historia de la Arquitectura, Facultad de Arquitectura, Universidad de la República, Montevideo

developed in his church in Atlántida (1958–60) and in his industrial buildings. Other important projects quickly emerged, transforming the landscape of the Montevideo neighborhood Pocitos and its section of La Rambla (fig. 4): the La Goleta (1952) and Panamericano (1958–64) buildings, by Sichero, and the El Pilar building (1957–59), by García Pardo. In older parts of town there were, among many others, the Gilpie (1955) and Positano (1957–63) buildings, by García Pardo; and the Mónaco building (1953), by Guillermo Jones Odriozola and Francisco Villegas Berro. The resorts along the east coast were significantly expanded both in number and size, and new housing appeared there as well: the Arcobaleno complex (1960), by Jones and Villegas; the Puerto building (1959), by Guillermo Gómez Platero and Rodolfo López Rey; and the urban project and houses in Punta Ballena (1946) by Antoni Bonet.

The role of the architect was changing as well, as many of them began taking responsibility for the investment, development, and construction of their projects, as well as the design. Public works were incorporating new concepts and aesthetics, ranging from the education buildings initiated by the Ministerio de Obras Públicas (Ministry of public works) to Nelson Bayardo's iconic columbarium (1960–62). At the Facultad de Arquitectura, radical changes were proposed to the curriculum in order to update it and deepen the school's social commitment: technology and social sciences were emphasized, and Beaux Arts practices gradually abandoned. New research was undertaken, and two new journals, one by the architecture school and the other by the students' association, were published; aside from these and the *Revista de la Sociedad de Arquitectos*, the only other regular writing on architecture was in a column in *Marcha*, a weekly paper, between 1950 and 1956.

Uruguayan society and culture were devastated during the brutal military regime that began in the early 1970s. An interesting new architectural phase had been taking shape, supported by the Ley de Vivienda, which allowed cooperative ownership of buildings; the Bulevar Artigas complex (1971–74, portfolio 11) and the Mesa cooperatives (1972–74) built by the young architects of the Centro Cooperativista Uruguayo are notable examples. But architecture entered a state of suspension during the crisis, and only a

4. **La Rambla, Playa Pocitos, Montevideo. 1968**. Archivo del Servicio de Medios Audiovisuales, Facultad de Arquitectura, Universidad de la República, Montevideo

few isolated interesting projects emerged, principally in luxury housing tied to real estate speculation. Among them are El Torreón (1980), by Estudio 5, and the Manantiales complex (1980), by Manteola, Sánchez Gómez, Santos, Solsona, Viñoly. It was only with the return to democracy, in 1984, that the country began to slowly shift toward its current situation.

The work of Uruguayan architects evinces a parallel gaze to modernist currents and local needs in works of unpremeditated coherence. To understand it one must delve into a critical history that makes a magnificent foundation of ideas that seek to understand architecture from within its very processes, themes, problems, and solutions. We should not simplify and devalue—via references, influences, and linear causalities—what happens when ideas take architectural form. Now is the time to formulate genuine critical arguments that might recover a passion—ever more fragile—for the discipline before the shifting times disperse the coherence of Uruguay's parallel gaze, before the sensibility that allows the joining together of small things disappears, before amicable coexistence and simple idiosyncrasy lead to forgetting.

3. **Hospital de Clínicas Dr. Manuel Quintela, Montevideo. 1929–30**. Carlos A. Surraco (Uruguayan, 1896–1976). Perspective. 1929. Pencil on paper, 39 ⅜ x 15 ¾ in. (100 x 40 cm). Archivo del Hospital de Clínicas, Universidad de la República, Montevideo

Mario Payssé Reyes (Uruguayan, 1913–1988)

Section. 1954. Ink on paper, 14 ⅝ x 26 ⅜ in. (37.2 x 67 cm). Instituto de Historia de
la Arquitectura, Facultad de Arquitectura, Universidad de la República, Montevideo

View of the veranda. 1967. Photograph by Julius Shulman.
Julius Shulman Photography Archive, Research Library at
the Getty Research Institute, Los Angeles

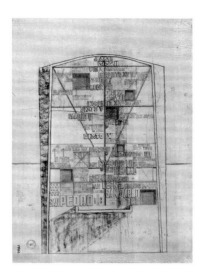

Above: Exterior view. 1967. Photograph by Julius Shulman. Julius Shulman Photography Archive, Research Library at the Getty Research Institute, Los Angeles

Top right: Study for the chapel's main facade. 1952. Pencil and chalk on paper, 31 ⅞ x 23 ¼ in. (81 x 59 cm). Instituto de Historia de la Arquitectura, Facultad de Arquitectura, Universidad de la República, Montevideo

Bottom right: View of the seminary chapel from the altar. 1967. Photograph by Julius Shulman. Julius Shulman Photography Archive, Research Library at the Getty Research Institute, Los Angeles

With its 1918 constitution, Uruguay established a legal separation of church and state, becoming one of the earliest Latin American countries to adopt a secular attitude. Nonetheless, and perhaps in resistance, numerous religious buildings were subsequently built in the 1940s and 1950s, most of them in a modernist vein. One such project was the Seminario Arquidiocesano de Montevideo, located 31 miles (50 kilometers) from the city, in Toledo. This includes both a secondary school and a grand seminary. The main building comprises a church and an assembly room for 500 people, with a library, auditorium, and residential accommodation for 250 pupils. The architect Mario Payssé Reyes, a devout Catholic born in Toledo in 1913, designed the winning entry in the 1952 competition to build the complex. The seminary is made up of several pavilions in brick, organized around a series of courtyards. The main element is the church, on whose monumental blind facade Payssé "wrote," in gigantic characters, the history of the church, set out as an ongoing dispute between *zelotes* (zealots)—supporters of individual initiative—and *herodianos*—supporters of collective objectives. Payssé, a classically trained architect, also maintained a strong relationship with the Uruguayan artist Joaquín Torres García. For the interior brick surfaces of the church, artists from Torres García's studio executed bas-reliefs and designed stained glass windows. These contributions, which continued into the early 1960s, were in keeping with the idea of the synthesis of the arts, a theory specific to Torres García but also parallel to *integración plastica*, a widespread concern at the time.   JFL

Iglesia de Cristo Obrero, Atlántida. 1958–60
(Church of Christ the worker)
Eladio Dieste (Uruguayan, 1917–2000)

View from the plaza. c. 1965. Photograph by Vicente del Amo Hernández. Instituto de Historia de
la Arquitectura, Facultad de Arquitectura, Universidad de la República, Montevideo

View toward the altar. 1967. Photograph by Julius Shulman.
Julius Shulman Photography Archive, Research Library at
the Getty Research Institute, Los Angeles

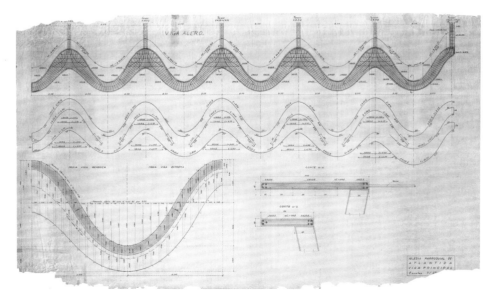

Plan of undulating supporting walls. 1958. Pencil on paper,
23 ⅜ x 33 ⅛ in. (59.4 x 84.1 cm)

View toward the altar. 2014. Photograph by Marcos Guiponi

View of the original neo-Romanesque church facade, from Plaza Independencia. 2014. Photograph by Marcos Guiponi

Perspective of the interior roof structure. 1967. Ink on paper, 23 ⅝ x 23 ⅝ in. (60 x 60 cm)

Urnario, Cementerio del Norte, Montevideo. 1960–62 (Columbarium)
Nelson Bayardo (Uruguayan, 1922–2002)

Exterior view. 2012. Photograph by Marcos Guiponi

Exterior view with a walkway. c. 1961.
Photograph by Julio Navarro

View of the courtyard. c. 1961. Photograph
by Julio Navarro

Interior view. 2012. Photograph by Marcos Guiponi

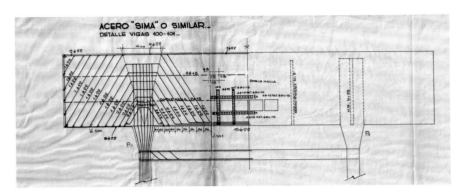

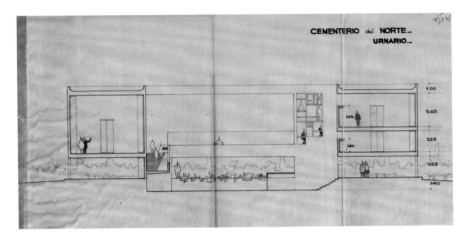

Top: Section showing steel rebar. 1959. Pencil on paper, 19 ¹¹⁄₁₆ x 23 ⅝ in. (50 x 60 cm).
Archivo de la Intendencia Municipal de Montevideo

Bottom: Longitudinal section (detail). 1959. Pencil on paper, 19 ¹¹⁄₁₆ x 23 ⅝ in. (50 x 60 cm).
Archivo de la Intendencia Municipal de Montevideo

Between 1960 and 1962 the municipal government of Montevideo undertook the construction of a building for the municipal cemetery that would house some eighteen thousand cremation urns. The commission went to Nelson Bayardo, an architect employed by the municipal services, who worked on the project with José Tizze, an engineering advisor. Set on a swelling mound in the park-like setting of the cemetery, the building is a prismatic box of reinforced concrete with facades unrelieved by openings, all held aloft on eight concrete piers. The prism is a *boîte à surprise*: once visitors cross the perimeter by entering under the box, they find themselves in an open courtyard with views into open loggias looking down on the central space. The loggias are reached via a gentle ramp that creates a promenade of ascent to the shelves of compartments for funerary urns. The whole supplies an experience of a singular sculptural richness. One interior facade is treated with a rich abstract bas-relief reminiscent of the work of the studio of Joaquín Torres García, by the sculptor Edwin Studer.   JFL

Raúl Sichero (Uruguayan, born 1916)

Exterior view. 2014. Photograph by Jorge Gambini

Uruguay was quite open to modernist experimentation in the 1950s and 1960s. There was a strong academic tradition at the architectural school of the Universidad de la República and a middle-class clientele that was culturally progressive and enjoying a period of economic prosperity. Many architects contributed to an urban landscape of very high quality, in urban centers large and small. Some of the finest expressions of International Style were explored in buildings such as the Edificio Pine Beach (1960), by Walter Pintos Risso; the Conjunto Recreacional Arcobaleno (1960), in Punta del Este, by Guillermo Jones Odriozola, Francisco Villegas Berro, and Héctor Vignale Peirano; and the more metropolitan expressions of Raúl Sichero's Panamericano building and the El Pilar and Positano apartment buildings by Luis García Pardo in Montevideo.

JFL

Photograph from a sales brocure, showing a model of the twin buildings. 1958. Collection Beatriz de Reizes

Luis García Pardo (Uruguayan, 1910–2006)
Adolfo Sommer Smith (Uruguayan)

Photomontage of El Pilar with model. 1957. Instituto de Historia de la Arquitectura, Facultad de Arquitectura, Universidad de la República, Montevideo

Views of El Pilar during and after construction. 1958 and 1959. Instituto de Historia de la Arquitectura, Facultad de Arquitectura, Universidad de la República, Montevideo

Presentation collage of the Positano building, with a photograph of a model. Black-and-white photographs and adhesive, 14 ⅜ x 9 1/16 in. (36.5 x 23 cm). Instituto de Historia de la Arquitectura, Facultad de Arqui-tectura, Universidad de la República, Montevideo

Exterior view of the Positano building. Instituto de Historia de la Arquitectura, Facultad de Arquitectura, Universidad de la República, Montevideo

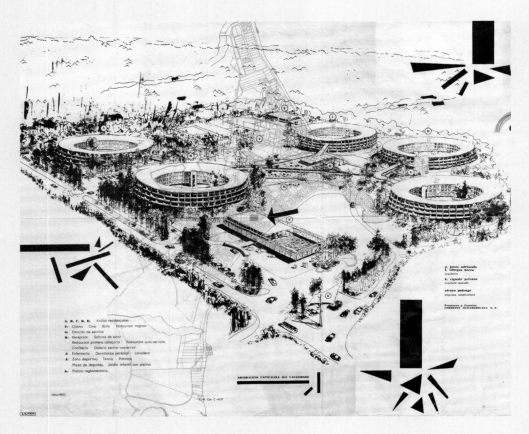

Conjunto Recreacional Arcobaleno, Punta del Este. 1960
Guillermo Jones Odriozola (Uruguayan, 1913–1994)
Franciso Villegas Berro (Uruguayan, born 1918)

Perspective, from a sales brochure. 1960

Complejo Habitacional Bulevar Artigas, Montevideo. 1971–74
Ramiro Bascáns (Uruguayan, 1936–2012)
Thomas Sprechmann (Uruguayan, born 1940)
Héctor Vigliecca (Uruguayan, born 1940)
Arturo Villaamil (Uruguayan, born 1947)

Above: Perspective. 1972. Pencil on paper, 9 ½ x 19 ⅛ in.
(24.1 x 48.6 cm). The Museum of Modern Art, New York. Gift
of the architects

Exterior view. 1974. The Museum of Modern Art, New York. Gift of the architects

Cooperativa Nuevo Amanecer, Mesa 1, Montevideo. 1972–74
Mario Spallanzani (Uruguayan, born 1935)
Luis Livni (Uruguayan, 1943–1996)
Rafael Lorente (Uruguayan, born 1940)

View of the facade. Instituto de Historia de la Arquitectura, Facultad de Arquitectura, Universidad de la República, Montevideo

View from the main access road. Instituto de Historia de la Arquitectura, Facultad de Arquitectura, Universidad de la República, Montevideo

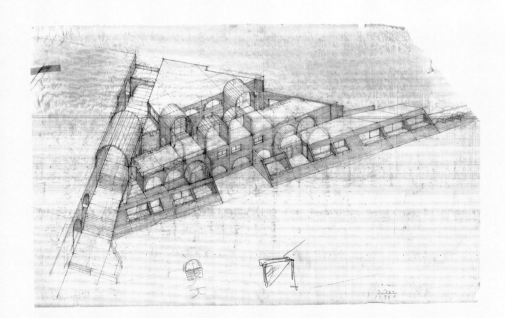

Terrazas de Manantiales. 1980
Manteola, Sánchez Gómez, Santos, Solsona, Viñoly (Argentina, est. 1966)

Axonometric view of the overall project. 1980. Pencil on tracing paper, 20 ⅞ x 32 ¼ in. (53 x 82 cm). The Museum of Modern Art, New York. Gift of the architects

View of the passageway between units. 1980. The Museum of Modern Art, New York. Gift of the architects

Residencia Son Pura, Punta del Este. 1960
Residencia Poyo Roc, Punta del Este. 1960
Guillermo Gómez Platero (Uruguayan, 1922–2014)
Rodolfo López Rey (Uruguayan, born 1932)

Exterior view of Son Pura. 1967. Photograph by Julius Shulman.
Julius Shulman Photography Archive, Research Library at the Getty Research
Institute, Los Angeles

Interior view of Poyo Roc. 1967. Photograph by Julius
Shulman. Julius Shulman Photography Archive, Research
Library at the Getty Research Institute, Los Angeles

Exterior view of Poyo Roc. 1967. Photograph by Julius Shulman.
Julius Shulman Photography Archive, Research Library at the
Getty Research Institute, Los Angeles

Residencia López Rey (Casa Ahel), Punta del Este. 1962
Rodolfo López Rey (Uruguayan, born 1932)
Residencia La Caldera, Punta del Este. 1966
Rodolfo López Rey (Uruguayan, born 1932)
Guillermo Gómez Platero (Uruguayan, 1922–2014)

Exterior view of Casa Ahel. 1962. Instituto de Historia de la Arquitectura, Facultad de Arquitectura, Universidad de la República, Montevideo

Above and right: Exterior views of La Caldera. 1967. Photographs by Julius Shulman. Julius Shulman Photography Archive, Research Library at the Getty Research Institute, Los Angeles

In the early 1920s, during the dictatorial rule of General Juan Vicente Gómez, Venezuela's oil boom made possible the onset of a clear and swift modernization.[1] In the decade after his death, in 1935, during the country's nascent democracy, Venezuelan architects adopted a hesitant approach toward modernism: although there was certainly a desire for buildings designed and constructed to advance modernization—which signaled unmistakable progress, thanks to increasingly efficient government administration—few architects wholeheartedly embraced the emerging canons of modern expression in architecture.

The Dirección de Urbanismo (Office of urban planning), created in 1938, promoted the Plan Rotival, an official master plan for modernization devised in 1939 by the French urban planner Maurice Rotival. This plan opened up the gridded colonial center of Caracas by introducing the Avenida Bolívar, a large triumphal thoroughfare running west to east, connecting El Calvario hill, on the west, with a proposed monumental plaza that would have extended the city eastward, although it was never built. Following, in part, Rotival's plan, Carlos Raúl Villanueva designed El Silencio (fig. 1), a working-class housing complex at the foot of El Calvario, with arcaded shopping streets around a civic plaza. One departure from Rotival's ideas was the construction, on the avenue, of the Centro Simón Bolívar (fig. 2), a multiuse complex by Cipriano Domínguez, with a twinned pair of skyscrapers that became a new visual reference for the valley of Caracas.

The 1950s marked the flourishing of Venezuelan modern architecture. The country was fully immersed in modernization, which was embraced with enthusiasm by architects and politicians. After the overthrow of the democratic order in late 1948, the dictator Marcos Pérez Jiménez dreamed of the creation of a great Venezuela and made resources available for ambitious public works. The plans were made possible by a new professional cadre of engineers, who were educated in recent building methods in Venezuela, and professional engineers from abroad, who were attracted to Venezuela's riches and public programs and brought with them knowledge about advanced techniques in concrete structures, the construction of which required a large immigrant workforce. The Danish firm Christiani & Nielsen, which designed and built such important structures as the Olympic stadium, is one example.

This new generation of architects developed projects that were attentive to Venezuela's climate, geography, and flora, in designs that tried out new ways of fusing interior and exterior, in public and private commissions, and in works that integrated painting, sculpture, and mosaic murals

Hotel Humboldt, Caracas. 1956. Tomás José Sanabria (Venezuelan, 1922–2008). Exterior view. 1956. Photograph by Tomás José Sanabria. Colección Tomás José Sanabria, Fundación Alberto Vollmer

1. **El Silencio housing complex, Caracas. 1941–45.** Carlos Raúl Villanueva (Venezuelan, born England. 1900–1975). View of the internal courtyard. c. 1944. Photograph by Alfredo Boulton. Fundación Alberto Vollmer

into spaces of unprecedented fluidity. The Plaza Cubierta (Covered plaza) at Caracas's Ciudad Universitaria, designed by Villanueva, integrates several significant buildings, among them the Biblioteca Central (fig. 3), a modern red box that constitutes a powerful sculptural element. This plaza creates an enchanting atmosphere of penumbral light effects—shelter from the sun and sudden explosions of focused light—and an ambitious program of newly commissioned artworks by Venezuelan and foreign artists, including Pascual Navarro, Fernand Léger, and Victor Vasarely. In the interior of the Aula Magna, Alexander Calder's "acoustic clouds" function as both sound modulators and monumental art (fig. 4). The university's individual buildings suggest a modern interpretation of the nineteenth-century notion of character, whereby buildings express something of their function principally

through their form, not least the powerful windowless facades of tall buildings such as the Facultad de Arquitectura y Urbanismo. Many of the tall prismatic housing projects that began to restructure the urban landscape during this period were enhanced with large-scale abstract murals intended, like the architectural forms, to awaken an intense feeling of modernity and to be read, as they are in the university buildings, both at a local scale and as urban beacons.

Creativity and boldness were hallmarks of Venezuelan architecture in the 1950s, and a number of urban landmarks emerged in the capital. Fruto Vivas, with his Club Táchira, designed while he was still a student, employed an innovative thin concrete shell with a distinctive double curvature, in collaboration with the Spanish engineer Eduardo Torroja. Sinuous floors meander under its protective canopy, with native plant species and custom-designed furnishings whose materials nod to Venezuelan tradition. The architects Jorge Romero Gutiérrez, Pedro Neuberger, and Dirk Bornhorst created El Helicoide (1958–61), a mixed-use building whose poetic geometry emerges out of the natural formation of the hill on which it is located. Alejandro Pietri designed the stations of the Teleférico del Ávila (Ávila aerial tramway) (1954–56) with interesting concrete folds of minimal thickness.The Teleférico is a recreational complex that places the city in contact with the port and beaches of the Caribbean coast and also provides access to Tomás José Sanabria's Hotel Humboldt (1956), located at the top of the mountain.

After the return of democracy in 1959, the 1960s and '70s were marked by important and imaginative efforts to achieve more sensitive architectural connections to place and a concomitant critique of the reigning modernist orthodoxy of buildings as simple rectilinear prisms with rectangular bases. Awareness of place was manifested in various ways. Jimmy Alcock's Altolar building in Caracas (1965) suggests a habitable wall that follows the terrain's topography and creates apartments that face the city and Cerro El Ávila in the distance; the living spaces are entered through a microclimate of various heights, with bridges, pierced walls, and tropical vegetation. Alcock created perhaps a more autonomous

2. **Centro Simón Bolívar, Caracas. 1949.** Cipriano Domínguez (Venezuelan, 1904–1995). **Model, as** seen in *Elite* magazine. Architecture & Design Study Center, The Museum of Modern Art, New York. Gift of Carlos Brillembourg

connection with the site in the house he designed for himself (1962), on the outskirts of Caracas, a modern metal structure that combines traditional materials, such as terra-cotta roof tiles, with tropical flora, including orchids and bromeliads, which can be enjoyed from delicate narrow balconies around the perimeter and a fragile bridge that connects the house to the site. Jorge Castillo designed his house at El Amarillo (1981) as a small greenhouse village, with a large overhanging roof and innovative colored enclosures set around a great central courtyard that evokes the traditional coffee haciendas of the Venezuelan countryside.

Jesús Tenreiro-Degwitz, in his headquarters for the Corporación Venezolana de Guayana (1967–68, portfolio 1), aspired to create an icon for the new and still-empty city. He designed the building as an unusual pyramidal form ringed by terraces. The terraces are sheltered by walls that seem to fly, made of brick panels set on delicate steel frames, creating an amiable relationship with the sun, rather than the typical defensive approach of the modernist brise-soleil. Protection from the sun was also the starting point for the design of the refined concrete facades at the headquarters of Sanabria's Banco Central de Venezuela in Caracas, begun in 1962, for which the architect drew meticulous diagrams mapping the effects of the sun at different times of day.

In other works the sense of place is explored through plants and art. Venezuelan flora creates spatial patterns in Caracas's Parque del Este (1956–61), designed by Roberto Burle Marx using plants discovered by a team of biologists and landscape designers who searched the forests all over the country for previously undiscovered species. Villanueva continued to pursue the idea of integrating art and architecture in landscape. His Venezuela Pavilion for Expo 67 in Montreal was conceived as a total work of art, with three simple, brightly colored cubic structures that contain inmersive environments by artists such as Jesús Soto. For the Museo de Arte Moderno Jesús Soto in Ciudad Bolívar (1970–73), Villanueva created an informal grouping of boxes freely dispersed within the site.

Venezuelan architecture became less spectacular in the 1970s, but it had reached a point of realist maturity thanks to the solidity and high quality of its architectural studios. One of the greatest concerns of the era was how to resolve the problem of mass housing on a national scale.[2] With their multiuse Parque Central complex, begun in 1969, which borders the Avenida Bolívar de Caracas to the south, Henrique Siso and Daniel Fernández Shaw attempted to move beyond the separation of functions. Among the more experimental visions for housing were Jorge Castillo's Casa Mara (1970–77)—a building system in polyester reinforced with fiberglass, which the architect had experimented with in El Conde park (1965)—both of them based on the possibilities suggested by the new plastics that were appearing as the petrochemical industry developed in Venezuela. Henrique Hernández designed his Casa de Cartón (Cardboard house) (1971) for plots with large amounts of uncompacted landfill, utilizing very light industrial materials. Vivas experimented with modular building systems of load-bearing metal frames, and with his *arboles para vivir* (trees for living) he hoped to create arborescent structures integrated with the landscape. Some architects made theoretical investigations into the capacity of inhabitants to resolve their own housing difficulties in rural neighborhoods; among these investigations, Teolinda Bolívar's meticulous studies particularly stand out for their direct and deeply engaged observation of some of the country's poorest communities.

The generation of architects that emerged during the 1960s and '70s would offer the country its best efforts in the years to come—years that would be still more complex and difficult.

1 See Carlos Rafael Silva, "Bosquejo histórico del desenvolvimiento de la economía venezolana en el siglo XX," in Ramón J. Velásquez, et al., *Venezuela moderna: Medio siglo de historia, 1926–1976* (Caracas: Ariel, 1979), pp. 765–67.

2 See Alfredo Cilento and Henrique Hernández, "Estructura, problemas y características de la industria de la construcción en Venezuela," *Punto*, no. 52 (October 1974): 17–29.

3. **Biblioteca Central, Ciudad Universitaria, Caracas. 1952–53.** Carlos Raúl Villanueva (Venezuelan, born England. 1900–1975). Exterior view. 2014. Photograph by Silvia Hernández de Lasala

4. **Aula Magna, Ciudad Universitaria, Caracas. 1952–53.** Carlos Raúl Villanueva (Venezuelan, born England. 1900–1975). Interior view, with acoustic clouds by Alexander Calder. 2014. Photograph by Silvia Hernández de Lasala

Aerial view. 1956. Photograph by Tomás José Sanabria. Colección Tomás José Sanabria,
Fundación Alberto Vollmer

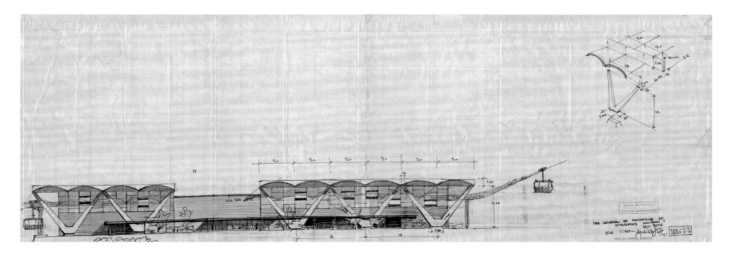

Elevation of the San José cable car station. 1956. Crayon and pencil on tracing paper,
24 7/16 x 68 7/8 in. (62 x 175 cm). Colección Tomás José Sanabria, Fundación Alberto Vollmer

Weather observations, Caracas. February 5, 1974. Pen, crayon, and marker on index card, 4 x 6 in. (10.2 x 15.2 cm). Colección Tomás José Sanabria, Fundación Alberto Vollmer

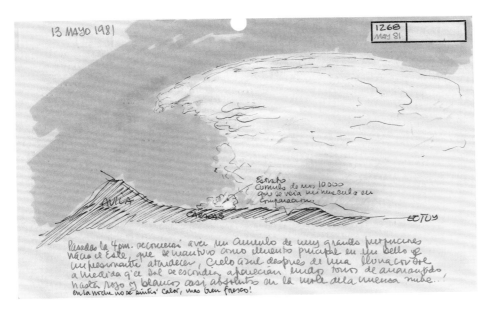

Weather observations, Caracas. May 13, 1981. Pen, crayon, and marker on index card, 4 x 6 in. (10.2 x 15.2 cm). Colección Tomás José Sanabria, Fundación Alberto Vollmer

Tomás José Sanabria's Hotel Humboldt was both an architectural beacon in Caracas's transforming landscape and a nodal point in an experiment that connected the Venezuelan coast with the high plateau of Caracas by cable car, via the mountaintop of Cerro El Ávila. Set near the end of the very trail that its namesake, the German explorer Alexander von Humboldt, had used to study the flora and fauna of the mountain, the hotel also embodied Sanabria's fascination with the city's climate, an interest he depicted in countless sketches and recorded in daily illustrated note cards created over several decades of watching the hotel disappear into and reappear from the clouds.   BB

Venezuela El Helicoide de la Roca Tarpeya, Caracas. 1958–61
Dirk Bornhorst (Venezuelan, born Germany, 1927)
Pedro Neuberger (Venezuelan, born Germany. 1923–2011)
Jorge Romero Gutiérrez (Venezuelan, born 1924)

View from the northeast. 1961. Photograph by Joseph Fabry. Architecture & Design
Study Center, The Museum of Modern Art, New York

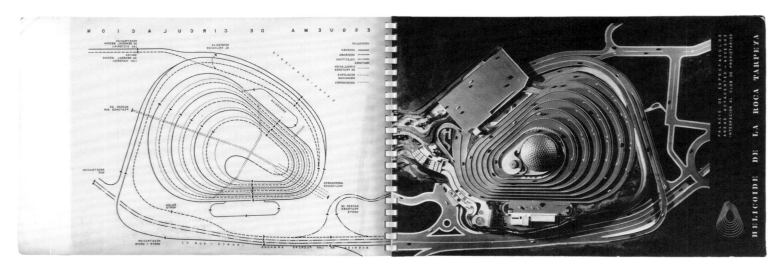

Sales brochure showing circulation plan (left) and aerial view of a model (right).
c. 1960. Architecture & Design Study Center, The Museum of Modern Art, New York

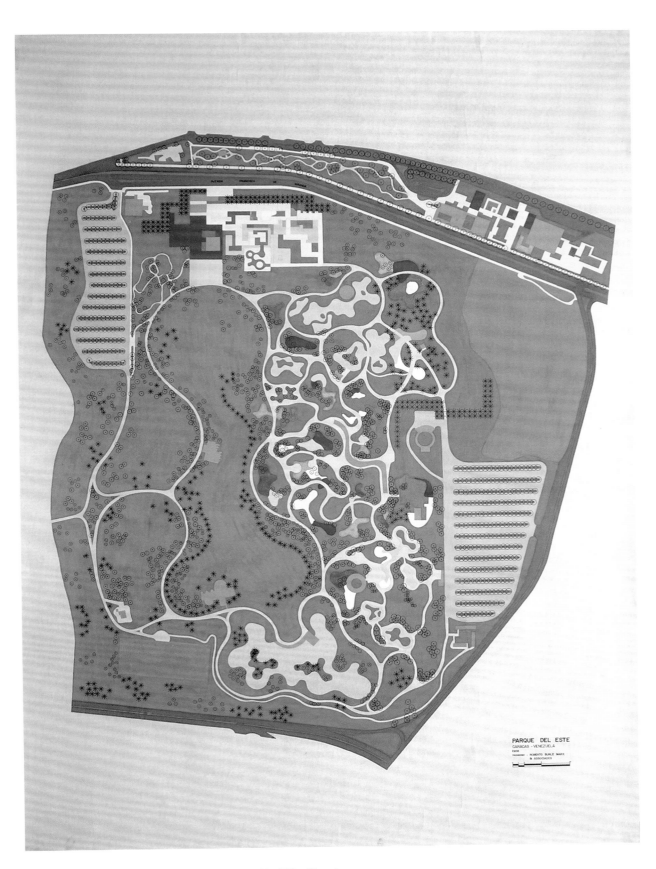

Site plan. c. 1956. Gouache on paper, 38 ⁹/₁₆ x 15 ³/₈ in. (98 x 39 cm)

Venezuela Facultad de Arquitectura y Urbanismo,
Universidad Central de Venezuela, Caracas. 1954–56
Carlos Raúl Villanueva (Venezuelan, born England. 1900–1975)

View of the northern facade. 1960. Photograph by
Paolo Gasparini. Fundación Villanueva

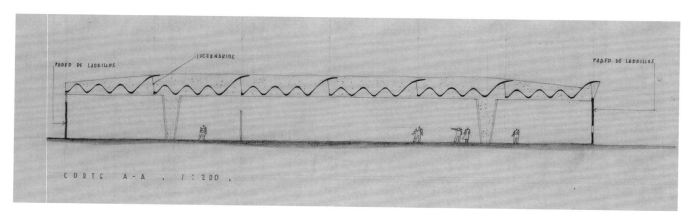

Section showing studios (detail). 1954. Pencil on paper, 19 x 19 ⁷⁄₁₆ in.
(48.2 x 49.4 cm). Colección Facultad de Arquitectura y Urbanismo,
Universidad Central de Venezuela

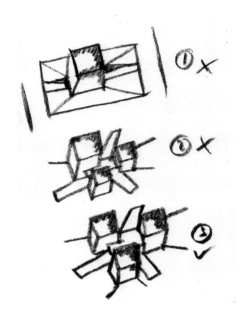

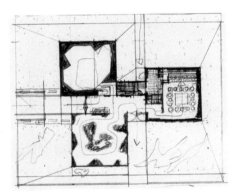

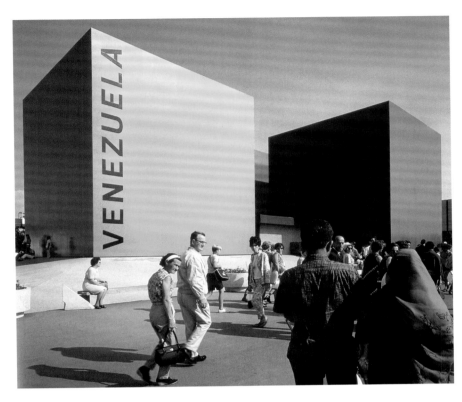

Above: Exterior view. 1967. Photograph by Paolo Gasparini. Fundación Villanueva

Top left: Massing studies for the pavilion. 1966. Pencil on paper, 11 ¹¹⁄₁₆ x 8 ¼ in. (29.7 x 21 cm). Galería de Arte Nacional, Caracas

Bottom left: Preliminary sketch of the ground-floor plan. Pencil and crayon on paper, 11 x 16 ⁹⁄₁₆ in. (27.9 x 42 cm). Galería de Arte Nacional, Caracas

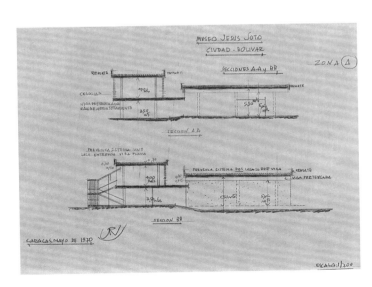

Sections of the museum. 1970. Pencil on paper, 10 ⅜ x 16 ¾ in. (26.4 x 42.5 cm). Colección Facultad de Arquitectura y Urbanismo, Universidad Central de Venezuela

Villanueva at the museum's front entrance. 1973. Photograph by Paolo Gasparini. Fundación Villanueva

Jimmy Alcock (Venezuelan, born 1932)

View from a nearby hill. 1998. Photograph by Paolo Gasparini. The Museum of Modern Art, New York.
Gift of the architect

View of a balcony. 1998. Photograph by Paolo
Gasparini. The Museum of Modern Art, New York.
Gift of the architect

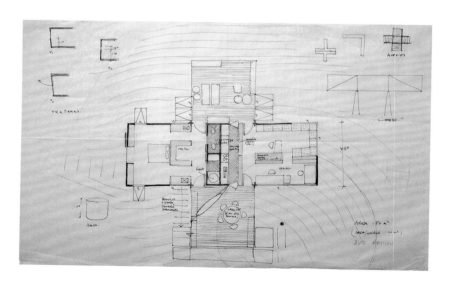

Early study for the piano nobile. 1962. Ink on paper, 16 9/16 × 23 3/8 in. (42 × 59.4 cm).
The Museum of Modern Art, New York. Gift of the architect

Casa El Amarillo, San Antonio de los Altos. 1981   Venezuela   287
Jorge Castillo (Venezuelan, born 1933)
Casa Marín, Caracas. 1975
Fruto Vivas (Venezuelan, born 1928)

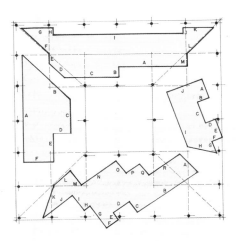

View of the interior courtyard of the El Amarillo house. 1983. Photograph by Jorge Andrés Castillo. The Museum of Modern Art, New York. Gift of the architect

Plan showing structural elements of the El Amarillo house, drawn by Alexandra Englert (detail). 1989. Ink on paper, 33 x 21 ⅝ in. (33 x 55 cm)

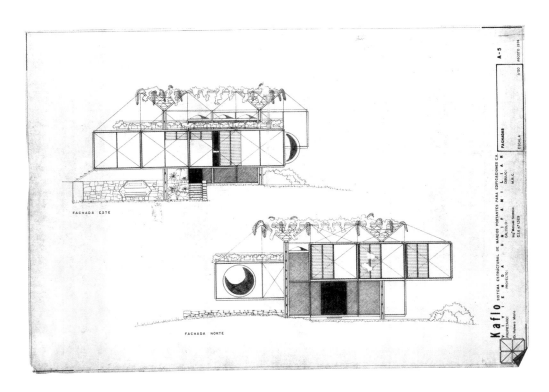

Elevations of the Marín house. 1975. Ink on paper. Museo de Arquitectura, Caracas

View of the central hallway of the Marín house. 2013. Photograph by Efraín Vivas

Headquarters for the Corporación Venezolana de Guayana–Electrificación de Caroní, Ciudad Guayana. 1967–68
Jesús Tenreiro-Degwitz (Venezuelan, 1936–2007)

Exterior view. 1970. Photograph by Paolo Gasparini

In a 2001 interview with the architect Carlos Brillembourg (*Bomb* 86 [Winter 2004]), Jesús Tenreiro-Degwitz recalled his intentions for Ciudad Guayana poetically but sanguinely:

The image of a stepped pyramid came to me at the very beginning. The site is the highest point in the Ciudad Guayana, and it was barren, with nothing built around it. There was no city plan establishing limitations on height or bulk. The CVG architects requested something like a landmark, and the pyramid came forth as a natural form for human beings living in a difficult tropical climate. . . . The stepped pyramid allows for the interaction of inner and outer space through a facade of continuous balconies with shaded gardens, a beautiful sight that is visible from almost all the working areas inside. It was to be the first building in the future center of Alta Vista, the heart of the new city, so it had the character of a foundation stone for an imagined beautiful metropolis—one that ultimately never came to be. The building stood lonely for many years. However, the archetypal image was strong enough to overcome the shameful city that eventually grew up around it. BB

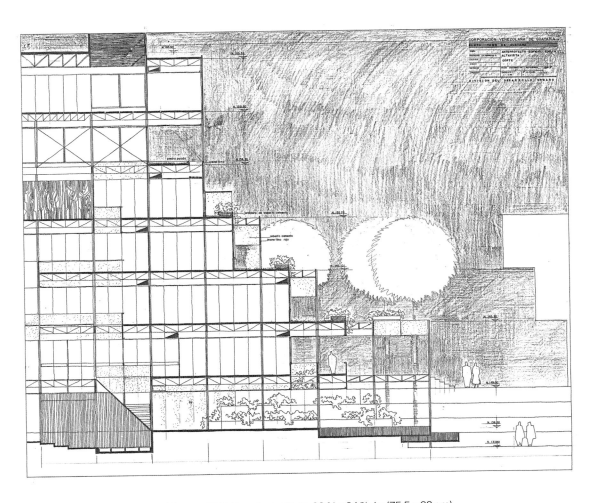

Section showing exterior corridors. c. 1970. Pencil on vellum, 29 ¾ x 24 ⁷⁄₁₆ in. (75.5 x 62 cm).
The Museum of Modern Art, New York. Gift of Ana Díaz de Tenreiro

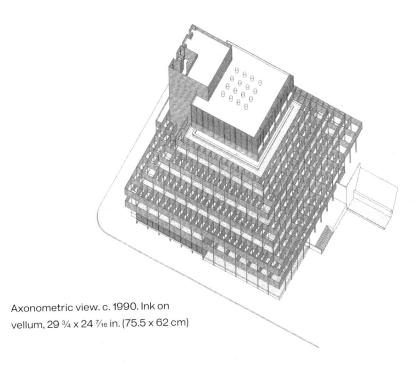

Axonometric view. c. 1990. Ink on
vellum, 29 ¾ x 24 ⁷⁄₁₆ in. (75.5 x 62 cm)

View through sun-shade structure. Photograph
by Antonio Puente. The Museum of Modern Art,
New York. Gift of Ana Díaz de Tenreiro

Unidad Residencial El Paraíso, Caracas. 1955
Carlos Raúl Villanueva (Venezuelan, born England. 1900–1975)
Banco Obrero (Venezuela, active 1928–1975)

Exterior view. 1955. Photograph by Paolo Gasparini.
Fundación Villanueva

Urbanización 2 de Diciembre (now 23 de Enero), Caracas. 1955–57
Carlos Raúl Villanueva (Venezuelan, born England. 1900–1975)
Banco Obrero (Venezuela, active 1928–1975)

Aerial view. 1955. Photograph by Paolo Gasparini. Fundación
Villanueva

Cerro Piloto, Caracas. 1955
Carlos Raúl Villanueva (Venezuelan, born England.
1900–1975)
Banco Obrero (Venezuela, active 1928–1975)

Aerial view. 1955. Photograph by Paolo Gasparini.
Fundación Villanueva

Revenues from Venezuela's thriving petroleum industry propelled the country's populist government to invest heavily in housing, in policies largely developed under the administration of General Marcos Pérez Jiménez in the 1950s. Through the Banco Obrero, created in 1928 under the Ministerio de Fomento (Ministry of development), the government financed the construction of enormous ensembles of housing blocks in various cities, most notably those designed and built in Caracas under the direction of Carlos Raúl Villanueva, such as the El Paraíso complex. Private investors also undertook important works for the middle class, such as the Pan-American Life Insurance Company (PALIC) building (1956), by Federico Guillermo Beckhoff, and the Altolar building, by Jimmy Alcock. In 1970 work began on the architect Daniel Fernández Shaw's Parque Central, in the heart of Caracas, which mixed housing with offices, commerce, and cultural functions in a complex of two 738-foot (225-meter) towers and eight buildings, the latter containing 314 apartments each.   JFL

Edificio Altolar, Caracas. 1965
Jimmy Alcock (Venezuelan, born 1932)

View of an interior corridor. 1998. Photograph by
Paolo Gasparini

Exterior view. 2014. Photograph by Leonardo Finotti

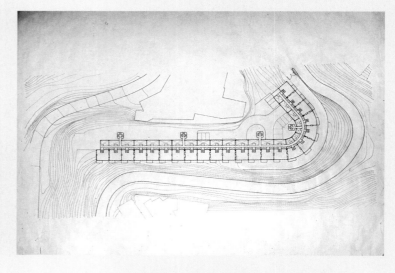

First floor and site plan. 1965. Ink on paper, 27 ½ x 39 in. (69.8 x 99 cm).
The Museum of Modern Art, New York. Gift of the architect

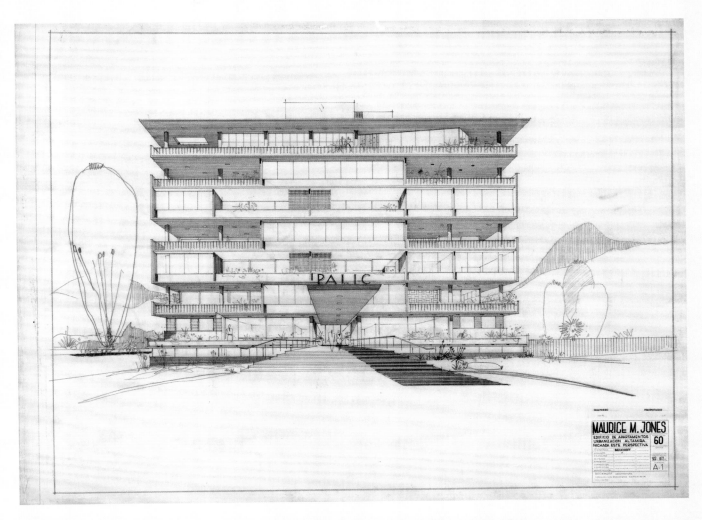

**Edificio PALIC apartments, Caracas. 1956
(Pan-American Life Insurance Company)**
Federico Guillermo Beckhoff (Venezuelan, born
Germany. 1919–1982)

Perspective of the eastern facade. Pencil on vellum,
23 ⅜ x 33 ⅛ in. (59.4 x 84.1 cm). The Museum of Modern Art,
New York. Gift of Bettina Beckhoff

View from Avenida Luis Roche. c. 1956. The Museum of Modern Art,
New York. Gift of Gift of Bettina Beckhoff

Casa Mara, San Antonio de los Altos, Caracas. 1970–77
Jorge Castillo (Venezuelan, born 1933)

View of a prefabricated housing module. 1977. Photograph
by Jorge Andrés Castillo

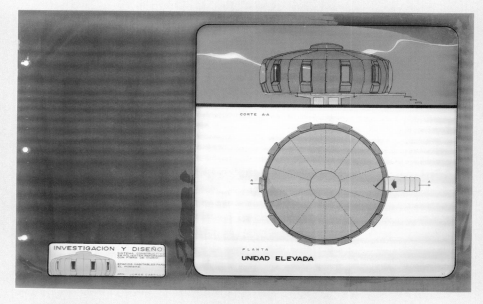

Plan and section of a typical raised unit. 1970. Zipatone on acetate,
15 ¾ x 23 ⅝ in. (40 x 60 cm). The Museum of Modern Art, New York.
Gift of the architect

Complejo Urbanístico Parque Central, Caracas. 1969–79
Sisto & Shaw Asociados Arquitectos (Venezuela, active 1964–1986)

Above: Brochure showing a model. 1971

Right: View of the courtyard. 1983. Photograph by Leo Matiz.
Fundación Leo Matiz

Project for *Caracas nodo de transferencia.* 1970   **Venezuela**   295
(Caracas transfer node)
Oasis. 1967
Jorge Rigamonti (Venezuelan, born Italy. 1940–2008)

Photocollage, 15 ¹⁄₁₆ x 9 ¼ in. (38.2 x 23.5 cm). The Museum of
Modern Art, New York. Latin American and Caribbean Fund

During Venezuela's precipitous postwar industrialization, the architect Jorge Rigamonti developed a highly original and provocative intellectual
position on the ways in which industrial and
transportation infrastructure was changing the
country. He would eventually be involved with
the development of the petroleum industry in
and around Lake Maracaibo, as well as with the
creation of the new city for the steel industry
at Ciudad Guayana, but earlier, in the years after
his graduation from the Universidad Central
de Venezuela, he created a powerful series of
Collages sobre la ciudad. These combined
photographs and found images from magazines
with imaginary drawings of architectural and
territorial interventions to reflect on both the triumphs and perils of large-scale industrialization.

BB

Photocollage, 6 ¹¹⁄₁₆ x 10 ¹⁄₁₆ in. (17 x 25.5 cm). The
Museum of Modern Art, New York. Gift of Helena
Correa de Rigamonti

Introduction   Patricio del Real

The written history of modern architecture in Latin America remains under construction, being a fairly recent enterprise intimately connected to the consolidation of a particular global imaginary after World War II and the hegemonic rise of North Atlantic cultural centers. The following essays discuss the publications in which the issues, terms, and ideas of modernism have appeared in individual countries, and the way the region's architecture was incorporated into general histories of modernism produced both locally and abroad. The bibliography itself has been placed online, at www.moma.org/laic_bibliography, where it will continue to grow.

Histories of modernism that incorporate the architecture of Latin America are conditioned by the changing strategies of assembling the region as a whole. The term "Latin America" was created in early-nineteenth-century France to advance a collective "Latin" identity rooted in culture, and ever since, it has been enriched, reinforced, questioned, and challenged by theoretical and practical assemblies that emphasize cultural, political, historical, and economic aspects of the region. Considerations of the nature of architectural modernism started early in the twentieth century, galvanized by ongoing debates on the development of national styles. Notions such as *nova arquitetura* in Brazil or *funcionalismo radical* in Mexico were debated in architecture and cultural journals. Early modernist developments were not put into a larger historical context, however, until after World War II, eventually coalescing first and foremost into national histories of modernism produced within the region. The historiography of modernism in Latin America oscillates between locally produced national histories—modulated by global overviews produced primarily in Spanish-speaking countries—and fragmentary incorporations of key moments in histories produced by scholars from outside the region. These latter histories have explained the emergence of modernism in Latin America primarily as an offshoot of European formal experiments that, responding to climate and culture, developed local stylistic idiosyncrasies with limited contributions to international discussions and formal explorations. In all, historical examinations from outside the region have been fragmentary, haphazard, and reductive, guided by the overarching aim of explaining the blossoming of modernism in Latin America in the mid-twentieth century.

Few histories of modern architecture produced outside Latin America have incorporated examples from the region, and those that do have treated only select developments in key countries as representative of the region as a whole. Latin American works first appeared in this literature in the context of the postwar polemic between functionalism and organicism, in Bruno Zevi's *Storia dell'architettura moderna* (1950), which mobilized examples in Brazil and Mexico to show the extent of the crisis of European rationalism. In *An Outline of European Architecture*, Nikolaus Pevsner summarily did the same by linking the "structural acrobatics" of Brazilian architecture to the postwar "expressionist" phase of Le Corbusier, signaled by his chapel of Notre Dame du Haut in Ronchamp, France. Zevi and Pevsner together inaugurated the tendency of viewing developments in the region as merely derivative of European movements. Moreover, these historians enabled the view of an exuberant or irrational "Latin American" style that would risk tainting "Western" modernism if it became too influential. In all, these histories argued that Latin American modernism tended toward baroque forms because, guided by Brazilian formal experiments, it was conditioned by a cultural predisposition for excessive formal experimentation, an overarching tropical geography, and an exuberant Latin sociological temperament coupled with a

deep colonial heritage. In these views, developments in Mexico, exemplified by the Ciudad Universitaria, fell too easily into folkloric nationalism and offered no positive counterbalance to Brazilian formalism.

In the 1950s ongoing developments were compiled in many surveys that captured the tremendous output of the region's architects. Two of the most singular were produced in 1955: Yuichi Ino and Shinji Koike's *Latin America* volume of the World's Contemporary Architecture series, published in Japan, and Henry-Russell Hitchcock's *Latin American Architecture since 1945*, accompanying the exhibition of the same name at The Museum of Modern Art. These surveys were enthusiastic about the work but had a limited impact on histories that attempted to explain the emergence and development of modern architecture. Three works of 1958—Hitchcock's *Architecture: Nineteenth and Twentieth Centuries*, Michel Ragon's *Livre de l'architecture moderne*, and Jürgen Joedicke's *Geschichte der modernen Architektur*—are paradigmatic examples of the integration of the region's architecture into the overall history of modernism. Unlike Ragon and Joedicke, Hitchcock included no works later than 1955, yet his history remains unparalleled for its unprecedented attempt to weave a complex tapestry of formal relationships that emphasized the rise of a new formal language along Miesian lines, being developed predominantly in Venezuela alongside the remarkable work of Carlos Raúl Villanueva. Although these histories reinforced the idea of the Corbusian origins of Latin American modernism, and helped to canonize the Ministério da Educação e Saúde in Rio de Janeiro as the singular point of modern architecture's introduction to the whole of South America, they acknowledged the level of independence and maturity reached in the region and thus tacitly rejected Zevi and Pevsner's initial outlook.

In *La arquitectura de las grandes culturas* (1957), the Cuban historian Joaquín Weiss emphasized this point and argued that the overall historical, climatic, and social conditions of Latin America favored the organic development of modernism without missionaries from abroad. A decade earlier, the Peruvian Luis Miró Quezada had advanced a similar humanistic and evolutionary thesis in *Espacio en el tiempo*. By 1958 and the dawn of Brasília, there was an overwhelming recognition of Brazilian modernism's contribution to the breaking of the rationalist and strict geometries of early functionalism. Opinions on the consequences of this liberation did not fall far from Pevsner's early warnings on its irrationalism, however, as most critics agreed that such formal explorations had become capricious. In contrast, Venezuelan developments were celebrated for their rigor and restraint, and for the restoration of a proper abstract universality to Latin American modernism.

Leonardo Benevolo's *Storia dell'architettura moderna* (1960) presented the Brazilian experience as an important shift in the geography of modernism. Yet Benevolo reduced the history of the entire region to that of Brazil, focusing on Brasília as the culminating point of this experience. Benevolo argued that Oscar Niemeyer's elemental and diagrammatic forms, decontextualized and disarticulated by the scale of the new capital city, had acquired surrealist tones that cast a shadow on the future of the city and, by implication, on the entire region. In all, as Sigfried Giedion argued in the 1962 fourth edition of *Space, Time and Architecture*, Brasília had closed the development of modernism in Latin America, which he summarized as a series of sudden bursts of activity that, although at times brilliant, were limited to regional and timely contributions.

In 1969 Francisco Bullrich met Benevolo and Giedion head-on, revising the story of the region's architecture after Brasília. His *Arquitectura latinoamericana, 1930–1970* was effectively the first book to consider the region's modern architecture as a whole, and it remains the key contribution from Latin America. Bullrich's book, published in both Spanish and English (with important differences, since the English-language edition contains more transnational thematic comparisons), revealed the tension between the necessity of presenting recent developments and the need to offer readers a historical overview. To manage this tension and address the enormous and diverse geography at hand, Bullrich advanced the notion of "common problems," in vogue in the political and social sciences of the period. Without abandoning "national features" and salient figures such as Villanueva, he accepted the regional frame by presenting a diversified production that rejected any form of authentic local or "Latin American" character. The roots of this overarching regional assembly based on perceived common traits can be found in the writings of the Spanish architectural historian Fernando Chueca Goitía, who inaugurated the idea of a common geocultural Iberian world in the 1940s.

Since the late 1960s, research centers, and journals such as *Summa*, have made efforts to go beyond Brasília. These efforts received impetus from the center-periphery model of dependency theory, deployed in works such as Rafael López Rangel's *Arquitectura y subdesarrollo en América Latina* (1975) and in collections of diverse voices such as Roberto Segre's *América Latina en su arquitectura* (1976) and Damián Bayón's *Panorámica de la arquitectura latinoamericana* (1977). These histories presented a tension between journalistic reporting and historical analysis; they also transformed the constraints of an architectural style, as described by Benevolo and Giedion, into the limitations of development in Latin America. The apparent impasse set by Brasília remained active in histories such as Manfredo Tafuri and Francesco Dal Co's *Architettura contemporanea* (1976). While the Italian historians did not reduce the entire region to a single country, they saw modern architecture there as unable to surpass its mid-twentieth-century developments, either by falling prey to the corporate modernism of US global hegemony, as in Mexican developments, or by wallowing in its own fashionable success, as in Brazil, where architecture had fallen into a manneristic repetition of scenographic forms. These summary judgments became the main historiographical line, repeated, for example, in William Curtis's *Modern Architecture since 1900* (1982) and Spiro Kostof's *A History of Architecture: Settings and Rituals* (1985).

The notion of commonality, first advanced by Bullrich and later reinforced by views on geography, politics, culture, and economy, became a key analytical frame, transforming into the shared problems of third world development, as in the 1982 Spanish edition of Benevolo's history, which included a chapter by the Catalan critic Josep María Montaner, or into the similarities of geography, culture, and identity in Critical Regionalism, as in Kenneth Frampton's *Modern Architecture: A Critical History* (1980). In Latin America, Ramón Gutiérrez (1983) and Leopoldo Castedo (1988) emphasized Iberian cultural similarities and colonial backgrounds to highlight the disruptive nature of modernism, and Bayón (1988) brought together architecture and art scholars to highlight the "points of contacts" enabled by modernity. International journals such as the French *Techniques et architecture*'s 1981 theme issue on Latin America, and the 1993 issue of the Italian *Zodiac*, gathered scholars and architects from key countries to present a synthesis of the development of modernism alongside the most salient works up until then. The historiographical impasse set by Benevolo and Giedion, however, remained active, as evidenced in Valerie Fraser's examination of Mexico, Venezuela, and Brazil in *Building the New World*, which stops in 1960.

The most pertinent architectural history to go beyond Brasília is Jorge Francisco Liernur's *America Latina: Architettura, gli ultimi vent'anni* (1990). Liernur assembled the region by bringing together diverse authors, and he developed the notion of common problems within architectural culture beyond stylistic considerations, examining topics such as the city, social housing, technology, and development from different positions. More important, he tackled the impasse set by Benevolo and Giedion by advancing the multiple futures imagined in the architecture produced after Brasília. In all, Liernur rejected the end of architecture in Latin America as announced by historians outside the region, and he gestured toward the future by examining architectural production in Latin America after 1960 as part of the ongoing history of its modern architecture.

This and other efforts have enabled the incorporation of nineteenth-century developments in Latin America in works such as Silvia Arango's *Ciudad y arquitectura: Seis generaciones que construyeron la América Latina moderna* (2012), and in genealogical compendiums of works along thematic, formal, and technological lines such as Luis Carranza and Fernando Lara's *Modern Architecture in Latin America: Art, Technology and Utopia* (2015). If the history of modern architecture in Latin America is on its way to being consolidated, a history of modernism as a whole, one that incorporates the region's development, produced both from outside and from within the region, remains very much in construction. This book offers another stone for that construction.

General References

Almandoz Marte, Arturo. *Planning Latin American Capital Cities, 1850–1950*. Planning, History, and the Environment Series. London: Routledge, 2002.

Arango, Silvia. *Ciudad y arquitectura: Seis generaciones que construyeron la América Latina moderna*. Mexico City: Fondo de Cultura Económica and Consejo Nacional para la Cultura y las Artes, 2012.

———. *Historia de un itinerario*. Bogotá: Universidad Nacional de Colombia, 2002.

———. "Historiografía latinoamericana reciente." *Archivos de arquitectura antillana* 9, no. 23 (January 2006): 163–69.

———. "Modos de actuar sentir y pensar en la arquitectura moderna latinoamericana." *Proa*, no. 407, 1991, pp. 30–36.

———. "Reflections upon Latin American Architecture: Sensorial Architecture and Contextuality." In Scott Marble, ed. *Architecture and Body*. New York: Rizzoli, 1988.

Bayón, Damián. *Arte moderno en América Latina*. Madrid: Taurus, 1985.

———. *Historia del arte hispanoamericano*. Madrid: Alhambra, 1987.

———. "Impressions of an Architecture: Colombia, Mexico, Venezuela." *Americas* 32 (January 1980): 13.

———. *Panorámica de la arquitectura latinoamericana*. Barcelona: Blume; Paris: UNESCO, 1977. Published in English as *The Changing Shape of Latin American Architecture: Conversations with Ten Leading Architects*. Chichester, U.K.: Wiley, 1979.

Boza, Cristián. *Las 100 obras de arquitectura latinoamericana del siglo XX*. Santiago: Editorial Los Andes, 2000.

Brillembourg, Carlos. *Latin American Architecture, 1929–1960: Contemporary Reflections*. New York: Monacelli Press, 2004.

Browne, Enrique. *Otra arquitectura en América Latina*. Naucalpan, Mexico: Gustavo Gili, 1988.

Bullrich, Francisco. *Arquitectura latinoamericana, 1930–1970*. Buenos Aires: Editorial Sudamericana, 1969.

———. *New Directions in Latin American Architecture*. New York: George Braziller, 1969.

Carranza, Luis E. "Expressions of Modernity in Latin American Architecture." *Journal of Architectural Education* 55, no. 4 (2002): 199–200.

Carranaza, Luis E., and Fernando Luiz Lara. *Historia del arte y de la arquitectura latinoamericana desde la época precolombina hasta hoy*. Santiago: Editorial Pomaire, 1970. Published in English as *A History of Latin American Art and Architecture from Pre-Columbian Times to the Present*. New York: Praeger, 1969.

———. *Historia del arte iberoamericano*. Madrid: Alianza Editorial, 1988.

———. *Modern Architecture in Latin America: Art, Technology and Utopia*. Austin: University of Texas Press, 2014.

Comas, Carlos Eduardo. "Memorandum latino americano: La ejemplaridad arquitectónica de lo marginal." Special issue on Latin America, *2G* (Barcelona), no. 8, 1998, pp. 130–43.

Comas, Carlos Eduardo, and Miquel Adrià. *La casa latinoamericana moderna: 20 paradigmas de mediados de siglo XX*. Naucalpan, Mexico: Gustavo Gili, 2003.

Comas, Carlos Eduardo, and Sérgio Marques, eds. *A segunda idade do vidro: Transparência e sombra na arquitetura moderna do Cone Sul Americano, 1930–1970*, Porto Alegre, Brazil: Centro Universitário Ritter dos Reis, Editora UniRitter, 2007.

Cuadra, Manuel. *Architektur in Lateinamerika: Die Andenstaaten Chile, Ecuador, Bolivien und Peru im 19. und 20. Jahrhundert: Geschichte, Theorie, Dokumente, mit 754 Abbildungen*. Darmstadt, Germany: J. Häusser, 1991.

Curtis, William J. R. *Modern Architecture since 1900*. Oxford: Phaidon, 1982.

Damaz, Paul. *Art in Latin American Architecture*. New York: Reinhold Publishing, 1963.

Filgueuras Gomes, Marco Aurélio A. de. *Urbanismo na América do Sul: Circulaçao de ideias e constituiçao do campo, 1929–1960*. Salvador, Brazil: Editora da Universidade Federal da Bahia, 2009.

Fraser, Valerie. *Building the New World: Studies in the Modern Architecture of Latin America, 1930–1960*. London: Verso, 2000.

Gasparini, Graziano, et al. "Situación de la historiografía de la arquitectura latinoamericana." Special issue, *Boletín del Centro de Investigaciones Históricas y Estéticas* (Caracas), no. 9 (April 1968).

Giedion, S. *A Decade of New Architecture*. Zurich: Girsberger, 1951.

———. "The State of Contemporary Architecture: The Regional Approach." *Architectural Record* 115, no. 1 (January 1954): 132–37.

Gonzales, Robert. *Designing Pan-America: U.S. Architectural Visions for the Western Hemisphere*. Austin: University of Texas Press, 2011.

Glusberg, Jorge. "Identidad y región: Recorrido crítico de la arquitectura en América Latina." *Summa*, no. 212 (May 1985): 47–52.

Glusberg, Jorge, and Kenneth Frampton, eds. *World Architecture, 1900—2000: A Critical Mosaic*. Vol. 2, *Latin America*. Vienna: Springer Verlag, 2000.

Guillen, Mauro F. "Modernism without Modernity: The Rise of Modernist Architecture in Mexico, Brazil, and Argentina, 1890–1940." *Latin American Research Review* 39, no. 2 (2004): 6–34.

Gutiérrez, Ramón. "Architectural Journals: The Means of Discourse in Latin America." *California Architect* 17, no. 2 (1995): 45–48.

———. *Architettura e società: L'America Latina nel XX secolo*. Milan: Jaca Book, 1996.

———. *Arquitectura y urbanismo en Iberoamérica*. Manuales Arte Cátedra. Madrid: Ediciones Cátedra, 1983.

———. "La historiografía de la arquitectura americana: Entre el desconcierto y la dependencia cultural, 1870–1985 (1)." *Archivos de arquitectura antillana*, no. 3, January 1997, pp. 88–91.

———. "La historiografía de la arquitectura americana: Entre el desconcierto y la dependencia cultural, 1870–1985 (3)." *Archivos de arquitectura antillana*, no. 5, September 1997, pp. 117–21.

Gutiérrez, Ramón, et al. *Arquitectura latinoamericana en el siglo XX*. Barcelona: Lunwerg; Milan: Jaca Book, 1998.

Gutiérrez, Ramón, and Centro de Documentación de Arquitectura Latinoamericana. *Le Corbusier en el Río de la Plata, 1929*. Buenos Aires: CEDODAL; Montevideo: Facultad de Arquitectura, Universidad de la República, 2009.

Gutiérrez, Ramón, Patricia Méndez, and Florencia Barcina. *Revistas de arquitectura de América Latina: 1900–2000*. San Juan: Universidad Politécnica de Puerto Rico, 2001.

Gutiérrez, Ramón, Jorge Tartarini, and Rubens Stagno. *Congresos panamericanos de arquitectos, 1920–2000: Aportes para su historia*. Buenos Aires: CEDODAL, 2007.

Hernández, Felipe, Mark Millington, and Iain Borden, eds. *Transculturation: Cities, Spaces, and Architectures in Latin America*. New York: Rodopi, 2005.

Hitchcock, Henry-Russell. *Architecture: Nineteenth and Twentieth Centuries*. 1958. Harmondsworth, U.K.: Penguin Books, 1975.

———. *Latin American Architecture since 1945*. New York: The Museum of Modern Art, 1955.

Ino, Yuichi, and Shinki Koike. *World's Contemporary Architecture: Latin America*. Tokyo: Shokokusha, 1955.

Joedicke, Jürgen. *Architecture since 1945: Sources and Directions*. New York: Praeger, 1969.

Koike, Shinki. *World's Contemporary Houses: Latin America*. Tokyo: Shokokusha, 1954.

Lejeune, Jean-François, and Centre International pour la Ville, l'Architecture et le Paysage. *Cruelty and Utopia: Cities and Landscapes of Latin America*. New York: Princeton Architectural Press, 2005.

Liernur, Jorge Francisco. *America Latina: Architettura, gli ultimi vent'anni. Tendenze dell'architettura contemporanea*. Milan: Electa, 1990.

———. "Cien años de soledad?: Identidad y modernidad en la cultura arquitectónica latinoamericana." *ARQ* 15, 1990, pp. 32–39.

———. *Escritos de arquitectura del siglo XX en América Latina*. Madrid: Tanais, 2002.

———. "Latin America: The Places of the Other." In Richard Koshalek et al. *At the End of the Century: One Hundred Years of Architecture*, pp. 277–318. Los Angeles: Museum of Contemporary Art, 1998.

———. "Menos es mísero: Notas sobre la recepción de la arquitectura de Mies van der Rohe en América Latina." *Arquine*, no. 18, 2001, pp. 66–79.

———. "Un nuovo mondo per lo spirito nuovo: Le scoperte dell'America Latina da parte della cultura architettonica del XX secolo." *Zodiac*, no. 8 (September 1992–February 1993): 84–121.

———. "The South American Way." *Block*, no. 4, 1999, pp. 23–41.

———. *Trazas de futuro: Episodios de la cultura arquitectónica de la modernidad en América Latina*. Santa Fe, Argentina: Ediciones UNL, 2008.

———. "Vanguardias versus expertos." *Block*, no. 6 (March 2004): 18–39.

López, Manuel. *Historia de la arquitectura y lucha de clases: Crítica a la historia de la arquitectura*. Caracas: Universidad Central de Venezuela, Facultad de Arquitectura y Urbanismo, División de Extensión Cultural, 1977.

López Rangel, Rafael. *Arquitectura y subdesarrollo en América Latina*. Puebla, Mexico: BUAP, 1975.

Marshall, P. J. "South American Scrapbook." *Architectural Review* 107, no. 638 (February 1950): 123–30.

Méndez Mosquera, Lala. "Arquitectura en Iberoamérica: Identidad y modernidad." *Summa*, no. 212, 1985, pp. 23–26.

Miró Quesada Garland, Luis. *Espacio en el tiempo: La arquitectura moderna como fenómeno cultural*. Lima, 1945.

Moholy-Nagy, Sibyl. "Some Aspects of South American Architecture." *Progressive Architecture*, April 1960, pp. 135–40.

Montaner, Josep Maria. "La arquitectura moderna en Latinoamérica." In Leonardo Benevolo, ed. *Historia de la arquitectura moderna*, pp. 917–58. Barcelona: Gustavo Gili, 1982.

Moré, Gustavo Luis, and Barry Bergdoll. "Caribbean Modernist Architecture." Special issue, *Archivos de arquitectura antillana,* 2009.

Moré, Gustavo Luis, and Eduardo Luis Rodríguez, eds. "El movimiento moderno en el Caribe insular." Special issue, *Docomomo Journal*, no. 33 (September 2005).

Morse, Richard M., and Jorge Enrique Hardoy. *Rethinking the Latin American City*. Washington, D.C.: Woodrow Wilson Center Press; Baltimore: Johns Hopkins University Press, 1992.

Pérez Oyarzún, Fernando. *Le Corbusier y Sudamérica: Viajes y proyectos*. Santiago: Ediciones Arq, 1991.

Posani, Juan Pedro, and Alberto Sato. "Thought from the Tropics." *Zodiac* 8, 1993, pp. 49–81.

Quantrill, Malcolm. *Latin American Architecture: Six Voices*. Studies in Architecture and Culture 5. College Station: Texas A&M University Press, 2000.

Real, Patricio del. "Simultaneous Territories: Unveiling the Geographies of Latin American Cities." *Architectural Design* 81, no. 3 (2011): 16–19.

Real, Patricio del, and Helen Gyger. *Latin American Modern Architectures: Ambiguous Territories* (New York: Routledge, 2012).

Ruiz Blanco, Manuel. *Vivienda colectiva estatal en Latinoamérica: Periodo 1930–1960*. Lima: Instituto de Investigación, Facultad de Arquitectura, Urbanismo y Artes, Universidad Nacional de Ingeniería, 2003.

Sambricio, Carlos, ed. *Ciudad y vivienda en América Latina (1930–1960)*. Madrid: Lampreave, 2013.

Sartoris, Alberto. *Encyclopédie de l'architecture nouvelle: Ordre et climat américains*. 1948. Milan: Hoepli, 1954.

———. *Gli elementi dell' architettura funzionale: Sintesi panoramica dell' architettura moderna*. 1932. Milan: Hoepli, 1935.

Sato Kotani, Alberto. "Simulacros urbanos en America Latina: Las ciudades de CIAM." *Astragalo*, no. 1 (June 1994): 55–67.

Segre, Roberto. *América Latina en su arquitectura*. América Latina en su cultura series. Paris: Unesco, 1975. Published in English as *Latin America in Its Architecture*. New York: Holmes and Meier, 1981.

———. *América Latina fim de milênio: Raízes e perspectivas de sua arquitetura*. São Paulo: Studio Nobel, 1991.

———. *Las estructuras ambientales en América Latina*. Havana: Universidad de La Habana, 1977.

Segre, Roberto, and Rafael López Rangel. *Arquitectura e territorio nell'America Latina*. Milan: Electa, 1982.

Segre, Roberto, Eliana Cárdenas, and Lohania Aruca. *Historia de la arquitectura y del urbanismo*. Vol. 3, *América Latina y Cuba*. Havana: Ediciones ENSPES, 1981.

Shmidt, Claudia. "A propósito de la 'posdata americana' de Pevsner." *Block*, no. 8 (March 2011): 42–47.

Suzuki, Makoto. "Latin America." Special issue on contemporary world architecture, *JA*, 1970, pp. 88–89.

Torre, Susana. "Cultural Identity and Modernity in Latin American Architecture." *Design Book Review*, nos. 32–33 (Spring–Summer 1994): 16–21.

Waisman, Marina. "Algunos conceptos críticos para el estudio de la arquitectura latinoamericana." *Boletín del Centro de Investigaciones Históricas y Estéticas* (Caracas) 18, 1974, p. 153.

———. *El interior de la historia: Historiografía arquitectónica para uso de latinoamericanos*. Colección historia y teoría latinoamericana. Bogotá: ESCALA, 1990.

———. "Para una caracterización de la arquitectura latinoamericana: Ponencia presentada en el IV seminario de arquitectura latinoamericana, Tlaxcala, México, 1989." *Arquitecturas del sur*, no. 66, 1989, p. 14.

———. "Paradojas de la utopía: Las dos últimas décadas." *A & V* 13, 1988, pp. 36–41.

Waisman, Marina, and César Naselli. *10 arquitectos latinoamericanos*. Seville: Consejería de Obras Públicas y Transportes, Dirección General de Arquitectura y Vivienda, 1989.

Weiss, Joaquín. *La arquitectura de las grandes culturas*. Havana: Editorial Minerva, 1957.

Argentina   Claudia Shmidt

The foundations of modern Argentine architecture began to be laid in the mid-1920s by specialist magazines such as *Revista de arquitectura* and *Nuestra arquitectura*, along with more widely ranging cultural journals such as *Martín Fierro* and *Sur*. More particularly the field was shaped by a group of principally young architects, including Alberto Prebisch, Antonio Vilar, and Wladimiro Acosta, whose works and whose aesthetic, technological, and urban ideas functioned to promote the new architecture. A turning point came in 1939 with the manifesto of Grupo Austral, signed by Antonio Bonet, Juan Kurchan, and Jorge Ferrari, which called for a humanistic rethinking of the relationship between urban planning and architecture. Historical research meanwhile supported a universal classicism over any specific national style.

World War II exposed a problem in the construction industry: a dependence on imports in a development-focused economy. But avant-garde magazines began to appear, including *Tecne* (1942), *Nueva visión* (1951), *Mirador* (1957), and *Obrador* (1963), and these, with the publishing houses NV and Infinito, articulated the challenges of contemporary architecture. Tomás Maldonado, Juan Manuel Borthagaray, Carlos Méndez Mosquera, Jorge Enrique Hardoy, César Janello, and Horacio Baliero were among those who addressed the problems of industrial modernization and changing ways of life.

This was the context in which, in 1963, Francisco Bullrich published *Arquitectura argentina contemporánea*, a first attempt to establish a canon of Argentine architects and their works. Bullrich initiated a history of a modern Argentine architecture located in a third world demanding drastic changes in the underlying conditions of production. For him the *casas blancas* (white houses) architectural movement had discovered another possible kind of classicism in the pre-Columbian and colonial world. Strong volumes, white walls, vaulted spaces, and terra-cotta tiles could be combined with concrete to produce organic forms with Corbusian echos that referenced a generic, atemporal history and signaled the necessity of a link between craft and technology. One approach to this goal looked toward an "industrial humanism" through the lens of the *Arte Concreto Invención* movement, which had called for good form, technical logic, and an integration of the arts. Another focused on individual creativity (Amancio Williams, Clorindo Testa). Meanwhile the magazine *Summa*, edited by Méndez Mosquera, first appeared in 1963 and sought to articulate the roots of an integrating common past—now termed Latin American—that might, in turn, construct a future through holistic design.

In the 1970s regionalist patrimonialism was linked to the appreciation for "national and popular" architecture manifested, with some variations, by Rafael Iglesia, Claudio Caveri, Ramón Gutiérrez, and others. From another perspective, Aldo Rossi's theory of the "analogue city," and the typological investigations of Antonio Díaz, Alberto Varas, and Justo Solsona, based on the tradition of city blocks, introduced a certain neutrality. In *Summarios*, Marina Waisman initiated an internationalist survey within a structuralist context.

In the late 1970s the modernist line opened by Bullrich began to be revalued, moving out of its position in the margins at the architectural workshop La Escuelita. Beginning in the 1980s the introduction of Frankfurt-inspired cultural history opened a parallel field, in tension with the dominance of Latin American Critical Regionalism. Jorge Francisco Liernur's critiques based on a "historical construction" of modern architecture in Argentina shifted the focal point; his work, together with that of figures like Ernesto Katzenstein, Roberto Fernández, the writers for the journal *Block*, and others, intervened in considerations of modern architecture and its foundational place in contemporary production

Acosta, Wladimiro. "Arquitectura contemporánea: Relaciones entre la industria y el arte de construer." *Nuestra arquitectura*, no. 23, 1931, pp. 920–21.
———. "El city-block integral." *Nuestra arquitectura*, no. 25, 1931, pp. 20–27.
———. *Vivienda y ciudad: Problemas de arquitectura contemporánea*. Buenos Aires: Anaconda, 1937.
Agrest, Diana, and Mario Gandelsonas. "arquitectura ARQUITECTURA." In *Summarios 13: Arquitectura crítica/Crítica arquitectónica*, pp. 5–8. Buenos Aires: Summa, 1970.
Alberto Prebisch: Una vanguardia con tradición. Buenos Aires: CEDODAL, 1999.
Baliero, Horacio, and Ernesto Katzenstein. "Reflexiones sobre el ladrillo en arquitectura." *Summa*, no. 199, 1984, pp. 50–51.
Borthagaray, Juan Manuel. "Industrialización liviana: Curtain Wall." *Summa*, no. 3, 1964, pp. 67–79.
Bullrich, Francisco. *Arquitectura argentina contemporánea*. Buenos Aires: Nueva Visión, 1963.
———. "Arquitectura industrial argentina." *Summa*, no. 5, 1966, pp. 23–24.
Caveri, Claudio. *El hombre a través de la arquitectura*. Buenos Aires: Carlos Lohlé, 1967.
"Coordenadas." *Tecné*, no. 1, 1942, pp. 1–2.
Córdova, Carmen. "Reflexiones." *Summa*, no. 199, 1984, p. 32.
Díaz, Antonio, Ernesto Katzenstein, Justo Solsona, and Rafael Viñoly. *La Escuelita: 5 años de enseñanza alternativa de arquitectura en la Argentina, 1976–1981*. Buenos Aires: Espacio Editora, 1981.
Fernández, Roberto. *La ilusión proyectual: Una historia de la arquitectura argentina, 1955–1995*. Mar del Plata, Argentina: Universidad, FADU, 1996.
Gazaneo, Jorge O., and Mabel Scarone. *Eduardo Catalano*. Buenos Aires: IAA, FAU, UBA, 1956.
González Capdevilla, Raúl. *Amancio Williams*. Buenos Aires: IAA, FAU, UBA, 1955.
Gorelik, Adrián. "La arquitectura de YPF: 1934–1943; Notas para una interpretación de las relaciones entre estado, modernidad e identidad en la arquitectura argentina de los años 30." *Anales del Instituto de Arte Americano e Investigaciones Estéticas,* no. 25, 1987, pp. 97–106.
Gorelik, Adrián, and Graciela Silvestri. "Arquitectura e ideología: Los recorridos de lo 'nacional y popular.'" *Revista de arquitectura*, no. 141, 1988, pp. 50–61.
Grupo Austral. "Voluntad y acción." Special issue on Grupo Austral, *Revista de arquitectura*, 1939.
Katzenstein, Ernesto. "Algo más sobre los 30." *Revista de arquitectura*, no. 144, 1989, pp. 90–97.
———. "Argentine Architecture of the Thirties." *Journal of the Decorative and Propaganda Arts*, no. 18, 1992, pp. 54–75.
Katzenstein, Ernesto, Jorge Francisco Liernur, and Jorge Sarquis. "Debate: Arquitectura argentina, 1930–1960." *Materiales*, no. 2, 1982, pp. 64–71.
Liernur, Jorge Francisco. *Arquitectura en la Argentina del siglo XX: La construcción de la modernidad*. Buenos Aires: Fondo Nacional de las Artes, 2001.
———. "The Bank of London and South America Head Office." *AA files*, no 34, 1997, pp. 24–44.

———. "El discreto encanto de nuestra arquitectura, 1930–1960." *Summa*, no. 223, 1986, pp. 60–79.

Liernur, Jorge Francisco, and Fernando Aliata. *Diccionario de arquitectura en la Argentina: Estilos, obras, biografías, instituciones, ciudades*. 6 vols. Buenos Aires: Agea, 2004.

Liernur, Jorge Francisco, and Anahí Ballent. *La casa y la multitud: Vivienda, política y cultura en la Argentina moderna*. Buenos Aires: Fondo de Cultura Económica, 2014.

Liernur, Jorge Francisco, Anahí Ballent, Jorge Mele, and Fernando Aliata. "Para una crítica: Concurso Nacional de Anteproyectos, la Biblioteca Nacional." *Materiales*, no. 1, 1982, pp. 12–80.

Liernur, Jorge Francisco, and Pablo Pschepiurca. *La red austral: Obras y proyectos de Le Corbusier y sus discípulos en la Argentina (1924–1965)*. Bernal, Argentina: Universidad Nacional de Quilmes, 2008.

Maldonado, Tomás. "Actualidad y porvenir del arte concreto." *Nueva visión*, no. 1, 1951, pp. 5–8.

Méndez Mosquera, Carlos. "Editorial." *Summa*, no. 1, 1963.

Ortiz, Federico. "Resumen de la arquitectura argentina desde 1925 hasta 1950." *Summa*, no. 106, 1976, pp. 87–90.

———. *SEPRA*. Buenos Aires: IAA, FAU, UBA, 1964.

Ortiz, Federico, and Ramón Gutiérrez. "La arquitectura en la Argentina, 1930–1970." Special issue, *Hogar y arquitectura*, 1972.

Prebisch, Alberto, and Ernesto Vautier. "Ensayo de estética contemporánea." *Revista de arquitectura*, no. 47, 1924, pp. 405–19.

Scarone, Mabel. *Antonio U. Vilar*. Buenos Aires: IAA, FAU, UBA, 1970.

Solsona, Justo. "Arquitectura: Año 1963." *Summa*, no. 2, 1963, pp. 83–84.

Suárez, Odilia. "El VIII Congreso Panamericano de Arquitectos: Una crónica." *Revista de arquitectura*, no. 368, 1952, pp. 49–51.

———. "En torno al concepto de desarrollo y su vinculación con la arquitectura." *Summa*, no. 127, 1978, pp. 34–38.

Trabucco, Marcelo. *Mario Roberto Álvarez*. Buenos Aires: IAA, FAU, UBA, 1965.

Vilar, Antonio. "Arquitectura contemporánea." *Nuestra arquitectura*, no. 25, 1931, pp. 18–19.

Waisman, Marina. "Argentina: La conflictiva década del '70." *Summa*, no. 157, 1980, pp 59–88.

———. "Una década revolucionaria: 1960–1970." *Summa*, nos. 200–201, 1984, pp. 58–63.

———. *La estructura histórica del entorno*. Buenos Aires: Nueva Visión, 1972.

———. "Integración nacional: Teorías; La cultura arquitectónica en el periodo de la integración nacional." *Summa*, no. 95, 1975, pp. 73–76.

———. "El lenguaje arquitectónico actual." *Nuestra arquitectura*, no. 337, 1957, pp. 25–36.

Williams, Amancio. "Arquitectura y urbanismo de nuestro tiempo." *Exposición arquitectura y urbanismo de nuestro tiempo: Exposición de obras originales*. Buenos Aires: Kraft, 1949.

Brazil Cláudia Costa Cabral

Philip Goodwin's exhibition and book *Brazil Builds*, produced by The Museum of Modern Art in 1943, provided the international launch for a school of modern architecture based in Rio, but it elicited controversy in the country itself: in 1948, the art critic Geraldo Ferraz demanded that Lucio Costa reverse Goodwin's "misrepresentation of information, which is beginning to determine the historiography of modern architecture in Brazil." According to Ferraz, Goodwin had ignored earlier modern works in São Paulo. Costa's response was to assert that the artistic value of Brazilian modern architecture, and its claim on international attention, derived not from the houses built by the Paulista Gregori Warchavchik in the late 1920s but from the original work of the Carioca Oscar Niemeyer, built on a Corbusian foundation.

The debate took another turn in the early 1950s, setting those who understood architecture as art ("construction conceived with plastic intention," in Costa's words) against those who understood architecture as service that provided housing for the people. Lina Bo and Pietro Maria Bardi, the founders and editors of the São Paulo–based magazine *Habitat*, opposed Niemeyer's "plastic complacencies" to the "severe morality" of João Batista Vilanova Artigas. Artigas himself, a communist like Niemeyer, denounced Le Corbusier's "reactionary ideology" and "servile formalism" in "Le Corbusier e o imperialismo." Writing from the southern city of Porto Alegre, Demétrio Ribeiro, another communist, asked for a national interpretation of Socialist Realism to achieve an architecture that the people could understand. Niemeyer launched *Modulo* magazine in 1955 to promote his ideas and refuted the criticisms of his architecture in "Problemas atuais da arquitetura moderna."

"To all appearances the modern movement had triumphed in Brazil," wrote Henrique E. Mindlin in *Modern Architecture in Brazil* (1956). "Unfortunately," he went on, "appearances are deceptive." Faced with the contradictions of the country's wide range of socioeconomic development, the literature on modern architecture and architects tends to deal with them in terms of responsibility for the future. In these terms, the idea of architecture as art, ratified once again by Niemeyer and Costa through the building of Brasília, represented a threat of degeneration for those who, like Ribeiro, considered formalism and "plastic acrobatics" unacceptable models, as "profligate opulence" was incompatible with Brazil's persistent underdevelopment. Pietro Maria Bardi's *Profile of the New Brazilian Art* (1970) made the opposite argument: Brazil could confront its gigantic size through its architecture, from Brasília on the plateau to Oswaldo Arthur Bratke's new cities in the Amazon, from works of engineering and infrastructure (the Jupiá and Ilha Solteira reservoirs, the Belém-Brasília highway) to large urban facilities such as Lina Bo Bardi's Museu de Arte de São Paulo, where the second generation of modern Brazilian architects emerged (Joaquim Guedes, Paulo Mendes da Rocha, Sérgio Ferro, and Rodrigo Lefèvre).

With the seizure of government by a military junta in 1964, these positions tended to become politicized, so that Bardi's vision came to be identified as conservative flag-waving, and the critique of the program of development as a posture of cultural resistance. In her article "Na América do Sul: Após Le Corbusier, o que está acontecendo" of 1967, Bo Bardi made an ironic reply to this latter position, and in particular to the "paternalistic advice" of the US journal *Progressive Architecture* (1967): South American architects should now seek inspiration in "Indian huts, little shacks and favelas of the poor, as befits underdeveloped architects who operate within an equally underdeveloped continent."

Yves Bruand's *Arquitetura contemporânea no Brasil* (1981) and Sylvia Ficher and Marlene Milan Acayaba's *Arquitetura moderna brasileira* (1982) brought this cycle to a close. Together these works constituted the first comprehensive history of modern Brazilian architecture, Bruand chronicling the eclectic work preceding the modern period and closing with the construction of Brasília, while Ficher and Acayaba addressed the 1970s and the regional developments of the modern legacy from north to south.

Le Corbusier e o Brasil (1987), by Cecilia Rodrigues dos Santos, Margareth Campos da Silva Pereira, Romão Veriano da Silva Pereira, and Vasco Caldeira da Silva, inaugurated a new cycle characterized by academic research. This cycle was nurtured by the growth of Brazilian postgraduate studies in architecture and by the establishment of national and international exchange networks (notably SAL—the Seminarios de Arquitectura Latinoamericana—and, since the late 1990s, Docomomo (the International Committee for Documentation and Conservation of Buildings, Sites and Neighborhoods of the Modern Movement). There has been a considerable expansion of documentary research, through not only general historiographical reviews (by Renato Anelli, Lauro Cavalcanti, Hugo Segawa, and Ruth Verde Zein) but thematic studies and monographs on the protagonists in the development of modern Brazilian architecture. New studies of foundational episodes (by Carlos Eduardo Dias Comas, Carlos Alberto Ferreira Martins, Pereira, Santos, and Zein) have provided the foundation for critical recognition of the modern legacy. Both approaches are rewriting the history of modern Brazilian architecture.

Andreoli, Elisabetta, and Adrian Forty, eds. *Brazil's Modern Architecture.* London: Phaidon, 2004.

Anelli, Renato, Abílio Guerra, and Nelson Kon. *Rino Levi: Arquitetura e cidade.* São Paulo: Romano Guerra, 2001.

Artigas, Rosa. *Paulo Mendes da Rocha: Projects, 1957–2007.* New York: Rizzoli, 2007.

Bastos, Maria Alice Junqueira. *Pós-Brasília: Rumos da arquitetura brasileira, discurso, prática e pensamento.* São Paulo: Perspectiva, 2003.

Bastos, Maria Alice Junqueira, and Ruth Verde Zein. *Brasil: Arquiteturas após 1950.* São Paulo: Perspectiva, 2010.

Bardi, Pietro Maria. *Profile of the New Brazilian Art.* Rio de Janeiro: Livraria Kosmos Editora, 1970.

Bo Bardi, Lina. "Na América do Sul: Após Le Corbusier, o que está acontecendo?" *Mirante das artes* (São Paulo), January–February 1967.

———. *Stones against Diamonds.* Edited by Silvana Rubino. Trans. Anthony Doyle and Pamela Johnston. London: AA Publications, 2012.

———. "Vilanova Artigas." *Habitat* (São Paulo), October 1950.

Bonduki, Nabil, org. *Affonso Eduardo Reidy.* Lisbon: Editorial Blau; São Paulo: Instituto Lina Bo e P. M. Bardi, 1999.

Braga, Milton. *O concurso de Brasília: Sete projetos para uma capital.* São Paulo: Cosac Naify, 2010.

Bruand, Yves. *Arquitetura contemporânea no Brasil.* São Paulo: Perspectiva, 1981.

Bruna, Paulo. *Arquitetura, industrialização e desenvolvimento.* São Paulo: Perspectiva, 1976.

———. *Os primeiros arquitetos modernos: Habitação social no Brasil, 1930–1950.* São Paulo: Edusp, 2010.

Camargo, Mônica Junqueira de. *Joaquim Guedes.* São Paulo: Cosac Naify, 2000.

Canez, Anna Paula, Carlos Eduardo Comas, and Glenio Bohrer. *Arquitecturas cisplatinas: Roman Fresnedo Siri e Eladio Dieste em Porto Alegre.* Porto Alegre, Brazil: UniRitter, 2004.

Cavalcanti, Lauro. *As preocupações do belo: Arquitetura moderna brasileira anos 1930/40.* Rio de Janeiro: Taurus, 1995.

———. *Sérgio Bernardes: Herói de uma tragédia moderna.* Rio de Janeiro: Relume-Dumara, 2004.

———. *When Brazil Was Modern: Guide to Architecture, 1928–1960.* New York: Princeton Architectural Press, 2003.

Cavalcanti, Lauro, and Fares El-Dahdah. *Roberto Burle Marx: A permanência do instável—100 anos.* Rio de Janeiro: Rocco, 2009.

Comas, Carlos Eduardo, ed. *Lucio Costa e as missões: Um museu em São Miguel.* Porto Alegre, Brazil: PROPAR/UFRGS, 2007.

Conduru, Roberto. *Vital Brazil.* São Paulo: Cosac Naify, 2000.

Costa, Lucio. "Carta-depoimento." 1948. In Costa, *Sobre arquitetura*, ed. Alberto Xavier. Porto Alegre, Brazil: CEUA, 1962.

———. *Considerações sobre arte contemporânea.* Rio de Janeiro: Ministéria da Educação e Cultura, 1952.

———. *Lucio Costa: Registro de uma vivência.* São Paulo: Empresa das Artes, 1995.

———. "Muita construção, alguma arquitetura e um milagre." *Correio da Manhã*, June 15, 1951. Republished in *Arquitetura brasileira: Depoimento de um arquiteto carioca.* Rio de Janeiro: Ministério da Educação e Cultura, 1952.

Czaikowski, Jorge, ed. *Jorge Machado Moreira.* Rio de Janeiro: Centro de Arquitetura e Urbanismo, 1999.

El-Dahdah, Fares. *Oscar 102 Brasília 50: Eight Cases in Brazil's Architectural Modernity.* Houston: Rice University, 2010.

El-Dahdah, Fares, ed. *Lucio Costa: Brasília's Superquadra.* New York: Prestel, 2005.

Evenson, Norma. *Two Brazilian Capitals: Architecture and Urbanism in Rio de Janeiro and Brasilia.* New Haven, Conn.: Yale University Press, 1973.

Fernandes de Oliveira, Olivia. *Lina Bo Bardi: Sutis substâncias da arquitetura.* São Paulo: Romano Guerra; Barcelona: Gustavo Gili, 2006.

Ferraz, Geraldo. "Falta o depoimento de Lucio Costa." *Diário de São Paulo*, February 1, 1948.

———. *Warchavchik e a introdução da nova arquitetura no Brasil.* São Paulo: MASP, 1965.

Ferraz, Marcelo, ed. *Lina Bo Bardi.* São Paulo: Instituto Lina Bo e P. M. Bardi, 1994.

Ficher, Sylvia, and Marlene Acayaba. *Arquitetura moderna brasileira.* São Paulo: Projeto, 1982.

Goodwin, Philip, and G. Kidder-Smith. *Brazil Builds: Architecture New and Old, 1652–1942.* New York: The Museum of Modern Art, 1943.

Guerra, Abilio, ed. *Textos fundamentais sobre historia da arquitetura brasileira.* 2 vols. São Paulo: Romano Guerra, 2010.

Guimarães, Eduardo Mendes. "Forma e racionalismo na arquitetura contemporânea brasileira." *Arquitetura e engenharia* (Belo Horizonte), January–February 1959.

Kamita, João. *Vilanova Artigas.* São Paulo: Cosac Naify, 2000.

Koury, Ana Paula. *Arquitetura nova: Flávio Império, Rodrigo Lefèvre, Sérgio Ferro.* São Paulo: Romano Guerra Editora, Edusp, Fapesp, 2004.

Latorraca, Giancarlo, ed. *João Filgueiras Lima: Lele.* Lisbon: Editorial Blau, 2000.

———. *Maneiras de expor: Arquitetura expostiva de Lina Bo Bardi/ Ways of Showing: The Exhibition Architecture of Lina Bo Bardi.* São Paulo: Museu de Casa Brasileira, 2014.

Lepik, Andres, and Vera Seimone Bader, eds. *Lina Bo Bardi 100: Brazil's Alternative Path to Modernism.* Ostfildern-Ruit, Germany: Hatje Cantz Verlag, 2014.

Lima, Zeuler. *Lina Bo Bardi.* New Haven, Conn.: Yale University Press, 2013.

Lira, José. *Warchavchik: Fraturas da vanguarda.* São Paulo: Cosac Naify, 2011.

Lissovsky, Mauricio, and Paulo Sérgio Moraes de Sá. *Colunas da educação: A construção do Ministério da Educação e Saúde.* Rio de Janeiro: MINC, IPHAN, 1996.

Luigi, Gilbert. *Oscar Niemeyer: Une Esthétique de la fluidité.* Marseille, France: Parenthèse, 1987.

Macedo, Danilo. *Da matéria à invenção: As obras de Oscar Niemeyer em Minas Gerais, 1938–1955.* Brasília: Câmara dos Deputados, 2008.

Magalhães, Sergio, ed. *Arquitetura brasileira após Brasília: Depoimentos.* 3 vols. Rio de Janeiro: Instituto dos Arquitetos do Brasil, 1978.

Mindlin, Henrique E. *Modern Architecture in Brazil.* New York: Reinhold, 1956.

Montezuma, Roberto, ed. *Arquitetura Brasil 500 anos/Architecture Brazil 500 Years.* 2 vols. Recife, Brazil: UFPE, 2002–08.

Niemeyer, Oscar. *Oscar Niemeyer.* Milan: Mondadori, 1975.

Nobre, Ana Luisa, João Masao Kamita, Octavio Leonidio, and Roberto Conduru, eds. *Lucio Costa: Um modo de ser moderno.* São Paulo: Cosac Naify, 2004.

Papadaki, Stamo. *The Work of Oscar Niemeyer.* New York: Rheinhold, 1950.

Penteado, Fábio. *Fábio Penteado: Ensaios e projetos.* São Paulo: Empresa das Artes, 1998.

Pessoa, José, Eduardo Vasconcellos, Elisabete Reis, and Maria Lobo, ed. *Moderno e nacional.* Niterói, Brazil: EDUFF, 2006.

Philippou, Styliane. *Oscar Niemeyer: Curves of Irreverence.* New Haven, Conn.: Yale University Press, 2008.

Pisani, Daniele. *Paulo Mendes da Rocha: Tutte le opere.* Milan: Mondadori–Electa Architettura, 2013.

Puppi, Marcelo. *Por uma história não moderna da arquitetura brasileira: Questões de historiografia.* Campinas, Brazil: Pontes, CPHA/IFCH, Unicamp, 1998.

Quesado Deckker, Zilah. *Brazil Built: The Architecture of the Modern Movement in Brazil.* London: Spon Press, 2001.

Ribeiro, Demétrio, José de Souza, and Enilda Ribeiro. "Situação da arquitetura brasileira." *Brasil: Arquitetura contemporânea* (Rio de Janeiro), no. 7, 1956.

Santos, Cecilia Rodrigues dos, et al. *Le Corbusier e o Brasil.* São Paulo: Projeto, Tessela, 1987.

Santos, Paulo F. *Quatro séculos de arquitetura.* Rio de Janeiro: Valença, 1977.

Segawa, Hugo. *Arquiteturas no Brasil, 1900–1990.* São Paulo: Edusp, 1998. Published in English as *The Architecture of Brazil, 1900–1990.* New York: Springer, 2013.

Segawa, Hugo, and Guilherme Mazza Dourado. *Oswaldo Arthur Bratke.* São Paulo: Pró-editores, 1997.

Segre, Roberto. *Ministério da Educação e Saúde: Ícone urbano da modernidade brasileira, 1935–1945.* São Paulo: Romano Guerra, 2013.

Silva, Elcio Gomes da. *Os palácios de Brasília.* Brasília: Camara dos Deputados, 2014.

Spiro, A. *Paulo Mendes da Rocha: Bauten und Projekte.* Sulgen, Switzerland: Niggli, 2002.

Tinem, Nelci. *O alvo do olhar estrangeiro: O Brasil na historiografia da arquitetura moderna.* João Pessoa, Brazil: Editora Universitária, 2006.

Tsiomis, Yannis, ed. *Le Corbusier: Rio de Janeiro, 1929–1936.* Rio de Janeiro: Centro de Arquitetura e Urbanismo, 1998.

Underwood, David. *Oscar Niemeyer and the Architecture of Brazil.* New York: Rizzoli, 1994.

Vilanova Artigas, João Batista. *Os caminhos da arquitetura.* São Paulo: Lech, 1981.

———. "Le Corbusier e o imperialismo." *Fundamentos* (São Paulo), January 1951. Republished in <author?> *Caminhos da arquitetura*, São Paulo: Lech, 1981.

Warchavchik, Gregori. "Importância e diretivas da arquitetura brasileira." *Acrópole*, February 1958.

Williams, Richard. *Brazil.* London: Reaktion Books, 2009.

Wisnik, Guilherme. *Lucio Costa.* São Paulo: Cosac Naify, 2001.

Xavier, Alberto, ed. *Arquitetura moderna brasileira: Depoimento de uma geração.* São Paulo: Pini, Associação Brasileira de Ensino da Arquitetura, Fundação Vilanova Artigas, 1987.

Xavier, Alberto, and Julio Roberto Katinsky, eds. *Brasília: Antologia crítica.* São Paulo: Cosac Naify, 2012.

Chile   Alejandro G. Crispiani

Publications on modern architecture began to appear in Chile at the end of the 1920s. The country's first debates on both the nature of the new architecture and the local possibilities of modern urban planning took place in the magazines *ARQuitectura* (1935–36), *Urbanismo y arquitectura* (1936–40), and others. The 1950s and '60s saw the development of various lines of theoretical thought—some of Chile's most original thinking on architectural culture in the twentieth century. Particularly significant was the production of the Escuela de Arquitectura de la Universidad Católica in Valparaíso, where Alberto Cruz and Godofredo Iommi were central figures. Their ideas tended toward the radically modern, foregrounding the relationship between architecture and poetry and finding expression in a range of different writings—indeed the most important text of this time and place was the collectively written poetry book *Amereida* (1967). The equally radical theories of Juan Borchers and, to a lesser extent, José Ricardo Morales must also be noted; approaching the subject from very different perspectives, both men tried to create a theoretical foundation for the practice of modern architecture.

Systematic studies of the history of modern architecture in Chile began in the late 1960s, and were later compiled in Manuel Moreno and Humberto Eliash's book *Arquitectura y modernidad en Chile, 1925–1965: Una realidad múltiple* (1989). In the last two decades, both subjects and methodologies have diversified, making space for a broad range of approaches. Although philosophical texts still appear, they have largely given way to a proliferation of historical studies, sometimes combining with criticism. Works like *Portales del laberinto* (2009), by Jorge Francisco Liernur, Fernando Pérez Oyarzún, Pedro Bannen, and

Federico Deambrosis; *Chilean Modern Architecture since 1950* (2011), by Pérez Oyarzún, Rodrigo Pérez de Arce, and Horacio Torrent); and a number of others show a rich perspective on Chilean architecture in the early twenty-first century.

The city of Santiago developed alongside the early debates on modern architecture. Karl Brunner's book *Santiago de Chile: Su estado actual y futura formación* (1932), which put forth both a plan for the Chilean capital and a criticism of Le Corbusier's theories and urban plans in the context of the Congrès Internationaux d'Architecture Moderne, is an early example of a historical approach. Although that approach was rejected by more radical groups, it is nonetheless relevant for both its judgments and its proposals. More thorough historical studies of Santiago developed slowly in the next decades. The planning theories of the 1970s, exemplified in John Friedmann's work on Santiago, contributed ideas but no historical analysis. In the 1970s and '80s, Juan Parrochia and Armando de Ramón, although they used different methodologies, helped to establish a historical view of Chile's capital.

Alongside the debates on modern architecture and urban planning there appeared studies of the history of so-called colonial Chilean architecture. Following an approach originally developed at the Universidad de Chile, the first fully systematic studies of this kind appeared in the 1930s and '40s, in the work of Alfredo Benavides and Manuel Eduardo Secchi. Pursuing this direction in the 1970s and beyond, Gabriel Guarda reasserted the value of history as an intellectual project.

Benavides, Juan. *Las razones de la nueva arquitectura*. Santiago: Editorial Universitaria, 1978.

Borchers, Juan. *Institución arquitectónica*. Santiago: Andrés Bello. c. 1968.

——. *Meta-arquitectura*. Santiago: Mathesis, 1975.

Brunner, Karl H. *Santiago de Chile: Su estado actual y futura formación*. Santiago: Imprenta La Tracción, 1932.

Cáceres, Osvaldo. *La arquitectura de Chile independiente*. Concepción, 1974.

Camus, Eduardo. "La arquitectura moderna en Chile." *Arquitectura y arte decorativo*, nos. 6–7 (October 1929): 235–60.

Colegio de Arquitectos de Chile. *La arquitectura chilena: Presentación al VI Congreso Panamericano de Arquitectos*. Santiago: Zig-Zag, 1947.

Cruz, Alberto, and Godofredo Iommi. "La ciudad abierta: De la utopía al espejismo." *Revista universitaria* 9, 1983, pp. 17–25.

Drifts and Derivations: Experiences, Journeys, and Morphologies/Desvíos de la deriva: Experiencias, travesías y morfologías. Madrid: Museo Nacional de Arte Reina Sofía, 2010.

Earwaker, Francis J., and John Friedmann. *Chile: La década del 70; Contribuciones a las políticas urbana, regional y habitacional*. Santiago: Fundación Ford, 1969.

Echeñique, Marcial. *Modelos en planificación y diseño urbano*. Santiago: Universidad de Chile, Facultad de Arquitectura y Urbanismo, 1971.

Eliash, Humberto, and Manuel Moreno. *Arquitectura y modernidad en Chile, 1925–1965: Una realidad múltiple*. Santiago: Universidad Católica de Chile, 1989.

Escuela de Arquitectura, Universidad Católica de Valparaíso. *Exposición 20 años Escuela de Arquitectura UCV*. Valparaíso: Escuela de Arquitectura, UCV, 1972.

Fernández Cox, Cristián. *Arquitectura y modernidad apropiada: Tres aproximaciones y un intento*. Santiago: Universitaria, 1990.

Friedmann, John, and Thomas Lackington. *La hiperurbanización y el desarrollo nacional en Chile*. Santiago: Universidad Católica de Chile, Comité Interdisciplinario de Desarrollo Urbano, 1967.

Greve Schlegel, Ernesto. *Historia de la ingeniería en Chile*. Santiago: Editorial Universitaria, 1938.

Gross, Patricio. *Arquitectura en Chile*. Santiago: Ministerio de Educación, Departamento de Extensión Cultural, c. 1978.

Iommi, Godofredo, et al. *Amereida*. Santiago: Editorial Cooperativa Lambda, 1967.

——. *Fundamentos de la Escuela de Arquitectura Universidad Católica de Valparaíso*. Valparaíso: Escuela de Arquitectura, UCV, 1971.

Irarrázaval C., Raúl. *Arquitectura chilena: La búsqueda de un orden espacial*. Santiago: Nueva Universidad, 1978.

Ministerio de la Vivienda y Urbanismo. *Política habitacional del gobierno popular: Programa 1972*. Santiago: Universitaria, 1972.

Morales, José Ricardo. *Arquitectónica: Sobre la idea y el sentido de la arquitectura*. Santiago: Universitaria, 1966–69.

Muñoz Lagos, Carlos A., et al. *Urbanización de Chile: Perspectivas y tendencias*. Santiago: Universidad de Chile, DEPUR, 1976.

Parrochia, Juan A. *Santiago en el tercer cuarto del s. XX*. Santiago: Universidad de Chile, DEPUR, 1979.

Peña, Carlos. *Santiago de siglo en siglo*. Santiago: Empresa Editora Zig-Zag, 1944.

Pendleton-Jullian, Ann M. *The Road That Is Not a Road and the Open City, Ritoque, Chile*. Cambridge, Mass.: MIT Press, 1996.

Pérez Oyarzún, Fernando. *Bresciani Valdés Castillo Huidobro*. Santiago: Editorial Arq, 2006.

Plaut, Jeannette, and Marcelo Sarovic. *CEPAL, 1961–1966*. Santiago: Constructo, 2012.

Quantrill, Malcolm, ed. *Chilean Modern Architecture since 1950*. College Station: Texas A&M Press, 2010.

Ramón, Armando de. *Historia urbana: Una metodología aplicada*. Buenos Aires: Clacso, Siap, 1978.

Rispa, Raúl, ed. *Valparaíso School: Open City Group*. Montreal: McGill–Queen's University Press, 2003.

Suárez, Isidro. *Organización, filosofía y lógica de la programación arquitectural*. Santiago: Universidad Católica de Chile, c. 1976–79.

——. *La refutación del espacio como sustancia en la arquitectura*. Santiago: Pontificia Universidad Católica de Chile, 1986.

Torrent, Horacio. "Una recepción diferente: La arquitectura moderna brasileña y la cultura arquitectónica chilena." *ARQ*, no. 78 (August 2011): 40–57.

Violich, Francis. *Urban Growth and Planning in Chile*. Berkeley, 1958.

Waisberg, Myriam. *En torno a la historia de la arquitectura chilena*. Santiago: Universidad de Chile Sede Valparaíso, Facultad de Arte y Tecnología, Departamento de Arquitectura y Urbanismo, 1978.

Colombia   Hugo Mondragón and Ricardo Daza

The story of modern architecture in Colombia begins with Carlos Martínez and Jorge Arango's book *Arquitectura en Colombia: Arquitectura colonial, 1538–1810; Arquitectura contemporánea en cinco años, 1946–1951*, published in 1951 by Editorial Proa. The book's structure resembles that of The Museum of Modern Art's exhibition catalogue *Brazil Builds* (1943): a selection of contemporary works preceded by an introduction attempting to link them with Colombian colonial architecture. With some nuances, this was the primary agenda of the magazine *Proa* during the thirty years that Martínez was its editor (1946–76), and it is also the evident agenda of *Arquitectura en Colombia*.

In 1981 Anne Berty published *Architectures colombiennes: Alternatives aux modèles internationaux*, a book that took a radical position against modernist architecture. Rather than seek a synthesis of the national and the international, Berty proposed the local as a project of resistance—resistance of the margin against the center, the local against the global. This ideological turn weighed heavily in the 1980s and '90s and in some areas still dominates today. Silvia Arango's essay "La evolución del pensamiento arquitectónico en Colombia, 1934–1984," published in the *Anuario de la arquitectura en Colombia* for 1984 and again in the 1989 *Historia de la arquitectura en Colombia*, follows a similar agenda. These historical narratives were constructed with the goal of homogenizing Rogelio Salmona's architectural program into a larger program of Colombian architecture.

As a body of critical writing that was particularly influential in its field, the writing of Germán Téllez Castañeda stands out for its distance from the ideological themes of nationalism versus internationalism and for its interest in the discipline of architecture. Recent studies also address concrete examples such as the Bogotá avenue Carrera Décima, Paul Lester Wiener and José Luis Sert's plans for Colombian cities, and Le Corbusier's much-studied encounter with Bogotá. Recent texts have recuperated the vision of ecological structure seen in Le Corbusier's plan for the city, as well as the role Bogotá played as an urban laboratory in his development scheme for Chandigarh, India.

Recent years have seen the publication of many monographs on individual architects, as well as case studies of specific cities. Carlos Niño's *Arquitectura y estado* examines the projects of the Ministerio de Obras Públicas. Essays such as Hugo Mondragón and Felipe Lanuza's "El intrincado juego de la identidad: Para una arqueología de la arquitectura colombiana" (2008) evidence the beginnings of critical reflection on the deliberate and militant practices of the history and critique produced in the 1980s and '90s.

Arango, Silvia. *Historia de la arquitectura en Colombia*. Bogotá: Editorial Universidad Nacional, 1989.

Arango Sanín, Jorge, and Carlos Martínez. *Arquitectura en Colombia: Arquitectura colonial, 1538–1810; Arquitectura contemporánea en cinco años, 1946–1951*. Bogotá. Ediciones Proa, 1951.

Arias Lemos, Fernando. *Le Corbusier en Bogotá: El proyecto del "grand immeuble," 1950–1951*. Bogotá: Universidad Nacional de Colombia, 2008.

Berty, Anne. *Architectures colombiennes: Alternatives aux modèles internationaux*. Paris: Le Moniteur, 1981.

Echeverría Castro, Nelcy. *La arquitectura de Aníbal Moreno Gómez, 1925–1990: La libertad espacial*. Bogotá: Universidad de La Salle, 2009.

Fonseca M., Lorenzo. *Aspectos de la arquitectura contemporánea en Colombia*. Bogotá: Centro Colombo-Americano, c. 1977.

Glusberg, Jorge. "Rogelio Salmona." *Dos puntos*, no. 5 (May–June 1982): 3–87.

Hofer, Andreas. *Karl Brunner y el urbanismo europeo en América Latina*. Bogotá: Corporación la Candelaria, 2003.

Martínez, Carlos, and Edgar Burbano. *Arquitectura en Colombia*. Bogotá: Ediciones Proa, 1963.

Mondragón López, Hugo. *Arquitectura en Colombia, 1946–1951: Lecturas críticas de la revista "Proa."* Santiago: Pontificia Universidad Católica de Chile, 2002.

———. "Arquitectura, modernización económica y nacionalismo: Una visión a partir de dos revistas de arquitecturalatinoamericanas de Posguerra: *Arquitectura* y *Construcción* y *Proa*." *Bitácora Urbano-Territorial* 1, no. 18 (2011): 55.

Montenegro Lizarralde, Fernando, and Carlos Niño Murcia. *Fernando Martínez Sanabria: Trabajos de arquitectura*. Bogotá: Escala, 1979.

———. *La vivienda de Guillermo Bermúdez*. Bogotá: Escala, 1981.

Niño Murcia, Carlos. *Arquitectura y estado*. Bogotá: Universidad Nacional, 1991.

Niño Murcia, Carlos, and Sandra Reina Mendoza. *La carrera de la modernidad: Construcción de la Carrera Décima; Bogotá, 1945–1960*. Bogotá: Alcaldía Mayor, Instituto Distrital de Patrimonio Cultural, 2010.

Orozco, María Cecilia O'Byrne, ed. *LC BOG: Le Corbusier en Bogotá, 1947–1951*. 2 vols. Bogotá: Ediciones Universidad de los Andes, 2010.

Rodríguez Botero, Germán Dario. *De la arquitectura orgánica a la arquitectura del lugar, en las casas Wilkie (1962) y Calderón (1963) de Fernando Martínez Sanabria (una aproximación a partir de la experiencia)*. Bogotá: Universidad Nacional de Colombia. Facultad de Artes, 2007.

Rother, Hans. *Arquitecto Leopoldo Rother*. Bogotá: Escala, 1984.

———. *Bruno Violi*. Bogotá: Universidad Nacional, 1986.

Samper Martínez, Eduardo. *Arquitectura moderna en Colombia: Época de oro*. Bogotá: Diego Samper Ediciones, 2000.

Schnitter, Patricia. *José Luis Sert y Colombia: De la Carta de Atenas a una carta del hábitat*. Medellín: Editorial Universidad Pontificia Bolivariana, 2004.

———. "Sert y Wiener en Colombia: La vivienda social en la aplicación del urbanismo moderno." *Scripta nova: Revista electrónica de geografía y ciencias sociales*, no. 7, 2003.

Serrano Camargo, Rafael. "Semblanza de Gabriel Serrano Camargo." *Cuaderno Proa*, no. 2, 1983.

Tascón, Rodrigo. *La arquitectura moderna en Cali: La obra de Borrero, Zamorano y Giovanelli*. Cali, Colombia: Fundación Civilis, n.d.

Téllez Castañeda, Germán. "La arquitectura y el urbanismo en la época actual, 1935–1979." *Manual de historia de Colombia*, vol. 3, pp. 343–412. Bogotá: Colcultura, 1980.

———. *Cuellar Serrano Gómez: Arquitectura, 1933–1983*. Bogotá: Escala, 1988.

———. *Rogelio Salmona: Obra completa, 1959–2005*. Bogotá: Escala, 2006.

Vélez-Ortiz, Cristina, Diego López Chalarca, Mauricio Gaviria Restrepo, and Nathalie Montoya Arango. *Arquitectura moderna en Medellín, 1947–1970*. Medellín: Editorial Universidad Nacional, 2010.

Villegas Jiménez, Benjamín, and Alberto Saldarriaga. *Casa moderna: Half a Century of Colombian Domestic Architecture*. Bogotá: Villegas Editores, 2001.

Cuba Belmont Freeman

Before the 1959 revolution and through the early 1960s, some of the most notable writing on Cuban architecture appeared in the pages of the journal *Arquitectura* (renamed *Arquitectura Cuba* in 1959). Starting in the 1930s the magazine's editors featured modernist works by Cuban practitioners and published widely read essays by critics and architects such as Eugenio Batista and Pedro Martínez Inclán. In 1951 the journal *Espacio*, produced by the students of the Escuela de Arquitectura in Havana, challenged the hegemony of *Arquitectura* and advanced the cause of modernism in multiple disciplines. The founding figure of the history of modernism in Cuba was Joaquín Weiss, who produced the first survey of contemporary Cuban architecture, in 1947, and one of Latin America's first histories of architecture worldwide, in 1957. Weiss's acute reflections on modernism fell into obscurity, however, overshadowed by his accomplished studies on colonial architecture and by the ideological turn that overtook Cuban scholarship after the revolution. During this period, governmental agencies such as the Ministerio de la Construcción produced good compendiums such as *La arquitectura escolar de la revolución cubana* (1973) and *Arquitectura y desarrollo nacional* (1978), which contextualize the building achievements of the revolution in terms of the larger history of social and economic development in Cuba.

Since 1970 two scholars who represent generationally divergent attitudes toward the subject have dominated the literature. Before his death in 2013, the Italian-Argentine architect Roberto Segre was a vigorous proponent of the Cuban Revolution. He went to Cuba in 1963, joined the faculty of the Universidad de La Habana, and was an influential teacher there for thirty years. His seminal 1970 publication *Diez años de arquitectura en Cuba revolucionária* valorized the work of the 1960s generation of Cuban architects as crucial to the socialist project while denigrating those who went into exile. Eduardo Luis Rodríguez was a student of Segre's. In writings beginning in the 1990s, Rodríguez has sought to depoliticize the narrative, to illuminate the work of the island's early modernists, and to reconnect the architecture of the postrevolution era to its antecedents in Cuban modernism of the 1940s and '50s. His 1997 essay "La década incógnita: Los cincuenta; modernidad, identidad y algo más" was the first work of Cuban scholarship to consider the masters of the 1950s free of guilt by association with the old regime.

Work on Cuban architecture since the revolution remains incomplete. John Loomis's 1999 *Revolution of Forms: Cuba's Forgotten Art Schools* brought international celebrity to the neglected Escuelas Nacionales de Arte buildings of 1959–64 and promoted the campus as a singular emblem of revolutionary ideals. In 2004 Rodríguez presented the broader scope of the remarkable architecture of the first decade of the revolution in an exhibition at New York's Storefront for Art and Architecture, *Architecture and Revolution in Cuba, 1959–1969*, though a publication has yet to emerge from the project. Timothy Hyde's recent *Constitutional Modernism*, which examines the process and form of civic architecture in the politically troubled decades before the revolution, is a significant achievement and an example for future scholarship on the longer history of Cuban modernism.

Congress of the International Union of Architects. *Cuba: La arquitectura en los países en vías de desarorollo.* Havana: UIA, 1963.

Coyula, Mario, Joseph Scarpaci, and Roberto Segre. *Havana: Two Faces of the Antillean Metropolis.* Chapel Hill: University of North Carolina Press, 2002.

Cuevas Toraya, Juan de las, Gonzalo Sala Santos, and Abelardo Padrón Valdés. *500 años de construcciones en Cuba.* Madrid: Chavín, Centro de Información de la Construcción, 2001.

Ferrari, A. "Architettura a Cuba." *Casabella* 354, 1970, pp. 9–15.

Freeman, Belmont. "Housing the Revolution: Cuba, 1959–1969." *Archivos de arquitectura antillana*, no. 34 (September 2009).

———. "What Is It About the Art Schools?" *Places Journal* website, February 27, 2012, placesjournal.org/article/what-is-it-about-the-art-schools.

Hyde, Timothy. *Constitutional Modernism: Architecture and Civil Society in Cuba, 1933–1959.* Minneapolis: University of Minnesota Press, 2012.

Lejeune, Jean-François. "The City as Landscape: Jean Claude Nicolas Forestier and the Great Urban Works of Havana, 1925–1930." *Journal of the Decorative and Propaganda Arts* 22, 1996, pp. 150–85.

Loomis, John. *Revolution of Forms: Cuba's Forgotten Art Schools.* New York: Princeton Architectural Press, 1999.

Quintana, Nicolás. "Evolución histórica de la arquitectura cubana." In Vicente Báez, ed. *La enciclopedia de Cuba*, pp. 1–115. San Juan: Enciclopedia y Clásicos Cubanos, 1977.

Richards, J. M. "Havana Pavilion for the 7th IUA Congress." *Architectural Record* 135 (February 1964): 145–47.

———. "Report from Cuba." *Architectural Record* 135 (November 1964): 222–24.

Rodríguez, Eduardo Luis. "The Architectural Avant-Garde: From Art Deco to Modern Regionalism." *Journal of the Decorative and Propaganda Arts* 22, 1996.

———. *"La década incógnita: Los cincuenta; Modernidad, identidad y algo más."* *Arquitectura Cuba*, no. 376 (December 1997): 36–43.

———. *La Habana: Arquitectura del siglo XX.* Barcelona: Blume, 1998.

———. *The Havana Guide: Modern Architecture, 1925–1965.* New York: Princeton Architectural Press, 2000.

———. *"Theory and Practice of Modern Regionalism in Cuba."* *Docomomo Journal* (Paris) 2005, pp. 12–20.

Rodríguez, Eduardo Luis, ed. *La arquitectura del movimiento moderno: Selección de obras del registro nacional.* Havana: Docomomo Cuba, Ediciones Unión, 2011.

Rodríguez, Eduardo Luis, and María Elena Martín Zequeira. *La Habana: An Architectural Guide.* Havana: Dirección Provincial de Planificación Física y Arquitectura, Ciudad de La Habana, 1998.

Rownstree, Diana. "New Architecture of Castro's Cuba." *Architectural Forum* 120 (April 1964): 122–25.

Salinas, Fernando, Roberto Segre, et al. *Ensayos sobre arquitectura e ideología en Cuba revolucionaria.* Havana: Universidad de La Habana, 1970.

Sambricio, Carlos, et al, *Arquitectura en la Ciudad de La Habana: Primera modernidad.* Madrid: Electa España, 2000.

Segre, Roberto. "Antillean Architecture of the First Modernity: 1930–1945." In Carlos Brillembourg, ed., *Latin American Architecture, 1929–1960: Contemporary Reflections*, pp. 116–35. New York: Monacelli Press, 2004.

───. *Arquitectura y urbanismo de la revolucion cubana*. Havana: Editorial Pueblo y Educación, 1990.

───. *Diez años de arquitectura en Cuba revolucionária*. Havana, 1970.

───. *La vivienda en Cuba en el siglo XX: República y revolución*, Mexico City: Concepto, 1980.

Torre, Susana. "Architecture and Revolution: Cuba, 1959 to 1974." *Progressive Architecture*, October 1974, pp. 84–91.

Weiss, Joaquin. "La nueva arquitectura y nosotros." *Revista Universidad de La Habana* 1, no. 3 (May–June 1934).

───. *Arquitectura cubana contemporánea*. Havana: Cultural SA, 1947.

The Dominican Republic   Gustavo Luis Moré

The Dominican Republic was one of the few Latin American countries missing from MoMA's famous 1955 exhibition *Latin American Architecture since 1945*. The country's modern architects appear nowhere in that show's remarkable catalogue. This absence may be attributed to two causes: first, the international hostility toward the dictator Rafael Leónidas Trujillo, who governed with an iron fist from 1930 until 1961, when he was assassinated; and second, the fact that many of the country's most recognized architectural works conformed to the early rationalism of the 1930s and '40s, making little allusion to the predominant tone of the buildings in the catalogue, with their curtain walls, brise-soleils, and surfaces clad in natural materials. This situation had a corollary in the literature: during that period, only one, almost apocryphal book, *La arquitectura dominicana en la era de Trujillo*, was published on the architecture of the time, and it was written by the architect most connected to the regime, Henry Gazón Bona.

With the end of the dictatorship, the country moved forward as a democracy. An architects' union was founded, and later became the Colegio Dominicano de Ingenieros Arquitectos, which produced, at irregular intervals, a magazine that was the only documentary record of the country's new architecture. In 1979 a group of young architects came together as the Grupo Nueva Arquitectura (GNA), a collective dedicated to the study, circulation, and promotion of the country's built heritage. Their initiatives inspired parallel developments in other countries in the region, including Cuba, Puerto Rico, and Guadalupe. The GNA published *Arquivox*, the Dominican Republic's first genuinely analytic magazine on architecture, and for a number of years contributed a widely influential architecture page to the newspaper *El nuevo diario*, published every Tuesday and later collected as a set in *100 hojas de arquitectura*.

The first wide-ranging study of the Dominican architecture of the period was Rafael Calventi Gaviño's *Arquitectura contemporánea en República Dominicana* (1986). Interest in the Greater Caribbean region, with its foundation in the CARIMOS/OEA Plan, was strengthened by various studies, including the *Manual bibliográfico de la arquitectura y el urbanismo en el Gran Caribe*, that opened the way to the appearance of the magazine *Archivos de arquitectura antillana* (*AAA*), which began publication in 1996. Issues no. 33 of the *Docomomo Journal* (2005) and no. 34 of *AAA* (2009) were devoted to the regional panorama; that issue of *AAA* was the product of a conference organized by The Museum of Modern Art and the University of Technology, Jamaica, on the theme of modernity in the Greater Caribbean.

Eugenio Pérez Montás brought together years of study and rigorous scholarship in his monumental volume *La ciudad del Ozama* (1998), a history of the city of Santo Domingo. Other texts with an urban focus are Antonio Vélez Catrain's *Ideas urbanas para Santo Domingo* (2002), Ramón Vargas Mera's *Tendencias urbanísticas en América Latina y el Caribe* (2004), José Enrique Delmonte's *Guía de arquitectura de Santo Domingo* (2006), and Cristóbal Valdez's *Reflexiones urbanas* (2007). Two texts published outside the country situated Dominican architecture in a wider perspective: the Panamanian scholar Eduardo Tejeira Davis's doctoral thesis "Roots of Modern Latin American Architecture," written in Heidelberg, on the Hispanic Caribbean, and Roberto Segre's pivotal *Arquitectura antillana del siglo XX*. (Segre was one of the most widely circulated and influential authors in the region.) My own *Historias para la construcción de la arquitectura dominicana, 1492–2008* and Delmonte's *60 años edificados* are two narrative texts on Dominican urban planning and architecture. Both address the country's recent architecture from historical as well as critical perspectives.

The view today is much more positive than it was three decades ago. Well-established journals such as *AAA*, *AAA/Pro_Files*, *Arquitexto*, *Hábitat*, and others maintain a variety of complementary perspectives on the national and regional scene, as do books focusing on more specific subjects and architectural projects that enrich our national inventory. A rigorous and updated critical vision is needed, however, the more precisely to situate the difficult and sometimes uncomfortable presence of the Dominican Republic within the diffuse Latin American panorama as seen from these paradoxically marginal shores.

Brea García, Emilio José, et al. *Santo Domingo: Guía de arquitectura/ An Architectural Guide*. Seville: Consejería de Obras Públicas y Transportes, 2006.

───. *60 años edificados: Memorias de la construcción de la nación*. Santo Domingo: Industria Nacional, 2008.

Grupo Nueva Arquitectura, ed. *100 hojas de arquitectura*. San Pedro de Macorís, Dominican Republic: Universidad Central del Este, 1984.

Martínez Suárez, Alex. "Universidad de Santo Domingo: Conjunto urbano moderno, 1944–1961." *Archivos de arquitectura antillana*, no. 46 (March 2013): 60–63.

Moré, Gustavo Luis, ed. *Historias para la construcción de la arquitectura dominicana, 1492–2008*. Santo Domingo: Grupo León Jiménez, 2008.

Rancier, Omar, and Emilio José Brea García, eds. *Arquitectura en el trayecto del sol: Entendiendo la modernidad dominicana/Architecture in the Path of the Sun: Understanding Dominican Modernity*. Santo Domingo: Laboratorio de Arquitectura Dominicana, 2014.

Tejeira-Davis, Eduardo. *Roots of Modern Latin American Architecture: The Hispano-Caribbean Region from the Late 19th Century to the Recent Past*. Heidelberg, Germany: Deutscher Akademischer Austauschdienst, 1987.

Waldheim, Charles. "Landscape as Monument: J. L. Gleave and the Colombus Lighthouse Competition." *Archivos de arquitectura antillana* 3, no. 7 (May 1998): 76–81.

Mexico   Cristina López Uribe

The history of Mexican modern architecture has for the most part been written by two important groups: people from outside Mexico, whose foreign perspective has allowed them to highlight specific characteristics of identity; and the country's own leading architects, who have written instrumental texts. This second group has tended to view modern architecture as an outgrowth of the Mexican Revolution of 1910—a socially responsible architecture, in other words, not subject to foreign influences.

The first magazine articles (whether published in Mexico or abroad), and Esther Born's groundbreaking survey of 1937, *The New Architecture in Mexico*, were clearly of great importance and demonstrated an optimism about the ability of modern architecture to create a better future. In fighting for that architecture, functionalists legitimated it through a schematic historical materialism that identified ornamentation as an instrument of the exploitation of the working classes. Conflicting ideas about modern architecture were evident in *Pláticas sobre arquitectura* of 1933. In 1937, in his book *El arte moderno en México: Breve historia siglos XIX y XX*, Justino Fernández for the first time proposed a genealogy of and a historical argument for Mexican modern architecture, launching ideas that would remain current for years about that architecture's origins, and ancestors, the negative reading of early forms of modern styles, and the condemnation of radical functionalism.

In the 1950s, under the spell of the Ciudad Universitaria, Carlos Obregón Santacilia and José Villagrán reviewed the past and identified the styles of the nineteenth century with the political powers of Mexico as it was before the revolution. They also described the "erroneous but necessary" paths taken to establish Mexican identity and break with academic traditions—the paths in question initially being those of the neocolonial style and, later, that of radical functionalism. They argued for a national consensus around an idea of modern architecture that would incorporate common features of past architectures, both indigenous and Spanish.

With the work of Israel Katzman and Mauricio Gómez Mayorga in the 1960s, architectural history became more professionalized, and architectural discourse was buoyed by optimism, related to an openness to influence from abroad and a view of modern architecture as being moved by industrial and technological development along a linear path of progress. In the 1970s critical historians such as Rafael López Rangel and Ramón Vargas reacted against these discourses, sharing a Marxist ideology and locating themselves in the context of an era of crisis and economic dependence. In a search for responses to this sense of crisis they looked to the past, focusing on the functionalist architecture of the 1930s, which they saw in heroic terms. In the 1980s and '90s Enrique de Anda, Antonio Toca, and Louise Noelle attempted to address history from a more neutral position and identified a continuity in the synthesis of Mexican identity and modernity achieved at Ciudad Universitaria and elsewhere. These projects led to the heights of architectural language seen in the work of Luis Barragán, whom Emilio Ambasz had introduced to an international audience through an exhibition at MoMA as early as 1976.

General studies have become scarcer in recent decades, making room for deeper study of specific cases. A focus on gathering, distributing, and safeguarding historiographic documents—as in the work of Carlos Ríos Garza—and a renewed interest on the part of North American academics such as Keith Eggener and Luis E. Carranza have allowed for critical reconsiderations that transcend linear discourse and arbitrary categories, bringing to light elements of Mexican modern architecture that had previously gone unnoticed.

Adrià, Miquel. *Mario Pani: La construcción de la modernidad*. Naucalpan, Mexico: Gustavo Gili, 2005.

———. *Teodoro González de León: Obra reunida*. Mexico City: CONACULTA, 2010.

Ambasz, Emilio. *The Architecture of Luis Barragán*. New York: The Museum of Modern Art, 1976.

Anda, Enrique X. de. *La arquitectura de la Revolución Mexicana: Corrientes y estilos en la década de los veinte*. 1990. Mexico City: UNAM-IIE, 2008.

———. *Historia de la arquitectura mexicana*. 1995. Barcelona: Gustavo Gili, 2013.

———. *Vivienda colectiva de la modernidad en México: Los multifamiliares durante el periodo presidencial de Miguel Alemán (1946–1952)*. Mexico City: UNAM-IIE, 2008.

Anda, Enrique de, and Salvador Lizárraga, eds. *Cultura arquitectónica de la modernidad Mexicana: Antología de textos, 1922–1963*. Mexico City: UNAM-IIE, 2010.

Apuntes para la historia y crítica de la arquitectura moderna mexicana del siglo XX: 1900–1980. 2 vols. Cuadernos de arquitectura y conservación del patrimonio artístico 21–22 and 22–23. Mexico City: INBA, 1982–83.

Born, Esther. *The New Architecture in Mexico*. New York: W. Morrow–Architectural Record, 1937.

Burian, Edward. *Modernity and the Architecture of Mexico*. Austin: University of Texas Press, 1997.

Canales, Fernanda. *Arquitectura en México, 1900-2010: La construcción de la modernidad: Obras, diseño, arte y pensamiento*. Mexico City: Arquine, 2014.

Canales, Fernanda, and Alejandro Hernández Gálvez. *100x100 arquitectos del sigo XX en México*. Mexico City: Arquine, 2011.

Carranza, Luis E. *Architecture as Revolution: Episodes in the History of Modern Mexico*. Austin: University of Texas Press, 2010.

———. "Mathias Goeritz: Architecture, Monochrome and Revolution." *Journal of the Decorative and Propaganda Arts* 26, 2010, pp. 248–77.

Castañeda, Luis. "Beyond Tlatelolco: Design, Media, and Politics at Mexico '68," *Grey Room* 40, Summer 2010.

Cetto, Max. *Arquitectura moderna en México/Modern Architecture in Mexico*. New York: Praeger, 1961.

Cruz González Franco, Lourdes. *Augusto H. Álvarez: Arquitecto de la modernidad*. Mexico City: UNAM, 2008.

Dussel Peters, Susanne. *Max Cetto, 1903–1980: Arquitecto mexicano-alemán*. Mexico City: Universidad Autónoma Metropolitana –Azcapotzalco, 1995.

Eggener, Keith. *Luis Barragán's Gardens of El Pedregal*. New York: Princeton Architectural Press, 2001.

Félix Candela, 1910–2010. Valencia: SECC, IVAM, 2010.

Fernández, Justino. *El arte moderno y contemporáneo de México*. 1952. Mexico City: UNAM-IIE, 1993.

Gallo, Ruben. *Mexican Modernity: The Avant-Garde and the Technological Revolution*. Cambridge, Mass: MIT Press, 2005.

Gómez, Lilia, and Miguel Ángel de Quevedo. *Testimonios vivos 20 arquitectos*. Cuadernos de arquitectura y conservación del patrimonio artístico 15–16. Mexico City: INBA, 1981.

Gómez Mayorga, Mauricio. "Notas polémicas." *Artes de México* 36, 1961.

González Gortázar, Fernando. *La arquitectura mexicana del siglo XX*. Mexico City: Consejo Nacional para la Cultura y las Artes, 1994.

Gorelik, Adrian, and Jorge Francisco Liernur. *La sombra de la vanguardia: Hannes Meyer en México, 1938–1949*. Buenos Aires: Universidad de Buenos Aires, Facultad de Arquitectura Diseño y Urbanismo, 1993.

Guía de arquitectura mexicana contemporánea. Mexico City: Espacios, 1952.

Hernández, Vicente Martín, and Victor Jiménez. *Catálogo de la exposición "La arquitectura en México: Porfiriato y movimiento moderno."* Mexico City: INBA, 1983.

Hernández Gálvez, Alejandro. "Juan O'Gorman: Architecture and Surface." Special Mexico issue, *Journal of the Decorative and Propaganda Arts* 26, 2010, pp. 206–29.

"Homenagem a México." Special issue, *Brasil: Arquitetura contemporânea* 6, 1955.

Jiménez, Victor. *Las casas de Juan O'Gorman para Diego y Frida*. Mexico City: INBA, 2001.

Kassner, Lily. *Mathias Goeritz: Una biografía, 1915–1990*. 2 vols. Mexico City: Conaculta, INBA, 1998.

Katzman, Israel. *La arquitectura contemporánea en México: Precedentes y desarrollo*. Mexico City: INBA, 1963.

Leduc, Carlos. "Arquitectura contemporánea." *Frente a frente* 5, 1936.

López Rangel, Rafael. *La crisis del racionalismo arquitectónico en México*. Cuadernos del museo 1. Mexico City: UNAM, 1972.

———. *La modernidad arquitectónica Mexicana: Antecedentes y vanguardias, 1900–1940*. Mexico City: Universidad Autónoma Metropolitana–Azcapotzalco, 1989.

———. *Orígenes de la arquitectura técnica en México, 1920–1933*. Mexico City: Universidad Autónoma Metropolitana–Xochimilco, 1984.

Manrique, Jorge Alberto. *Una visión del arte y de la historia*, vol. 5. Mexico City: UNAM-IIE, 2001.

Márquez, Luis. *En el mundo del mañana: La identidad mexicana y la Feria Mundial de Nueva York, 1939–40/In the World of Tomorrow: Mexican Identity and the 1939–40 New York World's Fair*. Mexico City: UNAM, 2012.

Martínez, Antonio Riggen. *Luis Barragán: Mexico's Modern Master, 1902–1988*. New York: Monacelli Press, 1996.

Moral, Enrique del. *El hombre y la arquitectura: Ensayos y testimonies*. Mexico City: UNAM, 1983.

Garlock, Maria Moreyra, and David Billington, eds. *Félix Candela: Engineer, Builder, Structural Artist*. New Haven, Conn.: Yale University Press, 2009.

Myers, Irwin Evan. *Mexico's Modern Architecture*. New York: Architectural Book Publishing, 1952.

Noelle, Louise. *Arquitectos contemporáneos de México*. Mexico City: Trillas, 1989.

———. *Regionalismo*. Cuadernos de arquitectura 10. Mexico City: Consejo Nacional para la Cultura y las Artes–INBA, 2003.

Obregón Santacilia, Carlos. *50 años de arquitectura mexicana (1900–1950)*. Mexico City: Patria, 1952.

———. *El maquinismo, la vida y la arquitectura*. Mexico City: Publicaciones Letras de México, 1939.

———. *México como eje de las antiguas arquitecturas de América*. Mexico City: Atlante, 1947.

O'Gorman, Juan. *Autobiografía*. Mexico City: UNAM, 2007.

Pérez-Méndez, Alfonso, and Alejandro Aptilon. *Las casas del Pedregal: 1947–1968*. Barcelona: Gustavo Gili, 2007.

Pláticas sobre arquitectura. Mexico City: Lumen, 1934. Mexico City: UNAM Facultad de Arquitectura, 2001.

Ramírez Vázquez, Pedro. *4,000 años de arquitectura en México*. Mexico City: CAM-SAM Editores Unidos, 1956.

Rodríguez Prampolini, Ida. *Juan O'Gorman: Arquitecto y pintor*. Mexico City: UNAM, 1982.

Rodríguez Prampolini, Ida, and Ferruccio Asta, eds. *Los ecos de Mathias Goeritz: Ensayos y testimonios*. Mexico City: INBA, 1997.

Smith, Clive Bamford. *Builders in the Sun: Five Mexican Architects*. New York: Architectural Book Publishing, 1967.

Toca Fernández, Antonio. *Arquitectura contemporánea en México*. Mexico City: Universidad Autónoma Metropolitana– Azcapotzalco, 1989.

Vargas, Ramón, ed. *Historia de la arquitectura y el urbanismo mexicanos*. Vol. 4, *El siglo XX: Arquitectura de la revolución y revolución de la Arquitectura*. Mexico City: UNAM, Facultad de Arquitectura–Fondo de Cultura Económica, 2009.

Vargas Salguero, Ramón, and Victor Arias, eds. *Ideario de los arquitectos mexicanos*. 3 vols. Mexico City: Instituto Nacional de Bellas Artes y Literatura, 2010.

Villagrán García, José. *Panorama de 50 años de arquitectura mexicana contemporánea: 1900–1950*. Cuadernos de arquitectura 10. Mexico City: INBA, 1963.

———. *Teoría de la arquitectura*. Mexico City: UNAM, 1988.

Yáñez, Enrique. *Del funcionalismo al post-racionalismo: Ensayo sobre la arquitectura contemporánea en México*. Mexico City: Universidad Autónoma Metropolitana–Azcapotzalco, 1990.

Zúñiga, Olivia. *Mathias Goeritz*. Mexico City: Editorial Intercontinental, 1963.

Peru   Sharif Kahatt

Theoretical and critical reflections on modern architecture have appeared only fleetingly in Peru; from the postwar period through to the present moment, they have gained no representative presence in the region. The few texts published in the first decades of the twentieth century addressed Neoclassical practices and, later, the establishment of a national style through directions such as the neocolonial, the "neo-Inca," and the "neo-Peruvian." Only at the end of the 1930s did the discourse begin to shift toward a form of modernism associated with the principles of architectural and urban functionalism.

These attempts to initiate a new architecture coincided with the publication of the first texts by Luis Miró Quesada and Fernando Belaunde Terry, the former, in essays in the newspaper *El comercio*, calling for advances in thinking on architecture, the city, and art, and the latter, as founder and editor of the magazine *El arquitecto peruano*, affirming the social responsibility of architecture. Only in 1945, however, was a book published that can be called a foundational text about modern architecture in Peru, Miró Quesada's *Espacio en el tiempo: La arquitectura moderna como tradición cultural*. Miró Quesada took an optimistic view of the modernist avant-garde and tried to interpret it from a Peruvian perspective. His book signaled the beginning of a consolidation of modern architecture at all levels, from academic teaching to actual construction.

By around 1955 the state, the private sector, and most of Peru's urban population had accepted modern architecture as a reality. Attempts to develop architectural discourse remained few, however, and were centered on discussion of the need for mass housing projects. Without critiquing modernist doctrine, Peruvian architects worked on adapting modern architecture to local realities, adjusting their practices to the country's political, social, cultural, environmental, and building conditions, as is evident from the magazine *El arquitecto peruano*.

In the context of these efforts, some of the most important essays and books relating to these new ideas regarding mass housing and urbanization efforts were published. The most important texts of the 1950s and 1960s—with a central focus on the population's lack of economic resources and the socio-political necessities that arose out of the explosive growth of Peruvian cities—concentrated on problems and solutions regarding affordable housing. Among these, the work of Adolfo Córdova is particularly outstanding.

In the 1970s, the last publication to make a real attempt to rethink architecture in Peru was the *Carta de Machu Picchu* (1977). Written by an international group of architects, this manifesto-like text—similar in its objectives to Le Corbusier's Athens Charter, published in 1943—focused on the urban responsibility of architecture, in a context where countries everywhere were experiencing crises around energy, ecology, and social issues. The *Carta de Machu Picchu* also shares in the worldwide concern with conceiving new forms of urbanism and rethinking the role of architecture in society.

Since the 1980s Peru's most important architectural writings have been dedicated to recuperating the work of important modern architects—their projects and ideas and their relation to the city. Many of these texts have involved analyses of the construction of modernity in Peru, and particularly of these architects' contributions to urban and architectural culture. A number of them have reflected on the relationship of modernity to notions of identity and urbanism; depending on the specific discourse, these ideas tend to be presented as contributions and recognitions of the local, the universal, and the interconnections between the two. In the early years of this century, urban culture, housing, the city, and, in particular, modernity continue to be the principal issues with which architectural thinking in Peru is concerned.

Agrupación Espacio. "Expresión de principios de la Agrupación Espacio." *El comercio* (Lima), May 15, 1947. Republished in *El arquitecto peruano* 11, no. 119 (June 1947).

Belaunde Terry, Fernando. "El barrio-unidad: Instrumento de descentralización." *El arquitecto peruano*, no. 83 (June 1944).

———. *La conquista del Perú por los peruanos*. Lima: Editorial Minerva, 1959.

———. "Estudios de planeamiento: La ruta Marginal de la Selva; Una visión de futuro." *El arquitecto peruano*, nos. 245–46 (November–December 1957).

———. "Nuestra propuesta al CIAM: La carta del hogar." *El arquitecto peruano*, no. 141 (April 1949).

———. "Perú: Precursor ignorado." *El arquitecto peruano*, nos. 288–90 (July–September 1961).

———. "El plan de vivienda del gobierno de peruano." *El arquitecto peruano*, no. 98 (September 1945).

———. "Planeamiento en el antiguo y moderno Perú." *El arquitecto peruano*, nos. 202–03 (May–June 1954).

———. "Vivienda individual o colectiva." *El arquitecto peruano*, no. 103 (February 1946).

Carta de Machu-Picchu. Lima-Cuzco: Congreso de la UIA, 1977.

Cayo, Javier. "La unidad arquitectónica y el panorama urbano." *El arquitecto peruano*, nos. 245–46 (November–December 1957).

Comisión para la Reforma Agraria y la Vivienda. *Informe sobre la vivienda en el Perú*. Lima: CRAV, 1958.

García-Huidobro, Fernando, Dielo Torres Torriti, and Nicolás Tugas. *Time Builds! The Experimental Housing Project (PREVI), Lima: Genesis and Outcome*. Barcelona: Gustavo Gili, 2008.

Kahatt, Sharif S. "Agrupación Espacio and the CIAM-Peru Group." In Duanfang Lu, ed. *Third World Modernism: Architecture, Development and Identity*. London: Routledge, 2010.

Ludeña, Wiley. *Lima: Historia y urbanismo en cifras, 1821–1970*. Lima: Ministerio de Vivienda, 2004.

———. *Tres buenos tigres: Vanguardias y urbanismo en el Perú del siglo XX*. Huancayo: Colegio de Arquitectos de Perú, 2004.

Martuccelli, Elio. *Arquitectura para una ciudad fragmentada: Ideas, proyectos y edificios en la Lima del siglo XX*. Lima: Universidad Ricardo Palma, 2000.

Matos Mar, José. *Las barriadas de Lima*. Lima: Instituto de Estudios Peruanos, 1966.

Miró Quesada, Luis. "Adecuacionismo, expresión estética." *El arquitecto peruano*, no. 74 (September 1943).

———. *Espacio en el tiempo: La arquitectura como fenómeno cultural*. Lima, 1945.

Velarde, Héctor. *Arquitectura peruana*. Lima: Ediciones Studium, 1946.

———. "Sobre un debate del CIAM." *El comercio* (Lima), February 12, 1950.

Zapata, Antonio. *El joven Belaunde: Historia de la revista El arquitecto peruano, 1937–1967*. Lima: Editorial Minerva, 1995.

Puerto Rico   Enrique Vivoni-Farage

In 1923, in *El libro de Puerto Rico/The Book of Puerto Rico*, the Bohemian architect Antonin Nechodoma took a theoretical view of design in the tropics for the first time in twentieth-century architecture literature on Puerto Rico; in so doing, he coined the term "ultra-modern style," for one "founded upon the urgent needs of the people who have chosen this tropical island for their abode." He described the need for the use of reinforced concrete walls, leaded colored-glass windows, and deep overhangs to protect from the "tropical light so injurious to the white races in the tropics." He further asserted that the "residents of the island have a tendency towards bright colors" because of the gorgeous and vivid colors of the tropics.

The influence of the tropics on architecture in Puerto Rico was a local issue from that point until 1945, when the work of the Committee for Design of Public Works (a product of the New Deal) was published by Richard Neutra in the March issue of *Architectural Forum*. For the committee the tropics and the socioeconomic condition of Puerto Rico were paramount, and it is in this context that architectural discussion would develop through the 1970s.

Most of the publications in journals were specific to projects; even the 1965 book *Arquitectura en Puerto Rico*, by José Fernández, is organized as a catalogue. Theoretical issues are absent from publications until Henry Klumb, in interviews and writings published in journals and books, began to expound on his ideas of living in nature. The work of Klumb's contemporaries, including

Osvaldo Toro, Miguel Ferrer, Jesús Amaral, Efrer Morales, Thomas Marvel, and Jorge del Río, appeared in various US and international architectural journals starting in 1949, but their work was generally presented as simply buildings in Puerto Rico, without their ideas on what architecture for the island should represent. But Efraín Pérez-Chanis provided a most vibrant voice, editorializing in his journal, *Urbe*, on architects and architecture in Puerto Rico. This journal, published from 1962 to 1973, argued in favor of both the Modern Movement and preservation, published architects' biographies, fought for the establishment of an architecture school, and proposed the URBE awards for architecture it considered deserving.

The first in-depth books about architecture in Puerto Rico were published in the 1990s, starting with Jorge Rigau's *Puerto Rico 1900* (1992), followed in 1997 by a series of books by the Archivo de Arquitectura y Construcción at the Universidad de Puerto Rico, which included biographies of architects and historical contextualization of their time.

In the 2000s the Colegio de Arquitectos published its first books, in a series called Colección Catálogos de Arquitectos and featuring Thomas Marvel, Jesús Amaral, and Luis Flores. The Amaral book was entirely written by Andrés Mignucci; the other contain essays by various architects and the featured architects themselves in monograph on their works.

Colección Catálogos de Arquitectura. *Luis Flores, Architect.* San Juan: Colegio de Arquitectos y Arquitectos Paisajistas de Puerto Rico, 2009.

———. *Thomas S. Marvel, Architect.* San Juan: Colegio de Arquitectos y Arquitectos Paisajistas de Puerto Rico, 2005.

Crisp-Ellert, J. A. "Henry Klumb in Puerto Rico: Architecture at the Service of Society." *AIA Journal*, July 1974, pp. 50–53.

Fernández García, Eugenio, ed. *El libro de Puerto Rico/The Book of Puerto Rico.* San Juan: El Libro Azul, 1923.

Figueroa Jiménez, Jósean, and Edric Vivoni González. *Henry Klumb: Principios para una arquitectura de integración.* San Juan: Colegio de Arquitectos y Arquitectos Paisajistas de Puerto Rico, 2007.

Gayá Nuño, J. A. "Henry Klumb y la arquitectura puertorriqueña." *Revista del Instituto de Cultura Puertorriqueña*, July–September 1962, pp. 39–42.

"Klumb of Puerto Rico." *Architectural Forum*, July 1962, pp. 87–89.

Marqués Mera, Juan. "Toro y Ferrer Architects: Ten Years of Reasonable Architecture in Puerto Rico." *Docomomo Journal*, no. 33 (September 2005): 38–42.

Marvel, Thomas S. *Antonin Nechodoma, Architect, 1877–1928: The Prairie School in the Caribbean.* Gainesville: University Press of Florida, 1994.

Mignucci Giannoni, Andrés. *[Con]textos: El Parque Muñoz Rivera y el Tribunal Supremo de Puerto Rico.* San Juan: La Rama Judicial de Puerto Rico, 2012.

———. *Jesús Eduardo Amaral, Architect.* San Juan: Colegio de Arquitectos y Arquitectos Paisajistas de Puerto Rico, 2011.

Moreno, María Luisa. *La arquitectura de la Universidad de Puerto Rico.* San Juan: Editorial de la Universidad de Puerto Rico, 2000.

Vivoni-Farage, Enrique. *Architect of Dreams: Pedro Adolfo de Castro y Besosa.* San Juan: Archivo de Arquitectura y Construcción de la Universidad de Puerto Rico, 1999.

———. "Modern Puerto Rico and Henry Klumb. *Docomomo Journal*, no. 33 (September 2005): 28–37.

Vivoni-Farage, Enrique, ed. *Ever New San Juan: Architecture and Modernization in the Twentieth Century.* San Juan: Archivo de Arquitectura y Construcción de la Universidad de Puerto Rico, 2000.

———. *Klumb: Una arquitectura de impronta social/An Architecture of Social Concern.* San Juan: Editorial de la Universidad de Puerto Rico/AACUPR, 2006.

Vivoni-Farage, Enrique, and Silvia Álvarez Curbelo, eds. *Hispanophilia: Architecture and Life in Puerto Rico, 1900-1950.* San Juan: Editorial de la Universidad de Puerto Rico/AACUPR, 1998.

Uruguay   Jorge Nudelman

Uruguayan architectural historiography proper began in 1955 with the publication of Juan Giuria's four-volume *La arquitectura en el Uruguay*, which described the national architecture from its colonial origins through the year 1900. Only a few years earlier, in 1952, the Facultad de Arquitectura—the architecture school at the Universidad de la República in Montevideo—had changed its curriculum, moving from a Beaux Arts model to a program that emphasized material production and organized theoretical courses of study in accordance with the Athens Charter. The school's antihistoricist tendency—and that of the authors who followed Giuria, including Aurelio Lucchini and, to a lesser extent, Leopoldo Carlos Artucio—would move the direction of research at the Instituto de Historia de la Arquitectura (earlier called the Instituto de Arqueología Americana) toward a scientific review of issues to do with the origins and evolution of "national" territory. The institute started to publish these studies in 1962 in its *Fascículos de información*, beginning with readings of land use, then later, though not to any great extent, moving on to other types of historiography, such as a debate between the architects Julio Vilamajó and Octavio de los Campos on the 1930 regulatory plan for Montevideo. In general, the writing of this period was oriented more toward cataloguing efforts than toward critique.

A military regime took over the government of Uruguay in 1973, and the following year its intervention in the university interrupted these projects. Lucchini, the director of the Instituto de Historia de la Arquitectura, had been working on a history of Uruguayan architecture; an unfinished version of this book would be published posthumously in 1988, under the title *El concepto de arquitectura y su traducción a formas en el territorio que hoy pertenece a la República Oriental del Uruguay*. The institute's faculty had constituted the largest concentration of architectural scholars in Uruguay, but a number of them resigned, and over the next decade the publication of architectural writing decreased and showed little innovation. When democracy returned in 1985, revisionist debates on modern architecture had advanced without the institute's participation. The leading writer of this period was Mariano Arana, and regionalist impulses were at the forefront; some younger writers, including Juan Bastarrica, Mariella Russi, and others, would work with these themes, but the continuity of archival and documentary work had been lost. A critical update seemed urgently necessary, and attempts were made in this direction, but their foundations in research were weak, and they mainly produced a growing number of opinion-based texts published in the 1990s in magazines such as *Elarqa* and by Julio Gaeta's Dos Puntos press. Today, a generation that grew out of that time—including Laura Alemán, Mary Méndez, Santiago Medero, Emilio

Nisivoccia, and Martín Cobas—has taken up the task of renewing the discourse with more documentary rigor and in an updated critical context.

Alberti, Mariana, Laura Cesio, Andrés Mazzini, and Cecilia Ortiz de Taranco. *Román Fresnedo Siri*. Montevideo: Facultad de Arquitectura, Instituto de Historia de la Arquitectura, Universidad de la República, 2013.

Alberti, Mariana, and Paula Gatti. *Juan Antonio Scasso*. Montevideo: Facultad de Arquitectura, Instituto de Historia de la Arquitectura, Universidad de la República, 2009.

Alemán, Laura. *Hilos rotos: Ideas de ciudad en el siglo XX*. Montevideo: Editorial Hum, 2013.

Alemán, Laura, Juan Carlos Apolo, and Pablo Kelbauskas. *Talleres, trazos y señas*. Montevideo: Departamento de Enseñanza de Anteproyectos y Proyectos de Arquitectura, Facultad de Arquitectura, Universidad de la República, 2006.

Altezor, Carlos, and Hugo Baracchini. *Historia urbanística y edilicia de la ciudad de Montevideo*. Montevideo: Junta Departamental de Montevideo, Biblioteca J. Artigas, 1971.

Anderson, Stanford. "Eladio Dieste: A Principled Builder." In Guy Nordenson, ed. *Seven Structural Engineers: The Félix Candela Lectures*, pp. 30–47. New York: The Museum of Modern Art, 2008.

Anderson, Stanford, ed. *Eladio Dieste: Innovation in Structural Art*. New York: Princeton Architectural Press, 2005.

Arana, Mariano. *Escritos*. Montevideo: Ediciones Banda Oriental, 1999.

Artucio, Leopoldo. *Montevideo y la arquitectura moderna*. Montevideo: Editorial Nuestra Tierra, 1971.

Ashfield, William Rey. *Arquitectura moderna en Montevideo: 1920–1960*. Montevideo: Facultad de Arquitectura, Universidad de la República, 2012.

Baldoira, Carlos, and Yolanda Boronat. *El edificio de apartamentos en altura: Su producción en las décadas del 50 y 60*. Montevideo: Instituto de Historia de la Arquitectura, Facultad de Arquitectura, 2009.

Boronat, Yolanda, and Marta Risso. *La vivienda de interés social en el Uruguay: 1970–1983*. Montevideo: Editorial Fundación de Cultura Universitaria, 1992.

Cobas, Martín. "Dieste redux: Máquinas hacia un orden tectónico infraestructural". *Plot* (Buenos Aires), no. 10 (December 2012–Februrary 2013): 210–15.

Conti, Nidia. *La vivienda de interés social en el Uruguay*. Montevideo: Facultad de Arquitectura, Instituto de Historia de la Arquitectura, Universidad de la República, 1972.

Eladio Dieste, 1917–2000. Seville: Consejería de Obras Públicas y Transportes; Montevideo: Dirección General de Arquitectura y Vivienda, 1998.

Gaeta, Julio, ed. *Guillermo Gómez Platero*. Monografías Elarqa 8. Montevideo: Dos Puntos, 2002.

———. *Luis García Pardo*. Monografías Elarqa 6. Montevideo: Dos Puntos, 2000.

———. *Mario Payssé Reyes*. Monografías Elarqa 3. Montevideo: Dos Puntos, c. 1999.

———. *Rafael Lorente Escudero*. Monografías Elarqa 1. Montevideo: Dos Puntos, 1993.

———. *Walter Pintos Risso*. Monografías Elarqa 7. Montevideo: Dos Puntos, 2001.

Jiménez Torrecillas, Antonio, ed. *Eladio Dieste: 1943–1996*. 2 vols. Seville: Consejería de Obras Públicas y Transportes, 1996.

Katzenstein, Ernesto, Gustavo Natanson, and Hugo Schvartzman. *Antonio Bonet: Arquitectura y urbanismo en el Río de la Plata y España*. Buenos Aires: Espacio Editorial, 1985.

Lorente Escudero, Rafael, ed. "50 años de arquitectura nacional." *Arquitectura* (Montevideo), November 1964.

Lorente Mourelle, Rafael, ed. *Ernesto Leborgne*. Montevideo: Editorial Agua;m, 2005.

———. *Rafael Lorente Escudero*. Montevideo: Editorial Agua;m, 2004.

Lucchini, Aurelio. *El concepto de arquitectura y su traducción a formas en el territorio que hoy pertenece a Uruguay*. Montevideo: Universidad de la República, 1986.

———. *Julio Vilamajó: Su arquitectura*. Montevideo: Universidad de la República, 1970.

Margenat, Juan Pedro. *Tiempos modernos: Arquitectura uruguaya afín a las vanguardias: 1940–1970*. 2 vols. Montevideo, 2013.

Mazzini, Elena, and Mary Méndez. *Polémicas de arquitectura en el Uruguay del siglo XX*. Montevideo: Departamento de Publicaciones, Unidad de Comunicación de la Universidad de la República, 2011.

Medero, Santiago. *Luis García Pardo*. Montevideo: Facultad de Arquitectura, Instituto de Historia de la Arquitectura, Universidad de la República, 2012.

Nisivoccia, Emilio. "Les Uruguayens: Le Corbusier, la política y la arquitectura en los sesenta." *dEspacio*, no. 2, 2005, p. 137.

Nudelman, Jorge. "Arquitectos uruguayos: Un intento de discernir tendencias." In Juan Manuel Bastarrica, ed. *Arquitectura en Uruguay, 1980–1990*, pp. 51–55. Montevideo: Grupo de Viaje CEDA G'84, 1991.

Pedreschi, Remo. *Eladio Dieste: The Engineer's Contribution to Contemporary Architecture*. London: Thomas Telford, 2000.

"Uruguay: Panorama de su arquitectura contemporánea." Special issue, *Revista Summa* (Buenos Aires), no. 27, 1970.

Venezuela   Guillermo Barrios

At the very moment when the process of establishing modern architecture in Venezuela reached its peak, in 1954 and 1955, Gio Ponti published a pair of articles in *Domus*, "Coraggio del Venezuela" and "A Caracas," highlighting the rapidity and the nature of the transformations in the architectural environment of Venezuela's capital city. The phenomenon not only attracted the attention of the international media but sparked the development of specialized journals within Venezuela, including, notably, *Integral* (1955–59). It was only in the 1960s, however, that the foundations of the country's architectural literature were laid. One milestone was the book *Caracas a través de su arquitectura* (1969), which balances Graziano Gasparini's valorization of a built heritage profoundly affected by new infrastructures against Juan Pedro Posani's sense of the multiple expressions, tendencies, and contradictions that came into play as these processes unfolded. A few years earlier, Carlos Raúl Villanueva had advanced an analytical approach based on historical comparisons in his book *Caracas en tres tiempos* (1966), which shows how this master architect's readings of traditional architecture generated intriguing insights into his own works. Villanueva's projects lie at the heart of Venezuelan modernity, as Sibyl Moholy-Nagy makes clear in her 1964 book *Carlos Raúl Villanueva and the Architecture of Venezuela*, which includes an insightful overview of the architectural panorama of the time.

The architectural literature of subsequent years often focused on particular architects working in the national context of Venezuela. This was true, for example, of Silvia Hernández de Lasala's book *Malaussena* (1990), a reference work focusing on the prelude to the country's modernist achievements, and of Alberto Sato's *José Miguel Galia* (2002), on the Uruguayan creator of many important examples of Venezuelan modernism. In addition to the tendency of focusing on individual figures, the literature also addressed the development of the modern city through analyses of urban-planning processes, for example in *La reurbanización "El Silencio"* (1988), by Ricardo De Sola, and *El Plan Rotival: La Caracas que no fue*, published in 1991 by the Instituto de Urbanismo at the Universidad Central de Venezuela. Other books inventoried notable points on the urban map. The origins of this kind of project include the series of articles "Guía arquitectónica de Caracas," begun by Manuel López in the magazine *Punto* in 1979, and Mariano Goldberg's *Guía de edificaciones contemporáneas de Caracas* (1982). In the mid-1980s *Los signos habitables*, organized by William Niño, launched a series of expository projects by Venezuelan museums whose catalogues would become important reference sources both on the works of specific architects and on tendencies and currents in the architecture of the immediately preceding decades. In *Venezuela y el problema de su identidad arquitectónica* (2006), Azier Calvo tried to smooth out the fragmentariness of the narrative of Venezuelan modernist architecture through both substantive analysis and a minutely detailed cataloguing of references and associations. That narrative remains an ongoing focus of academic research (whose results, however, are seldom published) and sporadic independent book and lecture projects, and has proven a popular subject of exchange on social networks.

Alcock, Walter James, Hannia Gómez, and William Niño Araque. *Alcock, arquitecto: Obras y proyectos, 1959–1992.* Caracas: Fundación Galería de Arte Nacional, 1992.

Appleyard, Donald. *Planning a Pluralist City: Conflicting Realities in Ciudad Guayana.* Cambridge, Mass.: MIT Press, 1976.

Berrizbeitia, Anita. *Roberto Burle Marx in Caracas: Parque del Este, 1956–1961.* Philadelphia: University of Pennsylvania Press, 2005.

Calvo, Azier. *Venezuela y el problema de su identidad arquitectónica.* Caracas: Ediciones FAU UCV, 2006.

De Sola, Ricardo. *La reurbanización "El Silencio": Crónica.* Caracas: Fundación Villanueva and INAVI, 1988.

De Sola, Ricardo, and Paulina Villanueva. *Villanueva: Crónica tres cubos en Montreal.* Caracas: Armitano Editores, 2007.

Galería de Arte Nacional. *Los signos habitables: Tendencias de la arquitectura venezolana contemporánea.* Caracas: Galería de Arte Nacional, 1985.

———. *Wallis, Domínguez y Guinand: Arquitectos pioneros de una época.* Caracas: Galería de Arte Nacional, 1998.

Gasparini, Graziano, and Juan Pedro Posani. *Caracas a través de su arquitectura.* Caracas: Fundación Fina Gómez, 1969.

Hernández de Lasala, Silvia. *En busca de lo sublime: Villanueva y la Ciudad Universitaria de Caracas.* Caracas: Redecorado UCV, 2006.

———. *Malaussena: Arquitectura académica en la Venezuela moderna.* Caracas: Fundación Pampero, 1990.

Jiménez, Ariel, ed. *Alfredo Boulton and His Contemporaries: Critical Dialogues in Venezuelan Art, 1912–1975.* New York: The Museum of Modern Art, 2008.

López, Manuel. "Guía arquitectónica de Caracas: Edificaciones del Banco Obrero, 1928–1958." *Punto*, no. 61 (June 1979).

Marta Sosa, Joaquín, Gregory Vertullo, and Federico Prieto. *Hotel Humboldt: Un milagro en el Ávila.* Caracas: Fundavag Ediciones, 2014.

Lo mejor del urbanismo y la arquitectura moderna en Caracas. Caracas: Mendoza & Mendoza Publicidad Editorial, 1957.

Moholy-Nagy, Sibyl. *Carlos Raúl Villanueva and the Architecture of Venezuela.* Caracas: Lectura, 1964.

Niño Araque, William. *Tomás José Sanabria, arquitecto: Aproximación a su obra.* Caracas: Galería de Arte Nacional, Caracas, 1995.

"Orientaciones de la arquitectura venezolana." *Integral*, no. 3 (April 1956).

Peattie, Lisa. *Planning: Rethinking Ciudad Guayana.* Ann Arbor: University of Michigan Press, 1987.

Pintó, Maciá. *Villanueva: La síntesis.* 2 vols. Caracas: Consejo de Preservación y Desarrollo de la Universidad Central de Venezuela, Fundación Telefónica, Fundación Villanueva, 2013.

"Planificación y función social del arquitecto: Temas fundamentales del IX Congreso Panamericano de Arquitectos." *Integral*, no. 2 (December 1955).

Ponti, Gio. "A Caracas." *Domus*, no. 307 (June 1955).

———. "Coraggio del Venezuela." *Domus*, no. 295 (June 1954).

Sato, Alberto. *José Miguel Galia, arquitecto.* Caracas: Ediciones del Instituto de Urbanismo, FAU UCV, 2002.

Vallmitjana, Marta, et al. *El Plan Rotival: La Caracas que no fue, 1939–1989; Un plano urbano para Caracas.* Caracas: Ediciones del Instituto de Urbanismo, FAU UCV, 1991.

Villanueva, Carlos Raúl. *Caracas en tres tiempos.* Caracas: Ediciones de la Comisión del Cuatricentenario, 1966.

Villanueva, Paulina, and Maciá Pintó. *Carlos Raúl Villanueva.* New York: Princeton Architectural Books, 2000.

Zawisza, Leszek. "La arquitectura moderna en Venezuela." *Anuario de arquitectura, Venezuela.* Caracas: Sociedad Bolivariana de Arquitectos y Proimagen, 1981.

Advisory Committee

Argentina
Fabio Grementieri
Justo Solsona
Claudio Williams

Brazil
Renato Anelli
Lauro Cavalcanti
André Aranha Corrêa do
    Lago
Maria Elisa Costa
Ana Lucia Niemeyer de
    Medeiros
Andrey Schlee

Chile
Fernando Pérez Oyarzún

Colombia
Silvia Arango
Maria Elvira Madriñan
Carlos Niño Murcia
Germán Samper
Germán Téllez

Cuba
Belmont Freeman
Eduardo Luis Rodríguez

Dominican Republic
Gustavo Luis Moré

Mexico
Lourdes Cruz
Louise Noelle
Sara Topelson de Grinberg

Peru
Frederick Llosa Cooper

Puerto Rico
Enrique Vivoni

Uruguay
Gustavo Scheps

Venezuela
Guillermo Barrios
Silvia Hernández de Lasala
Juan Pedro Posani
Paulina Villanueva
Sofia Vollmer de Maduro

United States
Carlos Brillembourg
Peter Land
Luis Pérez-Oramas
Jorge Silvetti

Lenders and Donors to the Exhibition

Argentina
Mario Roberto Álvarez y
    Asociados, Buenos Aires
Archivos Di Tella, Universidad
    Tocuato Di Tella, Buenos
    Aires
Archivo Manuel Gómez Piñeiro,
    Buenos Aires
Archivo Ernesto Katzenstein,
    Buenos Aires
Archivo Museo de la Cámara
    de Diputados de La Pampa,
    Santa Rosa
Archivo Soto Rivarola, Buenos
    Aires
Archivo Clorindo Testa,
    Buenos Aires
Archivo Amancio Williams,
    Buenos Aires
Bares Bares Bares Schnack:
    Estudio de Arquitectura,
    Buenos Aires
Colección Verónica Bidinost,
    Buenos Aires
Colección Esteban Caveri,
    Buenos Aires
Dirección de Archivos de
    Arquitectura y Diseños
    Argentinos, Facultad de
    Arquitectura, Diseño y
    Urbanismo, Universidad de
    Buenos Aires
Facultad de Arquitectura y
    Urbanismo, Universidad de
    Mendoza
MSGSSS (Manteola, Sánchez
    Gómez, Santos, Solsona,
    Sallaberry), Buenos Aires
Colección Lydia Ozsi, Mendoza
Sánchez Elia–SEPRA
    Arquitectos, Buenos Aires

Brazil
Arquivo João Filgueiras Lima
    (Lelé), Salvador
Arquivo Público do Distrito
    Federal, Brasília
Burle Marx & Cia Ltda, Rio de
    Janeiro
Casa de Lucio Costa, Rio de
    Janeiro

Decanato de Extensão,
    Universidade de Brasília
Departamento Técnico da
    Cãmara dos Deputados
    do Congresso Nacional,
    Brasília
Faculdade de Arquitetura e
    Urbanismo da Universidade
    de São Paulo
Fundação Oscar Niemeyer,
    Rio de Janeiro
Herdeiros Arquiteto Acácio Gil
    Borsoi, Recife
Herdeiros Arquiteto Joaquim
    Guedes, São Paulo
Instituto Lina Bo e Pietro Maria
    Bardi, São Paulo
Instituto Moreira Salles, Rio de
    Janeiro
Museu de Arte do Rio, Rio de
    Janeiro
Núcleo de Pesquisa e
    Documentação da
    Faculdade de Arquitetura
    e Urbanismo da
    Universidade Federal do
    Rio de Janeiro

Chile
Archivo Histórico José Vial
    Armstrong, Valparaíso
Archivo de Originales,
    Pontificia Universidad
    Católica de Chile, Santiago
Juan Ignacio Baixas, Santiago
Francisco Méndez Labbé,
    Santiago

Colombia
Archivo de Bogotá
Archivo Aníbal Moreno, Bogotá
Daniel Bermúdez, Bogotá
Fundación Rogelio Salmona,
    Bogotá
Instituto Distrital del
    Patrimonio Cultural/
    Museo de Bogotá
Museo de Arquitectura
    Leopoldo Rother,
    Universidad Nacional de
    Colombia, Bogotá

Cuba
Archivo Eduardo Luis
    Rodríguez, Havana

Dominican Republic
Laboratorio de Arquitectura
    Dominicana, Santo
    Domingo

Mexico
Colección Augusto F. Álvarez,
    Mexico City
Archivo de Arquitectos
    Mexicanos, Universidad
    Nacional Autónoma de
    México, Mexico City
Archivo de la Coordinación
    de Servicios de
    Información, Universidad
    Autónoma Metropolitana,
    Azcapotzalco, Mexico City
Archivo Pedro Ramírez
    Vázquez, Mexico City
Archivo Eduardo Terrazas,
    Mexico City
Archivo Alejandro Zohn,
    Guadalajara
Dirección General del
    Patrimonio Universitario,
    Universidad Nacional
    Autónoma de México,
    Mexico City
Fundacion Leo Matiz, Mexico
    City
Fundación Armando Salas
    Portugal, Mexico City
Teodoro González de León,
    Mexico City
Agustín Hernández Navarro,
    Mexico City
Instituto Nacional de Bellas
    Artes, Mexico City
Legorreta+Legorreta
    Arquitectos, Mexico City
Carmen Pesqueira de Attolini,
    Mexico City
Javier Sordo Madaleno
    Bringas, Mexico City

Peru
Colección Mercedes Alvariño,
    Lima
Archivo del Ministerio de
    Vivienda, Lima
Colección Enrique Ciriani, Lima
    and Paris
Cooper Graña Nicolini, Lima
Judith Rodrigo and Miguel
    Rodrigo Pérez-Aranibar,
    Lima
Universidad de Piura, Piura
Walter Weberhofer, Lima

Puerto Rico
Archivo de Arquitectura y
    Construcción de la
    Universidad de Puerto
    Rico, San Juan

Uruguay
Archivo General del Hospital de
    Clínicas, Montevideo
Archivo de la Secretaria de
    Planificación, Gestión y
    Diseño de la Intendencia,
    Montevideo
Ramiro Bascáns, Montevideo
Colección Susana and Daniel
    Bayardo, Montevideo
Centro de Documentación e
    Información, Instituto de
    Historia de la Arquitectura,
    Universidad de la
    República, Montevideo
Dieste y Montañez S.A.,
    Montevideo
Colección Virginia Monestier
    Lasnier, Montevideo
Colección Beatriz Perratone
    de Reizes, Montevideo
Thomas Sprechmann,
    Montevideo
Héctor Vigliecca, Montevideo
Arturo Villaamil, Montevideo
Colección Francisco Villegas,
    Punta del Este

Venezuela

Jimmy Alcock, Caracas
Bettina Beckhoff, Caracas
Jorge Castillo, Caracas
Consejo de Preservación y
    Desarrollo, Colección
    CUC-ICU, Universidad
    Central de Venezuela,
    Caracas
Helena Correa de Rigamonti,
    Caracas
Ana Díaz de Tenreiro, Caracas
Colección Facultad de
    Arquitectura y Urbanismo,
    Universidad Central de
    Venezuela, Caracas
Colección Daniel Fernández-
    Shaw, Caracas
Fundación Villanueva, Caracas
Fundación Alberto Vollmer,
    Caracas
Sylvia Magali Ruz de Galia,
    Caracas
Museo Nacional de
    Arquitectura, Caracas
Colección Tomás José
    Sanabria (Fundación
    Alberto Vollmer), Caracas
Sucesión Margot Arismendi
    de Villanueva, Caracas
Oscar Tenreiro-Degwitz,
    Caracas

United States and Canada

Archives of American Art,
    Washington, D.C.
Avery Architectural and Fine
    Arts Library, Drawings
    and Archives, Columbia
    University, New York
Centre Canadien d'Architec-
    ture/Canadian Centre for
    Architecture, Montreal
Ramiro Fernández Collection,
    New York
Mario Gandelsonas and Diana
    Agrest, New York
Getty Research Institute for
    the History of Art and the
    Humanities, Los Angeles
Eric Goldemberg Collection,
    Miami
Peter Land Collection,
    Chicago
Bernardo Villanueva
    Collection, New York

Europe

Barragan Foundation,
    Switzerland
Aldo van Eyck Archive,
    Rotterdam
Zofia & Oskar Hansen
    Foundation, Warsaw
Musée National d'Art
    Moderne/Centre de
    Création Industrielle,
    Centre Pompidou, Paris
Familia Justino Serralta,
    Nantes

Over the last seven years, this ambitious project has evolved with the help of many people, far too many to imagine that we can here record all the debts large and small the curatorial team has incurred. From the beginning *Latin America in Construction* was conceived as a workshop that would engage scholars from throughout the region, many of whom have followed the project on its advisory committee and written in this publication. Other workshops and public symposia have expanded our knowledge and our network, including "Caribbean Modernist Architecture," which took place at the University of Technology, Kingston, Jamaica, in winter 2008 and was published as a special issue of *Archivos de la arquitectura moderna* (*AAM* 034), which was in turn launched at a follow-up symposium in September 2009 at the Centro León in Santiago de los Caballeros, Dominican Republic. In autumn 2008 Wolfsonian-FIU and the University of Miami helped us by bringing together an international panel of experts, who provided excellent advice and who have continued to be involved in the project in ways both formal and informal. Present at that meeting, in addition to the curators, were Silvia Arango, Irma Arsestizabal, Enrique Fernández-Shaw, Timothy Hyde, Jean-François Lejeune, Marianne Lamonaca, Cathy Leff, Zeuler Lima, and Louise Noelle, as well as our MoMA colleague Luis Eduardo Pérez-Oramas, who has been a constant advisor and friend of this project.

The models in the exhibition were produced in workshops in exceptionally generous academic settings at the Pontificia Universidad Católica in Santiago de Chile and at the University of Miami. In Santiago the project was directed by Jeannette Plaut and Marcelo Sarovic of the cultural organization Constructo, who have provided precious advice since our early research trips to Chile. We thank most particularly Fernando Pérez Oyarzún, Director of the doctoral program; Dr. Ignacio Sánchez, Rector; Juan Larraín, Vice-Rector; Miryam Singer, Director, Artes y Cultura; Mario Ubilla, Dean, and Emilio de la Cerda, Director, Escuela de Arquitectura; and Francisco Quintana. The architectural students who devoted so many hours to the models were Carla Aldunate, José Miguel Armijo, Diego Avalos, Andrea Gómez, José Hernández, Juan José Mena, Juan Ramón Samaniego, Rafael Urcelay, and Guillermo Zilleruelo, aided by Santiago Vicuña and Constanza González. The work was supported by the Chilean Embassy in the United States (Juan Gabriel Valdés, Ambassador, and Javiera Parada, Cultural Attaché), the Consejo Nacional de la Cultura y las Artes (Claudia Barattini, Ministry of Culture, and Cristóbal Molina, Architecture Coordinator), Corporación LOMO, ARAUCO (Trupan/MDF), Hunter Douglas, Idealaser, and Color Animal. At the University of Miami we are grateful for the support of Dean Rodolphe El-Khoury, Associate Dean Denis Hector, and Professor Elizabeth Plater-Zyberk. The project was lead with great professionalism by Professors Jean-François Lejeune, Rafael Tapanes, and Allan T. Shulman. Thanks also to Professor Juhong Park, Adrian Villaraos,all the lab assistants, and to students Alberto Alfaro, Catherine J. Anderson, Zachary Anderson, Patrick A. Beck, Nicole Farah Cordero, Gerardo E. Delgadillo, Stefani Fachini de Araujo, Maria Carolina Fasano, Nora Gharib, Shusanik Ghazaryan, Divya Gosain, Sophie Juneau, Ekaterina Koroleva, Michael Lim, Natalie Loventhal, Stephanie Margarita, Madeliene Merck Hurtarte, Kalili Mella Pablo, Camilo Tirado, Riofrio Villegas, and Wang Hongyang.

It has been a huge pleasure to work again with the talented and resourceful Joey Forsyte, of Velocity Filmworks in Los Angeles, who was aided in editing by Luisa Martinez, Associate Producer Johnny Woods, and Zena Grey; in research in Buenos Aires by Graciela Rasponi; and in Montevideo by Susana Estavillo. Forsyte would like to thank, for assisting in securing archival footage, Jessica Berman-Bogdan, Patrick Montgomery, and Morgan Strong, Travel Film Archive at Global Imageworks; Joana Lima, Paulo Roberto da Rocha, Moema Müller, and Liana Correa, Centro Técnico Audiovisual–CTAv/SAV–MinC, Rio de Janeiro; Nahun Calleros Carriles, Image Bank Chief, Filmoteca UNAM, Mexico City; Lorena Pérez, Archivo de Films, Cinemateca Uruguaya, Montevideo; Julieta Keldijan Etchessarry, Universidad Católica de Uruguay, Montevideo; Carlos de Oteyz, Florianna Blanco, Alejandra Mendoza, and Gabriel Martinez, Bolívar Films Archive, Caracas; Vittorio Garatti, for footage of the Cuban art schools, with assistance from Alysa Nahmias and Benjamin Murray; Rick Prelinger, the Prelinger Film Collection; and the staff at the National Archives.

The Brazilian architectural photographer Leonardo Finotti has expanded his own remarkable collection of images of Latin American modern architecture with trips made expressly for this project. He was aided in the studio by Michelle Jean de Castro, Gustavo Hiriart, Alex Souza, Nelson Ferreira Litowtschenko, Kátia Harumi Gondo, Thomaz Harrell, and Shirley Paes Leme. Special thanks for assistance with permissions go to Janeth Ballen, Christian Beals, Miguel Braceli, Sol Camacho, José Castillo, Catalina Corcuera, Fernando Diez, Patricio Mardones, Cesário Melatonio Neto, Cristián Nanzer, Tomás Powell, Ricardo Sánchez P., Arturo Ortiz Struck, and Marcos Maurício Toba.

Our aim from the beginning of the project has been to find original materials, and our greatest debt is to institutions that have lent work to the exhibition or created high-quality digital reproductions. In addition to those members of the advisory committee, above, we would like to thank: in Argentina, Teresa Testa, Fina Santos, Daniela Nadalin, Ezequiel Segal, Gregorio Laferrere, Marcos Urcola, Alicia Braverman, Ines Katzenstein, Silvia Batlle, Sandra Méndez Mosquera, and Norma Durango; in Brazil, Julieta Sobral, Elicio Gomes da Silva, Danilo Matoso Macedo, José Manoel Morales Sanchez, Cynthia Roncaglio, Carlos Ricardo Niemeyer de Medeiros, Francisco and Teresa Guedes, Gabriel Penteado, Haruyoshi Ono, Isabela de Carvalho, Ana Carboncini, Eliana de Azevedo Marques, Valeria Valente, Clarissa Diniz, Paulo Herkenhoff, Mozart and Maria Teresa Serra, Denise Pinheiro Machado, Claudio Muniz, Elizabete Martins, Adriana R. Filgueiras Lima, Nivaldo Andrade Junior, Wilson Vieira Junior, and Anderson Couto; in Chile, Paloma Parrini, Hugo Mondragón, Jaime Reyes, Adolfo Espinosa, and Josefina Méndez; in Colombia, Ricardo Daza, Mehmet Charum Bayaz, Rodrigo Cortes Solano, Julien Petit, Marta Devia, Germán Samper, Gustavo Adolfo Ramírez Ariza, Angela Ovalle Bautista, Germán Téllez, and Octavio Moreno; in the Dominican Republic, Sachi Hoshikawa, Christy Cheng, and Rubén Hernández Fontana; in Mexico, María Eugenia Hernández, Marcos Mazari Hiriart, Iván Alvarado, Eduardo Terrazas, Salvador de Alba Martínez, Agustín Hernández, Roberto Hernández, Victor Legorreta, Romualdo López Zárate, Jorge Mercado Zelis, Adriana Miranda, Andrés Attolini, Javier Ramírez Campuzano, Karina García, Gina Zohn Muldoon, Dolores Martínez, Juan Manuel Ortiz Hijar, and Armando Salas; in Uruguay, Andrés Mazzini, Gonzalo

Larrambebere, Esteban Dieste, Eduardo Álvarez , Gonzalo Rodríguez Orozco, Ana Olivera, Beatriz Perratone, and Susana Bayardo; in Venezuela, Daniel Fernández-Shaw, Ana Díaz de Tenreiro, Alejandra Matiz, and Loly Sanabria de Pérez. We also thank lenders from outside Latin America and those who extended particular help in our research: Tess van Eyck Wickham in Rotterdam; Valentina Moimas and Olivier Cinqualbre at the Centre Pompidou, Paris; Federica Zanco and Martin Josephy at the Barragan Foundation, Switzerland; Carole Ann Fabian and Janet Parks at the Avery Library at Columbia University, New York; and Vittorio Garrati in Milan.

During our travels we were helped by many people, and we are profoundly grateful too all of them, even if some of their names are perhaps overlooked here. In particular we thank Rafael Romero and the staff of the Fundación Cisneros, and Patricia Phelps de Cisneros and Gustavo Cisneros for invaluable help and support in Caracas; Mery Méndez and Jorge Nudelman in Montevideo; Cristina López Uribe in Mexico City; and Jeannette Plaut and Marcelo Sarovic in Santiago de Chile. We want especially to thank, in Argentina, Eduardo Almirantearena, Juan Fontana, Oski Lorenti, Fernando Diez, Norma Durango, Ian Dutari, Jorge Hojman, Mauro Pozo, Facundo Savid, Juliá Sebastián, Christian Noetzly, and Marta Sirkis; in Brazil, Marcelo Carvalho Ferraz, Sylvia Ficher, Otavio Leonidio, Paulo Mendes da Rocha, Gustavo Rocha-Peixoto, Maria Helena Rohe Salomon, Fabiano Sobreira, and Nelson Tapias; in Chile, Pedro Alonso, Javiera Paz Parada Ortiz, Andres Ureta, Nikole Barkos, and José Salomón Gebhard; in Colombia, Diana Barco, Alejandro Beer, Enrique Colina, Giancarlo Mazzanti, Rafael Obregón, Catalina Samper, Eduardo Samper, Ximena Samper, Doris Tarchopulos Sierra, Olga Eusse González, Mauricio Pena Ceidel, Isabel Llanos, Juan Pablo Aschner, Alberto Miani Uribe, Juan Carlos Rojas, Juniata Santos, and Fernando Villa; in Costa Rica, Bruno Stagno and Jimena Ugarte de Stagno; in Cuba, Claudia Castillo de la Cruz, Orlando Inclán, and Christian Zecchin; in the Dominican Republic, Rafael Emilio Yuñen; in Ecuador, Milton Barragán, Katya Kohn Bernasconi, Ana María Durán Calisto, Mathieu de Genot de Nieukerken, Handel Guayasamin, and Alexis H. Mosquera Rivera; in Guatemala, Pablo Savid; in Mexico, Miquel Adrià, Fernanda Canales, Bettina Cetto, Adriana Ciklik Phillips, Eduardo Dávila, Candida Fernández de Calderón, María García Holley, José Grinburg, Salvador Lizárraga, Fernando Luna, Marcos Mazari Hiriart, Eduardo Prieto López, Penelope Torres, Moises Escarcega, Stephany Trazancos, Guillermo Schiaffino Pérez, Jose María Larios, Lucila Aguilar, Pablo Landa, Rosalba Rojas, and Humberto Menzoda; in Peru, Natalia Majluf, Pedro Mar Belaunde, Rubén Moreira, and Alexis Mosquera; in Puerto Rico, Elena García; in Uruguay, Eduardo Álvarez, Magela Bielli, Martín Cobas, Andrés Mazzini, Santiago Medero, Ana Olivera, Raquel Pereira, Magdalena Peña, Gonzalo Rodríguez Orozco, Adriana Rosenberg, Jorge Sierra, and Francisco Villegas; in Venezuela, Armando Figueredo, Jesús Fuenmayor, Hannia Gómez, Edwin Meyer, Franco Micucci, Carlos Oteyza, Maria Isabel Peña, Rafael Urbina, Ileana Vásquez, Henrique Vera Hernández, and Fruto Vivas. In New York Josef Asteinza, Belmont Freeman, and Holly Block gave us continual help in dealing with the complex issues of relations with Cuba.

Exceptional staff from nearly every department at The Museum of Modern Art have lent support to this project. Our utmost thanks go to Glenn

D. Lowry, Director. For essential leadership and counsel we thank Ramona Bannayan, Senior Deputy Director for Exhibitions, Collections, and Programs; Todd Bishop, Senior Deputy Director, External Affairs; James Gara, Chief Operating Officer; and Peter Reed, Senior Deputy Director for Curatorial Affairs; Trish Jeffers, Director of Human Resources; Laura Coppelli, Manager, Employee Relations and Recruitment; and Joyce Wong, Human Resources. The commitment of our colleagues in the Department of Development has been integral to the realization of this project, and we are grateful to Lauren Stakias, Sylvia Renner, and Claire Huddleston. For fashioning the exhibition's public presence, we thank the Departments of Marketing and Communications: Kim Mitchell, Chief Communications Officer; Margaret Doyle, Director of Communications; Paul Jackson, Communications Manager; Carolyn Kelly, Coordinating Editor; Rebecca Stokes, Director of Digital Marketing; Sara Beth Walsh Senior Publicist; Vistor Samra, Digital Media Marketing Manager; and Jason Persse, Manager. For Graphic Design and Advertising: Greg Hathaway, Creative Director; Hsien-yin Ingrid Chou, Associate Creative Director; Wendy Olson, Production Coordinator; Mike Abbnik, Senior Creative Director; and Claire Corey, Production Manager. For Marketing Partnerships and Research: Zoe Jackson, Assistant Director; and Gretchen Scott, Building Project Digital Marketing Manager. The Museum's Department of Conservation has been our guide in the care of works entrusted to us by the exhibition's lenders. We are especially grateful for the help of Roger Griffith, Associate Sculpture Conservator; Erika Mosier, Conservator, who specialized on the works on paper; and LeeAnne Daffner, Photography Conservator.

In the Department of Exhibition Design and Production, we extend our deep appreciation to Lana Hum, Director and to Mack Cole-Edelsack, Exhibition Designer. It has been a pleasure to work with Mack, for his discerning eye, patience, and encouragement. We are grateful to Peter Perez and his team in the frame shop, and to Aaron Louis, A/V Director; and Mike Gibbons, A/V Exhibitions Foreperson. We are indebted for support from our colleagues in the Department of Exhibitions: Erik Patton, Associate Director; Randolph Black, Associate Coordinator; and Jackie Verbitsky, Department Assistant. Nancy Adelson, Deputy General Counsel, has been our invaluable advisor on legal matters. In coordinating the exhibition's extensive checklist of works, we are beholden to the skill and resourcefulness of the Department of Collection Management and Exhibition Registration: Jessica Nielsen, Assistant Registrar; Jennifer Wolf, Associate Registrar; Cait Kelly, Senior Registrar Assistant; and Victoria Manning, Assistant Registrar. Our colleagues Tunji Adeniji, Director of Facilities and Safety; LJ Hartman, Director of Security; Louis Bedard and Joanne Hughes, Managers; and Frantz Guillaume, Department Manager; have been indispensable. In the Department of Education, we sincerely appreciate the support of Wendy Woon, The Edward John Noble Foundation Deputy Director of Education; Pablo Helguera, Director of Adult and Academic Education; Sara Bodinson, Director, Interpretation and Research; Susannah Brown, Associate Educator, Courses and Seminars; and Calder Zwicky, Associate Educator, Teen and Community Programs.

This book is the collective work of the indefatigable team in the Department of Publications. Christopher Hudson, Publisher; Chul R. Kim, Associate Publisher; David Frankel, Editorial Director; Marc Sapir, Production Director; Matthew Pimm, Production Manager; and Hannah Kim, Marketing and Book Development Coordinator, have structured our efforts and ensured our success. Our inspired editor, Emily Hall, took on the daunting task of editing texts from many authors spanning diverse languages and countries. Amanda Washburn's perceptive design gracefully weaves the book together as a whole and makes each page one on which to linger.

Finally, we are deeply grateful to the members of the Department of Architecture and Design. Encouragement has come from every corner. Our most special thanks go to Sarah Rafson, Editorial Assistant, who deftly orchestrated the many elements of the catalogue, from combing for image rights to doing bibliographic research, and from proofing pages to refining the captions. In various phases of its development the exhibition has been the work of many hands. For their versatile support, we thank Emma Presler, Department Manager; Marissa Beard, acting Departmental Manager; Paul Galloway, Study Center Supervisor; Pamela Popeson, Preparator; Luke Baker, Curatorial Assistant; and Bret Taboada, Assistant to the Chief Curator. Our interns have been invaluable on this project in its long gestation, including two yearlong interns Dimitra Nikoloú and Nuria Benítez, as well as Lilly Wong, Sarah Rosenthal, Dania Dávila, Anuj Daga and Rodrigo Zamora. At Columbia University, Anthony Graham lent a hand for research tasks.

Finally, each of the curators wishes to express thanks to their supportive families: Jorge Francisco Liernur to his wife, Maria Teresa Bonardo; Carlos Eduardo Comas to his wife, Ana Maria Alvares e Comas; Patricio del Real to his partner, Jerry Portwood; and Barry Bergdoll to his partner, William Ryall, and his indefatigable Spanish teacher and friend Marina Urbach.

Barry Bergdoll
Carlos Eduardo Comas
Jorge Francisco Liernur
Patricio del Real

Images have been provided in many cases by the owners or custodians of the work. Individual works of art appearing herein may be protected by copyright in the United States of America or elsewhere, and may not be reproduced in any form without the permission of the rights holders. In reproducing the images contained in this publication the Museum obtained the permission of the rights holders whenever possible. Should the Museum have been unable to locate a rights holder, notwithstanding good-faith efforts, it requests that any contact information concerning such rights holders be forwarded so that they may be contacted for future editions.

Published in conjunction with the exhibition *Latin America in Construction: Architecture, 1955–1980* at The Museum of Modern Art, New York, March 29– July 19, 2015. Organized by Barry Bergdoll, Curator in the Department of Architecture and Design, The Museum of Modern Art; Carlos Eduardo Comas, Professor of Architecture at the Universidade Federal do Rio Grande, Porto Alegre, Brazil; Jorge Francisco Liernur, Emeritus Professor of Architecture at the Universidad Torcuato Di Tella, Buenos Aires; and Patricio del Real, Curatorial Assistant in the Department of Architecture and Design, The Museum of Modern Art

A major contribution for the exhibition is provided by Emilio Ambasz.

Major support is provided by The International Council of The Museum of Modern Art.

Additional funding is provided by The Reed Foundation, the Mexican Agency for International Development Cooperation (AMEXCID) with the Mexican Cultural Institute of New York, the Government of Chile, the Consulate General of Brazil in New York, the Consulate General of the Argentine Republic in New York, and the MoMA Annual Exhibition Fund.

Produced by the Department of Publications
The Museum of Modern Art, New York
Christopher Hudson, Publisher
Chul R. Kim, Associate Publisher
David Frankel, Editorial Director
Marc Sapir, Production Director

Edited by Emily Hall, with Ron Broadhurst, Stephanie Emerson, and David Frankel
Designed by Amanda Washburn
Production by Matthew Pimm
Printed and bound by OGI/1010 Printing Group Ltd., China

This book is typeset in Acronym.
The paper is 157gsm Kinmari matt art paper.

The texts by Guillermo Barrios, Cláudia Costa Cabral, Alejandro G. Crispiani, Jean Pierre Crousse, Ricardo Daza, Sharif Kahatt, Silvia Hernández de Lasala, Hugo Mondragón, Gustavo Luis Moré, Carlos Niño Murcia, Louise Noelle, Jorge Nudelman, Fernando Peréz Oyarzún, Silvio Plotquin, Eduardo Luis Rodríguez, Gustavo Scheps, and Cristina López Uribe were translated from the Spanish by Jen Hofer.

The essay by Jorge Francisco Liernur was translated from the Spanish by Laura Martínez de Guereñu.

The texts by Claudia Shmidt and Ruth Verde Zein were translated from the Portuguese by Steve Berg.

Published by The Museum of Modern Art, New York
11 West 53 Street, New York, New York 10019-5497

Distributed in the United States and Canada by ARTBOOK | D.A.P.
155 Sixth Avenue, New York, New York 10013. www.artbook.com

Distributed outside the United States and Canada by Thames & Hudson Ltd.
181A High Holborn, London, WC1V 7QX. www.thamesandhudson.com

Library of Congress Control Number: 2015930700
ISBN: 978-0-87070-963-0

Printed in China

Portfolio of photographs by Leonardo Finotti

1. Headquarters of the Corporación Venezolana de Ciudad Guayana– Electrificación de Caroní, Ciudad Guayana, Venezuela. 1967–68. Jesús Tenreiro-Degwitz (Venezuelan, 1936–2007). View of a terrace and sunshade structure. 2014. The Museum of Modern Art, New York. Gift of André Aranha Corrêa do Lago
2. Iglesia de San Pedro, Durazno, Uruguay. 1967. Eladio Dieste (Urugayan, 1917–2000). View of the vaulted ceiling above the sanctuary and nave. 2011
3. Church for the Benedictine monastery of Santísima Trinidad de Las Condes, Santiago, Chile. 1963–64. Hermano Martin Corréa (Chilean, born 1928), Hermano Gabriel Guarda (Chilean, born 1928). View of the ramp to the nave. 2010
4. Museu de Arte Moderna (MAM), Rio de Janeiro, Brazil. 1953–67. Affonso Eduardo Reidy (Brazilian, born France. 1909–1964). View of the northern facade at night. 2012
5. Aula Magna, Universidad Central de Venezuela, Caracas. 1952–53. Carlos Raúl Villanueva (Venezuelan, born England. 1900–1975). View of the covered plaza. 2014
6. Palácio do Itamaraty (Ministério das Relaçãoes Exteriores [Ministry of Foreign Relations], Brasília, Brazil. 1962. Oscar Niemeyer (Brazilian, 1907–2012). View of the honorific staircase leading to the curved mezzanine. 2007
7. Edificio Palmas 555, Mexico City. 1975. Juan Sordo Madaleno (Mexican, 1916–1985). View from Avenida de Las Palmas. 2007
8. Niemeyer apartment building, Belo Horizonte, Brazil. 1954–60. Oscar Niemeyer (Brazilian, 1907–2012). View of the facade. 2007
9. Congresso Nacional, Brasília, Brazil. 1958–60. Oscar Niemeyer (Brazilian, 1907–2012). View from the Esplanada dos Ministérios. 2007. The Museum of Modern Art, New York. Gift of Elise Jaffe + Jeffrey Brown
10. Edificio Girón, Havana, Cuba. 1967. Antonio Quintana (Cuban, 1919–1993). Exterior view. 2014
11. Complejo Habitacional Bulevar Artigas, Montevideo, Uruguay. 1971–74. Ramiro Bascáns (Uruguayan, 1936–2012), Thomas Sprechmann (Uruguayan, born 1940), Héctor Vigliecca (Uruguayan, born 1940), Arturo Villaamil (Uruguayan, born 1947). View of the northeastern wing. 2011
12. Headquarters for the Banco de Londres y América del Sur, Buenos Aires, Argentina. 1959–66. SEPRA Arquitectos (est. 1936), Clorindo Testa (Argentine, born Italy. 1923–2013). View of the mezzanine. 2014

Front cover: Mercado de la Merced, Mexico City. 1957. Enrique del Moral (Mexican, 1905–1987). Photograph by Guillermo Zamora. Archivo Enrique del Moral, DACPAI, INBA
Back cover: Residencias El Parque (Torres del Parque), Bogotá. 1964–70. Rogelio Salmona (Colombian, born France. 1929–2007). View with Plaza de Toros bullfighting ring (1931). 2014. Photograph by Leonardo Finotti

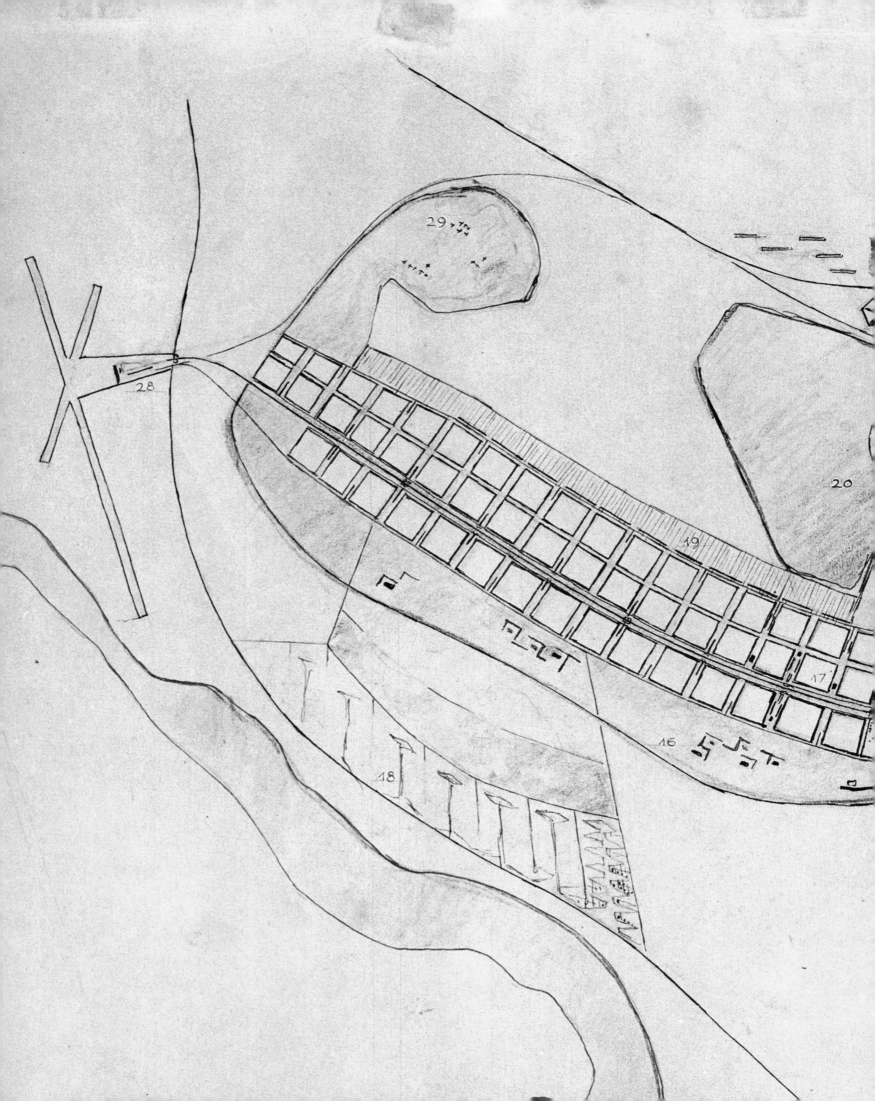